THE NEW CAMBRIDGE SHAKESPEARE

GENERAL EDITOR
Brian Gibbons, *University of Münster*

ASSOCIATE GENERAL EDITOR
A. R. Braunmuller, *University of California, Los Angeles*

From the publication of the first volumes in 1984 the General Editor of the New Cambridge Shakespeare was Philip Brockbank and the Associate General Editors were Brian Gibbons and Robin Hood. From 1990 to 1994 the General Editor was Brian Gibbons and the Associate General Editors were A. R. Braunmuller and Robin Hood.

THE FIRST PART OF KING HENRY IV

This edition offers a strongly theatrical perspective on the origins of *The First Part of King Henry IV* and the history of its interpretation. In their Introduction the editors clarify the play's surprising, de-centred dramatic structure, questioning the current assumption that the drama focuses on the education of Prince Hal. They call attention to the effects of civil war upon a broad range of relationships. Falstaff's unpredictable vitality is explored, together with important contemporary values of honour, friendship, festivity, and reformation.

Extensive lexical glosses of obscure, ambiguous, or archaic meanings make the rich word-play accessible. The notes also provide a thorough commentary on Shakespeare's transformation of his sources (particularly Holinshed's *Chronicles*) and suggest alternative stagings. The stage history features detailed accounts of major productions since 1945.

THE NEW CAMBRIDGE SHAKESPEARE

All's Well That Ends Well, edited by Russell Fraser
Antony and Cleopatra, edited by David Bevington
The Comedy of Errors, edited by T. S. Dorsch
Hamlet, edited by Philip Edwards
Julius Caesar, edited by Marvin Spevack
The First Part of King Henry IV, edited by Herbert Weil and Judith Weil
The Second Part of King Henry IV, edited by Giorgio Melchiori
King Henry V, edited by Andrew Gurr
The First Part of King Henry VI, edited by Michael Hattaway
The Second Part of King Henry VI, edited by Michael Hattaway
The Third Part of King Henry VI, edited by Michael Hattaway
King Henry VIII, edited by John Margeson
King John, edited by L. A. Beaurline
King Lear, edited by Jay L. Halio
King Richard II, edited by Andrew Gurr
Macbeth, edited by A. R. Braunmuller
Measure for Measure, edited by Brian Gibbons
The Merchant of Venice, edited by M. M. Mahood
The Merry Wives of Windsor, edited by David Crane
A Midsummer Night's Dream, edited by R. A. Foakes
Much Ado About Nothing, edited by F. H. Mares
Othello, edited by Norman Sanders
The Poems, edited by John Roe
Romeo and Juliet, edited by G. Blakemore Evans
The Sonnets, edited by G. Blakemore Evans
The Taming of the Shrew, edited by Ann Thompson
Titus Andronicus, edited by Alan Hughes
Twelfth Night, edited by Elizabeth Story Donno
The Two Gentlemen of Verona, edited by Kurt Schlueter

THE EARLY QUARTOS

The First Quarto of King Lear, edited by Jay L. Halio
The First Quarto of King Richard III, edited by Peter Davison

THE FIRST PART OF
KING HENRY IV

Edited by

HERBERT WEIL

Professor of English, University of Manitoba

JUDITH WEIL

Associate Professor of English, University of Manitoba

CAMBRIDGE
UNIVERSITY PRESS

Published by the Press Syndicate of the University of Cambridge
The Pitt Building, Trumpington Street, Cambridge CB2 1RP
40 West 20th Street, New York, NY 10011-4211, USA
10 Stamford Road, Oakleigh, Melbourne 3166, Australia

First published 1997

Printed in Great Britain at the University Press, Cambridge

A catalogue record for this book is available from the British Library

Library of Congress cataloguing in publication data

Shakespeare, William, 1564–1616.
(King Henry IV.   Part 1)
The first part of King Henry IV / edited by Herbert Weil, Judith Weil.
     p.   cm. – (New Cambridge Shakespeare)
Includes bibliographical references
ISBN 0 521 22682 1 (hardback) – ISBN 0 521 29615 3 (paperback)
  1. Henry IV, King of England, 1367–1413–Drama.   2. Great Britain–History–Henry IV,
1399–1413–Drama.   I. Weil, Herbert (Herbert S.)   II. Weil, Judith.   III. Series: Shakespeare,
William, 1564–1616.   Works.   1984.   Cambridge University Press.
PR2810.A2W45   1996
822.3'3 – dc20   96-10278 CIP

ISBN 0521 22682 1 hardback
ISBN 0521 29615 3 paperback

BT

CONTENTS

read
these

ILLUSTRATIONS

Illustrations 1, 3*a*, and 7*b* are reproduced by permission of Laurence Burns; illustration 4 by permission of the Shakespeare Centre Library, Stratford-upon-Avon; illustration 5 by permission of the Angus McBean estate; illustration 6 by permission of Chris Davies and illustrations 7*a* and 8 by permission of the Shakespeare Centre Library: Joe Cocks Studio Collection.

PREFACE

This edition owes a special debt to a pair of scholars no longer here to read it: Philip Brockbank who followed his initial invitation with continuing encouragement and Richard David who criticised an earlier draft in the kindest possible light. Giorgio Melchiori shared many questions and concerns while he was editing *2 Henry IV*. With his learning and patience, Brian Gibbons has been responsible for improvements on almost every page. At Cambridge University Press, Sarah Stanton has astutely smoothed many ways over many years; Paul Chipchase and Margaret Berrill have provided expert advice. C. Walter Hodges at a very early stage vividly illustrated our inchoate suggestions. A. R. Humphreys and David Bevington, editors of the Arden and Oxford editions of *1 Henry IV*, helpfully answered our queries.

Among the many friends and colleagues who have listened, argued, criticised drafts, or sent us their own work in progress, we wish especially to thank Scott McMillin, Miriam Gilbert, Edward Pechter, Ernst Honigmann, Patrick Boyde, George Hunter, Barbara Hodgdon, Victor Cowie, Kenneth Muir, George Toles, Tom Roberts, Patricia Tatspaugh, and Inga-Stina Ewbank. At the Shakespeare Centre in Stratford-upon-Avon, Marian Pringle, Sylvia Morris, and Mary White gave invaluable help with illustrations and production records; the staff of the Cambridge English Faculty Library, too, has been exceptionally generous. We are also grateful to the staffs of the University of Manitoba Library, the Cambridge University Library, the Folger Library, and the Huntington Library. Lucia Flynn has often saved us with her skills at the computer. For financial support and research leaves, we are indebted to the University of Manitoba Faculty of Arts, the University of Manitoba Institute for the Humanities, and the Social Sciences and Humanities Research Council of Canada. Clare Hall and Robinson College, Cambridge, helped us work in a stimulating environment.

We would also like to express our gratitude to the larger communities of critics, scholars, and directors who keep testing the value of Shakespeare's plays. Many of them have, in effect, questioned a widespread assumption that *1 Henry IV* presents an inclusive picture of society. But relative absences – particularly those of women, or of middle- and lower-class characters – may figure as important presences. By identifying such presences in small roles or in the transforming energies of languge and action, we have tried to indicate some of the newer ways in which *1 Henry IV* continues to challenge its audience. Finally, we acknowledge that any errors or misguided opinions which remain here are our own.

We dedicate this edition to our son and daughter, Fred and Leslie Weil, who have grown up in the company of Shakespeare and Shakespeareans, bearing our arguments and adventures with lively humour and grace.

ABBREVIATIONS AND CONVENTIONS

Shakespeare's plays, when cited in this edition, are abbreviated in a style modified slightly from that used in the *Harvard Concordance to Shakespeare*. Other editions of Shakespeare are abbreviated under the editor's surname (Theobald, Duthie) unless they are the work of more than one editor. In such cases, an abbreviated series title is used (Cam.). When more than one edition by the same editor is cited, later editions are discriminated with a raised figure (Rowe³). All quotations from Shakespeare, except those from *1 Henry IV*, use the text and lineation of *The Riverside Shakespeare*, under the general editorship of G. Blakemore Evans.

1. Shakespeare's plays

Ado	*Much Ado About Nothing*
Ant.	*Antony and Cleopatra*
AWW	*All's Well That Ends Well*
AYLI	*As You Like It*
Cor.	*Coriolanus*
Cym.	*Cymbeline*
Err.	*The Comedy of Errors*
Ham.	*Hamlet*
1H4	*The First Part of King Henry the Fourth*
2H4	*The Second Part of King Henry the Fourth*
H5	*King Henry the Fifth*
1H6	*The First Part of King Henry the Sixth*
2H6	*The Second Part of King Henry the Sixth*
3H6	*The Third Part of King Henry the Sixth*
H8	*King Henry the Eighth*
JC	*Julius Caesar*
John	*King John*
Lear	*King Lear*
LLL	*Love's Labour's Lost*
Mac.	*Macbeth*
MM	*Measure for Measure*
MND	*A Midsummer Night's Dream*
MV	*The Merchant of Venice*
Oth.	*Othello*
Per.	*Pericles*
R2	*King Richard the Second*
R3	*King Richard the Third*
Rom.	*Romeo and Juliet*
Shr.	*The Taming of the Shrew*
STM	*Sir Thomas More*
Temp.	*The Tempest*
TGV	*The Two Gentlemen of Verona*
Tim.	*Timon of Athens*

Tit.	*Titus Andronicus*
TN	*Twelfth Night*
TNK	*The Two Noble Kinsmen*
Tro.	*Troilus and Cressida*
Wiv.	*The Merry Wives of Windsor*
WT	*The Winter's Tale*

2. Other works cited and general references

Abbott	E. A. Abbott, *A Shakespearian Grammar*, 1894 (references are to numbered paragraphs)
AEB	*Analytical and Enumerative Bibliography*
Auden	W. H. Auden, *The Dyer's Hand and Other Essays*, 1962
Bailey	Nathaniel Bailey, *Dictionary of Cant Words*, added to *The New English Dictionary*, 4th edn, 1759
Barber	C. L. Barber, *Shakespeare's Festive Comedy*, 1959
Beaumont and Fletcher	*Dramatic Works in the Beaumont and Fletcher Canon*, ed. Fredson Bowers, 1966
Bevington	*Henry IV, Part I*, ed. David Bevington, 1987 (Oxford Shakespeare)
Bullough	*Narrative and Dramatic Sources of Shakespeare*, ed. Geoffrey Bullough, IV, 1962
Cam.	*The Works of William Shakespeare*, ed. W. G. Clark, J. Glover, and W. A. Wright, 9 vols., 1863–6 (Cambridge Shakespeare)
Capell	*Mr. William Shakespeare his Comedies, Histories, and Tragedies*, ed. Edward Capell, 10 vols., 1767–8
Cercignani	Fausto Cercignani, *Shakespeare's Works and Elizabethan Pronunciation*, 1981
Chambers, *Shakespeare*	E. K. Chambers, *William Shakespeare: A Study of Facts and Problems*, 2 vols., 1930
Chambers, *Stage*	E. K. Chambers, *The Elizabethan Stage*, 4 vols., 1923
Child	Harold Child, 'The stage history of *King Henry IV*', in Wilson, pp. xxix–xlvi
Collier	*The Works of William Shakespeare*, ed. John Payne Collier, 8 vols., 1842–4
Collier[3]	*Shakespeare's Comedies, Histories, Tragedies, and Poems*, 6 vols., 1858
Colman	E. A. M. Colman, *The Dramatic Use of Bawdy in Shakespeare*, 1974
conj.	conjecture
corr.	corrected
Cowl and Morgan	*The First Part of King Henry the Fourth*, ed. R. P. Cowl and A. E. Morgan, 1930 (Arden Shakespeare)
CQ	*Critical Quarterly*
Daniel	Samuel Daniel, *The First Fowre Bookes of the Civile Wars Between the Two Houses of Lancaster and Yorke*, 1595. Excerpts from Book III reprinted in Bullough, pp. 208–15
Davison	*The First Part of King Henry the Fourth*, ed. P. H. Davison, 1968 (New Penguin)

Dekker	*The Non-Dramatic Works of Thomas Dekker*, ed. A. B. Grosart, 5 vols., 1884–6
Dent	R. W. Dent, *Shakespeare's Proverbial Language: An Index*, 1981 (references are to numbered proverbs)
Dering MS.	*The History of King Henry the Fourth as revised by Sir Edward Dering, Bart.* (1623), a facsimile edition, ed. G. Walton Williams and G. Blakemore Evans, 1974
DNB	*Dictionary of National Biography*, 1953
Drake	Nathan Drake, *Shakespeare and his Times*, 1817
Dyce	*The Works of William Shakespeare*, ed. Alexander Dyce, 6 vols., 1857
Dyce²	*The Works of William Shakespeare*, ed. Alexander Dyce, 9 vols., 1864–7
Empson	William Empson, *Essays on Shakespeare*, 1986
ESC	English Shakespeare Company
Evans	*The Riverside Shakespeare*, ed. G. Blakemore Evans *et al.*, 1974
F	*Mr William Shakespeares Comedies, Histories, and Tragedies*, 1623 (First Folio)
F2	*Mr William Shakespeares Comedies, Histories, and Tragedies*, 1632 (Second Folio)
F3	*Mr William Shakespear's Comedies, Histories and Tragedies*, 1664 (Third Folio)
F4	*Mr William Shakespear's Comedies, Histories and Tragedies*, 1685 (Fourth Folio)
FV	*The Famous Victories of Henry the fifth*, 1598, reprinted in Bullough, pp. 299–343
Geneva	Geneva translation of the Bible, 1560
Gibbons	*Measure for Measure*, ed. Brian Gibbons, 1991 (New Cambridge Shakespeare)
Gurr	*King Richard II*, ed. Andrew Gurr, 1984 (New Cambridge Shakespeare)
Gurr, *Stage*	Andrew Gurr, *The Shakespearean Stage 1574–1642*, 3rd edn, 1991
Hall	Edward Hall, *The Union of the two noble and illustre famelies of Lancastre and Yorke*, 1548 and 1550; 1809 edn, reprinted 1965
Hanmer	*The Works of Shakespear*, ed. Thomas Hanmer, 6 vols., 1743–4
Hazlitt	*Characters of Shakespear's Plays*, ed. P. P. Howe, 1930
Hemingway	*Henry The Fourth, Part I*, ed. Samuel Burdett Hemingway, 1936 (New Variorum)
Hinman	*Henry the Fourth, Part I*, Shakespeare Quarto Facsimiles no. 14, ed. Charlton Hinman, 1966
Holinshed	*Holinshed's Chronicles of England, Scotland, and Ireland*, 6 vols., 1587, 1808 edn, reprinted 1965
Humphreys	*The First Part of King Henry IV*, ed. A. R. Humphreys, 1960 (Arden Shakespeare)
Johnson	*The Plays of William Shakespeare*, ed. Samuel Johnson, 8 vols., 1765
T. Johnson	*The Works of Mr William Shakespear*, pub. T. Johnson, 1710
Jonson	*Ben Jonson*, ed. C. H. Herford and Percy Simpson, 11 vols., 1925–52

KR	*Kenyon Review*
Kittredge	*Sixteen Plays of Shakespeare*, ed. George Lyman Kittredge, 1946
Lyly	*The Complete Works of John Lyly*, ed. R. Warwick Bond, 3 vols., 1902
Mahood, *Bit Parts*	M. M. Mahood, *Bit Parts in Shakespeare's Plays*, 1992
Mahood, *Wordplay*	M. M. Mahood, *Shakespeare's Wordplay*, 1957
Malone	*The Plays and Poems of William Shakespeare*, ed. Edmond Malone, 10 vols., 1790
Marlowe	*The Complete Works of Christopher Marlowe*, ed. Fredson Bowers, 2 vols., 1973
McMillin	Scott McMillin, *Shakespeare in Performance: Henry IV, Part One*, 1991
Melchiori	*The Second Part of King Henry IV*, ed. Giorgio Melchiori, 1989 (New Cambridge Shakespeare)
MLN	*Modern Language Notes*
MLQ	*Modern Language Quarterly*
MLR	*Modern Language Review*
Morgann	Maurice Morgann, *Shakespearean Criticism*, ed. Daniel A. Fineman, 1972
Nashe	*The Works of Thomas Nashe*, ed. R. B. McKerrow, 5 vols., 1904–10; rev. edn F. P. Wilson, 1958
N&Q	*Notes and Queries*
Odell	George C. D. Odell, *Shakespeare from Betterton to Irving*, 2 vols., 1966
OED	*The Oxford English Dictionary*, 20 vols., 1989
Onions	C. T. Onions, *A Shakespeare Glossary*, revised by Robert D. Eagleson, 1986
Oxford	*William Shakespeare: The Complete Works*, ed. Stanley Wells and Gary Taylor, 1986
Oxford OS	*William Shakespeare: The Complete Works*, Original Spelling Edition, ed. Stanley Wells and Gary Taylor, 1987
Partridge	Eric Partridge, *Shakespeare's Bawdy*, 3rd edn, 1969
Patterson	Annabel Patterson, *Reading Holinshed's Chronicles*, 1994
Pope	*The Works of Shakespear*, ed. Alexander Pope, 6 vols., 1723–5
Pope[2]	*The Works of Shakespear*, ed. Alexander Pope, 10 vols., 1728
PBA	*Proceedings of the British Academy*
PMLA	*Publications of the Modern Language Association*
Q0	sig. C1–C4^v (fragment), 1598
Q1	*The History of Henrie the Fourth*, 1598 (first quarto)
Q2	*The History of Henrie the Fourth*, 1599 (second quarto)
Q3	*The History of Henrie the Fourth*, 1604 (third quarto)
Q4	*The History of Henry the Fourth*, 1608 (fourth quarto)
Q5	*The History of Henrie the Fourth*, 1613 (fifth quarto)
Q6	*The Historie of Henry the Fourth*, 1622 (sixth quarto)
Q7	*The Historie of Henry the Fourth*, 1632 (seventh quarto)
Qq	quartos
RES	*Review of English Studies*
Rowe	*The Works of Mr William Shakespear*, ed. Nicholas Rowe, 7 vols., 1709

Rowe[3]   *The Works of Mr William Shakespeare*, ed. Nicholas Rowe, 3rd
                                     edn, 8 vols., 1714
RSC   Royal Shakespeare Company
Salgādo   Gāmini Salgādo, *Eyewitnesses of Shakespeare: First Hand Accounts
                                     of Performances 1590–1890*, 1975
SB   *Studies in Bibliography*
Schäfer   Jürgen Schäfer, *Documentation in the OED: Shakespeare and
                                     Nashe as Test Cases*, 1980
SD   stage direction
SH   speech heading
Spenser   *The Works of Edmund Spenser*, ed. Edwin Greenlaw *et al.*, 8 vols.,
                                     1932–49 (Variorum)
Sprague, *Histories*   Arthur Colby Sprague, *Shakespeare's Histories*, 1975
Sprague and Trewin   Arthur Colby Sprague and J. C. Trewin, *Shakespeare's Plays
                                     Today*, 1970
SQ   *Shakespeare Quarterly*
S.St.   *Shakespeare Studies*
S.Sur.   *Shakespeare Survey*
Staunton   *The Plays of Shakespeare*, ed. Howard Staunton, 3 vols., 1858–60
Steevens   *The Plays of William Shakespeare*, notes by Samuel Johnson and
                                     George Steevens, 3rd edn, 10 vols., 1785
Stow, *Chronicles*   John Stow, *The Chronicles of England*, 1580. Excerpts reprinted in
                                     Bullough, pp. 215–19
Stow, *Survey*   John Stow, *A Survey of London*, ed. Charles L. Kingsford, 2 vols.,
                                     1908
subst.   substantively
Sugden   E. H. Sugden, *A Topographical Dictionary to the Works of Shake-
                                     speare and his Fellow Dramatists*, 1925
Textual Companion   Stanley Wells and Gary Taylor, with John Jowett and William
                                     Montgomery, *William Shakespeare: A Textual Companion*, 1987
Theobald   *The Works of Shakespeare*, ed. Lewis Theobald, 7 vols., 1733
Tilley   M. P. Tilley, *A Dictionary of the Proverbs in England in the
                                     Sixteenth and Seventeenth Centuries*, 1950 (references are to
                                     numbered proverbs)
Trewin   J. C. Trewin, *Shakespeare on the English Stage*, 1964
TSLL   *Texas Studies in Literature and Language*
uncorr.   uncorrected
Van Lennep   William Van Lennep, ed., *The London Stage: 1660–1800, Part I
                                     1660–1700*, 1965
Var. 1773   *The Plays of William Shakespeare*, ed. Samuel Johnson and
                                     George Steevens, 10 vols., 1773
Var. 1778   *The Plays of William Shakespeare*, ed. Samuel Johnson and
                                     George Steevens, 10 vols., 1778
Walker   William S. Walker, *A Critical Examination of the Text of Shake-
                                     speare*, 3 vols., 1860
Warburton   *The Works of Shakespeare*, ed. William Warburton, 8 vols., 1747
West   Gilian West, '"Titan", "onyers", and other difficulties in the text
                                     of *1 Henry IV*', *SQ* 34 (1983), 330–33
Wilson   *The First Part of the History of Henry IV*, ed. John Dover Wilson,
                                     1946 (New Shakespeare)

Wilson, *Fortunes*	John Dover Wilson, *The Fortunes of Falstaff*, 1943
Wright	*The First Part of King Henry IV*, ed. W. A. Wright, 1897 (Clarendon Press Series)
G. Wright	George T. Wright, *Shakespeare's Metrical Art*, 1991

Biblical quotations are from the Geneva edition, 1560, unless otherwise noted.

INTRODUCTION

Reputation

In the most highly regarded twentieth-century study of history plays from different periods and nationalities, Herbert Lindenberger argues: '*Henry IV* surely provides the supreme example of a complex and serious approach to history that diverts in the very act of instructing.'[1] G. R. Hibbard represents many leading critics and directors when he expands this evaluation beyond the confines of genre: 'In size, in significance, and above all, in the sheer wealth of invention that has gone into its making, *Henry IV* is among the major achievements.'[2]

For *1 Henry IV*, undisputed facts concerning the play's reception support these superlatives. From its first appearance, probably in 1597, *Part One* has enjoyed great popularity and has been performed with exceptional frequency. Between 1598 and 1622, before the First Folio of 1623, there were seven quarto editions – more than for any other play by Shakespeare. *Part One* continues to be among the plays most often published in general texts and anthologies of literature for students around the world.

Readers and audiences familiar with the reputation of *1 Henry IV* will often be surprised when they approach the play itself for the first time. If they anticipate stirring action or expect to laugh whole-heartedly with Falstaff, the first two scenes may seem relatively subdued. They contain a stimulating but unstable mixture of serious and comic qualities. During the third scene, political conflict does disrupt the King's Council, yet the next episodes, which focus on the robbery at Gad's Hill and on Hotspur's argument with his wife, Lady Percy, may even diffuse such political momentum as has built up during the Council scene. Only with the three great scenes of the central action – in the tavern with the Prince and Falstaff, in the household of Glendower, and in the court of Henry IV – does the dramatic intensity and richness for which the play has been celebrated burst upon us.

This delay between expectation and fulfilment provides evidence of the play's basic design: a restless, de-centred opening movement, followed by a mid-section filled with astonishing, highly theatrical surprises, and a concluding movement which powerfully intensifies the already discordant rhythms of uneasiness and elation. Shakespeare's willingness to postpone satisfactions reveals the confidence with which he reshaped historical and theatrical sources in composing his play. Early audiences, acquainted with some of these materials and aware of Shakespeare's prior history plays, were probably even more surprised by this first movement than are audiences today. For example, anyone who had recently watched *Richard II* (1595–6) would already know that, according to Shakespeare, Henry's reign had begun with a rebellion which the

---

[1] *Historical Drama: The Relation of Literature and Reality*, 1975, p. 108.
[2] *The Making of Shakespeare's Dramatic Poetry*, 1981, p. 162.

I

Percys helped put down, and with the assassination of Richard himself. The King's pointed reference to his 'unthrifty' son as a dissolute prodigal (*Richard II* 5.3.1) would prepare an audience to behold a ruffian Prince of Wales. So would the popular legends circulated through ballads and tales as well as in plays like *The Famous Victories of Henry the fifth* which celebrated the Prince's wild youth. But when the Prince suddenly confides to the audience his secret plans for self-reform – plans which necessarily 'falsify men's hopes' (1.2.171) – the audience realises that Shakespeare intends to give them something fresh and surprising.

The Prince's soliloquy offers the most emphatic among many examples of how, early in the play, Shakespeare unsettles preconceptions. If audiences believe the King in the opening scene, they may expect the Prince to be stained with 'riot and dishonour' (1.1.84). They may also surmise that Glendower, 'irregular and wild' (1.1.40) is a barbarian, that Hotspur is princely, and that the King, admiring Hotspur's virtues, will treat him with respect when they meet 'Wednesday next' (1.1.102) at Westminster. Expectations about all these matters will prove to be mistaken, at least in part.

Shakespeare fashions *1 Henry IV* as a sequence of three movements. Although his seventh play about English history, it is striking for its originality. Shakespeare forgoes the ceremonious, highly symbolic style of dramaturgy on which he had relied in *Richard II*. He leads the audience to a more gradual, detached understanding of complex characters who repeatedly foist their interpretations of the past upon one another. What is distinctive about Prince Henry is not that he so fervently remembers and predicts events, but that he ultimately succeeds in imposing his will on these events. With Henry IV, Shakespeare turned his attention to a king who had barely escaped the violent sacrificial death suffered by Henry VI, Richard III, and Richard II. He thereby freed himself to explore the volatile, disconcerting strategies of other would-be survivors.

Falstaff is probably the best-known survivor in western literature. Generations of spectators have watched to see if he can dodge the trap set for him by the Prince and Poins, and have been astonished by the way he escapes death at the battle of Shrewsbury. Falstaff's dramatic impact has become inseparable from his reputation. However widely critical responses to him may diverge, they are usually informed by some sense of his fame, of the debates he has inspired, and of the rejection he must ultimately experience. His reputation tends to enhance the vitality which shines through this extraordinary character, so that he may seem to enjoy a life almost independent of the play's design. Falstaff is an unpredictable presence throughout the three movements; his theatrical range extends from intimate banter to brilliant and uproarious scene-stealing. He is never more likely to surprise us than when he apparently adopts conventional roles or when he passes shrewd judgements upon the Prince – or on himself.

To elaborate a design which could register the energies of his characters in this history play, Shakespeare drew upon his own experiments with comedy; he also enriched *1 Henry IV* with imitations of popular festivity and entertainment. But when

1 'What trick, what device . . . canst thou now find out?' Act 2, Scene 4. Michael Pennington as the
Prince and John Woodvine as Falstaff in Michael Bogdanov's English Shakespeare Company touring
production, 1986

he transferred his own grasp of exciting surprise and reversal to suspicious rulers and
ambitious courtiers, he moved far beyond the characterisation of such earlier self-
conscious tricksters as Richard of Gloucester in *Richard III* or the Bastard in *King
John*. Richard knows what he is doing and does it; the Bastard openly experiments.
But Henry IV, his son, and Falstaff deny us full confidence that they can or will
attempt to do what they say, for their success may at times depend on obscuring their
motives, both to others and to themselves.

As a consequence, this history play will divert and instruct different audiences in
remarkably different ways. Recorded critical reaction to the play begins with a nar-
rowly partisan response by the powerful Cobham family who apparently protested
against Shakespeare's treatment of their supposed ancestor Sir John Oldcastle,
thereby causing his name to be changed to Sir John Falstaff. The controversy that
seems to have arisen over Falstaff's name provides important information about both
the date and the early reception of *1 Henry IV*. These topics, to some extent inseparable, will be distinguished for the sake of clarity. 'Date' focuses upon matters of

chronology – perhaps the last subjects we might expect to find closely associated with Falstaff. The early reception of the play will be considered later, as a preface to selected contexts for interpretation.

Date

The few accepted facts about the date of *1 Henry IV* have enabled scholars to place its first performances tentatively in the early months of 1597. As we consider this limited evidence, it is helpful to remember that early performances of this play probably overlapped those of *The Merchant of Venice* (1596–7) and closely preceded those of *Much Ado About Nothing* (1598), *Julius Caesar* (1599), and *Hamlet* (1600–1). Furthermore, the text of Shakespeare's new play would have been especially flexible, subject to the pressure of contemporary political and theatrical circumstances.

On 25 February 1598, a play entitled *Henry IV* was entered in the Stationers' Register to Andrew Wyse:

1597 [1598, new style] xxv die ffebruariji. Andrew Wyse. Entred for his Copie, under t[he] handes of Master Dix: and master Warden man a booke intituled The historye of HENRY the IIIJth with his battaile of Shrewsburye against HENRY HOTTSPURRE of the Northe with The conceipted mirthe of Sr John Ffalstoff.

This entry makes no mention of 'Part One' or of 'The first Part', which may indicate that *Part Two* had not yet been written or performed, or that, if it had been, those who entered the copy saw no reason to identify this second play in any way.

Two separate quarto editions of *1 Henry IV* were printed in 1598, but only a fragment of the first (Q0) survives (see Textual Analysis, pp. 199–200). The second (Q1) was reprinted from the first by the same printing house, that of Peter Short. Its title modifies slightly the entry above:

THE / HISTORY OF / HENRIE THE / FOVRTH; / With the battell at Shrewsburie, / *betweene the King and Lord* / Henry Percy, surnamed / Henrie Hotspur of / the North. / *With the humorous conceits of Sir* / Iohn Fastalffe.

Only when, some months later, Francis Meres praised Shakespeare for his excellence in both comedy and tragedy in *Palladis Tamia* (entered in the Stationers' Register, 7 September 1598) do we have firmer evidence to support Shakespeare's authorship. As examples of 'tragedy', Meres submitted 'Richard the 2. Richard the 3. Henry the 4.' The titles of the quartos printed between 1599 and 1613 credit Shakespeare with having 'newly corrected' his play. None of the early quarto titles of the play show that it had an immediate sequel; our earliest specific reference to 'the firste part' comes from a Stationers' Register entry of 1603. In contrast, the sole quarto of *Part Two*, printed in 1600 as *THE Second part of Henrie the fourth . . . Written by William Shakespeare*, clearly indicates its relationship to *Part One*.

That the play was well received is beyond doubt. Following the two quarto editions of 1598, additional quartos were printed in 1599, 1604, 1608, 1613, and 1622, before the First Folio publication in 1623. New quartos in 1632 and 1639 strongly indicate the continuing appeal of the play. From the beginning, as the titles above suggest,

Falstaff must have been counted upon to attract audiences. Indeed, Shakespeare's success in making Falstaff notorious seems to have displeased a small but influential group of courtiers.

In the earliest staged version of *1 Henry IV*, Falstaff was apparently called Oldcastle, while Bardolph and Peto seem to have been named Rossill and Harvey. These names angered powerful aristocratic families, particularly the Cobhams who were descendants of Oldcastle's wife. The fifteenth-century Lollard, Sir John Oldcastle (d. 1417), would have been widely revered as a precursor of Protestant Reformation martyrs. Shakespeare changed these names, perhaps modifying the play in the process, but also leaving relics of his earlier intentions in his text. Two of the early names survive as speech headings, 'Ross.' in Q1 of *Part One* at 2.4.147, 149, and 153, and 'Old.' in Q of *Part Two* at 1.2.114. Poins names the four robbers-to-be as 'Falstaffe, Harvey, Rossill and Gadshill' in Q1 1.2.130–1, a line that endured through over twenty years of 'newly corrected' reprintings to appear in the Folio.[1]

The relationship of this controversy to the probable earliest performance of *1 Henry IV* is indirect but significant. Original performances are particularly elusive; the editors of *William Shakespeare: A Textual Companion* (1987) conclude, 'We can identify the first performances of only two plays: *All Is True* [usually called *Henry VIII*, 1613] and *1 Henry VI*.'[2] E. K. Chambers speculated that *1 Henry IV* may have been published 'unusually soon after its production. This can hardly have been earlier than 1597.'[3] He reasoned that the company would have wished 'to advertise the purging of the offence' which they had managed to give through the treatment of Oldcastle and others. An important consideration here is that William Brooke, Lord Cobham, served briefly as Queen Elizabeth's Lord Chamberlain between August 1596 and his death on 5 March 1597. Only then was he in a position to stop performances of a play which seemed to satirise his ancestor. Original performances before his death but fairly late in the season 1596–7 would also be consistent with the agreement among scholars that *Richard II*, entered in the Stationers' Register on 29 August 1597, had probably been first performed late in 1595. On the theory that Lord Cobham was responding to both parts of *Henry IV*, which 'increasingly misrepresent his ancestor', A. R. Humphreys conjectures that *Part One* might have been performed earlier in the season.[4]

Two other issues are closely bound up with the changing of names: the influence of censorship in reshaping the play and the form in which such a shape might be considered 'final'. We have no proof that Lord Cobham actively intervened, using his authority over the Revels Office or the licensing of plays. Why, one may wonder, would Shakespeare's normally cautious company have gone out of its way to antago-

---

[1] On the premise that Lord Cobham required the name changes, they have been altered in the Oxford *Complete Works*, 1986; Falstaff becomes 'Sir John'; Bardolph becomes 'Russill'; and Peto becomes 'Harvey'.

[2] S. Wells and G. Taylor with J. Jowett and W. Montgomery, p. 89.

[3] Chambers, *Shakespeare*, 1, 382–3.

[4] Humphreys, p. xiv. Gary Taylor argues that 'Oldcastle' was changed to 'Falstaff' before performance at court, Christmas 1596, in 'William Shakespeare, Richard James and the house of Cobham', *RES* 38 (1987), 347–9.

nise a Lord Chamberlain?[1] In the summer following the conjectured first performances of *Henry IV*, when the second Lord Hunsdon, the patron of Shakespeare's
company, had become the new Lord Chamberlain, the Privy Council actually prohibited *all* performances from 28 July to about 10 October 1597. They were both reacting
to an allegation from the City fathers that 'unruly apprentices' were gathering at plays,
and terminating production of *The Isle of Dogs* by Jonson and Nashe, which they
judged to be inflammatory.[2] In the light of such regulatory powers and attitudes,
Gary Taylor argues credibly that official censors insisted that the name 'Oldcastle'
be eliminated.[3] Yet no evidence has so far appeared which would suggest that
Shakespeare resisted changing Oldcastle and the other names. Indeed, it is possible
that having touched the nerves of honour and piety with 'Oldcastle', he would probe
them more deeply with 'Falstaff', especially if, early in 1598, he were still developing
his character for performance of *Part Two*.[4]

Whether 'Rossill' and 'Harvey', the original names of Bardolph and Peto, actually
pleased or displeased powerful lords has been matter for careful but inconclusive
speculation about Elizabethan patronage.[5] That these names survive in speech headings or in a list of thieves may give us evidence of another kind by contributing
suggestions about playhouse practices. In the theatres, composition, rehearsal, revision, and performance may have overlapped extensively.[6] This could have been
particularly true when the playwright, Shakespeare, as both a shareholder and an actor
in the company, might well have exercised the powers of a modern director in
preparing plays for the stage. From this theatrical perspective, survival of the names
could reveal playhouse nonchalance where groups of attendants are concerned or
reflect the irrelevance of precise identities where a deliberately confusing robbery,
enlivened with improvisation, must have been enacted.[7] Because the naming of the
thieves has contributed to the largest group of textual problems in *1 Henry IV*, further
discussion is reserved for the Textual Analysis (pp. 200–1). In later productions, as
well as in allusions to the play, Falstaff is occasionally called Oldcastle. Even if
intended merely as neutral substitutions, such references might have stirred up the
embers of ill will.

---

[1] See Bullough, p. 171; Robert J. Fehrenbach, 'When Lord Cobham and Edmund Tilney "were att odds":
Oldcastle, Falstaff and the date of *1 Henry IV*', *S.St.* 18 (1986), 87–101. E. A. J. Honigmann believes
that Shakespeare and his company deliberately provoked the Cobhams in order to please the
Essex faction. See 'Sir John Oldcastle: Shakespeare's martyr', in *Fanned and Winnowed Opinions: Shakespearean Essays Presented to Harold Jenkins*, ed. John W. Mahon and Thomas A. Pendleton, 1987, pp. 118–
32.
[2] See Chambers, *Stage*, I, 298–9. He argues that the new Chamberlain may have persuaded the Council to
permit performances to resume in October.
[3] 'The fortunes of Oldcastle', *S.Sur.* 38 (1985), 85–100. Janet Clare describes the 'Oldcastle' controversy in
the context of developing regulation in *'Art Made Tongue-Tied by Authority': Elizabethan and Jacobean
Dramatic Censorship*, 1990, pp. 76–9.
[4] Melchiori argues that *Part Two* was composed in 'late 1597/early 1598' and first performed 'after March
1598', p. 3.
[5] See John Jowett, 'The thieves in *1 Henry IV*', *RES* 38 (1987), 325–33.
[6] Scott McMillin, *The Elizabethan Theatre and 'The Book of Sir Thomas More'*, 1987, pp. 37–9.
[7] Mahood, *Bit Parts*, pp. 8–9, 15–16.

The design of the play

Who in Shakespeare's original audiences could have anticipated that he would take up the sober figure of a Lollard knight, regarded as a martyr by sixteenth-century religious reformers, and give him the theatrical genius of a great entertainer? *1 Henry IV* incorporates surprise within overall expectation as a principle of design. Shakespeare's skill at crafting an interplay of expectation and surprise, convention and experiment, becomes evident in the three-phase movement of his drama. The first movement of *1 Henry IV*, which includes six scenes, extends from the briefing session of Act 1, Scene 1, to the wrangling between Hotspur and Lady Percy in Act 2, Scene 3. The second movement begins with a long and vigorous scene set in the Eastcheap tavern (2.4) and ends two scenes later with the confrontation, so vividly anticipated in the tavern, between King and Prince at court (3.2). The third and final movement of ten scenes starts with another tavern gathering in Act 3, Scene 3 and ends after the victory by the King's party over Hotspur and his army at the long-awaited battle of Shrewsbury. Even so brief a survey can suggest some of the play's most important features: the economy with which Shakespeare links episodes; the combativeness of characters living in readiness for war; and the entanglement of public with private, political with domestic spheres of action. What such a survey of the play as a whole omits are the ways in which each movement differs from the other two. These are important differences; they may help to explain why, for many, the comic genre of *1 Henry IV* is a belated discovery rather than a foregone conclusion. Comedy arises surprisingly and with evident strain and stress from the grimly efficient dramaturgy of the third movement.

THE FIRST MOVEMENT: 'THEREFOR WE MEET NOT NOW'
In the opening speech King Henry describes his hopes for a crusade to the remote Holy Land which both he and his lords probably know will not take place: 'Therefor we meet not now' (1.1.30). They do meet to consider news from England's own borders: Mortimer's defeat and capture by the Welsh rebel, Glendower, and Henry Percy's (Hotspur's) victory at Holmedon, with his capture of several Scottish lords. Potential controversy over this 'honourable spoil' will become the occasion of the Council at the beginning of Scene 3. Shakespeare quickly plunges his audience into the political confusions for which the King is largely responsible. He has usurped power from his first cousin, King Richard II, and has caused Richard to be assassinated. Edward Hall, the Tudor chronicler, characterised as 'unquiet' the early years of Henry's reign. They were frequently disrupted when other rebels attempted to imitate the King's success and thereby replace him. By demonstrating that a king could be deposed, in spite of the divine sanctions which, all were taught, supported his rule, Henry had undermined a major prop of feudal monarchy. Feudal rulers were idealised as the first among equals in the legends of King Arthur supported by his Round Table; nevertheless such rulers were at the mercy of great landed noblemen, on whom they depended for arms and services. As *1 Henry IV* begins, the powerful Percy family who helped Henry become king is testing his authority.

In terms of staging, it is significant that this beginning has a business-like quality. Shakespeare may well have reserved for his third scene the striking visual props of royal power. There, a central throne and a spectacular display of crown and sceptre might serve as royal weapons with which to awe the unruly Percys.[1] Here, however, we appear to be in the royal equivalent of that workaday world which Shakespeare evokes throughout the first movement of his play, a world which includes household chambers and an innyard as well as the public highway where both the King's 'auditor' (2.1.46) and Falstaff will be robbed. A subdued conference in 1.1, followed by a surprising exhibition of regal might in 1.3, would not only deploy the resources of the Elizabethan stage; it would conform to the policy later explained by Henry to his son in Act 3, Scene 2. A ruler who avoids frequent and showy public appearances can have, he believes, the effect of a 'comet' when he does display his 'presence' (3.2.47, 54).

In terms of a developing structure, the opening scene introduces a series of episodes in which 'Therefor we meet not now' becomes almost a leitmotif. The King summons Hotspur to court, then drives him to rebel; the Prince agrees to participate in a robbery but robs the robbers; Hotspur talks of battle in his sleep yet refuses to confide his plans to his wife. Perhaps the King does more than any other character to establish a sense of uneasiness and mistrust during this first movement of the play. Although he is physically present in only two scenes, he epitomises, as cause and focus of rebellion, a range of political and familial disorders. He provides memorable and misleading accounts of Hotspur's honour and the Prince's 'dishonour' (1.1.84), initiating an opposition which he will accentuate when he has an opportunity. In Act 1, Scene 3, he imposes his own pessimistic interpretations upon the puzzling behaviour of Mortimer.

To set off the King from the characters who try to imitate or mimic him, Shakespeare creates a distinctive style.[2] In Henry's opening speech, images of body parts – 'lips' and 'blood' (6), 'hoofs' (8), and 'eyes' (9) – suggest dismemberment rather than identifiable wholes. By vaguely picturing uncontrollable forces – 'frighted peace' (2) or the 'edge of war' (17) – King Henry insinuates the divisions which trouble his kingdom and communicates a potential for violence.[3] Through a series of prophetic statements linked by the repetition of 'No more . . .', Henry promises peace but rhetorically stresses war. Such language is appropriate for a politician who, from his first appearance in *Richard II*, has been adept at activating the darker motives of others and at obscuring his own. The King's conduct raises questions to which there can be no reliable answers: would he really have gone crusading if not thwarted by rebellion? Is his rage at Hotspur calculated?

[1] On the theatrical dimensions of kingship, see Anne Righter [Barton], *Shakespeare and the Idea of the Play*, 1962, pp. 113–38; Stephen Orgel, *The Illusion of Power: Political Theatre in the English Renaissance*, 1975; David Scott Kastan, 'Proud majesty made a subject: Shakespeare and the spectacle of rule', *SQ* 37 (1986), 459–75.

[2] For the use of images which individualise characters, see Wolfgang Clemen, *The Development of Shakespeare's Imagery*, 1951, pp. 5 ff.; Katherine Eisaman Maus, 'Taking tropes seriously: language and violence in Shakespeare's *Rape of Lucrece*', *SQ* 37 (1986), 66–82.

[3] For a different view of allegorical language here, see Madeleine Doran, 'Imagery in *Richard II* and in *Henry IV*', *MLR* 37 (1942), 113–22.

The opening episode of *1 Henry IV* demonstrates Shakespeare's skill in writing scenes which have the coherence of miniature plays, yet reflect and support his overall design. Scene 1 foreshadows the rhythm of subsequent scenes which move from irresolution to decisiveness. It also anticipates the shape of the overall dramatic narrative. King Henry controls the discourse of the conference through his questions.[1] By the end of the scene, the King has begun to recover the firmness which will be so conspicuous in Scene 3: 'I will from henceforth rather be myself, / Mighty and to be feared . . .' (5–6). When he emphatically concludes the third and final movement of the play, he has, at least for the time being, consolidated his authority.

The drama of moral choice

Showing how Shakespeare could achieve a 'continuous flow of action' on a bare thrust stage, Anthony Brennan observes: 'The progress of characters in time is embroidered in a pattern of contrasts and parallels, echoes and distortions.'[2] We may therefore notice again in Scene 2 several of the elements which both typify the first movement and echo Scene 1: informality; distinctive styles of speech; conscious anticipation of later events. Just as Scene 1 leads to a second and more complex court scene, Scene 2 points towards the first tavern scene, 2.4, which in turn pulls together and builds upon Hal's first appearance with Falstaff and the pair of robbery scenes, 2.1 and 2.2.

Yet such similarities bring out striking differences which repay very close attention. Falstaff's reiterated 'when thou art king' (1.2.12–13, 19, 47, 49) repeats King Henry's 'No more . . . no more', but in a far more hopeful key. The fluent prose style of the jests between Falstaff and the Prince introduces us to an unusual 'friendship' (see below, pp. 31–3). This style helps us begin to distinguish Falstaff's world from those of the King and of the Percy faction.[3] Falstaff exaggerates his freedom and social stature as a highwayman: 'Let us be Diana's foresters, gentlemen of the shade, minions of the moon' (1.2.20–2). His fantasies and his wonderful caricature of social order as 'the rusty curb of old Father Antic the law' (48) provoke the Prince's responses: imagining dire consequences for Falstaff's crimes and taunting him with the promise that he will be made official hangman.

The Prince and Falstaff are alone together onstage for the first eighty-five lines of Scene 2 and exchange thirty-three speeches. But the exact rapport between the two characters will vary from one production or reading to the next. A phrase like Falstaff's, 'Indeed, you come near me now, Hal' (10) can express a wide range of tones, from delighted approval and applause to ironic resentment. The productions described in 'Stage History' have shown that this relatively brief dialogue at the beginning of Scene 2 quickly suggests the nature of the bond between Falstaff and the Prince and is crucial for its later richer development.

Much more clear than the nature of their feelings for each other are the tacit rules which guide the relationship between them. As they plan the joke of the Gad's Hill

[1] Joseph A. Porter, *The Drama of Speech Acts: Shakespeare's Lancastrian Tetralogy*, 1979, pp. 60–1.
[2] *Shakespeare's Dramatic Structures*, 1986, p. 5.
[3] See Jean E. Howard, *Shakespeare's Art of Orchestration: Stage Technique and Audience Response*, 1984, p. 27.

robbery, the Prince and Poins count on Falstaff to amuse them in predictable ways. The repartee between Falstaff and the Prince is impersonal enough to accommodate other characters; Poins can enter into their non-stop bantering and baiting as if he had been present all along.

The Prince, having side-stepped questions about his future, suddenly reveals in his soliloquy that his behaviour has been intended to create a misleading impression. His speech probably surprises many readers and spectators, reversing their expectations about his character. The Prince's clear motives and plans contrast with his father's opaque calculations; his promises imply both a star performance as Henry V, and a unified dramatic narrative about his development. For Shakespeare, such a narrative model already existed in the form of popular Morality plays and Interludes which represented the testing of Christian youth beset by the temptations of the world, the flesh, and the Devil. Morality plays showed the influence of ingenious preaching techniques, as well as of folktales. They embodied, according to Robert Potter, archetypal narratives of innocence lost and salvation achieved through conversion and repentance.[1] Although this particular Morality pattern had flourished in the late fifteenth and earlier sixteenth centuries, it could probably still be recognised by Elizabethan audiences and reinforced through contemporary enthusiasm for the biblical theme of the prodigal son.[2]

Modern audiences and readers have often responded to the Prince's dramatic function by perceiving its similarity to more recent versions of the spiritual quest archetype: romantic and post-romantic stories of education and self-discovery, rebellion and initiation. Lindenberger points out that for a 'generation' of interpreters, the play explores the 'balance' which the Prince achieves or the ambivalence he learns to negotiate between values typified by Hotspur and Falstaff.[3] Yet this coming-of-age story provides only one of the conventions on which Shakespeare relied in designing *1 Henry IV*. Also important are chronicle histories, history plays, and poems which develop more sequentially as well as romance narratives like that of Edmund Spenser's *The Faerie Queene* (1590), composed of interlaced stories occurring simultaneously. Then too, we should reckon with traditions of celebration and entertainment which could have prepared Elizabethan audiences to find established conventions used in theatrically self-conscious and unconventional forms. Falstaff joyfully plays the Morality role of the Vice or 'Iniquity', but other functions of the Vice, tempting, mocking, and entertaining, seem to be shared out more equally between Falstaff and the Prince himself. Even the division of comic from serious scenes, often practised in Morality plays and stipulated by Renaissance theorists mindful of classical decorum, breaks down when Hotspur provokes laughter or when the Prince promises to cast off his closest friend during the tavern revels of 2.4.

The Morality pattern of spiritual reform that underlies the Prince's soliloquy may be one method of inviting an audience into the play; it can engage concern with a

[1] *The English Morality Play: Origin, History and Influence of a Dramatic Tradition*, 1975, pp. 8–10, 16–20.
[2] See Richard Helgerson, *The Elizabethan Prodigals*, 1976, pp. 2–3, 12–15. On similarities between Falstaff and the tempters in such plays, see Wilson, *Fortunes*, pp. 17–23, 31.
[3] Lindenberger, pp. 100, 180 n. 5.

2 'I know you all': a possible staging of Prince Hal's soliloquy, Act 1, Scene 2, as drawn by
C. Walter Hodges. The position and stance of the Prince will determine whether he includes the audience
in the theatre as part of 'you all'

whole series of moral choices rather than provide a sturdy framework for any one
character's dilemma. Indeed, Shakespeare gave up a more conventional form of sus-
pense by presenting a Prince who has already made his choice and feels armed against
surprise: 'I know you all' (1.2.155). His soliloquy shows that he has the capacity later
described by Hamlet, 'a large discourse, / Looking before and after' (4.4.36–7), but
King Henry and the rebellious Percys will set the political agenda. Moreover, the
Prince's speech operates 'before and after' in ways he cannot have intended. It fur-
nishes one of several moments when the play appears to pivot on a fulcrum. In Walter
Hodges' illustration for 'I know you all', the Prince looks back at least momentarily
towards his departed friend, Poins, before facing forward towards the audience (see
illustration 2). If we hear the speech while thinking back ourselves, we may remember
the ambiguities in the King's overture. Within a few moments and a mere five lines
into the next scene, we can recognise a strong likeness between the Prince, a hidden
'sun' who will eventually 'please again to be himself' (160) and the King who resolves,

'I will from henceforth rather be myself.' His 'all', which briefly stretches the world of the play, making a few characters stand for an entire society, will toll through the Prince's speeches even after, late in *Part Two*, he becomes King Henry V, suggesting his comprehensive sense of responsibility. He may prove successful, in part, because he youthfully underestimates the obstacles he faces.

Shakespeare complicates the pattern of moral choice in *Part One* by bringing Hotspur onstage right after the Prince's soliloquy. Perhaps he is reflecting here the designs of late sixteenth-century Morality plays which often present two antagonists rather than one central figure.[1] Through Hotspur's two long and brilliant speeches to the King in 1.3 – an alibi for ignoring the King's agent at Holmedon and an apology for Mortimer's honour – audiences discover why a king might want him for a son. In addition to his sincere passion for chivalry, he is humorous and imaginative – qualities markedly absent in his father, his uncle, and the King. That a naive Hotspur should regard the departed King as a 'vile politician' (238) and fail to notice how his own father and uncle 'train him on' (5.2.21) is one of the tragic ironies of the play.[2] Surfacing early, it encourages an audience to compare his relations to his elders with the Prince's and to look for more evidence of growth under pressure than one might otherwise expect from the Prince. Both young men are committed to redeeming not only the times but also their fathers (see Commentary on 1.2.177 and 1.3.85).

Shakespeare juxtaposes the joke played by Poins and the Prince when they hide Falstaff's horse at Gad's Hill – 'Falstaff sweats to death, / And lards the lean earth as he walks along' (2.2.90–1) – with Hotspur's sharp satire on the 'frosty-spirited rogue' who runs away from the Percy plot (2.3.17). At the same time, he sets off a more subdued reverberation between two emotional bonds: Falstaff's friendship with the 'rogue' who has tricked him ('If the rascal have not given me medicines to make me love him, I'll be hanged' 2.2.15–16) and Lady Percy's compassionate dependence upon a husband almost wholly preoccupied with riding his horse into battle. Suggestions of good life, disrupted by robbers and rebels, run through the play from the flea-ridden inn of 2.1 to the later scenes set in Eastcheap and Wales. When Lady Percy asks, 'For what offence have I this fortnight been / A banished woman from my Harry's bed?' (2.3.32–3), Shakespeare brings the personal cost of such disorder home to his audiences.

THE SECOND MOVEMENT: '. . . BANISH ALL THE WORLD'
The second movement of *1 Henry IV* bursts forth with three exuberant scenes which have more lines than did the first six. All three are filled with mercurial changes of character, surprising images, and strikingly resonant clashes of personality. Although distinct in rhythm and mood, each of these scenes represents a fullness and richness of experience withheld during the first movement. That set in Eastcheap (2.4) and the

---

[1] Alan C. Dessen, *Shakespeare and the Late Moral Plays*, 1986, pp. 55–90.
[2] See Robert Ornstein, *A Kingdom for a Stage: The Achievement of Shakespeare's History Plays*, 1972, p. 133. For an especially stimulating and influential argument on the complexity of 'two opposed value-judgements' that are necessary for any full experience of the plays, see A. P. Rossiter, 'Ambivalence: the dialectic of the Histories' in *Angel with Horns: Fifteen Lectures on Shakespeare*, 1961, p. 51.

latter part of the following scene, set in Wales (3.1), create a holiday humour. The duping of Falstaff, so easily brought off, hardly prepares us for his ability, within a frame of satisfied expectations, to surprise everyone, turning 2.4 into a feast of theatrical invention. And, after earlier references to Glendower as 'irregular and wild' (1.1.40) and as 'damned' (1.3.82), who would expect to find in Wales a haven of civility? C. L. Barber's observation that Shakespeare 'dramatizes not only holiday but also the need for holiday and the need to limit holiday' is especially pertinent to the second movement.[1] The festive energies of the tavern scene and the Welsh scene enhance the seriousness of the third (3.2) – an interview of great tension through which the Prince, here meeting his father for the first time in the play, earns his confidence. King Henry concludes the movement with grim and sharpened purpose: 'let's away, / Advantage feeds'him fat while men delay'.

The first tavern scene, 2.4, easily the longest in the play with four hundred and sixty-one lines, has proved for many readers and spectators to be the most memorable. Like the play as a whole, this scene has three movements: an introduction during which the Prince, awaiting Falstaff, passes time by teasing Francis, the apprentice drawer; a mid-section devoted to the expected and the unexpected consequences of the joke played on Falstaff; and a climactic, more surprising pair of short plays improvised by the Prince and Falstaff (312–99), followed by a brief passage or coda in which the Prince hides Falstaff from the Sheriff, vows to make Falstaff 'answerable' for the money if he has 'robbed these men' (437–8), and, with Peto, picks Falstaff's pockets of their tavern reckonings. Although critics differ about the relative weighting of these components, most would probably agree that 'when examined, it is seen to be not at all a meandering effusion but a controlled structure, a skilfully threaded series of small firm units'.[2]

However carefully planned, this exuberance has led to great diversity of theatrical and critical interpretation.[3] As the plot thickens with the delayed entry of Falstaff and as the theatrical powers of the scene multiply, so too do possibilities for understanding Falstaff, the Prince, and the significance of their relationship. Falstaff incarnates humour 'unyoked' (1.2.156) – a tendency to claim too much and go too far – but a similar extravagance has been unleashed in the Prince: 'I am now of all humours that have showed themselves humours since the old days of goodman Adam to the pupil age of this present twelve o'clock at midnight' (2.4.81–3). Their imitations of Hotspur, Douglas, and the King are inspired. As T. S. Eliot said of Ben Jonson's satire, such parody is 'great in the end not by hitting off its object, but by creating it'.[4] Falstaff escalates his count of men said to have attacked him from two to eleven figures in

[1] Barber, p. 192.
[2] Emrys Jones, *Scenic Form in Shakespeare*, 1971, p. 30; he sees a two-part structure 'bridged' by the news of Northern and Western Rebellions. See also Mark Rose, *Shakespearean Design*, 1972, pp. 49–59.
[3] For extended discussion of 2.4 and of its relation to the rest of the play, see Gareth Lloyd Evans, 'The comical–tragical–historical method – *Henry IV*', *Stratford-upon-Avon Studies*, 3 (1961), 144–63; J. McLaverty, 'No abuse: the Prince and Falstaff in the tavern scenes of *Henry IV*', *S.Sur.* 34 (1981), 105–110; Edward Pechter, 'Falsifying men's hopes: the ending of *1 Henry IV*', *MLQ* 41 (1980), 211–30; John Shaw, 'The staging of parody and parallels in *1 Henry IV*', *S.Sur.* 20 (1967), 61–73.
[4] *Elizabethan Dramatists*, 1963, p. 80.

buckram, then tosses in 'three misbegotten knaves in Kendal green' (186–7). The Prince expects to deflate Falstaff with his revelation that 'we two set on you four, and, with a word, out-faced you from your prize', but Falstaff in some productions and readings out-faces the Prince with his defence: 'By the Lord, I knew ye as well as he that made ye' (212–13, 221).

The climax of this unyoked humour comes when Falstaff, impersonating the Prince, pleads, 'Banish plump Jack, and banish all the world' (397–8). By replying 'I do. I will', the Prince (in some interpretations) brings the game, with its free spirits, to a close (see below pp. 49, 54 and Commentary). Whether he momentarily reveals his long-range strategy and whether Falstaff grasps the nature of his game are indeed crucial problems. How they may be resolved depends upon these considerations: the wariness or warmth with which both the Prince and Falstaff play their roles; the degree to which their emotional dynamism is supported or ignored by the audience onstage; inclinations of readers or spectators either to trust or distrust acting and games; varying hypotheses about the 'history', social order, and royal power which interrupt and re-direct revelry when Falstaff returns to announce 'villainous news' (276) – that the King has summoned the Prince to court and that civil war has begun. Charged with hopes and desires which neither character can fully reveal, their improvised playing resonates far beyond its length. Energetic accusations and defences make their sport resemble a public trial. Yet despite the crowded stage, the Prince and Falstaff can seem to be acting out a two-handed drama essentially for one another. Their final exchange suggests both a common preoccupation with self and a gulf between their loyalties and commitments.

The tavern scene can function within the play much as does the Prince's soliloquy in 1.2 – as a fulcrum prompting revaluations of the past (did Falstaff see through the Prince's disguise at Gad's Hill?) and shaping expectations of the future (will the Prince be able to manage his father?). 'Depose me?', asks Falstaff when the Prince abruptly commands, 'Do thou stand for me, and I'll play my father' (2.4.357–8). But although this change of roles might symbolise King Henry's past usurpation and the Prince's future succession, it does not fulfil the immediate purpose proposed for their theatrical game, enabling the Prince to 'practise an answer' to the King (309). Both characters seize on another opportunity for competitive wit and caricature. Then, almost as if he had wished to distract audiences from focusing on English family politics, Shakespeare follows the first tavern scene with a Welsh episode, distinguished from the scenes surrounding it both by social climate, and by an independent time-scheme. Whereas 3.2 takes place later the same morning that began in 2.4, 3.1 shows the rebels still planning their rendezvous at Shrewsbury. Yet in the next scene, King Henry reports the rebel gathering there as an event already past.[1]

In Wales, the revels, if not the dialogue, are dominated by Glendower, a man who, historically, sought to be prince of an independent realm.[2] Whereas 2.4 seems to

---

[1] On the complex time-scheme employed in *1 Henry IV*, see Ricardo J. Quinones, *The Renaissance Discovery of Time*, 1972, pp. 340–1.

[2] Arthur Granville Bradley, *Owen Glyndwr and the Last Struggle for Welsh Independence, with a Brief Sketch of Welsh History*, 1901.

mirror aspects of the entire play, 3.1 (the third longest scene in *1 Henry IV*) dramatises qualities which would otherwise largely be absent. Just how strongly readers or spectators perceive these exceptional qualities may depend on how they are encouraged to view Glendower's response to Hotspur. If he becomes too angry, in the theatre or in our readings, Hotspur's spirited lines will make him seem a fool. If he graciously restrains himself, it may appear that at least one major character does not always assume a self either imposed by or addressed to others. Instead, he confidently proclaims his achievements, including three substantive defeats of the English King (here treated as a predatory troublemaker), as well as his skill in music, poetry, and occult science. Some stage Glendowers, while looking bizarre, have behaved tactfully, making it seem that Hotspur, with one of those delayed reactions for which he is noted, is exploiting an opportunity to bait the King who broke off their dialogue in 1.3.

During recent productions, Glendower's musicians and the Welsh singing of his daughter, almost invariably omitted for over two hundred years, have conveyed the enchantment which Mortimer finds in his wife's strange tongue; it seems 'as sweet', he says, 'as ditties highly penned, / Sung by a fair queen in a summer's bower / With ravishing division to her lute' (202–4). Within Glendower's court, love is not merely a distraction from politics. Interpretations of the play which ignore the exceptional qualities of 3.1 may erase a brief holiday from the attitudes and anxieties which emphatically return in 3.2.

Where Glendower is 'wondrous affable' (162), King Henry is often wondrous harsh. Peremptory with Hotspur for refusing to send him the Scottish prisoners, he gains the support of his own son by challenging his honour. In marked contrast to the 'play extempore' (2.4.231) with its balanced exchanges and more equal division of lines, the King has five of the scene's nine speeches, including the first and last, and utters one hundred and thirty lines to the Prince's forty-four. Shakespeare points for his hearers the repetitive nature of experience by giving father and son similar language. The Prince's vow, 'I shall hereafter, my thrice-gracious lord, / Be more myself' (3.2.92–3) echoes his father's earlier threat to the Percys: 'I will from henceforth rather be myself' (1.3.5); the King's conviction that his 'being seldom seen' caused him to be 'wondered at' like a comet (3.2.46–7) parallels the Prince's plan in his soliloquy to 'imitate the sun', which 'Being wanted . . . may be more wondered at' (1.2.157, 161), and his opinion that people only wish for holidays when they 'seldom come' (166). Yet the scene can surprise an audience with the possibility that if anyone does teach the Prince how to answer his father, it may well be the mistrustful King himself.

THE THIRD MOVEMENT: '. . . IF A LIE MAY DO THEE GRACE'
Comparing Shakespeare's dramaturgy to that of medieval plays where a character may well have his own 'house' set up onstage, John Wilders comments that 'the action of *Henry IV* is distributed between different physical worlds or locations, each dominated by a unique and uniquely demanding character'.[1] In the third movement of the play, however, the Prince has a strong impact in spite of his relatively brief appear-

---

[1] *The Lost Garden: A View of Shakespeare's English and Roman History Plays*, 1978, p. 87.

ances onstage. Falstaff often becomes a more dominant theatrical presence, yet tends, at times, to lose some of his dramatic force. In contrast to their earlier scenes, Falstaff occupies the stage throughout 3.3 and 4.2, while the Prince arrives late and leaves before Falstaff. And beginning with 3.3, Falstaff not only gets the last, sometimes rude, word in five scenes (3.3, 4.2, 5.1, 5.3, and 5.4) but also speaks in soliloquy, as did the Prince at the end of 1.2.

Falstaff's questions which open 3.3, 'Bardolph, am I not fallen away vilely since this last action? Do I not bate? Do I not dwindle?' invert the King's call to action which closes 3.2: 'let's away, / Advantage feeds him fat while men delay'. They introduce a movement which 'bates' from its predecessor. Of the last ten scenes, only this second tavern scene lasts more than one hundred and seventy lines. Except for 3.3 and 5.4, these scenes replace complex interaction and vigorous repartee with political self-justification. The richness of language and character becomes less complex as the choreography of battle becomes increasingly important. Falstaff's new role of scavenging recruiter who leads his starving troops 'where they are peppered' (5.3.35) complements a new emphasis on the chivalric side of Prince Henry. The prospect of battle seems to simplify the life of this great play, although the fighting, when it does come, takes up only the first parts of two scenes in the text. Most of the scenes conclude in an anticlimactic vein.

Falstaff's lines about his own bating also parallel the lines with which the King opens the play, 'So shaken as we are, so wan with care.' In the third movement, Falstaff's resemblance to King Henry becomes more obvious. His anxieties about decline and death forshadow a major motif associating the King and Falstaff in *Part Two*. Through this dwindling Falstaff, Shakespeare explores the ethical border between loyalty to others and self-preservation. In 3.3, Falstaff provokes the Hostess into a hilariously damning self-defence against his back-handed compliment to her as an 'otter': 'She's neither fish nor flesh, a man knows not where to have her.' 'Thou art an unjust man in saying so', protests the enraged Hostess, 'thou or any man knows where to have me, thou knave, thou' (102–7).

Responses to Falstaff's soliloquy on 'honour' may depend to an unusual extent not only on the values supported by particular interpretations or productions, but also on the views about war already held by readers and spectators. To confirm his own opinions, Falstaff employs the catechism, a device for indoctrinating students by teaching them correct answers to prescribed questions. While his technique helps him reduce military obligation to absurdity, his affirmation of life may be irresistible. Like the Prince's soliloquy, Falstaff's speech invites us to measure an emphatic viewpoint against other possibilities. After Falstaff attacks the vanity of dying to save face, the audience witnesses the King's strategy to protect his life by disguising loyal lords in his 'coats'. The Prince risks his life to save the King and then to kill Hotspur. In turn, Falstaff pretends that he is dead, then that Hotspur may revive, 'Why may not he rise as well as I?' (5.4.121–2), before claiming the honour he has mocked.

Shakespeare seems to limit diversity of experience and attitude during this third movement, then release them at its conclusion. But he does prepare for a comic ending, in part by transposing roles. Hotspur's similarity to the King as rebel and potential regicide grows, while the Prince takes up the role Hotspur played in earlier scenes: the forthright and generous young warrior. For the first time, in 5.4, the Prince meets Hotspur who has dismissed his challenge to single combat with rueful realism: 'O, would the quarrel lay upon our heads, / And that no man might draw short breath today / But I and Harry Monmouth!' (5.2.47–9). The dead Hotspur lies momentarily side-by-side with the supposedly dead Falstaff. Falstaff's ultimate resurgence when he takes credit, earned by the Prince, for killing Hotspur, will mirror the King's victory.

Belated comedy

King Henry's success is a strong probability based on well-known facts. The ending, however, could have been given a more tragic or a more heroic emphasis. Perhaps Shakespeare discovered, as he composed, how controlling was a comic vision for the action of *Part One*.[1] Shakespeare had learned to shape his dramatic presentation of history throughout groups of plays so that moments of humiliation, sacrifice, and festive joy would resonate with one another. By echoing earlier sequences in his own work, he produced effects often analogous to the typological repetitions which connected events of biblical history within the English mystery plays. (These popular cycles were still being staged in Shakespeare's youth, and he might well have seen one performed at Coventry, near Stratford-upon-Avon.)[2]

The primary type or model for the comic ending of *1 Henry IV* could well have been the first tavern scene. Act 5, Scene 4, the climactic episode in the final sequence, often recalls 2.4 because of its exceptional polish and tight-knit three-part design: (1) a 'breather' or pause in battle, emphasising the Prince's new solidarity with his brother and father, whose life he then saves from Douglas; (2) the verbal and physical combat between 'Harry' Monmouth and 'Harry' Hotspur, which ends with Hotspur's death and the Prince's epitaphs for Hotspur and Falstaff; and (3) the revival of Falstaff, leading to his virtual theft of the Prince's prize. Both scenes build on bustling entrances and exits. But the 'unyoked humour' of the first tavern scene has become the unyoked violence of the battlefield, while the illusion of two-handed performance by the Prince and Falstaff has turned into a series of deadly duels. Before his mock death, Falstaff, an enormous target, wanders miraculously unhurt through the thick of battle, like a spectre from the comic world of Eastcheap. 'Art thou alive? . . . I prithee speak' (5.4.129–31), says the Prince to his resurrected companion. By gaining credit for defeating Hotspur, Falstaff enjoys a splendid fool's revenge for the jokes practised upon him in the tavern. This vengeance proves truly comic, because the Prince graciously agrees, 'if a lie may do thee grace, / I'll gild it with the happiest terms I have' (5.4.148–9).

As in 2.4, the third episode serves as a fulcrum for reassessments and forecasts. In a broader view of Shakespeare's design, this play may be approached as the first of two plays about Henry IV, as the first play in the 'Henriad' of three plays, or as the second play in a larger group of either four or eight. If we recall that Falstaff will ultimately

[1] See Leonard F. Dean, 'From *Richard II* to *Henry IV*: a closer view', in *Studies in Honor of DeWitt T. Starnes*, ed. Thomas P. Harrison *et al.* (1967), pp. 37–52.

[2] Emrys Jones, *The Origins of Shakespeare*, 1977, pp. 35, 51.

be rejected by the Prince or that Henry V will die young, after his triumph at Agincourt, this will darken our sense of the ending with the shadows of events that are '[p]ast and to come' (*2 Henry IV* 1.3.108). But for now the King's side has won. The final mood is improbably benign – comparable to those interludes of happiness in the mystery cycles, which are eventually swallowed up in a succession of harrowing episodes and violent sacrifices. Or to the elation shared by fans of a sports team after a rare season of success.

Transforming the sources

Among the sources for *1 Henry IV* are not only quite different narrative and dramatic histories, but also popular and widely accessible materials such as ballads, proverbs, and biblical passages. Following his own practice in *Richard II*, Shakespeare sifted historical accounts with care, at the same time treating them more independently. He frequently developed characters or situations from minimal suggestions, or re-combined hints provided by his sources. Two of these are especially influential: one, Holinshed's *Chronicles* (1587) for the King's struggle with the Percys, leading to the

a

3 Two battle scenes from Act 5, Scene 4:
   a The Prince saves the King from Douglas in the touring production of the English Shakespeare Company, directed by Michael Bogdanov, 1986
   b Hotspur fights the Prince while Douglas 'kills' Falstaff. A possible Elizabethan staging drawn by C. Walter Hodges

Hotspur

Prince

Douglas

Falstaff

b

battle of Shrewsbury; and the other, popular dramatic traditions for the behaviour of the prodigal Prince and his riotous companions. But as consideration of the play's design and of Falstaff's original name, Oldcastle, has already suggested, Shakespeare was able to cross the seriousness of civil disorder with the comic humours of popular entertainment, recalling his earlier experiments in the history play, but with significant differences.

HISTORY PLAYS
The genre of history play seems to have been largely created by Shakespeare himself. In his first historical tetralogy, the three parts of *Henry VI*, and *Richard III* (probably

1589–93) and subsequently in *King John* (probably 1595–6), Shakespeare began to develop a form of drama which could represent the ongoing nature of political conflicts and suggest their complicated, interactive causes. These early histories resemble contemporary tragedies and plays about conquerors which employ multiple story lines and portray sensational violence. Like these plays, they also emphasise the strategies and consequences of intrigue and revenge, especially in *Richard III*. But through a proliferation of agents and motives, such coherent patterns often lose their shaping force in the history plays and become more incidental. Conflict and crisis may occur at any time in the action, revealing how closely the dramatist depends on the apparent incoherence of history.

The possibility that such open and chaotic formal structures might be unified by concepts which contemporaries would have recognised has provided a focus for most twentieth-century studies of the Elizabethan history play. E. M. W. Tillyard maintained that both of Shakespeare's tetralogies express a divine plan: God punished the English people for the deposition and murder of Richard II, and redeemed them through the victory of Henry VII over Richard III at the battle of Bosworth in 1485. Tillyard's case for the authority of this 'Tudor myth' in Shakespeare's age rested on the arguments of Tudor historians and theologians, and on the preaching of homilies (sermons) against rebellion.[1] Irving Ribner contended that a structure derived from Morality plays helped to shape English historical drama by emphasising the struggle between good and evil forces.[2] Lily B. Campbell's investigation of how the plays are informed by Renaissance historiographic practices on one hand and addressed to current political concerns on the other, has been followed by numerous studies which stress historical thought and literature, the political themes of kingship, constitution, and popular resistance, and the social and political crises of the 1590s.[3] Those who approach the histories in secular terms have often agreed with Tillyard and other exponents of ideological interpretation that Shakespeare wrote a national epic of fall and redemption, achieving Miltonic scope through an integrated sequence stretching through eighty-seven years and eight plays, from *Richard II* to *Richard III*.

While there can be no doubt that Shakespeare responded to such schemes of interpretation as the 'Tudor myth' – his characters expressed them and his spectators could have been quick to apply them – it is important to remember that Shakespeare's own plans were subject to the financial realities of theatrical production. Whether or not he conceived whole cycles of plays, his company seems never to have performed them as cycles; even two-part dramas like the *Henry IV* plays were not, as far as we know, staged on consecutive days. Shakespeare's company might have enjoyed more financial security, and have therefore planned more ambitious projects towards the end of the 1590s.[4] Yet, as the partisan responses of the Cobhams and the general theatre closing of 1597 (referred to above, pp. 5–6) make clear, theatrical fortunes remained precarious. It is safer to surmise that any design imposed by Shakespeare

[1] *Shakespeare's History Plays*, 1944.
[2] *The English History Play in the Age of Shakespeare*, 1957.
[3] *Shakespeare's 'Histories': Mirrors of Elizabethan Policy*, 1947.
[4] Gurr, pp. 3–4.

upon the endless disorders of fifteenth-century history would have been retrospective, emerging as he wrote, rather than as part of a consistent plan.

Although valuable not only for stimulating speculation about what history meant to Shakespeare and his audience, but also for the thematic continuities they have helped us to identify, theories of unity and order can also efface important differences between and within Shakespeare's tetralogies. *Richard II*, which begins the second tetralogy (1595), was composed perhaps three years after *Richard III* which concludes the first. The second group seems to be more deeply engaged with the role of private character in public life. It dramatises a far more problematic symbiosis between rulers and ruled. For extended passages in the *Henry IV* plays, overt political conflict like that which animates the first tetralogy or *King John* appears to recede. As we have seen, the style and movement of *1 Henry IV* distinguish it from *Richard II*. Moving from the comic design of *1 Henry IV*, Shakespeare presented in *Part Two* a more satiric anatomy of old King Henry's world, and approached tragedy with the turning away of Falstaff by the newly crowned King. Then, in *Henry V*, Shakespeare submitted the beliefs which sustain the social contract between king and people to rigorous testing. To understand the 'history' in any one play, therefore, is to understand distinctive combinations of characters and events, to recognise that important experiences and values may indeed occur only once, while others reverberate over long dramatic periods of time.

HISTORY IN THE PLAY

In addition to the 1587 edition of Holinshed's *Chronicles*, Shakespeare consulted and used less extensively Edward Hall's *The Union of the two noble and illustre famelies of Lancastre and Yorke* (1548), the *Chronicles* collected by John Stow (1580) and Stow's *Annals* (1592), as well as Thomas Phaer's verse portrait entitled 'Owen Glendower' from *A Mirror for Magistrates* (1559). Closely associated with these accounts, both as a source for *1 Henry IV* and as an analogue based on the same period of history, is Samuel Daniel's epic poem *The Civile Wars Between the Two Houses of Lancaster and Yorke* (1595).[1]

The group of middle-class writers, who together produced the volumes known as Holinshed's *Chronicles* (after their first editor, Raphael Holinshed, who died in 1586), nourished, and responded to, a growing fascination with historical writing of many kinds. The 1587 edition addresses those who are 'studious in antiquities, or take pleasure in the grounds of ancient histories'. Louis B. Wright believed that in Elizabethan eyes, history was 'the greatest of secular studies'. But earlier he stressed a more questionable 'middle-class' view: that history was 'safe, entertaining, instructive and useful'.[2] When Shakespeare had Richard of Gloucester boast in *3 Henry VI* of his ability to 'set the murtherous Machevil to school' (3.2.193), some spectators may have linked his villain to a stereotype for evil politicians. But members of the audience whose knowledge of historical writing included Machiavelli's political analyses might

[1] Bullough reprints excerpts from Holinshed, Stow's *Chronicles*, *A Mirror for Magistrates*, and Daniel, with several analogues including *The Famous Victories of Henry the fifth*.
[2] *Middle-Class Culture in Elizabethan England*, 1935, pp. 337, 301.

have brought to performances some of his attitudes towards causation.[1] These were famous or infamous, depending on one's viewpoint, because they stressed such secondary causes of events as character and accident, rather than the supposed primary cause, divine providence. That 'history' in its more restricted meaning, i.e. a narrative of government and political affairs, was not at all 'safe' became strikingly obvious when Sir John Hayward was imprisoned in the Tower of London in 1600.[2] Hayward had dedicated his *The First Part of the Life and Raigne of King Henrie IIII* to the Earl of Essex; he was suspected of having supported the Earl's ambitions by emphasising the deposition of Richard II. After the trial and execution of Essex in 1601, it became unwise for playwrights to scrutinise the postures and policies of English royalty. Shakespeare turned his attention to still more 'ancient' sources, the legends of early Britain, and the sophisticated biographies and histories by classical writers.

The fact that Shakespeare had anticipated and had helped to create strong interest in historical subjects does not mean that he relied on his audience to remember either *Richard II* or the chronicle descriptions of Henry's reign. Through the speeches of his characters, he quickly introduces necessary information: the play opens in 1400 (1.1.26), there is trouble on both borders (34–61), the royal Council will meet next Wednesday (102). If spectators *did* recall *Richard II*, they might well infer that the usurping King has ruled a year; he had concluded *Richard II* with a vow to expiate his guilt for the assassination of Richard by making a 'voyage to the Holy Land' (5.6.49), and he admits, during the speech which opens *1 Henry IV*, that 'our purpose now is twelve month old' (1.1.28).

In comparing Shakespeare's versions of English history with chronicle accounts, there is always some risk that a focus upon source materials will over-emphasise details which Shakespeare has effectively submerged, co-ordinated or transformed. Another risk is that a broader sense of the chronicles and of their power to excite Shakespeare's imagination will be lost. Readers curious about the potential significance of Shakespeare's omissions or about his extraction of voices and opinions from Holinshed may consult the Appendix. Annabel Patterson has argued that one of the main purposes guiding the compilation of chronicles by Holinshed and others was the wish to represent conflicting viewpoints, which he terms 'indifference'.[3] Apparent inconsistencies, therefore, result from a wary and self-critical attempt to preserve the texture of controversy. If the writers identified as 'Holinshed' were as careful to achieve 'indifference' as they were to record rare documents, the inclusiveness for which they have been criticised was more discriminating than it appears. For our understanding of how Shakespeare used this archive, Patterson's revaluation of Holinshed has several implications: that Shakespeare's primary source was simultaneously a model of multiplicity and caution, that particular details or anecdotes may have resonated for Shakespeare

---

[1] Felix Raab devotes the second chapter of *The English Face of Machiavelli: A Changing Interpretation 1500–1700*, 1964, to 'Machiavelli's reception in Tudor England'.

[2] To write about politics rather than antiquarian matters, some historians believed, required personal experience in government. See D. R. Woolf, *The Idea of History in Early Stuart England: Erudition, Ideology and 'The Light of Truth' from the Accession of James I to the Civil War*, 1990, p. 22.

[3] Patterson, pp. vii–x, 15.

because of far-flung connections in the chronicles themselves, and that serious students of the history in Shakespeare's plays can no longer limit their attention to 'Shakespeare's Holinshed' – those often cited passages on which he most heavily relied.

King Henry IV corresponds more closely than any other major character in this play to his prototype in Holinshed. Shakespeare seized upon his use of anticipatory violence ('policie often-times preventeth perill') and skill in fathoming the 'cloaked drift' of the Percy faction.[1] He attributed to Henry himself the fatalistic sense of retribution which in Holinshed, as earlier in Hall, becomes pervasive soon after Henry's coronation and recurs during the narrative of his reign. Bent upon staving off rebellions similar to his own, Shakespeare's King intends his rare public apearances to resemble the effects of a comet (3.2.47). Here Shakespeare probably picked up and transfigured Holinshed's belief that the comet or 'blasing starre' of 1402 was an omen for 'the great effusion of bloud that followed' (p. 19). Shakespeare apparently made his King more dependent on mental than on physical strength; Holinshed had credited him with killing thirty-six of his enemies at Shrewsbury, implying that his deeds inspired an unidentified 'other' to attack and kill Hotspur. Holinshed's Henry is partly victorious through the fighting of the 'lustie' Prince, but requires no life-saving intervention. Both kings are poisoned by guilt, but only Shakespeare's King claims, after one year of rule, that he might unify the English by leading them on a crusade to Jerusalem. In contrast, the year before he died (1412), according to Holinshed Henry did make preparations for a voyage to the Holy Land, 'there to recover the citie of Ierusalem from the Infidels' (p. 57). His motive, however, was more international than civil; he was disturbed by the 'malice' of Christian princes who fought one another rather than the enemies of their faith.

Shakespeare developed both Hotspur and the Prince in a more original manner which meshes with his alteration of historical fact. He condensed the period between 1400 when his play begins and 1403, the date of the battle of Shrewsbury. At the same time, he greatly reduced the age of Hotspur, who was born in 1364, before the King (1367); this change is already apparent in *Richard II* when young Henry Percy makes his first appearance as a sober, loyal, and hard-working supporter of the rebellion against Richard II. The fiery and imaginative warrior so envied by the King in *1 Henry IV* is Shakespeare's invention, tinged perhaps with memories of stirring ballads about Northumbrian battles, *The Hunting of the Cheviot* and *The Battle of Otterburn*. By adding several years to the Prince's age, Shakespeare supported other parallels between 'Harry' Percy and 'Harry' Monmouth; one 'star' of England is made to extinguish the other in single combat at the end of the play. It is probable that Shakespeare derived his sense of rivalry between the two young men from Samuel Daniel's heroic lines in the *Civile Wars*:

> There shall young *Hotespur* with a fury lead
> Meete with thy forward sonne as fierce as he.   (III, st. 97)

---

[1] Holinshed, III, 16, 23. References to this edition and volume will be placed in the text within parentheses.

Daniel credits the Prince with rescuing his father from Douglas, but not with killing Hotspur. Where Daniel blames Hotspur for being furious and violent as well as 'wrong counsail'd' (III, st. 109), Shakespeare makes possible a more rueful response to Hotspur's death. He turns the sickness of Northumberland, reported as occurring earlier by both Holinshed and Daniel, into a last-minute excuse and he follows Holinshed in stressing the role of Worcester, who betrayed Hotspur by misrepresenting the King's final terms for peace and then whetting him on to fight. Shakespeare surrounds the final encounter of the Prince and Hotspur with intimations of a brotherhood they might have shared in less tragic circumstances.

The characterisation of Prince Hal builds on specific sources, but branches off from the myths and popular dramatic traditions described in more detail below. Hall and Holinshed mention his military service on the Welsh marches, not his carousing in London taverns. According to Holinshed, towards the end of the reign King Henry feared that the Prince might be planning to 'usurpe the crowne' (p. 53). He had heard 'tales' from his servants, not only about the Prince's 'evill rule', but also about the large number of people who followed him. The Prince then publicly vowed his loyalty to the King. Otherwise Holinshed records no evidence that Henry seriously doubted his son's allegiance. In his *Chronicles* (1580), John Stow picks up several stories about the legendary wild Prince which Shakespeare may have noticed. For example, he describes how the Prince and his men would waylay the Prince's 'own receivers' in disguise, and 'distresse them of theyr money'. When they later complained to him, the Prince would pay them back and reward them for their trouble. This particular tale may be more historically accurate than others because it derives from the recollections of the Earl of Ormonde, a contemporary of the Prince, who later knighted him in France shortly before Agincourt.[1]

'O that Glendower were come!' (4.1.124), exclaims Hotspur before the battle. Welsh fighters did assist the Percys at Shrewsbury according to Holinshed; in the play, however, we learn from the Archbishop of York that Glendower 'comes not in, o'er-ruled by prophecies' (4.4.18). The first rebel to be mentioned in Scene 1 and the reason why King Henry must march to Wales at the end (in Holinshed he marches to York), Shakespeare's puzzling Glendower owes little to historical accounts. His prototype studied law in England; Holinshed says that he served Richard II, but records the chronicler Walsingham's contrary view that he served Henry Bullingbrook. Holinshed refers obscurely to '[s]trange wonders' at Glendower's birth (p. 21), (perhaps confusing the birth of Glendower with that of Mortimer), and is emphatic about quoting Hall on the folly of Welsh prophets (p. 23). Thomas Phaer, author of 'Owen Glendower' in *A Mirror for Magistrates*, zestfully describes how this foolish rebel died of exposure in the Welsh mountains. Shakespeare borrows Phaer's sentiment, echoed by Holinshed, to fuel the King's rage at Mortimer's defection: 'on the barren mountains let him starve' (1.3.88), but prolongs the dramatic life of Glendower himself, who is certainly the last rebel defeated in *Part Two*.[2]

---

[1] Charles L. Kingford, ed., *The First English Life of King Henry the Fifth*, 1911, pp. xvii, xix, 17.

[2] For the supposition that the Welsh Captain of *Richard II* might be Glendower, see Peter Ure, ed., *King Richard II*, 1956, note to 3.1.43.

THE WILD PRINCE

Shakespeare probably knew earlier dramatic versions of the material which he presented in his three plays about Henry IV and Henry V. Thomas Nashe had referred in *Pierce Penilesse his Supplication to the Divell* (1592) to '*Henrie* the fifth represented on the stage', while Henslowe's *Diary* recorded that a 'harey the v' was performed as 'ne' (new) by his company the Admiral's Men in 1595–6.[1] Kenneth Muir concludes his survey of sources for the *Henry IV* plays with a particularly tantalising allusion by Gabriel Harvey, who mentioned in *Foure Letters* (1592), ' "clownes; gowty Divels, and buckram Giants . . . hypocritical hoat spurres" and "some old lads of the Castell" '. 'Was there', asks Muir, 'a play as early as 1592 in which Oldcastle talked of men in buckram?'[2]

One of these popular plays has survived, but in a text that many scholars consider corrupt. *The Famous Victories of Henry the fifth* may have been first acted in the late 1580s or early 1590s; its title page (1598) links it to 'the Queenes Majesties Players', a prominent earlier troupe that had been disbanded. A play of the same title was entered in the Stationers' Register for 1594. *The Famous Victories* appears to abridge a longer play which covered the career of Henry V, from his youthful escapades to his victory at Agincourt and his marriage to Katherine of France. It therefore corresponds roughly to the plots of *1 Henry IV*, *2 Henry IV*, and *Henry V*.

That *The Famous Victories* can have been a direct source for much of *1 Henry IV* seems unlikely. As an analogue, it throws light on two major aspects of Shakespeare's play: the character of the Prince and the comic liveliness of Falstaff. The robbery episode which constitutes the main link between *The Famous Victories* and *Part One* quickly demonstrates that the Prince is a prodigal son. The King's receivers who have been attacked (before the play begins) suspect what has happened. When they enter, they cannot help but see the stolen money, laid out in a 'brave shewe'; they recognise the horses and identify the 'bignesse' of the Prince himself. One of them claims that he has 'belambd' this figure 'about the shoulders'. The Prince bullies the receivers into re-telling their 'tale' of robbery by 'foure', debunks the beating he has been given ('Gog's wounds you lamd them faierly, / So that they have carried away your money' *FV* 70–1), and threatens to have them hanged 'and all your kin' if they report him.

No delight in 'incomprehensible' lies inflates this jest or redeems its perpetrators from vindictiveness; no money is given back. Sir John ('Jockey') Oldcastle, a cautious flatterer scarcely distinguishable from the other companions, Ned and Tom, tamely echoes the Prince's lawless, parricidal schemes: 'Nobly spoken *Harry*, we shall never have a mery world til the old king be dead' (*FV* 475–6). With good reason, 'the old king' calls himself 'thrice accursed' for getting a son who 'with greefe / Will end his fathers days' (*FV* 262–4). In *The Famous Victories*, the Prince's relationship with the King is never complicated by the Percy rebellion. Shakespeare seems to have invented the scene in which Henry uses his grievances to turn the Prince against the Percys in the third Act of *1 Henry IV*; it owes little to the historical reconciliation which

---

[1] Nashe, I, 213; *Henslowe's Diary*, ed. R. A. Foakes and R. T. Rickert, 1961, p. 33.
[2] *The Sources of Shakespeare's Plays*, 1978, p. 103.

occurred shortly before the King's death, a scene described at length by Holinshed and Stow and dramatised in both *The Famous Victories* and *2 Henry IV*.

Incidents comparable to the robbery portraying the wild youth of Henry V were introduced and passed down through Thomas Walsingham's *Historia Anglicana* (1418), Tito Livio's *Vita Henrici Quinti* (1437), the *Brut* chronicle (1479), Fabyan's *Chronicle* (1516), and the English manuscript translation of Livio (1513) which added new matter from de Monstrelet's *Chroniques* and from the reminiscences of the Earl of Ormonde. John Stow, as we have seen, picks up the story about the Prince robbing his own receivers. Playwrights surely noted the potential appeal of such stories, replete with drunken brawling and a radical conversion by the prodigal son; in *The Famous Victories*, he approaches his father with dagger in hand and the King weeps. Shakespeare could turn, therefore, to a popular dramatic tradition centred on the life of Henry V which combined serious and comic styles of presentation.

This popular tradition tended to juxtapose rather than mingle serious and comic elements, enhancing the autonomy of comedians and clowns. An anecdote in *Tarlton's Jests*, an informal collection of practical jokes, shows how a resourceful clown might exaggerate his independence by improvising. Richard Tarlton (d. 1588), seems to have played a role similar to that of the clown, Dericke, in *The Famous Victories*. Referring to his performance at the 'Bull' in 'a play of *Henry the fift* wherein the judge was to take a box on the eare', the jest-book describes what happened when the actor playing the judge was apparently absent. Tarlton, therefore, 'ever forward to please, tooke upon him to play the same judge, besides his owne part of the clowne'.[1] After the corresponding scene in *The Famous Victories*, which focuses on the legend that the Prince struck the Lord Chief Justice, Dericke talks John Cobbler into impersonating a judge, then beats him for thinking he really is one.

By mingling comedy and history, Shakespeare made his play potentially more subversive. He altered the dramatic convention of juxtaposing history and comedy by fusing them within a more complex, provocative synthesis. Simultaneously, he upset social decorum by presenting the aristocratic Oldcastle as a notorious wit; the Cobhams were offended when Oldcastle, a colourless follower in *The Famous Victories*, merged with a figure 'ever forward to please' and entertain. Above all, by drawing the clown into his serious plot, Shakespeare transformed his role and heightened tensions between the truths of history and of drama.

HISTORY AND TRUTH

Two established attitudes would have influenced ways of perceiving the truth of history plays. On one hand, many people believed that staging could create a verisimilar effect so that history would appear to transpire before the eyes of the spectators. On the other hand, they thought that, after careful assessment and reconciliation of available evidence, historians could reach an understanding of the past which was largely accurate.[2] Just how powerful the first type of truth might have seemed in a dramatic history is suggested by Thomas Nashe's defence of drama in *Pierce Penilesse*:

---

[1] *Tarlton's Jests*, 1611, ed. J. O. Halliwell-Phillips, *Shakespeare Society* 20 (1844), 24–5.
[2] Woolf, p. 34.

How would it have joyed brave *Talbot* . . . to thinke that after he had lyne two hundred years in his Tomb, hee should triumphe againe on the Stage, and have his bones newe embalmed with the teares of ten thousand spectators . . . who, in the Tragedian that represents his person, imagine they behold him fresh bleeding.[1]

Attackers and defenders of the theatre recognised the force of such illusions. Titles of the period which repeatedly assert that history plays are 'true' may appeal both to the exciting effects of verisimilitude and to a faith in historical accuracy little mediated by fiction or art.[2]

Falstaff's resurrection at Shrewsbury activates these two senses of truth. As a clown who can suddenly improvise his death and rebirth, he seems to be filled with a dramatic life of his own. At the same time, Shakespeare partly created this rebirth by combining scattered facts and observations in Holinshed. From the first year of Henry V's reign came the information that Sir John Oldcastle, 'highlie in the kings favour' (p. 62) was accused of heresy but escaped from the Tower of London. He seems to have drawn, too, on rumours that had surfaced early in the reign of Henry IV, that Richard II was alive after all. And one especially striking detail from Holinshed's account of Shrewsbury (1403) surely helped to sow another seed for Falstaff's resurgence. Following Douglas' response when he has killed Blunt and three others in king's clothing – 'I marvell to see so many kings thus suddenlie arise one in the necke of an other' – the chronicler comments, 'The king in deed was raised' (p. 26). By connecting some of this wonder and relief to Falstaff, Shakespeare fashioned a theatrical miracle.

Shakespeare, finally, gave an unforgettable twist to the narrative and to the whole question of historical truth. How can the Prince, who has killed Hotspur and seen Falstaff 'dead', contradict Falstaff's revision of the facts: 'we rose both at an instant, and fought a long hour by Shrewsbury clock' (5.4.139–40)? Through the Prince, spectators may experience the slipperiness of history, which within the play often means to the characters what they remember or choose to believe.[3]

A multitude of competing views within an open-ended play about civil war would not necessarily create scepticism or undermine a faith that history might attain truth. Shakespeare the dramatist seems to be more interested in the visible results of ideas and arguments than in their philosophical significance. It seems ironically appropriate that Falstaff can transform history by carrying away the corpse of Hotspur – the character who has naively assented to a partisan version of history. But the incongruous image of Falstaff with Hotspur on his back lodges in our memories whether or not we unravel the complex of truths which knots it together.

The appeal of Falstaff and the contexts of interpretation

The popularity of *1 Henry IV* has always depended upon the great appeal of Falstaff, who engages readers and audiences through his surprising wit. In his numerous roles

[1] *Pierce Pennilesse his Supplication to the Divell* in Nashe I, 212.
[2] G. K. Hunter, 'Truth and art in history plays', *S.Sur.* 42 (1990), 15–24, finds thirteen examples in titles between 1573 and 1616. See also Herschel Baker, *The Race of Time: Three Lectures in Renaissance Historiography*, 1967, chap. 1, 'The truth of history'.
[3] Robert C. Jones, *These Valiant Dead: Renewing the Past in Shakespeare's Histories*, 1991, pp. 100–7.

– including companion, entertainer, father-figure, satirist, and thief – Falstaff brings us to the heart of the play's key relationships and draws our attention to its problematic themes. At the same time, his theatrical genius opens up the stricter boundaries of political and familial strife to a reflection of issues which have concerned different spectators, then and now. Decisions about which issues and which contexts of interpretation are appropriate have traditionally been inseparable from choices among Falstaff's many roles. He rarely leads us towards the whole truth, but he can never be ignored. We have therefore included many references to or opinions about Falstaff in the following discussion of contexts which can expand a view of the play. It begins with echoes and reverberations of the Oldcastle controversy (see Date, pp. 5–6). To conclude this survey, we look briefly at the most influential responses to Falstaff's character.

EARLY RECEPTION

In an Epilogue written for *Part Two* (but omitted from the 1600 quarto) before *Henry V* was performed, Shakespeare promised the audience that in the following play 'Sir John' will 'make you merry' and perhaps 'die of a sweat, unless already 'a be killed with your hard opinions, for Oldcastle died [a] martyr, and this is not the man'. Public 'opinions' may have surprised the playwright, causing him to reshape his game of arousing an audience's curiosity. Falstaff makes no one 'merry' in expected ways in *Henry V*; he dies offstage, leaving the audience to decide whether to blame his 'sweat', or the young King who has 'kill'd his heart' (2.1.88), or the 'hard' and contentious responses he had provoked offstage. By 1599 the reception of Falstaff generated a competing dramatic interpretation of the 'martyr' by the Lord Admiral's Men, entitled *The first part of the true and honorable historie, of the life of Sir John Old-castle, the good Lord Cobham*. The authors, Michael Drayton, Richard Hathway, Antony Munday, and Robert Wilson, warn their audience, 'It is no pampered glutton we present, / Nor agèd counsellor to youthful sins; / But one whose virtues shone above the rest, / A valiant martyr, and a virtuous peer.'[1]

Topical references to Falstaff/Oldcastle confirm his powerful effect upon early viewers, and clarify in retrospect the displeasure of the Cobham family. The Earl of Essex seems to have been referring contemptuously to Henry Brooke, the son of Lord Cobham, when he wrote to Sir Robert Cecil in February 1598, encouraging him to tell their friend, Sir Alex Ratcliffe, that 'his sister is maryed to Sr Jo. Falstaff'.[2] Much later, in 1633, Richard James, the librarian to Sir Robert Cotton, attempted to explain in a dedicatory epistle why Shakespeare had replaced 'Oldcastle' with the name of another historical figure who in fact outlived both Oldcastle and Henry V:

in Shakespeare's first show of Harrie the Fifth, the person with which he undertook to play a buffoon was not Falstaffe, but Sir Jhon Oldcastle, and that offence being worthily taken by personages descended from his title, as peradventure by many others also who ought to have

---

[1] Prologue 6–9 in *The Oldcastle controversy: Sir John Oldcastle, Part I and The Famous Victories of Henry V*, ed. Peter Corbin and Douglas Sedge, 1991.
[2] Leslie Hotson, *Shakespeare's Sonnets Dated and Other Essays*, 1949, p. 147.

him in honourable memory, the poet was put to make an ignorant shift of abusing Sir Jhon Fastolphe, a man not inferior of virtue though not so famous in piety as the other . . .[1]

James' judgement on Shakespeare as an unscrupulous entertainer and on his Falstaff as a buffoon was repeated by George Daniel of Beswick in his poem *Trinarchordia* (1647) and by the influential Thomas Fuller, both in *The Church History of Britain* (1655) and in his *Worthies of England* (1662).

Such reactions sever many of the lines mooring Falstaff to the larger vessel of Shakespeare's play. Although informed by condescension towards popular theatre, they help initiate a tendency, also evident in the quarto titles, to give Falstaff independent stature as a source of humours and 'conceits'. On one hand, their bias might well have been encouraged by Falstaff's growing prominence within a dramatic design which Francis Meres (above, p. 4), perhaps thinking of both parts, had in 1598 regarded as tragic. By treating Falstaff as a buffoon, James and others testify to his kinship with such fools and clowns as Richard Tarlton and William Kemp who were famous for pleasing crowds and stealing shows. On the other hand, the Oldcastle controversy exemplifies the kind of intensely topical interpretation from which the editors of the First Folio sought to free Shakespeare.[2] 'He was not of an age, but for all time', wrote Ben Jonson in his Folio poem celebrating Shakespeare's memory. The Oldcastle controversy reminds us that Shakespeare was also 'of an age', one in which Reformation passions ran high. It invites us to rethink the attitudes of spectators who needed either to censure Falstaff or to enjoy him mainly as a welcome distraction from their own concerns.

HONOUR

During the last decade of the sixteenth century, the rising fortunes of the Earl of Essex demonstrated the continuing power of 'honour' as a political value. Becoming the Queen's favourite, Essex also attracted a large group of dependent supporters. Chivalry had become largely ceremonial and recreational, an occasion for tournaments and jousts, while the English nobility had lost many of its feudal privileges to the centralised power of the crown. Yet the great prestige of mighty war lords lived on in an age which offered many opportunities for violent adventure. Mervyn James has shown that Essex defined himself and his objectives through a proud and militant code of honour which preserved medieval features.[3] Hotspur, 'the theme of honour's tongue' (1.1.80), might not have seemed anachronistic to Shakespeare's first audience.

A particularly interesting manifestation of 'honour' relevant to conflicts in *1 Henry IV* appears in the reason which Essex later gave to justify his treacherous behaviour: he sought only to circumvent 'flatterers' who surrounded the Queen, cutting off his channels of communication and keeping him from fulfilling his obligations.[4] A similar excuse was used by the leaders of the Northern Rebellion of 1569, and by the earlier representatives of the same Percy family, who in 1403 send out letters explaining that

[1] Samuel Schoenbaum, *William Shakespeare: A Compact Documentary Life*, 1978, pp. 195–6.
[2] Leah S. Marcus, *Puzzling Shakespeare: Local Reading and its Discontents*, 1988, p. 28.
[3] *Society, Politics and Culture: Studies in Early Modern England*, 1986, pp. 416–65.
[4] *Ibid.*, p. 445.

they cannot directly approach the King with their grievances because of 'the slander-
ous reports of their enimies' (Holinshed, p. 23). In the rebellion of 1405, which he
leads with Northumberland, the Archbishop of York maintains that he is in arms for
'feare of the king, to whom he could have no free accesse, by reason of such a multitude
of flatterers as were about him' (p. 37). In *Richard II*, Henry Bullingbrook removes
and destroys the King's 'flatterers', claiming that his aim is reform, not revolution.
And in *1 Henry IV*, Worcester explains to the King that the Percys, 'the first and
dearest of your friends', have rebelled to protect themselves against 'unkind usage,
dangerous countenance, / And violation of all faith and troth / Sworn to us in your
younger enterprise' (5.1.69–71). Here, 'dangerous countenance' implies not only that
the King's 'looks of love' (1.3.284) have vanished, but also that the Percys can no
longer rely upon support from a relationship characterised at best by what Marc Bloch
has called 'reciprocity in unequal obligations'.[1]

The 'honour' at stake in these exchanges refers to the capacities which equip an
individual for public trust or responsibility, to the opinions or 'credit' which make
possible the performance of tasks or duties, and to the primary reward of such
performance in a time when most public or governing roles were unsalaried.[2] Falstaff's
allegation that 'honour' is merely a 'word' (5.1.132) aptly represents its fleeting quality. Sixteenth-century advice on noble behaviour or military conduct rarely emphasises the interactive fluidity of reputation, although this quality may help to explain
why the honourable man had to be 'constant' and true to his word. What Falstaff
himself misses by equating honour with a quick recipe for death ('I like not such
grinning honour as Sir Walter hath' (5.3.56–7)) is that honour may have helped to
reduce violence. Honour communities flourish where the means of control exerted by
elite groups are precarious and personal. In Thomas Hobbes' opinion, honour provides the power to secure obedience.[3] It may also have functioned for Elizabethans as
a method of turning envy into emulation, as a stimulus for hospitality, and as a means
of policing the borders of gender and class.[4] At one extreme, honour brightened into
the armour of reputation and public faith which made it possible for Queen Elizabeth
to rule without a standing army. At the other, it shaded into confidence tricks and
protection rackets, not to mention robberies in which thieves 'cannot be true one to
another' (2.2.22–3).

A much darker depiction of 'honour' within both parts of *Henry IV* occurs when
Falstaff abuses his authority as a captain; Shakespeare directly reflects current scandals
by showing how Falstaff robs the wealthier citizens (who buy out of military service)
and exploits the poorer ones who are helpless. When Falstaff leads his 'ragamuffins'

[1] *Feudal Society*, vol. I, *The Growth of Ties of Dependence*, 1961, p. 228. Bloch is referring to vassalage at an
earlier period, but the description is pertinent here. Graham Holderness, *Shakespeare's History*, 1985, pp.
30–9, argues that Shakespeare understood and consciously reconstructed feudalism.
[2] See Anthony J. Fletcher, 'Honour, reputation, and local office-holding in Elizabethan and Stuart
England', in Fletcher and John Stevenson, eds., *Order and Disorder in Early Modern England*, 1985, pp.
92–115.
[3] *Leviathan*, ed. Michael Oakeshott, 1946, p. 58.
[4] Felicity Heal, *Hospitality in Early Modern England*, 1990, p. 23; Michael Hattaway, 'Fleshing his will in
the spoil of her honour: desire, misogyny and the perils of chivalry', *S.Sur.* 46 (1994), 121–35.

where they are 'peppered' (5.3.34–5) and maimed for life, he abandons a responsibility 'which, in its paternalism, far exceeded the normal duty of an officer towards his troops'.[1] Falstaff applies this duty only in one direction; he has already asked the Prince to stand over him if he falls in battle: '. . .'tis a point of friendship', he suggests (5.1.121–2). The Prince's answer offers an example of how 'detraction', as Falstaff soon remarks, does not 'suffer' honour to 'live with the living' (136). He reduces Falstaff's point of honour to grotesque absurdity: 'Nothing but a Colossus can do thee that friendship' (123).

FRIENDSHIP

The examples above suggest that Elizabethan friendship would often have been entangled with political alliances, codes of conduct, and public opinions. As Essex knew, one method of acquiring honour was to attract a large following.[2] This practice continued well into the next century. Troops of such 'friends' are temporarily assembled by the hero of Thomas Middleton's *A Mad World My Masters* (1604–7) so that he will be mistaken for a lord. Five hundred followers, an extraordinarily large group, lost the security of 'good lordship' when Prince Henry suddenly died in 1611.[3] Hotspur deplores the contaminating effects of alliance upon the 'bright honour' of the Percy family, which he longs to redeem from 'half-faced fellowship' with the King, a 'vile politician' (1.3.206, 238). To the King, the Prince's choice of friends is inevitably a public, political issue which brings dishonour upon his son. Anxious in Holinshed, as we have seen, when he hears about a 'great resort of people' at the Prince's house, the King suffers in Shakespeare because the Prince has one follower who is evidently 'known as well as Paul's' (2.4.442).

Montaigne believed that princes must forgo friendship altogether, for 'no friendship can be knit where there is so little relation and correspondence'. Men follow not the prince but his fortune, hoping 'by countenance and custom' to increase their own.[4] Montaigne was convinced that a true friendship like his bond with Etienne de La Boétie must be 'free', that is, unencumbered by kinship, marriage, domestic ties, or questions of benefit and obligation. It would be impossible to sustain two such friendships because one's friends might require competing services. The complete mingling of souls and wills in genuine as opposed to 'common' friendships, which were short-lived, might occur but once in a lifetime, he thought.[5]

With his emphasis on disinterested virtue and suspicion of allies or flattering dependants, Montaigne echoes discussions of friendship by Cicero and Plutarch. His influential contribution to an important humanist theme and literary topic strongly implies that many friendships must have been fraught with social and political differences. In a society built upon patronage and hierarchy, true marriages of male minds

---

[1] Lindsay Boynton, *The Elizabethan Militia 1558–1638*, 1967, p. 104.
[2] On large contemporary households, see G. R. Batho, ed., *The Household Papers of Henry Percy Ninth Earl of Northumberland 1564–1632*, 1962, pp. xxii–iii.
[3] See Leonard Tennenhouse, 'Sir Walter Ralegh and the literature of clientage', in Guy Fitch Lytle and Stephen Orgel, eds., *Patronage in the Renaissance*, 1981, p. 253.
[4] 'Of the inequality that is between us', in *Complete Works*, trans. Donald M. Frame, 1958, p. 195.
[5] *Ibid.*, 'Of friendship', pp. 135–44.

would have been almost impossible. As if drawn to complicated attachments, Shakespeare represents friendships which are marked by conspicuous disparities of age, rank, and emotional need. Perhaps the most challenging and unlikely of all these friendships is the one between Falstaff and the Prince. Paradoxically, their relationship, by far the closest in the play, achieves the freedom which Montaigne prized, not in spite of, but because of obstacles and constraints.

By approaching Falstaff in the ambiguous terms of Renaissance friendship, we may be able to balance interpretations which treat him as a temptation to cast away, a problem to outgrow, or as the occasion for indulgences which can be wilder because they are also temporary.[1] Barbara Everett appeals from a recent critical tradition preoccupied with the Prince's growth to an earlier focus upon Falstaff, once 'widely agreed to be the dramatist's greatest character'.[2] Because the play so effectively fuses history and comedy, one may also appeal to a perspective which emphasises relations between characters: without their friendship, neither Falstaff nor the Prince would engage our attention so fully. Ronald A. Sharp explains the power of friends to transform each other by using an analogy with Edward Hyde's theory of the gift. Gifts, according to Hyde, accumulate value as they circulate; they create abundance by sharing it.[3] So conceived, friendship becomes a comic art, one that is richer and riskier for its inclusion of utilitarian selfishness, competition, and the occasional reckoning.

Through his patronage, the Prince extends hospitality to Falstaff by paying his bills. Through his imagination, Falstaff gives the Prince opportunities to play serious games. Together they turn patriarchal society upside down and inside out, when the young Prince becomes a nurturing and protective lord or the old man mentors him by playing the roles of prodigal youth and childlike dependant. As a father who can be mocked or manipulated, or as a 'plump' maternal figure who serves up food for the Prince's keen wit, Falstaff has frequently been approached in the context of psycho-analytic theories oriented, like many political readings, towards the future of the developing young man.[4] It is also possible, however, that Falstaff's familial traits reflect ways, especially in great households like Burleigh's, in which roles overlap among friends, followers, servants, wives, and children.[5]

Flourishing outside the court, which was often seen as inimical to friendship, these friends speak a social and physical language of burlesque, rather than the erotic language of compliment more typical of ideal and instrumental male friendships.[6] The Prince uses the words 'friend' or 'friends' nineteen times to Falstaff's one, but never about Falstaff. Except during the first part of Act 1, Scene 2 (a mere eighty-five

[1] For example, see D. J. Palmer, 'Casting off the old man: history and St Paul in *Henry IV*', *CQ* 12 (1970), 267–83.
[2] 'The fatness of Falstaff: Shakespeare and character', *PBA* 76 (1991), 109.
[3] *Friendship and Literature: Spirit and Form*, 1986, pp. 84–8, 93.
[4] Valerie Traub, *Desire and Anxiety: Circulations of Sexuality in Shakespearean Drama*, 1992, pp. 50–70.
[5] See Richard C. Barnett, *Place, Profit, and Power: A Study of the Servants of William Cecil, Elizabethan Statesman*, 1969, pp. 5, 9.
[6] Alan Bray, 'Homosexuality and the signs of male friendship in Elizabethan England', *History Workshop Journal* 29 (1990), 1–19.

lines) and on three brief occasions in Act 5, these friends are never alone together onstage. Falstaff complains, when his fellow thieves hide his horse and themselves, that

I have forsworn his company hourly any time this two-and-twenty years, and yet I am be-witched with the rogue's company. If the rascal have not given me medicines to make me love him, I'll be hanged. It could not be else. I have drunk medicines.   (2.2.13–16)

To speak of his love at all, Falstaff resorts to a superstitious explanation favoured by the fathers of rebellious daughters; he also speaks very loudly for an audience just offstage: the Prince, who has surely not known Falstaff for twenty-two years, and Poins, who just as surely bewitches no one during *1 Henry IV*. His one other mention of love for the Prince could be taken as an indirect confession, but it also signals to the Prince that their balancing act demands some restraint. When Falstaff first proposes 'a play extempore', Hal, hanging on to Falstaff's supposed cowardice, replies, 'Content, and the argument shall be thy running away.' In one of the most poignant lines of the play, Falstaff responds, 'Ah, no more of that Hal, an thou lovest me' (2.4.230–33).

Falstaff seems to understand that one friend can only win a battle of wits if both do, hard as each must try to top the other. And so he urges the Prince: 'Play out the play' (2.4.402). Trust in their bond makes possible such experiments with the self, just as it allows Falstaff to fall asleep confidently behind the arras. Perhaps the Prince forgets, in the heroic loneliness of his conquest over Hotspur, that his 'old acquaintance', apparently slain, has been more to him than a 'vanity' (5.4.105). Falstaff soon puts him out of this simple, honourable humour. With an independence typical of their friend-ship, he acts out a duplicity often typical of honour, and beats the Prince at his new chivalric game.

FESTIVITY

Holiday in *1 Henry IV* is both a basic principle of structure and a rich trove of dramatic experience. To early modern religious reformers who sharply regulated or even elimi-nated holidays, viewed as pagan disorders, plays themselves seemed dangerous.[1] In addition to exploiting the theatricality associated with unruly entertainment and revelry, Shakespeare draws upon archetypes familiar from sports and celebrations as one clear way to identify his characters and to associate them with the forces of time and change, ritualised through festivity.

Popular dramatic traditions had long been animated through physical proximity of performer to spectator in dining-halls, churchyards, streets, and market-places.[2] Elizabethan clowns like Richard Tarlton were notorious for adopting the actor's potential autonomy as their special privilege. David Wiles has argued that William Kemp, an enormously popular and talented clown, would have played Falstaff.

---

[1] See Jonas A. Barish, *The Antitheatrical Prejudice*, 1981; Jean E. Howard, *The Stage and Social Struggle in Early Modern England*, 1994.
[2] Robert Weimann, *Shakespeare and the Popular Tradition in the Theatre: Studies in the Social Dimension of Dramatic Form and Function*, 1978.

Because Kemp left the company before *Henry V* was completed, Wiles believes, Shakespeare chose to make Falstaff die offstage.[1] Some sense of the clown's irrepressible vigour might have prepared early audiences at *Part One* for Falstaff's resurrection. Perhaps they might also have noticed how Shakespeare gives *his* clown an added challenge, that of provoking laughter in the midst of violence and death. By tempering sympathy for Falstaff, Shakespeare seems to play him against the grain of a convention which would otherwise have given him overwhelming dramatic advantages.

When he jokingly impersonates the King, Falstaff resembles household jesters and fools, whose wisdom and careful observation taught them how and when to subvert authority.[2] When he wildly insults the Prince, or conjures up attackers in Kendal green, he embodies the excessive energies of carnival.[3] As with their Morality-play roles of Vice and Prodigal, both Falstaff and the Prince self-consciously portray the battle between Shrovetide (the English equivalent of carnival) and Lent, between an old fat man and a young lean one, a 'huge hill of flesh' and a 'starveling' (2.4.202–3).[4] They compete, as well, for control of their jokes and games, recalling the Lords of Misrule chosen to preside over amateur entertainments, especially during the Christmas season. The Prince, who as Henry V will found the feast of Crispin Crispianus to commemorate his victory at Agincourt, already shows an English monarch's sensitivity to the political powers of spectacle and holiday.[5] In effect, he censors Falstaff's performance as king, and tries to turn the 'play extempore' into an exhibition of royal displeasure. Whereas Falstaff prefers to fuse holiday and everyday, the Prince draws a line between them, culminating on the battlefield when he throws Falstaff's own bottle of sack at him, demanding whether it is 'a time to jest and dally now' (5.3.52). In a society where special clothing, dishes, foods, and pastimes were reserved for use on particular holidays, the Prince's attitude might have found a more sympathetic response at other times as well.

Whether festivals provided outlets for social tensions or methods of sustaining resistance to authority, they seem to have been deeply rooted in popular practices. Shakespeare's play suggests that such roots may be tapped for negative as well as positive purposes, and that festive liberties may even be used against the people. Prince Hal wins the hearts of his drinking companions, the tavern drawers, who, he claims, consider him 'no proud Jack like Falstaff' (2.4.9–10), then urges Francis to rebel against his master by breaking his indentures and running away (38–40). Even when his own festive humour runs away with him, the Prince may be trying to find out how popularity works to empower one king or to get rid of another.[6] Perhaps

---

[1] *Shakespeare's Clown: Actor and Text in the Elizabethan Playhouse*, 1987, p. 128; see also Wilson, *Fortunes*, pp. 124–5.

[2] Walter J. Kaiser, *Praisers of Folly: Erasmus, Rabelais, Shakespeare*, 1964, pp. 267–75; Enid Welsford, *The Fool: His Social and Literary History*, 1961, pp. 163 ff.

[3] Michael D. Bristol, *Carnival and Theatre: Plebeian Culture and the Structure of Authority in Renaissance England*, 1985, pp. 204–7.

[4] For an illuminating discussion of Shrovetide customs, see François Laroque, *Shakespeare's Festive World: Elizabethan Seasonal Entertainment and the Professional Stage*, 1993, pp. 96–104.

[5] David Cressy, *Bonfires and Bells: National Memory and the Protestant Calendar in Elizabethan and Stuart England*, 1989, pp. xii, 67.

[6] Sheldon Zitner, 'Anon, anon: or a Mirror for a Magistrate', *SQ* 19 (1968), 63–70.

he is sometimes inclined to get back, through Falstaff, at the people of England, the very people, Holinshed said, who had been 'so readie to joine and clappe hands' with his usurping father (p. 58). Holinshed commended the Prince for 'recreations, exercises, and delights' which were not 'offensive or at least tending to the damage of anie bodie' (p. 54). But Shakespeare emphasised his determination to 'make offence a skill' (1.2.176). By taunting Falstaff for his fat body and repeatedly comparing him to slaughtered meat, the Prince may prefigure the end of carnival and the rejection of his friend.

C. L. Barber argued, in his seminal treatment of Shakespearean festivity, that characters experience a ritual process which moves them 'through release to clarification'.[1] Barber's formula accords with the way in which the Prince and Falstaff can test and strengthen one another through their differences. It illuminates Falstaff's unparalleled candour about his own weaknesses and connects his resurrection, through folk plays and motifs, to fertility rituals which reconcile human with natural cycles. What Barber's harmonising concept does not address are the repeated hints within the play of rituals which are far more contradictory and sacrificial.

REFORMATION

How would Falstaff have appealed to those concerned with religious issues? When Ben Jonson anatomised English society in *Bartholomew Fair* (1614), he included references to the slaughter of the innocents ('childermass'), the martyrdom of St Bartholomew (patron saint of butchers), the massacre of Protestant Huguenots by Catholics in France on St Bartholomew's Day, 1572, and the burning of English Protestants in adjoining Smithfield during the reign of Queen Mary (1553–8). Through a travesty of epic heroes and Puritan zealots, Jonson encouraged his audience to laugh at the fears and hatreds which eventually helped propel England into a religious civil war. It is possible that passages from *1 Henry IV* could have been written in a similar spirit; Falstaff's biblical citations should have been amusing for the audience and safe for Shakespeare because Falstaff mocks his own pretensions, along with those of pious Puritans.[2] But Shakespeare was sailing much closer than Jonson to the high winds of Reformation controversy. Instead of merely alluding to a dark history of religious violence, he took it upon himself to burlesque Oldcastle the martyr, and to treat Falstaff's promises of 'amendment' as a running joke. Emphasising the Prince's plan for '[r]edeeming time' (see 1.2.177 and note), he initiated an exploration of this reformer's career.

Whereas 'honour' and 'festivity' tend to be associated with impulses which fix social patterns, 'friendship' and 'reformation' have more dynamic properties. Gerhart B. Ladner emphasises a definition of reform which is theologically Catholic but also consistent with the comic design of *1 Henry IV*. He distinguishes reform from revolution which claims total improvement, from the cyclical Machiavellian 'ricorso'

---

[1] Barber, pp. 6–10.
[2] Naseeb Shaheen points out that twenty-six of the fifty-four biblical allusions that he counts in *Part One* are spoken by Falstaff, 'probably suggested by Oldcastle's religious background', in *Biblical References in Shakespeare's History Plays*, 1989, p. 137.

which minimises human agency, and from the Protestant spiritual rebirth which occurs once. Reform is a process of *multiple* repetition which permits the most inventive elements in human history to survive.[1] So defined, reformation in *Part One* can point ahead, to *2 Henry IV*, with its numerous meditations on time, and to the secular apocalypse of Agincourt in *Henry V*. In his edition of *2 Henry IV*, Giorgio Melchiori explores the hypothesis that for Shakespeare, who was trying to put new shapes on old and familiar dramatic materials, the entire 'Henriad' is a 'remake'.[2]

Within *1 Henry IV*, the evidence of reformation in Ladner's sense is more limited but nonetheless vivid. When the King lectures his son on the lessons of his own past, he employs a highly tendentious parallel between then and now, between King Richard and Henry Bullingbrook as they were, the Prince and Hotspur as they are. These equations slot Richard into the role of a 'skipping King' who

> ambled up and down,
> With shallow jesters, and rash bavin wits,
> Soon kindled and soon burnt, carded his state,
> Mingled his royalty with capering fools . . .   (3.2.60–3)

So described, Richard himself resembles a lively theatre clown; William Kemp, who perhaps played Falstaff, would later dance from London to Norwich in 1599. Long before he literally digs up King Richard and re-buries him (*Henry V*, 4.1.295–305), the Prince, by 'mingling' with Falstaff, may be redeeming both Richard's time and his own.

Whether Shakespeare lighted by accident or intention upon Oldcastle as a figure to couple with his princely reformer, there is wonderful propriety in his choice. For after the Reformation, Oldcastle the Lollard became 'one of those cultural icons in which are epitomized a society's conflicting and shifting values'.[3] There are also multiple ironies in the fact that the Cobham descendants of Oldcastle belonged not to a persecuted sectarian minority but to a ruling class which fervently supported the union of church and state. For all their disagreements over the regulation of religion, members of this consensus came together in attacking religious independents who questioned such a union.[4] Because Lollard views frequently coincided with those of the later radical independents and sectarians, Oldcastle's theology could have been as embarrassing to his heirs as was his alleged rebellion against Henry V – and not so easily explained away.[5] In an intellectual climate hostile to unorthodox attitudes, Shakespeare may have managed to approach religious radicalism by couching a 'damnable iteration' (1.2.72) of the Bible in the language of folly.

---

[1] *The Idea of Reform: Its Impact on Christian Thought and Action in the Age of the Fathers*, 1959, pp. 25–35, 436.
[2] Melchiori, pp. 9–15.
[3] Patterson, p. 131.
[4] G. H. Williams, *The Radical Reformation*, 1962, pp. xxiii–xxxi. See also, for a 'third body of ideas' that was rejected by the court and the established church on one hand, and by orthodox Puritanism on the other, Christopher Hill, *Milton and the English Revolution*, 1979, p. 69.
[5] A. G. Dickens, *The English Reformation*, 1967, chap. 2, describes the survival of Lollardry into the sixteenth century.

APOLOGIES FOR FALSTAFF

Falstaff may not be the central figure in his play, but during four hundred years he has become more familiar than almost every hero and heroine. Like Hamlet and Cleopatra, Falstaff enjoys a privileged existence in our cultural awareness; many feel they 'know' him, including some who have neither read nor seen any of the three plays in which he appears. He has lent his name to an opera, a novel, and, most appropriately, a beer. As Shakespeare does for his greatest heroes and villains, he gives Falstaff weaknesses which are never completely effaced by the qualities which please audiences, qualities which are much easier to experience than to describe or recapture.

For over three hundred years after the play was first performed, allusions to and commentary about *1 Henry IV* overwhelmingly emphasised Falstaff. Most of these writers appear to assume that enthusiasm for Falstaff is general. At the same time, they try to explain why Falstaff should be so charismatic when his faults are so glaring. By far the most influential earlier commentaries are those by Samuel Johnson in the notes to his edition of 1765, and by Maurice Morgann in his monograph, *Essay on the Dramatic Character of Sir John Falstaff* (1777).

Johnson considered the two parts of *Henry IV* to be more widely read than Shakespeare's other works; no two plays had ever 'afforded so much delight'. He apostrophised Falstaff as 'unimitated, unimitable', then asked, '[H]ow shall I describe thee?' Answering his own question must have strained Johnson's professed admiration for Shakespeare's 'mingled drama'; it would be difficult to find, in the many critical references to Falstaff as a parasite or tempter, a stronger condemnation than Johnson's. 'Falstaff is a character loaded with faults, and with those faults which naturally produce contempt . . . At once obsequious and malignant, he satirises in their absence those whom he lives by flattering. He is familiar with the Prince only as an agent of vice . . .' But in explaining Falstaff's necessity to 'the prince that despises him', Johnson shifted quickly to an unsentimental appreciation of Falstaff's 'perpetual gaiety', which, he suggested, is in no way criminal or ambitious. We are left, then, to ponder Johnson's final harshness and to puzzle over his emotional withdrawal in declaring that 'neither wit nor honesty ought to think themselves safe with such a companion when they see Henry seduced by Falstaff'.[1]

Johnson revealed his disproportionate interest in Falstaff by spending in his concluding note more than twice as many words upon him as upon the Prince and Hotspur combined. Maurice Morgann, defending Falstaff against what he takes to be a universal verdict on his cowardice, wrote the longest and the most often cited early discussion of any Shakespeare character. 'There is no better piece of Shakespearian criticism in the world', said A. C. Bradley (1902). Certainly, as Jonathan Bate suggests, there can be few more 'generous' ones.[2]

Like Johnson, Morgann saw how repellent Falstaff's vices may become: 'here we shall behold him most villainously unprincipled and debauched; possessing indeed the same Courage and ability, yet stained with numerous vices'. These vices 'become still

[1] *Johnson on Shakespeare*, ed. Arthur Sherbo, *The Works of Samuel Johnson*, vol. VII, 1968, pp. 522–4.
[2] Ed., *The Romantics on Shakespeare*, 1992, p. 8. Bradley's praise is cited by Fineman in Morgann, p. 27.

more intolerable by an excess of unfeeling insolence on one hand, and of base accommodation on the other'.[1] But by coupling these traits with the 'leading quality' of quick wit, by showing what happens when such an individual is 'grouped' with or related to others, and by imposing upon him the limits of genre and artifice, Shakespeare produced a comic figure who 'passes thro' the Play as a lawless meteor, and we wish to know what course he is afterwards likely to take'.[2]

This paradox – a carefully wrought character who is simultaneously a 'lawless meteor' – seems designed to astound a 'jury' of moralistic readers and spectators. Distracted by the issue of Falstaff's cowardice, critics and theatre historians often neglect Morgann's implicit attack upon this audience. His defence of a constitutional or 'natural' courage, of a capacity for pragmatic behaviour which may even 'avail itself of flight', is a way of demonstrating that Shakespeare 'makes a character act and speak from those parts of the composition, which are *inferred* only, and not directly shown'.[3] In building his case, Morgann wrote as if Falstaff had a past: 'He found himself esteemed and beloved with all his faults, nay *for* his faults, which were all connected with humour, and for the most part, grew out of it.'[4] But Morgann also undertook, as the 'jury' he cajoled did not, a disciplined scrutiny of the evidence against his own argument. The guilty parties in this trial were those who responded to Falstaff superficially, missing the substance and the true pleasure of Shakespeare's art.

Morgann was followed by A. W. Schlegel (1808), William Hazlitt (1817), and A. C. Bradley, while James Gillray and Isaac Cruikshank, cartoonists active in the 1790s, and later Samuel Taylor Coleridge (1812–13), carried on Johnson's view of Falstaff as an immoral, destructive tempter. Coleridge associated Falstaff with the dynamic villains Richard III and Iago.[5] (Alexander Pushkin would later group him with Angelo and Shylock.) Falstaff's defenders emphasised instead his love of life, laughter, and society. For Hazlitt, he was 'the most substantial comic character that ever was invented'. The same keen mind which Coleridge thought corrupt, seemed for Hazlitt to be 'an emanation of a fine constitution; an exuberance of good-humour and good nature'. Hazlitt regarded his vices as 'characters' assumed by Falstaff:

He is represented as a liar, a braggart, a coward, a glutton, etc. and yet we are not offended but delighted with him; for he is all these as much to amuse others as to gratify himself . . . The unrestrained indulgence of his own ease, appetites, and convenience, has neither malice nor hypocrisy in it.[6]

Although the rejection of Falstaff was not treated as a major issue before Bradley, both Morgann and Hazlitt seem to have been disturbed by the ending of *Part Two*.[7] Morgann assumed that the Prince knew Falstaff's faults as well as he did, but unlike Hal, he wanted to rescue Falstaff from detractors anyway. Hazlitt conceded that

---

[1] Morgann, p. 210.
[2] *Ibid.*, pp. 214–15.
[3] *Ibid.*, pp. 154, 168.
[4] *Ibid.*, pp. 151–2.
[5] *Lectures 1808–1819 on Literature*, ed. R. A. Foakes, *The Collected Works of Samuel Taylor Coleridge*, vol. V, pt 1, 1987, pp. 575–6.
[6] Hazlitt, p. 279.
[7] See G. K. Hunter, 'Shakespeare's politics and the rejection of Falstaff', *CQ* 1 (1959), 232–3.

Shakespeare himself knew best, but admitted,. 'we never could forgive the Prince's treatment of Falstaff'.[1] Bradley largely discounted Falstaff's vices while stressing his novelty, as had Morgann. Bradley celebrated Falstaff's 'freedom of soul' which was 'illusory only in part, and attainable only by a mind which had received from Shakespeare's own the inexplicable touch of infinity which he bestowed on Hamlet and MacBeth and Cleopatra, but denied to Henry the Fifth'.[2]

In reaction against a romantic tendency to take characters out of their contexts in plays, early twentieth-century critics often approached Falstaff as a dramatic role or function. They also subordinated his vitality to the unifying effects of more general themes and images. The most influential study, John Dover Wilson's *The Fortunes of Falstaff*, emphasised his similarities to the Vice, the conventional tempter–entertainer of the Morality plays.

Dissenting from this paradigm, W. H. Auden and William Empson took their own strong responses in surprising directions. Without the Falstaff scenes, Auden suggested, *Henry IV* would become the 'middle section of a political trilogy, which could be entitled *Looking for the Doctor*'.[3] He reflected that Falstaff's love for the Prince was 'tragic' because Falstaff himself, lacking any sense of time or consequences, cannot see it is hopeless. This ever youthful and creative figure (a fat man, wrote Auden, looks like 'a cross between a very young child and a pregnant mother') is both a 'Lord of Misrule' and 'a comic symbol for the supernatural order of Charity'.[4]

Empson's qualified defence of Falstaff ('It is hard to defend this strange figure without doing it too much') questioned the lack of ambivalence in Dover Wilson's view. To explain why Falstaff has a 'heart' that can be broken when the new King rejects him, Empson joined the conflicting insights of Johnson and Morgann in a new apology. As Morgann acknowledged, Falstaff had 'sordid' inner vices; and as Johnson suggested, Falstaff 'feels in himself the pain of deformity' even if he does 'make sport of it among those whom it is in his interest to please'. If Falstaff was Dover Wilson's medieval Vice, thought Empson, he would have no inner life, 'no interior at all'.[5]

Empson's tact, so unexpected, in accounting for the 'heart' of a Falstaff 'driven on by an obscure personal shame of an amoral sort' was remarkably similar to the tact he found in Shakespeare, who included what had to be made 'obvious' for his first audiences but, going beyond unambiguous meanings, 'rode remarkably near the edge'.[6] What seemed clear to Empson was Falstaff's Renaissance role as an aristocratic, Machiavellian tutor who initiated a future ruler into a flawed world. What seemed more perplexing was the 'power' of Falstaff, connected to his 'shame' and somehow realised in 'love': the love which attracted the 'young thieves' he tutored, and the 'love' he himself expressed for them. Baffled, he admitted, by the potent

---

[1] Hazlitt, p. 285.
[2] 'The rejection of Falstaff' in *Oxford Lectures on Poetry*, 1909, p. 273.
[3] Auden, p. 186.
[4] *Ibid.*, pp. 195–8.
[5] Empson, p. 65. This chapter is a revision of 'Falstaff and Mr Dover Wilson', *KR* 15 (1953), 213–62. Johnson's comment on 'deformity' comes from his note on 'the Burning Lamp' (3.3.20); he suggested that Falstaff bitterly resents insults about his being fat.
[6] Empson, p. 39.

compound of shame, charm, desire, and drink in Falstaff's 'heart', Empson stated unforgettably, 'Indeed, if you compare Hal to his brother and his father, whom the plays describe so very unflinchingly, it is surely obvious that to love Falstaff was a liberal education for him.'[1]

Stage history

PLAYHOUSE BEGINNINGS

When *1 Henry IV* was first performed in 1596–7, Shakespeare's company may have been in transition among several playhouses. Until the former Theatre was taken apart, moved from the northern edge of the City to the south bank of the Thames, and reconstructed as the Globe (1599), they probably used either the Curtain or the Swan.[2] *1 Henry IV* would have been well adapted to travel within London – or beyond, when the theatres were temporarily closed. From the text we can conjecture that the players must have required only a few portable properties: a crown, a throne, a joint stool, Falstaff's mug, cushion, and bottle, Hotspur's letter, and assorted weapons. Spectators entering the playhouse might well have seen a stage which would be bare except, perhaps, for a throne, some rushes on the floor, and hangings at the rear. An upper playing area, used to represent castle battlements in *Richard II*, would not be required.

The Curtain and the Swan were probably, like the Globe, capable of holding three thousand spectators who sat in tiers of galleries or stood in the yard or 'pit' which was lower than a platform stage thrust out from one side of the amphitheatre.[3] During daylight performances in the open air, spectators would have seen one another, and their faces would have been visible to the actors. Other distinctive features of Elizabethan staging were the rapid pace of performance and the symbolic quality of some techniques.[4] Within the 'two hours traffic of the stage' (Prologue, *Rom.*), the rhythm of scenes was enhanced by their continuity. Not only costumes or actions, but also different parts of the stage and its structure could quickly take on significant meanings. A flurry of entrances and exits, as in the tavern scene of *1 Henry IV*, might distinguish a public from a more private setting.

Of all the arts used to engage spectators in the Elizabethan theatre, the most important would have been the skills of the actors who could exploit their physical proximity to the audience.[5] Specific speeches would have created immediate and flexible relationships between actors and audiences, varying not only with cast changes but also from day to day. Because many plays encouraged actors to address the

---

[1] *Ibid.*, p. 67.
[2] Gurr, *Stage*, pp. 45–8, 118–20.
[3] Gurr, *ibid.*, pp. 123–31, describes the excavations of the Rose Theatre site in 1989 which indicated differences in the designs of the Southwark playhouses.
[4] Glynne Wickham stresses the shift from an 'emblematic' towards a more naturalistic staging style during this period, in *Early English Stages 1300–1600*, 3 vols., 1959–81.
[5] John Russell Brown discusses the new naturalism of Elizabethan acting in *Shakespeare's Plays in Performance*, 1969, pp. 22–39. Cf. Gurr, *Stage*, pp. 100–3. For the influence of playhouse conditions on acting, see Bernard Beckerman, *Shakespeare at the Globe 1599–1609*, 1962, pp. 127–37.

audience directly, even using 'asides' when other actors were onstage, it may be difficult to determine the inwardness or privacy of speeches in which a character seems to think aloud. The Prince's soliloquy in 1.2 plainly provides, in a non-realistic manner, necessary information about his secret plans. But by stepping forward to say 'I know you all', the actor can also implicate the audience, catching the attention of spectators who might have been waiting for the next appearance of Falstaff and ready to chime in whenever the comedy became more raucous.[1] The development of modern theatres which simulate the dimensions of Shakespeare's playhouses has not extended to the inclusion of noisy 'groundlings' like the ones referred to by Sir Thomas Palmer, in a commendatory poem prefaced to the Folio edition of Beaumont and Fletcher in 1647: 'I could praise Heywood now, or tell how long / Falstaff from cracking nuts hath kept the throng.'

Writing his plays for his own company of all male actors, Shakespeare must often have shaped the script to the performer. He would have anticipated the skills of his players, a group which included thirteen men (some of whom were shareholders in the company) and four boys. For example, he could only have written the part of Lady Mortimer, Glendower's daughter, if he could count upon the talents of a boy able to act and sing in Welsh (see 3.1.191 SD and note). Continuing experience with one another and specialisation in particular types of role equipped this company to develop and sustain a remarkably large repertoire. In performing *1 Henry IV*, which presents thirty-three characters and additional attendants, travellers, and soldiers, the majority of actors in Shakespeare's company must have played several roles. The question of which actors took major parts in *1 Henry IV* has caused much speculation: Richard Burbage has been proposed as the Prince; John Heminges, Thomas Pope, and Will Kemp (the clown) as Falstaff. Shakespeare perhaps conceived Falstaff's role as a clown part; then, when the role became more challenging, it might have been assumed by the actor who would eventually play the King to Burbage's Hamlet.[2]

THE GROWTH OF ACTING TRADITIONS

The allusions and references which substantiate the Oldcastle controversy show that Falstaff must have made a strong immediate impression. But evidence for actual early performances of *1 Henry IV* is minimal. After 1700, with much more frequent staging, evidence increases; spectators and actors add their memories and biographers add their lives of theatre personalities to the record supplied by acting editions, official documents, and cast lists. Later, surviving playbills and newspaper reviews become valuable historical sources, while editors, essayists, and critics begin to take notice of current stage practices. In the twentieth century, most aspects of production have become the objects of careful study by scholars and critics interested in performance and its traditions.

The first recorded production of *1 Henry IV* may be the play put on for the Lord

---

[1] See Herbert Weil, 'On expectation and surprise: Shakespeare's construction of character', *S.Sur.* 34 (1981), 39–50.
[2] Useful, but not authoritative, are T. W. Baldwin, *The Organization and Personnel of the Shakespearean Company*, 1927, p. 312 and Henry David Gray, 'The roles of William Kemp', *MLR* 25 (1930), 261–73.

Chamberlain's private entertainment of the Flemish ambassador in 1600; a letter from Rowland Whyte to Sir Robert Sidney referred to it as 'Sir John Old Castell', which could mean either *Part One* or *Part Two*.[1] In 1612–13, one or both parts were among twenty plays staged at court during celebrations for the marriage of Princess Elizabeth to the Elector Palatine.[2] *The First Part of Sir John Falstaff* was staged at Whitehall in 1625. Before all theatres were closed by Parliament in 1642, the only other performance recorded was of 'ould Castel', probably Shakespeare's play, at the 'Cocpit' at court in 1638.[3] In this early period, information about the popular, as opposed to the courtly, appeal of *1 Henry IV* comes primarily from the repeated publication of quarto editions, from Palmer's poem, cited above, and from an allusion by Leonard Digges in some lines prefaced to the 1640 edition of Shakespeare's poems. Digges declared that 'though the Fox and subtill Alchimist, / Long intermitted could not quite be mist . . . when let but Falstaffe come, / Hall, Poines, the rest you shall scarce have a roome, / All is so pester'd'.[4]

A manuscript discovered in 1844 preserves a conflation and adaptation of both parts for private performance in 1622–3. Named after Sir Edward Dering (1598–1644), this manuscript is of special interest because, of its 3,401 lines, roughly two-thirds come from *Part One*. The Dering MS. cut only 11 per cent of *Part One* – two complete scenes (2.1 and 4.4) and some two hundred additional lines. The second longest deletion was the final eighty lines of Glendower's scene with Lady Mortimer. These changes eliminated eight characters, all of them minor except Westmoreland, whose lines in the first scene were spoken by Prince John and by Sir Walter Blunt. These deletions reveal close knowledge of the text and anticipate those in later acting editions and adaptations, especially John Barton's *When Thou Art King* in 1969 (see below, pp. 52–3).

With the restoration of kingship and the re-opening of the theatres in 1660, *1 Henry IV* seems to have been revived almost immediately. It played three times before the year was out, at the Red Bull theatre, and later at the Vere.[5] In the division of the existing repertory between two companies, Davenant's and Killigrew's, the play went with a mere handful of Shakespeare's works to Killigrew's troupe. Samuel Pepys, who was to record his attendance at some three hundred and fifty London performances between 1660 and 1669, saw *1 Henry IV* in December 1660 and complained that reading the play beforehand reduced his pleasure in the production, 'my expectation being too great'.[6]

1 Henry IV seems to have been acted even when Shakespeare became temporarily unfashionable in the 1670s.[7] The publication of a 'droll' or skit entitled *The Bouncing Knight, or The Robbers Robbed*, in *The Wits, or, Sport upon Sport* (1662, 1672), which

[1] Chambers, *Shakespeare*, II, 322.
[2] Chambers, *Stage*, II, 217; IV, 127, 180.
[3] Chambers, *Shakespeare*, II, 353.
[4] *The Shakespeare Allusion Book: A Collection of Allusions to Shakespeare from 1591 to 1700*, ed. John Munro, 1932, I, 457.
[5] Van Lennep, pp. 12, 19, 23.
[6] *Ibid.*, p. 23.
[7] Odell, I, 42.

portrays Falstaff and the Hostess on its frontispiece, suggests that the tavern scenes, exploited in the skit, may have helped to keep the play itself upon the boards.

In 1682, the two London theatre companies merged, and *1 Henry IV* came under the control of Thomas Betterton. Colley Cibber, the actor, would later recall how Betterton played Hotspur (at the age of forty-seven) with 'wild impatient starts' and 'fierce and flashing fire'.[1] Betterton initiated two significant traditions when, eighteen years later in 1700, he acted Falstaff at Lincoln's Inn Fields in a performance billed as 'King Henry the Fourth: With the Humours of Sir John Falstaff'. Praised for hitting these humours, Betterton became the first in a succession of stage Falstaffs who, playing the role year after year, could be compared with one another. The cuts which he made in the text established patterns which John Bell and John Kemble later used in their editions of Shakespeare, 1773–5 and 1815.[2] Betterton trimmed the King's opening speech to ten lines and removed nearly thirty of his lines from Act 3, Scene 2. Also cut were a large segment of Lady Percy's speech to Hotspur in 2.3, a portion of the 'play extempore' in 2.4, 3.1 after line 140, all of 4.4, and the Prince's rescue of the King before Hotspur's entry (5.4.1–57).[3] This revival seems to have been planned as competition for Cibber's thoroughly altered *Richard III* at Drury Lane, and its capacity to draw 'all the town' proved to one observer that 'Shakespeare's wit will always last.'[4]

According to Harold Child, 'the vogue of *Henry IV* reached its zenith in the eighteenth century ... [with] two hundred and twenty performances of *Part One* in London, 1704–50 [in contrast to] eighty of *Part Two* for ... 1720–50'.[5] After Betterton, the most successful Falstaff was James Quin (1693–1766). He too began with Hotspur (1718), went on to King Henry two seasons later, and regularly played Falstaff from 1722 until his retirement in 1751. The bookseller Thomas Davies praised this intelligent Falstaff for his excellence at 'satire and sarcasm', while Francis Gentleman, editor of the Bell edition (1773–5), later recalled his 'glow of feature and expression' when exposed by the Prince and Poins.[6] Quin further reduced the acting script for *1 Henry IV* by curtailing Falstaff's role in the robbery and by eliminating the 'play extempore' altogether. Gentleman said that it 'rather choaked and loaded the main business'.[7] Quin also created the gag of introducing Falstaff's escape from 'open and apparent shame' with 'Ha, ha, ha! d'ye think I did not know ye?' This trick was still being used in Sir Herbert Beerbohm Tree's production in 1896.[8]

Compared with the many references to Falstaff, comments on other roles are extremely rare during these years. After Cibber described Edward Kynaston (1619–

---

[1] Child, p. xxxiii.
[2] Bell's edition was printed from the prompt-books of two Theatres Royal, Drury Lane and Covent Garden. See Odell, II, 15–19, 40–1.
[3] C. B. Hogan, *Shakespeare in the Theatre, 1701–1800*, vol. I, *London 1701–50*, 1952, p. 144. See also Odell, I, 84.
[4] Van Lennep, p. 523.
[5] Child, p. xxxv.
[6] Davies' *Dramatic Miscellanies*, 1785, reprinted in Salgādo, p. 176; Sprague, *Histories*, p. 61. Sprague emphasises the frequent mention of Falstaff's eyes.
[7] Child, p. xxxvii.
[8] *Ibid.*, p. xxxvi.

87) as Henry IV, noting the 'terrible menace' of a whispered 'Send us your prisoners' to Betterton's Hotspur and his 'affecting scene' with his son in 3.2, the King and the Prince received little attention.[1] David Garrick, perceived to be miscast as Hotspur, because of his flexible voice and small size (Quin could easily carry him off), quickly dropped the part. Of the many eighteenth-century Falstaffs besides Quin, the most popular seems to have been John Henderson (1747–85). Contrasting his 'frolicksome, gay, and humorous' qualities with Quin's 'impudent dignity', Davies remembered his description of his 'ragamuffin regiment' and his pleasure at misusing 'the king's press money'.[2]

INNOVATIONS: 1800–1945

The enthusiasm of earlier audiences apparently promoted tendencies to 'exalt the Falstaff scenes at the expense of the historical part of the play'.[3] Gentleman was reflecting one extreme contemporary attitude to *1 Henry IV*, when he declared that 'want of ladies, and matter to interest female auditors, lies so heavy on it' that only 'an excellent Falstaff' can give it 'occasional life'.[4] This trend continues into the nineteenth century as actors build reputations by playing Falstaff, often sacrificing subtlety for new stage business and costumes. The common practice of dressing Falstaff in thick, high boots probably began as a means of disguising an actor's thin legs. Because his role at Shrewsbury could be strenuous, it became customary to send him into stage battle without armour.[5] By the late eighteenth century, Davies claimed, 'No joke ever raised such loud and repeated mirth, in the galleries, as Sir John's labour in getting the body of Hotspur on his back.'[6] Morgann strongly objected to seated Falstaffs so fat that they had to be picked up off the edge of the stage by the Prince and Poins disguised as robbers, or who resembled 'piteous' tortoises while the Prince fought Hotspur.[7] Some later Falstaffs seem to have been so badly beaten in the robbery scene that they crawled from the stage, and to have emphasised their cowardice upon rising from the dead.[8] When in 1816 Stephen Kemble needed no padding to play Falstaff, he provoked Hazlitt into a cascade of insults rivalling the Prince's; another spectator recalled that it had been 'painful' to watch the obese Kemble, who 'evidently suffered under the exertion'.[9] Kemble began the tradition of discovering Falstaff asleep in 1.2, continued by many later productions.[10] Sharp differences of opinion began to appear in recollections of specific stage Falstaffs, just as they have always attached themselves to the character. Samuel Phelps was both noted for 'unctuosity' and pronounced

[1] Citations in Salgādo, pp. 174–5.
[2] *Ibid.*, p. 177.
[3] Child, p. xxxiv.
[4] Odell, II, 41.
[5] Sprague and Trewin, pp. 80–1.
[6] Davies, cited by Child, p. xxxvii.
[7] Morgann, p. 154.
[8] Arthur Colby Sprague, *Shakespeare and the Actors: The Stage Business in His Plays, 1660–1905*, 1945, p. 85; Sprague, *Histories*, p. 71.
[9] J. R. Planché, *Recollections and Reflections*, 1901, reprinted in Salgādo, pp. 180–1.
[10] Sprague and Trewin, p. 28.

lacking in 'unction'.[1] In mid-century, Phelps carried on the tradition of specialising in Falstaff by acting him more than three hundred times.[2] In the United States, James Hackett portrayed Falstaff, starting in 1828, for over forty years.[3]

More innovative was the attempt to achieve authenticity in scenes and costumes. A 'bill' advertising Charles Kemble's 1824 production at Covent Garden listed, among other authorities for its period accuracy, effigies, portraits, stained glass, illuminated manuscripts, sumptuary laws, and chronicles.[4] This production closely followed and was influenced by a spectacular *2 Henry IV* staged for the coronation of George IV in 1821 and a highly successful, 'picturesque' *King John*. For the 1864 centenary production directed by Phelps (playing Falstaff), there appear to have been thirteen painted scenes, plus a sunset.[5] Between each of the fifteen scene changes in Beerbohm Tree's 1914 production, the curtain fell and the band played.[6] Such a production style, described by J. C. Trewin as 'the great canvas pavilions of spectacular Shakespeare', also depended upon crowds of supernumeraries.[7]

In the long run, the 1864 production may have been more important for its text than for its scenery. Phelps, who had restored the 'play extempore' in 1846 and taken it out again in 1856, decisively returned it in 1864, along with all of Act 3, Scene 1. Reviews of Beerbohm Tree's 1896 production disagreed about the merits of Tree's believable Falstaff, but recognised a new kind of acting which appeared less mannered or 'tragic'.[8] In the twentieth century, influenced by the boldly simplified stagings of Granville Barker and by William Poel's attempt to revive Elizabethan conventions, directors began to seek a more 'classical' style. Poel's impact seems to have been apparent in Robert Atkins' 1935 production, although the great vaudeville comedian and crowd-pleaser, George Robey, alleged to have 'hardly ever seen a Shakespearean performance', stole the show as Falstaff. Reviewing the first night, James Agate suggested that Robey only fell into his music-hall trick of raising his eyebrows when he needed time to recall his lines, but that the delighted crowd kept him going.[9] In a purer theatrical experiment designed to reproduce Elizabethan stage conditions in the Harrow School Speech Room, Ronald Watkins worked with '[n]o curtain here in front, no darkened hall, no scenery, no lights, nothing at all'.[10] Such developments were behind the simple timber framework set up on the stage of the Memorial Theatre at Stratford in 1951 for the performance of the entire second tetralogy.

One other significant development, originating in nineteenth-century Germany, was the production of *1 Henry IV* as part of a group or cycle. Franz Dingelstadt

[1] Hemingway, 'Appendix on stage history', p. 490.
[2] *Ibid.*
[3] George C. D. Odell, *Annals of the New York Stage*, 1931, II, 493.
[4] Odell II, 173.
[5] *Ibid.*, p. 361.
[6] Sprague, *Histories*, p. 52.
[7] Trewin, p. 58; Odell, II, 174.
[8] Child, p. xlii.
[9] *Brief Chronicles: A Survey of the Plays of Shakespeare and the Elizabethans in Actual Performance*, 1943, p. 102.
[10] Trewin, p. 207, n. 1.

directed *1 Henry IV* in Munich in 1851 and began to work on a series of seven histories from the two 'tetralogies'. In 1864, to celebrate the tercentenary of Shakespeare's birth, Dingelstadt produced these histories in Weimar, taking a week to complete his cycle.[1] At Stratford-upon-Avon, between 1899 and 1916, F. R. Benson regularly directed productions of plays from the 'second tetralogy', emphasising *Richard II* and *Henry V*; he apparently presented all four plays on consecutive days in May 1905.[2] The two parts of *Henry IV* were finally staged together on Shakespeare's birthday by Sir Barry Jackson for the Birmingham Repertory Company in 1921, and again, for the opening of the new Memorial Theatre building at Stratford in 1932.

PERFORMANCES, CELEBRATIONS, AND NEW AUDIENCES: 1945–91
Because performances of *1 Henry IV* often reach a broad spectrum of the theatre-going public, modern English companies have produced the play for special occasions. During the Festival of Britain, 1951, and the centenary year of Shakespeare's birth, 1964, it was staged as part of a cycle of histories. The Royal Shakespeare Company selected *1 Henry IV* as the play to open its new London theatre, the Barbican, in 1982. Again, in 1991, beginning his term as artistic director for the RSC, Adrian Noble directed *1* and *2 Henry IV* as the featured plays on the main stage in Stratford-upon-Avon. While such productions have affirmed the vitality of the play for contemporary audiences, cycle stagings, developing much further the experiments of Dingelstadt, Benson, and Jackson (above), have radically changed its meanings. Audiences have been able to observe *1 Henry IV* as the first of two or of three, or as the second of four plays. In 1951 and in 1964, the Royal Shakespeare Company performed the entire second tetralogy; spectators in 1964 might have seen their three-play version of the first tetralogy in 1963. Then in 1988 the touring English Shakespeare Company presented both tetralogies within a single season. Eager addicts could see seven plays in less than sixty-two hours. New dimensions of *1 Henry IV* have also been revealed by one major film adaptation, a television production, and a video based directly upon a stage performance.

This account of stage history after the Second World War concentrates on the most influential productions. Whereas resources for the study of earlier stage history are often meagre – anecdotes or generalities abound, but only for Falstaff's role do we have much evidence – contemporary productions have been much more thoroughly documented. Because recent studies have described some of these productions extensively, we will focus upon their most innovative qualities and emphasise their dramatisation of four important sequences: the soliloquy of the Prince; the 'play extempore'; the reconciliation of the King and the Prince; and the combat between Hotspur and the Prince with its sequel.[3]

---

[1] Simon Williams, *Shakespeare on the German Stage*, 1990, I, 153–4.
[2] Michael Mullin, ed. *Theatre at Stratford-upon-Avon: A Catalogue Index to Productions of the Shakespeare Memorial/Royal Shakespeare Theatre, 1879–1978*, 1980, I, 395, 139, 146, 153.
[3] See especially McMillin; Barbara Hodgdon, *The End Crowns All: Closure and Contradiction in Shakespeare's History*, 1991; T. F. Wharton, *Text and Performance: Henry the Fourth, Parts 1 and 2*, 1983; and Sprague, *Histories*.

4   A non-theatrical version of the robbery, Act 2, Scene 2: Falstaff, a 'huge hill of flesh', nimbly runs away.
Etching by George Cruikshank, 1858. In 1945, Ralph Richardson was praised for his agile footwork,
surprising when combined with his heavily padded figure

John Burrell's production for the Old Vic Company in 1945 was part of a classical
repertory planned to show 'that the London Theatre had not only survived the years
of devastating air raids but had survived with unmatchable ability'.[1] In at least one key
respect, this extremely popular production followed stage tradition: the leading actors
played Hotspur and Falstaff. They received by far the most comments from reviewers.
Laurence Olivier, who had recently triumphed as the hero in his film of *Henry V*,
chose to play Henry Percy rather than the future Henry V. His romantic, inscrutable
Hotspur spoke quickly, even incomprehensibly, with a stammer which culminated in
his last broken line, 'food for w – w –'. (The idea of having Hotspur stammer, probably
based upon a misreading of 'speaking thick', i.e. 'fast', in *2 Henry IV* 2.3.24, dates at
least from the Beerbohm Tree production of 1914.) Olivier concluded Hotspur's
speech and life by pitching face forward in full armour down some steps.[2] The young
and relatively inexperienced actor who played the Prince was overshadowed by Ralph
Richardson's engaging Falstaff. Spectators saw 'little of the glutton or the sensualist'
in a performance distinguished for great mental and physical agility. Although
Richardson followed Robey and other stage Falstaffs who had exaggerated the expres-
siveness of their eyes, he dispensed with one traditional gag, a shield used to hide his

[1] McMillin, p. 14.
[2] Trewin, p. 195.

face before he peeped out from behind it and exclaimed in his next line, 'By the Lord, I knew ye, as well as he that made ye.'¹ Richardson's mobile countenance told the story of his exposure and joyous recovery; caught out when his invention of men in buckram ran away with him, he was defenceless until his wit suggested an escape route. For Kenneth Tynan, recalling this production, Richardson's humane and vulnerable performance, with its 'charity', 'magnanimity', and 'grief', seemed to confirm W. H. Auden's hyperbolic suggestion that Falstaff was a comic symbol for Jesus Christ.²

It is striking that in a company of such overall strength as the Old Vic's in 1945, well-known actors in minor roles – Harcourt Williams as Glendower, Sybil Thorndike as Mistress Quickly, Margaret Leighton as Lady Percy – should have received more praise than did Nicholas Hannen as the King or Michael Warre as the Prince. Compared with later interpretations, these roles seem to have been presented in relatively straightforward fashion: a capable, conscientious ruler and father; a Prince who used his soliloquy more for information than for self-expression. Later though, after 'I do, I will', he playfully threw the royal cushion back to Falstaff.

In the next major production, directed by Anthony Quayle at Stratford-upon-Avon in 1951, Falstaff and Hotspur drew less attention, while, probably for the first time, the characters of the King and the Prince and the relationship between them became more prominent. This occurred both through staging the entire second tetralogy and through strong casting: Harry Andrews as the King, and Richard Burton as the Prince. Quayle himself acted Falstaff, not as a scene-stealing charmer but as a potentially vicious clown. The exceptionally large company of forty-six (the Old Vic had twenty-seven), including seventeen supernumeraries, presented all four plays within a frame structure, created by designer Tanya Moiseiwitsch to simulate a more Elizabethan theatrical environment.

In the eighteenth century, Edmond Malone believed that Nicholas Rowe's edition (1709) enhanced the stage popularity of *1 Henry IV*.³ Scholarship seems to have had a large, if indirect, influence upon the 1951 production, visible not only in the more authentic staging but in the conception of Falstaff as a tempter. Above all, Tillyard's approach to Shakespeare's eight histories as a national epic seemed particularly attractive while the struggle to recover from the Second World War continued. It may well have given confidence to directors and actors staging a cycle of plays in the year of the Festival of Britain, celebrated throughout the country.⁴

When *1 Henry IV* opened a month after *Richard II*, audiences could see for themselves that King Henry was declining from his role as energetic, ambitious usurper in *Richard II*. They could experience the anxieties of kingship when they recognised Michael Redgrave, the assassinated Richard II, returning in the role of Hotspur. They would have seen in Richard Burton a far more complex Prince, already somewhat alienated from his companions and so preoccupied with his future that he

---

¹ On persistent gags, see Sprague, *Histories*, p. 61.
² *Showpeople: Profiles in Entertainment*, 1970, p. 43. For Tynan's early review, stressing Richardson's dignity and youthful heart, see *He That Plays the King: A View of the Theatre*, 1950, pp. 49–50.
³ Hemingway, p. 480.
⁴ McMillin, p. 36.

5 A typical publicity photograph: Prince Hal (Richard Burton) and Poins taunt Falstaff (Anthony Quayle) while Bardolph looks on in Act 2, Scene 4. Quayle directed this production at Stratford-upon-Avon in 1951

developed minimally through the cycle. Richard David's description of the Prince's soliloquy suggests Burton's 'sobriety and self-knowledge': 'Hal had turned to watch [Poins] leave the stage; for a moment he stood looking after him; then his head moved slowly to regard the audience over his shoulder.' His soliloquy 'followed, with a curious simplicity and tonelessness, and yet with a suggestion of strong emotion held in check'.[1] In the first tavern scene, the Prince turned jovial play to deadly earnest assault so that the laughter of the watchers became uneasy and stopped with the momentous pause, preceding Prince Hal's 'I do, I will.' Never until he thought Falstaff dead did Burton's Prince reveal any friendly feeling. In the scene of reconciliation (3.2), father and son spoke at cross-purposes and with mutual mistrust.

Playing Falstaff to this much less responsive Prince, Quayle, said the *Times* reviewer, 'speaks the jests with metallic precision; and his smile when it appears is a painted smile'.[2] After he was criticised for make-up which turned him into 'a cross between an aged circus clown and a Hallowe'en turnip', Quayle subdued his appearance. Nevertheless, spectators found him too cold and unsympathetic. By letting audiences glimpse the evil behind his jester's mask, Quayle prepared them early for his

[1] David, 'Shakespeare's history plays: epic or drama?', *S.Sur.* 6 (1953), 136.
[2] John Dover Wilson and T. C. Worsley, *Shakespeare's Histories at Stratford, 1951*, 1952, p. 67.

ultimate rejection. Redgrave's Hotspur was a simpler and far cruder figure, who spoke his own version of a dialect he had studied in the pubs of Northumberland. Hotspur's wife, played by Barbara Jefford, shared his rough manners, so that their boisterous physical argument received new emphasis; it has since been copied frequently. Quayle included all of 2.1 (Gadshill had often been cut because of his obscure language), 4.4, and 3.1. This last 'was given in full, with long and passionate speeches in Welsh for Glendower's daughter ... there was no sense of flagging'. Hugh Griffith as Glendower captured the 'dangerous, enigmatical, and compelling personality that alone can cast the spell the scene demands'.[1]

By the time that Peter Hall and the newly named Royal Shakespeare Company returned to the four plays thirteen years later, in 1964, the heroic temper of 1951 had diminished. Influenced by the Theatre of the Absurd, by the Theatre of Alienation, and probably by excitement over Bertolt Brecht's Berliner Ensemble, which had performed in England beginning in 1956, this production of *1 Henry IV* had little in common with its most influential predecessors: Quayle's 1951 epic or the more tempered mingling of comedy and history in Douglas Seale's production for the Old Vic in 1954–5.[2] In 1963 the RSC had achieved great success with *The Wars of the Roses*, John Barton's adaptation of the three parts of *Henry VI* and *Richard III* as a trilogy. Therefore, when audiences came to see the second tetralogy, staged in 1964, many would have been familiar with the bleak, anti-military *Wars of the Roses*, which begin just after Henry V has died, leaving an infant ruler, Henry VI, who will prove temperamentally incapable of controlling factions at home or of holding on to his father's French conquests. They watched Ian Holm, who had starred in the role of the tyrant Richard III, now portray the Prince who becomes Henry V. Reviewers found more similarities than contrasts between the Machiavellian villain and the model ruler. All four plays used John Bury's set which consisted of large, movable, oppressive armoured walls to present a world of corrupt power politics.

Audiences seem to have been enthusiastic about the vision and style of these cycles. Harold Hobson wrote, 'I doubt if anything as valuable has ever been done for Shakespeare in the whole previous history of the world's stage.'[3] When the company revived their productions of the second tetralogy in 1966 some critics, looking back over Hall's reign, praised the unified direction given to the histories as his greatest achievement.[4]

Individual performances, as opposed to company style, however, evoked mixed reactions. King Henry, strongly acted first by Eric Porter and then in 1966 by Tony Church, was an unpredictable but also obviously sick and exhausted figure. Holm, playing the Prince as another unpredictable character, was criticised for his detachment. Gareth Lloyd Evans wrote, 'He tends ... to act from the outside of a character,

[1] David, 'Shakespeare's history plays', 135.
[2] For an account of Seale's production, see Tynan, *A View of the English Stage*, 1975, pp. 153–4.
[3] *Sunday Times*, 19 April 1964, cited by McMillin, pp. 60–1.
[4] In contrast, Ronald Bryden (*New Statesman*, 24 April 1964) astutely questioned this unifying conception, emphasising both distinctions among the plays and the inadequacy of the Prince's education as a coherent organising theme.

and to engage in tricksiness of speech and gesture.'¹ The small Holm physically dominated much larger actors playing Falstaff (Hugh Griffith) and Hotspur (Roy Dotrice). Merciless when promising to banish Falstaff, he killed Hotspur and then dumped him into a pig trough. The most disputed performance was that of Hugh Griffith. He came to *1 Henry IV* not, with the rest of the company, from the ironic *Wars of the Roses* but from the robust comedy of the *Tom Jones* film, in which he portrayed Squire Western. Perhaps because his performance seemed reminiscent of kinder Falstaffs like Richardson's, reviewers were disoriented. He would, McMillin concludes, 'have been more at home in another production of the play'.²

Audiences who watched the RSC tetralogy revived for London in 1966 could also have gone to see the extraordinary rearrangement of lines and episodes from this tetralogy in Orson Welles' film, *Chimes at Midnight*. By transposition and cutting (principally Glendower and Douglas), Welles crammed into one hundred and fifteen minutes much of *Part One*, a medley of materials from *Part Two*, and brief passages from both *Richard II* and *Henry V*. In this bravura adaptation, Welles played Falstaff, recalling the tradition of actor-managers like Betterton and Beerbohm Tree. At the same time, he explored the play in the film medium with a genius that most critics were slow to appreciate.³

The film begins by showing two figures in the distance slowly struggling through snow towards an ancient oak tree, before it cuts to a beamed room with an immense roaring fire. The first lines heard, taken from late in *Part Two*, are those of the frail Justice Shallow, who croaks, 'Jesus, Sir John, the days that we have seen.' The rest of the film creates the effect of a flash-back remembered by Falstaff shortly before he dies. After the film credits – displayed against a background of marching troops, with lively music and a voice-over based on Holinshed ('King Richard the Second was murdered, some say at the command of Henry Bolingbroke . . .'), the film moves to Westminster where King Henry, his lines superbly spoken by John Gielgud, coldly confronts the rebels (1.3). This scene was shot in the cathedral of Cardona in Spain, using a low-angle perspective that makes emphatic the elevation, distance, and rigidity of the King. In a remarkably surreal effect, only the King's breath is visible as a rising vapour.

The camera then shifts to a close-up of a pot of ale (probably suggested here by Hotspur's threat to poison the Prince), moves back to reveal the Prince drinking, and searches through several rooms, up and down stairs, for the missing Falstaff. We are in the Boar's Head tavern instead of the Prince's chamber. When the camera and the Prince find the sleeping Falstaff, Poins has already picked his pocket (2.4), which, in this film, Falstaff quickly discovers. Three tavern scenes in quick succession incorporate lines from 1.2, 2.4, and 3.3, as well as passages from *Part Two*. In contrast to the technique for the Westminster scene, the camera tracks, cuts, and wheels about in the

¹ 'Shakespeare, the twentieth century and behaviourism', *S.Sur.* 20 (1967), 137.
² McMillin, p. 62.
³ This film has itself become legendary, the subject of many articles and several books; we do know that major financial difficulties led to filming in Spain, that very long delays (some lasting over a year) caused many in the international cast to leave, and – reportedly – that the financier believed he was paying for a movie of *Treasure Island*.

tavern sequence, suggesting both the intricacy and festivity of the tavern world, especially when we see Falstaff chase the Prince down a twisting staircase. The escaping Prince will become more and more eager, as the film continues, to get away from Falstaff once and for all.

Through a series of staged adaptations, beginning in 1938, Welles had evolved this version with his view of Falstaff as 'the most completely good man in all drama', an interpretation that no critic found in the finished film. Yet Welles wanted Falstaff to be no more important than the Prince in the film as a whole. A melancholy and transparent figure, he conveyed an affection for the Prince which more than balanced his vices and frivolity. Welles made it clear that Falstaff, anxious about the Prince's feelings, does not foresee his rejection.

For the soliloquy, 'I know you all', the Prince stood at the tavern gate, faced both the camera and the ramparts of his father's castle, and spoke with his back towards Falstaff, who, we see, is standing on the edge of the frame. The film viewer may observe that Falstaff strains but manages to hear few words, if any. Then, on 'offend', the Prince turns and winks at Falstaff, who smiles back. Soon, after the Prince's 'I do, I will', during a long silence before the rapping on the door, the camera catches the same bemused expression on Falstaff's face. Samuel Crowl comments that for all Falstaff's 'alertness to the sham hollowness of the political rhetoric . . . the one person he does not see through is his own pupil, Hal – the most powerfully shrewd character in the play'.[1]

To escape the Sheriff, Falstaff does not hide behind an arras, but is dropped through a trap-door. This foreshadows his rejection and burial in the last two sequences. Welles edits the battle of Shrewsbury so that it illustrates Falstaff's vision of honour. Falstaff and the camera bear witness to terrible violence which lasts for ten minutes before a word is spoken. Pauline Kael considered this sequence, 'the most brutally sombre battle ever filmed'.[2] Both the Prince and Hotspur seem worn out when they begin to fight. Later, as the Prince tells Falstaff's dead body, 'I could have better spared a better man', he sees vapour rising through Falstaff's visor. Changing tone in mid-speech, he angrily taunts the corpse, 'Embowelled will I see thee by and by.' Welles altered the conclusion of *Part One* even more drastically by having Falstaff drag Hotspur into the presence of the King. He thereby trapped and humiliated the Prince, who lost both his prize and his father's regard by failing to contradict Falstaff's lie. When Falstaff follows up this victory by delivering his speech in praise of sherris-sack from *Part Two*, the Prince throws down his tankard and follows his father towards the castle.

Of special interest for the light it cast upon Elizabethan stagings outside the London theatres was the history cycle entitled *When Thou Art King*. Adapted by John Barton from the second tetralogy, and directed by Barton and Gareth Morgan for the RSC's

[1] 'The long goodbye: Welles and Falstaff', *SQ* 31 (1980), 376. For the development of Welles' version, see Robert Hapgood, '*Chimes at Midnight* from stage to screen: the art of adaptation', *S.Sur.* 39 (1987), 39–52; and, for Welles' treatment of Shakespeare's text, Jack Jorgens, *Shakespeare on Film*, 1977, pp. 106–21.

[2] *Kiss Kiss Bang Bang*, 1968, p. 202.

Theatregoround, this production toured schools and community centres in 1969 and
1970. *Part One*, called *The Battle of Shrewsbury*, lasted ninety-five minutes, while *Part
Two*, called *The Rejection of Falstaff*, and *Henry V*, titled *The Battle of Agincourt*, each
ran about eighty minutes. The Theatregoround company could present any one
segment alone without an interval, two with a single break, and on special occasions,
all three with one short interval and another long enough for a meal. This company of
ten actors included eight men and two women; it mingled established leading actors,
veteran players of secondary roles, and young apprentices, replicating the make-up
(except for the women) of Shakespeare's own somewhat larger company. Only two
actors never doubled: Charles Thomas, fresh from playing Mark Antony on the
company's main stage, who acted the Prince of Wales and Henry V, and Brewster
Mason who played Falstaff but no part in *Henry V*. Other actors played multiple roles,
notably Jeffrey Dench as King Henry IV and Gadshill (and later, Pistol and King
Charles of France), and Peter Geddes who was Poins and Sir Walter Blunt (and later,
the Chorus and Gower). *The Battle of Shrewsbury* included twenty-three characters
(six without individual or personal names) and deleted eight: Westmoreland (with
some of his lines given to Prince John and some to Blunt), Worcester, Vernon,
Glendower, Mortimer, Lady Mortimer, the Archbishop, and Sir Michael.

Sets for the Theatregoround production were simple, flexible, and portable, easily
set up in a variety of acting spaces. Ideas from the directors' rehearsal notes that were
reprinted in the programme suggest that Barton and Morgan tried to see the action
through Elizabethan eyes. The Prince is said to experience a 'Morality school': 'After
contact with all kinds of humanity, Hal returns to the palace better equipped to govern
himself and his people.' Both Hotspur and Falstaff are figures of 'Vanity'. To prevent
Falstaff from winning audience sympathy too quickly or too thoroughly, Barton
borrowed from *The Famous Victories* the Prince's conflict with the Lord Chief Justice
and used it to open *The Battle of Shrewsbury*.[1]

In 1975, Terry Hands transformed the original sequence of the plays by beginning
with *Henry V*. *Part One* followed several weeks later, then *Part Two*, and finally, before
the end of the season, *The Merry Wives of Windsor*. His productions exaggerated a
theatrically self-conscious style which had been given stong impetus by Peter Brook in
his *A Midsummer Night's Dream* (1970). They also created a much more informal
mood, partly a response to a much tighter budget. Spectators who arrived early for
Henry V saw on the stage, apparently in rehearsal clothing, twenty-five actors who
gradually put on historical costumes and became a coherent group.

Because of the re-ordering by Hands, many in the audiences came to *Part One*
having recently seen, not the assassination of Richard II, but the triumphs of Henry V.
Alan Howard presented this Henry as a consummate role-player; his voice and stage
presence seemed convincingly to inspire his army. Those who had seen *Henry V* might
therefore have been particularly surprised to discover, during the first tavern scene of
1 Henry IV, that Howard, as the young Prince, had been genuinely afraid of 'that fiend
Douglas, that spirit Percy, and that devil Glendower' (2.4.304–5). The 'play extem-

[1] These explanations come from unpublished conversations between Barton and H. Weil, who was an
observer at rehearsals for this production.

pore' became a device which the Prince could use to control his terror. In the process, Richard David pointed out, Howard showed such aversion to Falstaff that he seemed 'to freeze the whole company at the inn'.[1]

Central to both parts of *Henry IV* in Hands' cycle, was a particularly vexed relationship of the Prince with his two 'fathers', the King and Falstaff. Emrys James, who acted Henry IV, had previously played the Chorus in *Henry V* as a fervent supporter of that young King. But in the role of Henry IV he became a guilt-racked autocrat; his behaviour under stress removed any basis for a convincing reconciliation with his son. By contrast, Brewster Mason, returning to Falstaff after *The Merry Wives of Windsor* (1968) and *When Thou Art King* (1969–70), seemed gentlemanly and restrained, a counterbalance to the sometimes hysterical monarch. Hands intensified the Prince's father-complex by treating the centre of the play, from the first to the second tavern scene, as one unusually long act between the two intervals. He also drew attention to overtly theatrical techniques throughout this cycle: characters from one scene repeatedly would watch what happened in another, while props as well as furniture could be used by characters separated in time and space. After his soliloquy, the Prince remained onstage at the beginning of 1.3 to observe the quarrel between his father and Hotspur, neither of whom he would otherwise meet for many scenes. During the reconciliation scene (3.2), father and son could at first observe the end of the scene in Wales (3.1), then later drink out of the same cup of sack, left from the tavern scene (2.4).

The BBC, with major support from Time–Life publishers, created for television another cycle of histories which aimed for a 'definitive' and 'neutral' style. *1* and *2 Henry IV* and *Henry V*, all directed by David Giles, appeared in 1979, the second year of the new series, when the original producer, Cedric Messina, asserted that the plays should be allowed to 'speak for themselves'. Like *Chimes at Midnight* in at least this one respect, these productions were filmed without the long rehearsal periods and the two seasons of repertory playing which so often strengthened RSC productions. Falstaff (Anthony Quayle) and Hotspur (Tim Piggott Smith) overshadowed the rest of the characters, in a throwback to the days before the staging of cycles. Returning to a role he had performed nearly thirty years before in 1951, Quayle played to the cameras with a zest which qualified his brutal stabbing of Hotspur's corpse. But this Falstaff also owed something to cycle-thinking in that his essential corruption seemed to have worked backwards from Quayle's conception of *Part Two*. Because this production lacked a strong directorial theme or strategy, specific scenes like the Council episode (1.3) and the Welsh sequence proved more memorable than most of the film.

To launch the long-heralded RSC theatre at the Barbican in London on 7 May 1982, Trevor Nunn chose to direct *1 Henry IV*. *Part Two* followed six nights later. Nunn introduced as a prologue a hymn and a procession of monks bearing candles. John Napier's set, three towering wooden structures moved by hydraulic trucks, provided 'a magnificent folly of balconies, gangways, rotting beams and rusting armour'.[2] Robert Smallwood observed, 'It is a big set, on a very big stage, and it is one

---

[1] *Shakespeare in the Theatre*, 1978, p. 197.
[2] Michael Coveney, *Financial Times*, 14 May 1982.

6   King Henry (Patrick Stewart) steps from a procession to speak the first lines in the Royal Shakespeare Company production which opened the Barbican Theatre, London in 1982. Trevor Nunn gave Scene 1, often presented more intimately, a ceremonial style

of the great successes of the production that one never feels that the company is failing to fill it.'[1] More direct engagement of actors with audiences was created by the architecture of the Barbican itself, which, despite its capacity of 1,160 seats, reduced the usual distance between auditorium and stage, and eliminated a proscenium arch. Another of the company's successes, reviewers agreed, was their depth and strength as a group, called by Stephen Wall their 'flair for the communal and the collective', which had been widely acclaimed in their recent adaptation of *Nicholas Nickleby*.[2]

To the extent that this energetic, highly physical production had any specific emphasis, it explored new versions of father–son relationships. Both Hotspur and the Prince were boyish, immature. The Prince clearly preferred the animated, friendly world of Eastcheap to a severe and lonely court; Patrick Stewart played King Henry as a priest-like figure who stepped out of the monastic procession to emerge as an individual. This King chose to repress his affection for his son. Joss Ackland's tough and ambitious Falstaff, on the other hand, occasionally showed the Prince genuine warmth. During their first scene, Gerard Murphy's Prince sat on Falstaff's knee and embraced his friend while he insulted him; another embrace followed 'I do, I will.'

[1] '*Henry IV, Parts 1 and 2* at the Barbican Theatre', *CQ* 25 (1983), 15.
[2] *TLS*, 25 June 1982.

Wall commented that 'As modern criticism has often dourly insisted, it is clear that Falstaff is impossible. Ackland reminds us that he is irresistible.' Whether Murphy's Prince had the intelligence to learn anything from Falstaff seemed less certain. One reviewer saw as the key moment in the production the encounter between the Prince's two fathers. Just before the battle (5.1), 'Hal finds himself poised between his two fathers, but instinctively responds to Falstaff's cry of "Hal" as the King regretfully departs.'[1]

In 1986–7, Michael Bogdanov directed his new English Shakespeare Company in productions of *1* and *2 Henry IV* and *Henry V* which toured Britain, Europe, and North America. Bogdanov's were probably the most praised and most disputed theatrical interpretations of these history plays during the past twenty years. Each play was presented in a nearly full text, with *Part One* lasting almost three hours. Eager spectators could join in a single-day marathon: *Part One* in the late morning; *Part Two* after a long break for lunch; and *Henry V* in the evening after a longer break for dinner. Then the next year, the company expanded its repertory to perform all the plays from both tetralogies, combining the three plays of *Henry VI* into two; it travelled to Hong Kong, Tokyo, the United States, Australia, and Europe, and toured Britain, before playing a London season in 1989.

To reduce what he called 'repetition' in *Part Two*, Bogdanov sacrificed some of the more affirmative qualities in *1 Henry IV*. When the Prince first met his father onstage in 3.2, Michael Pennington delivered his lines in the bored, insolent manner of a truant teenager. The Prince seemed to be telling the King what he wanted to hear – almost as if he had memorised a text composed by his father – but suggested that he did not mean a word of it. The effect of this interpretation was to emphasise sincerity of feeling when father and son are really reconciled, shortly before the King's death in *Part Two*. Interestingly, when the ESC revived its productions the following year, but performed them after the first tetralogy and *Richard II*, Pennington played 3.2 in *Part One* without irony. Another alteration apparently drew upon and simplified Orson Welles' treatment of Falstaff's lie about killing Hotspur. In Bogdanov's revision of Shakespeare and Welles, the Prince receives praise from the King for his deed, only to be interrupted by the entry of Falstaff carrying the body of Hotspur. Both the King and Prince John, neither present in the text, clearly believe Falstaff's version. They stare at the Prince in disgust and depart without a word, suggesting that, for them, the Prince's account of his combat – and implicitly, his promises to reform – are worthless. This change gives *Part One* a forceful conclusion, but the Prince's generous offer to Falstaff, 'If a lie may do thee grace', turns into an unrooted, perhaps futile gesture.

Like the RSC, the new ESC was using *1 Henry IV* and the other histories to display its range. But unlike the cycles which had focused on the education of the good ruler, Machiavellian kingship, or family psychology, Bogdanov's productions were explicitly anti-Establishment and charged with class-consciousness. Both the social consensus and the inexpensive tickets which had helped the Burrell production become so popular in 1945 were things of the past. King, court, rebels, and Sir John Falstaff all

[1] *Guardian*, 11 June 1982.

7 Two versions of the 'play extempore' in Act 2, Scene 4:

   a Alan Howard, as the Prince, playing the King in the 1975 production directed by Terry Hands

   b John Woodvine as Falstaff plays the King to Michael Pennington's Prince Hal in Michael Bogdanov's touring production, 1986. Both Howard and Pennington played the young Prince only after starring at the Royal Shakespeare Company in larger roles for older men

embodied the corruption and selfishness of the aristocracy. In its *Henry V*, the company outrageously parodied the chauvinistic violence of the campaign against the French. *Part One* began upon a stage littered with grubby props. A group of actors, dressed in rehearsal clothes, was singing a 'Ballad of Harry le Roy'; the Prince, in blue jeans, stepped out of this ensemble and watched the other actors prepare for the beginning of Scene 1. Although the chilly detachment of Pennington's Prince could make his presence and behaviour arresting, it was given an obnoxious twist on the battlefield. When Hotspur disarmed the Prince and chivalrously returned his sword, the Prince promptly stabbed him in the back.

Such a 'hunter', as John Peter termed him, had little to learn from John Woodvine's Falstaff, also portrayed as selfish and watchful.[1] Woodvine's outstanding performance gained part of its vitality, McMillin has argued, from a bizarre contrast between his wearing the green velvet jacket and red-checked trousers of a seedy gentleman, and the chaotic jumble of clothing styles on the other actors. 'Through it all, Woodvine's Falstaff was, of all things, a centre of stability, a classical performance visible through those outlandish costumes, a figure one could almost count on in the midst of the image-breaking around him.'[2] Both the subtlety and the accuracy of his acting were exceptional. Indeed, Woodvine's appeal so overbalanced the flaws he made no effort to hide, that when he appeared as the Chorus at the beginning of *Henry V*, slimmed down and tossing out the cushions that had filled Falstaff's baggy costumes, he regularly received a standing ovation.

At the end of its second season (1989), Bogdanov's entire seven-play cycle was filmed in the Grand Theatre, Swansea. Distributed primarily on educational television, in schools and universities, the video of *Part One* provides a faithful record of its theatrical life. Some skilful camera work in the tavern scenes, incorporating close-ups of Bardolph and Mistress Quickly shouting and banging on tables, captures the contagious skills of Barry Stanton, who replaced Woodvine for the second season. One reviewer epitomised his technique and vision: 'He keeps buffoonery at a minimum, and doesn't even strive for wit. Like all great comics he simply describes the world as he sees it, and is appalled.'[3] Another strong new performance was that of Andrew Jarvis, who followed the late John Price in the role of Hotspur. Jarvis himself had been both a flute-playing Gadshill and a fanatic Douglas during the first ESC season. Ingeniously he turned what might have been a broad caricature of Percy – this bow-legged Northumbrian centaur clomped across the stage – into an engaging sketch of trust barely tainted by prevailing decadence.

In 1991, Adrian Noble directed for the RSC a production which was remarkable for its staging and its fresh conception of characters. As in the productions of Welles, Nunn, and Bogdanov, a carnivalesque tavern was opposed to an austere court. The elaborate tavern set, presenting a multi-level flourishing bordello, recalled the Barbican set of 1982. But in staging the battle, Noble emphatically distinguished this

---

[1] *Sunday Times*, 29 March 1987.
[2] McMillin, p. 111.
[3] Thomas M. Disch, *The Nation*, 25 June 1988, cited by Barbara Hodgdon, *Shakespeare in Performance: Henry IV, Part Two*, 1993, p. 134.

8 The tavern scene in Act 2, Scene 4 was dominated by Robert Stephens as Falstaff in Adrian Noble's production for the Royal Shakespeare Company, 1991

production from its predecessors. Trucking off the massive tavern structures at the Barbican had exposed the empty space upstage used for the battlefield. At Stratford, to the sound of drumming with a Japanese timbre, a tableau of the battlefield was lifted hydraulically from under the stage. Robert Smallwood's description captures the effect of this spectacle, with the King 'in the center, a heaving mass of armored soldiers on either side, seething and writhing in slow-motion combat around him, the clash and cacophony of the music and the falling bits of arms and armor seeming to catch something of the futile destructiveness of war'.[1] The swift transition from stylised tableau to intense realism when Prince Harry fought Harry Hotspur was extraordinary. Vertical dynamics were emphasised by other staging devices: a small replica of the Sepulchre Church of Jerusalem, which resembled a golden crown, and hung high above the stage, where it was flown after the King prayed to it at the beginning of Scene 1; a very high ladder which the Prince climbed part way, in order to speak with Falstaff on the march through Warwickshire (4.2); traffic up and down stairs in the tavern. Playing the second tavern scene (3.3) before a front cloth, Falstaff arrived and left through a trap; after his stabbing of Hotspur, they sank down together through this trap while Falstaff kissed the top of Hotspur's head.

Especially rich and resonant were the performances of Robert Stephens as Falstaff and Julian Glover as King Henry. Stephens provided an exceptional example of

[1] 'Shakespeare at Stratford-upon-Avon, 1991', *SQ* 43 (1992), 342.

casting against type. In his first season with the company, after a long career of leading parts both onstage and in films, his only other role was Julius Caesar. After two years of playing Falstaff, he would assume the title role in *King Lear*. Stephens' awkward bulk and his absurd leather doublet were at odds with his cunning face or the delicate, expressive hands which he scrutinised for evidence of decay on 'Do I not dwindle?' He managed to suggest that he delighted in the Prince's youth and wished to gaze upon or touch it because he himself might once have been a charismatic charmer; his melancholy lay in his perception that few fat old men, however companionable, are likely to be loved. '*Part One*', wrote Peter Holland, 'seemed to hinge on the search for an embrace' that Hal could not give to this childless Falstaff, an embrace like the one which the Prince so deeply wanted from his father and could not receive.[1]

What sort of father could have moved his son's feelings in so surprising a way? Julian Glover's King Henry superbly complemented Stephens' imposing Falstaff, as if one performance had heightened the other. Glover was unquestionably majestic, a wise and authoritative ruler who made few mistakes and no uncalculated moves. He saw through young men like Hotspur and his son whom he had to control. If the Prince himself had been presented as a Machiavellian street-fighter or proto-Henry V, this characterisation of the King might have been ineffective. But Michael Maloney's Prince, though nimble and wholesome, was also young, confused, unformed, and small enough to be over-shadowed by tall old men and by the vertical dimensions of his stage environment. Even when the battle tableau lifted into the air, the Prince was tucked in behind his father, seemingly unready to emerge on his own.

In the stage history of the past fifty years, when *Part Two* has regularly followed *Part One*, we cannot always treat either as an independent work. But throughout the preceding three hundred and fifty years of performance, *Part One*, almost without exception, stood alone. We have seen that its reputation among audiences, scholars, and the public has made it the most admired of all Shakespeare's histories. And not the least of reasons for this acclaim is its ending. *Part Two* ends with Henry V's near-definitive rejection of Falstaff after the death of Henry IV and long after the death of Henry Percy. In the last two hundred lines of *Part One*, each major character reaches an oddly affirmative conclusion. Hotspur, who would not want life without honour, dies heroically. Each of the other three – the Prince, the King, and Falstaff – fights his own battle by vastly different rules. Who could have predicted that all three would win the day?

[1] 'Shakespeare performances in England 1990–91', *S.Sur.* 45 (1993), 143.

NOTE ON THE TEXT

The text for this edition is based on the first quarto (Q1, 1598), with the exception of 1.3.199–2.2.104. This passage relies primarily upon the only surviving fragment of a slightly earlier quarto (Q0, also 1598), from which Q1 was faithfully reprinted. Q0 and Q1 are widely acknowledged to be among the most carefully printed quartos for any play by Shakespeare. They provide the only authoritative copy-text for *1 Henry IV*. Most spellings have been modernised in accordance with the conventions of the *New Cambridge Shakespeare*. In one case, an earlier form, 'Bullingbrook', indicates pronunciation ('Bullinbrook') and has been retained, as in the *NCS Richard II*, ed. Gurr. Speech headings have been regularised, including 'Prince' for 'Prin.' and 'Pr.' (rather than 'Prince of Wales' or 'Prince Hal').

'Falstaff', the familiar version for the name of the most famous character in *1 Henry IV*, has been used throughout as a speech heading. Although Sir John 'Oldcastle' is known to have been the character's original name, we have no evidence that Shakespeare resisted changing it to Falstaff. To adopt 'Sir John' as the speech heading would unduly weight a class-inflected form used most often by the Hostess and Bardolph in a single scene (3.3), and thereby undervalue other contexts in which Falstaff vigorously participates. For a discussion of 'Oldcastle', 'Rossill', and 'Harvey', the names altered after the earliest performances of the play, see Introduction pp. 5–6 and Textual Analysis, pp. 200–1. This edition follows Melchiori, ed., *2 Henry IV*, in identifying 'Bardolph' as a name change for 'Rossill' (red nose), hence 'Peto' for 'Harvey'.

The light punctuation of Qq01 has been retained when it offers more flexible choices to the actor and the reader. Changes in punctuation which significantly alter the meaning of the copy-text have been collated. Several elisions have been introduced, in keeping with Qq01's general preference for these colloquial forms. A grave accent in verse (as in armèd, impressèd) shows that the vowel should be pronounced. Elision of 'ed' or 'd' may otherwise be assumed. The treatment of short or irregular verse lines is explained in the Textual Analysis pp. 208–9, where special attention is given to 'shared' or 'split' lines.

When stage directions are added, they (like other changes to the copy-text) are enclosed in square brackets and recorded in the Collation. Such directions either replace obvious omissions or make explicit specific actions which are clearly indicated by lines in the copy-text.

In the format used for the Collation, a lemma or citation from the text is followed, after a square bracket, by the authority for the reading given. When additional readings help to illustrate the history of interpretation, these follow in chronological order. The Collation includes: (1) all significant departures from Qq01; (2) plausible emendations from later editions that have not been adopted; and (3) several emendations, which have historical importance even though they no longer seem to be credible choices. Spelling variants are not normally considered to be significant departures from the copy-text.

The Commentary explains meanings of terms, phrases, and short passages. When meanings are numbered in a sequence, each is acceptable; the first is not necessarily preferred. Illustrative examples often include conjectures about original staging, supplemented by reference to recent productions. To ensure that the basic historical background for *1 Henry IV* is immediately accessible, pertinent information has been incorporated in head-notes and in numerous glosses.

The First Part of King Henry IV

LIST OF CHARACTERS
In order of appearance (for speaking characters only)

KING *Henry the Fourth*
Lord John of LANCASTER
Earl of WESTMORELAND
Sir Walter BLUNT

PRINCE *Henry*

Sir John FALSTAFF
POINS

Earl of NORTHUMBERLAND
Earl of WORCESTER
HOTSPUR, *Sir Henry Percy*

FIRST CARRIER
OSTLER
SECOND CARRIER
GADSHILL
CHAMBERLAIN
PETO
BARDOLPH
FIRST TRAVELLER
SECOND TRAVELLER

LADY PERCY
SERVANT *to Hotspur*

FRANCIS
VINTNER
HOSTESS
SHERIFF

Lord Edmund MORTIMER
Owen GLENDOWER
LADY MORTIMER
DOUGLAS
MESSENGER
Sir Richard VERNON
ARCHBISHOP *of York*
SIR MICHAEL
Soldiers, other travellers, and attendants

Notes

QQF of *Henry IV, Part One* do not have a list of characters. The first list was provided by Rowe. The following notes are selective; they contain information on biography and on the significance of some names.

KING *Henry the Fourth* (1367–1413) Son of John of Gaunt, the Duke of Lancaster, and first cousin of Richard II, whom he supplanted in 1399. Hotspur calls him 'Bullingbrook' (his place of birth in Lincolnshire); Glendower calls him 'Lancaster' (his inherited ducal title). Both men question his legitimacy as monarch. He dies in *Part Two* 5.2.

Lord John of LANCASTER (1389–1435) The third son of Henry IV. He was made Duke of Bedford by his brother, Henry V, and became Regent of France in the reign of Henry VI. He presided over the execution of Sir John Oldcastle, was responsible for burning Joan of Arc, and caused Douglas to fall in battle.

Earl of WESTMORELAND (1364–1425) Ralph Neville, a northern baron and a kinsman of the King through marriage ('my gentle cousin', 1.1.31). Although never mentioned in *R2*, he had been one of King Henry's earliest supporters.

Sir Walter BLUNT An older knight. Not mentioned in *R2*, he had been a loyal follower of John of Gaunt and of his son, King Henry.

PRINCE *Henry* (1387–1422) The Prince of Wales, eldest son and heir to Henry IV, later crowned Henry V (1413). He is called 'the Prince of Wales' and 'Harry' by the King, 'Hal' primarily by Falstaff, and 'Harry Monmouth' (for his birthplace in Wales) by Hotspur.

Sir John FALSTAFF The Prince's companion. In the earliest version of the play, he was called 'Sir John Oldcastle', the name of a character in *FV* and, historically, a Lollard knight burned as a heretic in 1417. 'Falstaff' may have been suggested by 'Fastolffe', a historical figure who appears in *1H6* (spelled 'Falstaffe' in F and subsequent editions). It is possible, however, that his name (perhaps an ironic analogy to 'Shake-spear') symbolises his disposition. See Robert F. Willson, 'Falstaff in *1 Henry IV*: what's in a name?', *SQ* 27 (1976), 19–20, and George Walton Williams, 'Some thoughts on Falstaff's name', *SQ* 30 (1979), 82–4.

POINS A companion of the Prince and of Falstaff, self-described in *2H4* as a 'second brother', 2.2.67, i.e. a wild 'gallant' or a gentleman with little money (see *Wiv.* 3.2.73). He is also called 'Ned' and 'Yedward'.

Earl of NORTHUMBERLAND Henry Percy (1342–1408), the greatest of the northern barons and the most powerful of King Henry's early supporters in *R2*. In *2H4*, he flees to Scotland; after he returns he is 'overthrown' by the shrieve of Yorkshire, 4.4.97–9.

Earl of WORCESTER Thomas Percy (1344–1403), the younger brother of Henry. In *R2*, he forsook his position as steward of the royal household to support Bullingbrook.

HOTSPUR Sir Henry Percy (1364–1403), the eldest son of the Earl of Northumberland, generally referred to by his 'adopted name of privilege', 5.2.18, or nickname, which his historical prototype earned in border warfare with the Scots. He inspires other titles and epithets, ranging from 'Harry Percy' to 'the Hotspur of the North' or 'this gun-powder Percy'.

GADSHILL The 'setter' who arranges the robbery. His name probably comes from *FV*, where it is the nickname of the thief Cutbert Cutter, said to be 'a taking fellow / upon Gad's Hill in Kent', 165–6. Confusion often arises because of the similar names of the character and the location.

PETO A follower of the Prince. He is given an 'honourable' position in the arrangements preceding the battle, 2.4.456–7. He appears briefly as a messenger in *2H4*. In the early version of *1H4*, he was apparently called 'Harvey'. No historical significance has been found for 'Peto', a Warwickshire family name.

BARDOLPH Falstaff's companion and attendant of many years. He reappears in *2H4* and *Wiv.*, and is executed in *H5* for having stolen a 'pax' from a church, 3.6. He probably was first named 'Rossill', perhaps to annoy the Russell family. See Q 1.2.131; Melchiori, ed. *2H4*, p. 5, suggests a play upon the Italian '*rosso*', i.e. red, because of his nose. 'Bardolph', confusingly, is also the name of a rebel lord in *2H4*.

LADY PERCY Katherine (1371–1444?), Hotspur's wife and Edmund Mortimer's sister, called 'Elianor' in Holinshed (probably through confusion with her niece), but, in fact, named Elizabeth. Shakespeare may have made her a Katherine because he associated her with qualities represented by 'Kates' in *Shr.* and later in *H5*. See Laurie Maguire, ' "Household Kates": *chez* Petruchio, Percy, and Plantagenet', in *Gloriana's Face: Women Public and Private in the English Renaissance*, ed. S. P. Cerasano and Marion Wynne-Davies, 1992, pp. 129–65.

FRANCIS An apprentice drawer or tapster. He will assist the Prince and Poins in *2H4* when they disguise themselves in 'two of our jerkins and aprons', 2.4.16–17.

HOSTESS The landlady of the tavern in Eastcheap. The Prince and his companions in *FV* 83–4 refer to 'our old hostess / At *Feversham*', and to 'a prettie wench / That can talke well' at the 'olde Taverne in Eastcheape', 87–9. Also called 'Mistress Quickly', in *2H4* she becomes 'Helen of thy noble thoughts' (5.5.33) and in *H5*, married to ancient Pistol, 'Nell'. In *Wiv.*, Mistress Quickly is servant to Dr Caius.

Lord Edmund MORTIMER (1376–1409) The son of the third Earl of March and the brother-in-law of Hotspur. Holinshed and Shakespeare incorrectly identify him as the legitimate heir of Richard II. Edmund's elder brother, Roger, fourth Earl of March, was proclaimed heir presumptive in 1385 (Holinshed, II, 768). When Roger was killed in Ireland in 1398, his title and royal claim descended to his son, another Edmund (b. 1391), nephew of Shakespeare's character. The latter continued to support Glendower and died in the siege of Harlech (Barkloughly) castle.

Owen GLENDOWER (1359?–1416?) In Welsh, Owain ab Gruffydd (*DNB*). He 'dwelled . . . in a place called Glindourwie', i.e. 'The vallie by the side of the water of Dee, by occasion whereof he was surnamed Glindour Dew' (Holinshed, III, 17). He led the Welsh rebellion, both a movement for independence and a protest against the deposition of Richard. He may well be the Welsh Captain in *R2* 2.4, and is reported dead in *2H4* 3.1.103. Historically he was offered a pardon on the accession of Henry V, but refused it. Some report that he died of starvation in the mountains, others that he reached a ripe old age.

DOUGLAS (1369–1424) Archibald, fourth Earl of Douglas, often referred to as 'the' Douglas to indicate that he is the head of a noble Scottish family. Known in history as a great warrior and a poor general, he was killed at the battle of Verneuil by the English forces under the Duke of Bedford (Prince John).

ARCHBISHOP *of York* Richard Scroop (1350?–1405), the leader of the ongoing rebellion in *2H4*, entrapped and executed at Gaultree Forest by Prince John and Westmoreland, 4.1. He was the cousin (not the brother, as in Holinshed and Shakespeare) of William Scroop, Earl of Wiltshire and Lord Treasurer under Richard II, who was beheaded by Bullingbrook in 1399.

THE FIRST PART OF KING HENRY IV

[1.1] *Enter the* KING, LORD JOHN OF LANCASTER, EARL OF WESTMORELAND, [SIR WALTER BLUNT,] *with others*

KING So shaken as we are, so wan with care, ~~Pause~~ high rhetoric
Find we a time for frighted peace to pant, Pause
And breathe short-winded accents of new broils
To be commenced in strands afar remote;
No more the thirsty entrance of this soil   more poetic   5

Title] F (The First Part of Henry the Fourth); THE / HISTORY OF / HENRIE THE / FOVRTH Q1; KING Hanmer 1.1] *Actus Primus, Scœna Prima*. F; *not in* Qq 0 SD.1–2 EARL OF WESTMORELAND] QqF (Earle of Westmerland) *throughout* 0 SD.2 SIR WALTER BLUNT] *Dering MS., Capell; not in* QqF 4 strands] QqF (stronds)

Act 1, Scene 1

[1.1] Q marks neither act nor scene divisions. This edition uses the divisions in F except when noted.

[1.1] Shakespeare compresses the first two years of Henry's reign, beginning in 1399, into one; the Welsh victory described by Westmoreland, 38 ff., came in 1401. According to Holinshed (III, 16), the new King was almost immediately threatened by civil disturbances and border wars. In contrast to the formal Council meeting in 1.3, Shakespeare here presents an informal exchange of views, dominated by a general mood of uncertainty.

The stage could be bare or there might be a throne. In the latter case, decision must be made whether the King confidently takes this seat or leaves the throne conspicuously vacant.

0 SD John, younger brother of the Prince, appears only in this scene and in Act 5; he has no lines to speak until 5.4. The copy-text, Q1, provides no entry for Sir Walter Blunt, who is referred to as 'here' at 62–3 below. If he is included with the group as the scene opens, the King, who will already know the good news he brings, may speak more forcefully. If the King has already dispatched a messenger to Hotspur (99), he might have learned from Blunt, just before the scene begins, of Hotspur's victory at Holmedon. Alternatively, Blunt is 'here' in court, but remains offstage. Much like the 'post from Wales' of the preceding night (37), he could interrupt the scene at 62 and change its mood by encouraging the King. This might require more stage business: a letter from which the King reads

(67–73, 91–4) and a silent gesture as he sends a messenger to summon Hotspur. A sense of urgency created by rapid reassessments may be more important than the clarity of the King's motivation. On Shakespeare's imprecision about some entries and exits for messengers and minor characters, see Textual Analysis, pp. 201–2.

1 we The royal pronoun, and perhaps the nation as well.

1 wan pale, also weary and melancholy.

2–3 Find . . . breathe The grammar is ambiguous, either 'we' or 'peace' being the subject of 'pant'. Because 'we' governs line 3's 'breathe', a pause after 'peace' could indicate that 'we' also governs 'find', and 'pant'.

2 Find we (1) Let us try to find, (2) We happen to find.

3 breathe This verb is intransitive and here means 'speak' (though in 1.3.101 'breathed' is intransitive, meaning 'paused', rested for breath).

3 accents words, language.

3 broils fighting.

4 strands i.e. 'the shore of the Holy Land, to which, in *Richard II* (5.6.49), King Henry vowed a crusade' (Bevington).

5 thirsty entrance . . . soil i.e. dry mouth. The metaphor presents the earth as an unnatural mother devouring her own children. It has strong biblical overtones. Compare Gen. 4.11: the earth 'opened her mouth to receive thy brothers blood from thine hand'. This initiates a sequence of images which convey the horror of civil war.

prophesies of John of L coming to pess

grand speech
England - Northland

Shall daub her lips with her own children's blood,
No more shall trenching war channel her fields
Nor bruise her flow'rets with the armèd hoofs
Of hostile paces. Those opposèd eyes
Which, like the meteors of a troubled heaven,   10
All of one nature, of one substance bred,
Did lately meet in the intestine shock
And furious close of civil butchery,
Shall now in mutual well-beseeming ranks
March all one way, and be no more opposed   15
Against acquaintance, kindred, and allies.
The edge of war, like an ill-sheathèd knife,
No more shall cut his master. Therefore, friends,
As far as to the sepulchre of Christ –
Whose soldier now, under whose blessèd cross   20
We are impressèd and engaged to fight –
Forthwith a power of English shall we levy,
Whose arms were moulded in their mother's womb

23 mother's] QqF (mothers)

6 daub (1) cover with plaster or clay, (2) soil (*OED sv v* 1 and 3).

7 trenching ploughing (*OED sv v* 3b) and in a military sense, the use of ditches as fortification (*OED sv v* 5). As does the suggestion of white-washing in 'daub', 6, the agricultural metaphor obscures the responsibility of the participants, including King Henry, for their destructive actions. Blood, running down the channels like rain, ferti-lises the gashed earth.

8 flow'rets small flowers.

8 armèd hoofs i.e. horses' hoofs that have been shod. Henry's imagery resembles the use of vivid montage in Eisenstein's films.

9 paces the gait or swift motion of war-horses.

9 opposèd eyes hostile as well as physically op-posite. This use of the rhetorical figure metonymy, representing armies through some of their parts, carries ironic undertones of the body politic being dismembered by civil war.

10 meteors of a troubled heaven Meteors are taken as ominous (see *1H6* 1.1.1–5). An anxious concern for portents, omens, and prophecies typi-fies many characters in this play.

12 intestine internal, domestic (with a sugges-tion of the physiological sense). A choice of grave yet showy words, which preserve latinate or archaic meanings, distinguishes the King's personal idiom. Compare 'impressèd' (21), 'expedience' (33), 'in-dustrious' (62), 'adventure' (92), and 'utterèd' (106).

13 close grappling, hand-to-hand fighting.

13 civil civic or communal. Mahood (*Wordplay*, p. 26) suggests that the phrase 'civil butchery' gains vigour through a 'mainly unconscious' rejection of the meaning 'polite'.

14 mutual well-beseeming interdependent, well-ordered (Humphreys).

17–18 ill-sheathèd . . . master A common saying as in *WT* 1.2.156–7. That he adds this well-worn metaphor may hint at Henry's exhaustion, belying his more hopeful syntax, 'No more . . . , no more'.

18–27 Therefore . . . bitter cross The King concludes his speech with a momentum designed to emphasise the necessity for union and express his own impatience to seek absolution for his guilt.

19–22 As far . . . levy By advancing Henry's wish to go on a crusade from the end of his reign (Holinshed III, 57) to a time near its inception, Shakespeare links the opening of *1H4* more tightly to the concluding scene of *R2*.

21 impressèd and engaged conscripted and pledged by oath.

22 power army, force.

23 arms Punning on weapons/limbs (as 'chase' implies, 24).

23 mother England. The metaphor of soldiers born from the earth may echo the myths of Cadmus and of Medea.

To chase these pagans in those holy fields
Over whose acres walked those blessèd feet   25
Which fourteen hundred years ago were nailed
For our advantage on the bitter cross.
But this our purpose now is twelve month old,
And bootless 'tis to tell you we will go.
Therefor we meet not now. Then let me hear   30
Of you, my gentle cousin Westmoreland,
What yesternight our Council did decree
In forwarding this dear expedience.
WESTMORELAND My liege, this haste was hot in question,
And many limits of the charge set down   35
But yesternight, when all athwart there came
A post from Wales, loaden with heavy news,
Whose worst was that the noble Mortimer,
Leading the men of Herefordshire to fight
Against the irregular and wild Glendower,   40
Was by the rude hands of that Welshman taken,
A thousand of his people butcherèd,
Upon whose dead corpse there was such misuse,

---

26 fourteen hundred] Q (1400)   30 Therefor] *Davison;* Therefore QqF   31 Westmoreland] QqF (Westmerland) *through-*
out   39 Herefordshire] F; Herdforshire Qq1–3; Herdfordshire Qq4, 5   43 corpse] Q1, F (corpes); corps Qq2–5; corses
Staunton conj.

26–7 **Which . . . cross** The emphasis falls not on
'advantage' but on 'nailed' and 'bitter cross'. This is
significant for the speaker and for the action to
come. See Introduction, p. 8.

29 **bootless** useless, without reward.

30 **Therefor . . . now** That is not the reason we
now meet. The short sentence ending in mid-line
signals a major shift in tone.

31 **Of** From.

31 **gentle cousin** noble kinsman. 'Cousin' can
indicate any relationship of kin except direct
descent.

33 **dear expedience** urgent and cherished enterprise; 'expedience' carries the sense (now obsolete)
of an expedition that requires speed (*OED* 1a); compare *Ant.* 1.2.178.

34 **liege** liege lord, the 'superior to whom one
owes feudal allegiance and service' (*OED* sv *sb* 1).

34 **hot in question** i.e. being planned with zeal.
Compare 'hot incursions and great name in arms'
(3.2.108).

35 **limits of the charge** specified orders and
defined responsibilities for military and financial
needs.

36 **all athwart** contradicting our purposes.

37 **post** messenger who rides hastily.

37 **heavy** grave, of great importance (*OED* sv *a*[1]
12, citing 2.3.57).

38 **the noble Mortimer** See List of Characters
for a detailed explanation of Shakespeare's confusing Lord Edmund Mortimer, captured by
Glendower, with his nephew Edmund, the fifth
Earl of March. This same confused substitution
follows at 1.3.83, 142–4.

40 **irregular** engaged in guerilla warfare, i.e. not
observing the rules.

43 **corpse** corpses. The Elizabethan usage of
'corpse' in a plural sense is common.

43–6 **Upon . . . spoken** of Westmoreland's relatively tactful version rephrases Holinshed, 'The
shamefull villanie used by the Welshwomen towards the dead carcasses, was such, as honest eares
would be ashamed to heare, and continent toongs to
speak thereof' III, 20. For a much more explicit
account of the women's atrocities, see Holinshed III,
34.

Such beastly shameless transformation,
By those Welshwomen done, as may not be   45
Without much shame retold or spoken of.
KING It seems then that the tidings of this broil
Brake off our business for the Holy Land.
WESTMORELAND This, matched with other, did, my gracious lord,
For more uneven and unwelcome news   50
Came from the north, and thus it did import:
On Holy-rood day, the gallant Hotspur there,
Young Harry Percy, and brave Archibald,
That ever valiant and approvèd Scot,
At Holmedon met, where they did spend   55
A sad and bloody hour;
As by discharge of their artillery,
And shape of likelihood, the news was told;
For he that brought them, in the very heat
And pride of their contention did take horse,   60
Uncertain of the issue any way.
KING Here is a dear and true industrious friend,
Sir Walter Blunt, new lighted from his horse,
Stained with the variation of each soil
Betwixt that Holmedon and this seat of ours;   65
And he hath brought us smooth and welcome news.
The Earl of Douglas is discomfited.
Ten thousand bold Scots, two-and-twenty knights,

55–6 At . . . spend / A . . . hour] QQF; At . . . met / Where . . . hour *Capell*   62 a dear and true] Q5, F; deere, a true QQ1–4

49–55 This . . . met Shakespeare brings the two events together to show how the King's authority is being challenged on the borders of his realm. The battle of Holmedon, according to Holinshed, took place three months after Mortimer's capture.
50 uneven (1) not uniform or 'smooth', as 66, (2) uncertain.
52 Holy-rood day 14 September, the day dedicated to the Holy Cross in the church calendar. This is an ironic coincidence in the light of the King's deferred crusade to the Holy Land.
53 Archibald The fourth Earl of Douglas. See List of Characters.
54 approvèd tested by experience.
55 Holmedon In Northumberland, near Wooler (there are many variant spellings, e.g. Humbleton), where in 1402 the Percys stopped one of the frequent invasions of northern England by the Scots.
57–8 As by discharge . . . told The severity of

the fighting is being estimated from the amount of shooting. Holinshed speaks of archery, but 'artillery' could refer to any missile, as well as to the engine used to fire it (*OED* 2). At 2.3.47 Hotspur dreams of basilisks, cannon, and culverin.
60 pride highest pitch, intensity.
62–3 Here . . . Blunt See 0 SD.
62 dear and true This F reading is more consistent with the King's style. He often couples words and phrases as in 'smooth and welcome', 66. The copy-text Q's 'Here is deere, a true' clearly requires some emendation.
62 industrious painstaking, attentive (*OED* 2).
64 Stained with the variation of each soil The King praises Blunt's diligence and may suggest his native integrity. His figures do not necessarily describe the way Blunt looks.
66 smooth pleasant.
67 discomfited overthrown, routed in battle.

Balked in their own blood, did Sir Walter see
On Holmedon's plains. Of prisoners Hotspur took   70
Mordake, Earl of Fife and eldest son
To beaten Douglas, and the Earl of Atholl,
Of Murray, Angus, and Menteith.
And is not this an honourable spoil?
A gallant prize? Ha, cousin, is it not?   75
WESTMORELAND In faith, it is a conquest for a prince to boast of.
KING Yea, there thou makest me sad, and makest me sin
        In envy that my Lord Northumberland
        Should be the father to so blest a son –
        A son who is the theme of honour's tongue,   80
        Amongst a grove the very straightest plant,
        Who is sweet Fortune's minion and her pride –
        Whilst I by looking on the praise of him
        See riot and dishonour stain the brow
        Of my young Harry. O that it could be proved   85
        That some night-tripping fairy had exchanged
        In cradle-clothes our children where they lay,
        And called mine Percy, his Plantagenet!
        Then would I have his Harry, and he mine.
        But let him from my thoughts. What think you, coz, 90
        Of this young Percy's pride? The prisoners

---

69 blood, did] Q5, F (blood did); bloud. Did QQ1–4   76 SH WESTMORELAND] QQF (Westmerland) (*throughout*)
76 WESTMORELAND In faith . . . boast of] *As Bevington;* [*King*] In faith . . . is. / *West.* A conquest . . . of QQF

69 **Balked** Heaped up, perhaps in rows. A 'balk' was a ridge between two furrows.

70 **prisoners** Henry seems to know that Hotspur has captured Douglas, but his name is not included in the list of prisoners. Compare 3.2.112–17.

71 **Mordake** Shakespeare may have wrongly identified him as Douglas' son because of a missing comma in Holinshed's list of prisoners (III, 21). Murdoch Stewart was the eldest son of Robert, Duke of Albany, Regent of Scotland.

73 **Menteith** One of 'Mordake's' titles, not a separate person historically (an apparent mistake by the dramatist).

74 **honourable spoil** Henry may be contrasting Hotspur's behaviour with that of the Welshwomen. He maintains his public commitment to chivalric standards.

82 **minion** Here, favourite; elsewhere, servant or lover, as at 1.2.21.

84 **riot** debauchery of the worst kind (*OED* sv *sb* 1a) or (more mildly), wanton revelling. The term,

used only three times in *1* and *2 H4*, always refers to the Prince.

84 **stain the brow** From his first appearance in *R2* Henry conceptualises dishonour or shame in physical terms.

85–7 **O that . . . lay** Shakespeare probably follows Daniel in making Hal and Hotspur the same age. Historically Hotspur was twenty-one years older than Hal and two years older than the King himself. See Introduction, pp. 23–4.

86 **fairy had exchanged** Alluding to the folk belief that fairies exchanged their own ugly offspring for beautiful human children. This shows an atypical side of Henry who is often hard-headed.

88 **Plantagenet** The dynastic surname of the royal family.

90 **coz** cousin, kinsman.

91–4 **The prisoners . . . Fife** According to the law of arms (referred to in *H5* 4.7.2), Hotspur could hold for ransom all prisoners except those of royal blood. He was therefore obliged to surrender only Mordake, grandson of Robert II of Scotland.

Which he in this adventure hath surprised
To his own use he keeps, and sends me word
I shall have none but Mordake, Earl of Fife.

WESTMORELAND This is his uncle's teaching, this is Worcester,   95
Malevolent to you in all aspects,
Which makes him prune himself, and bristle up
The crest of youth against your dignity.

KING But I have sent for him to answer this;
And for this cause a while we must neglect   100
Our holy purpose to Jerusalem.
Cousin, on Wednesday next our Council we
Will hold at Windsor, so inform the lords.
But come yourself with speed to us again,
For more is to be said and to be done   105
Than out of anger can be utterèd.

WESTMORELAND I will, my liege.

Exeunt

most imp. figure in 2nd scene – usually H.S.

[1.2] *Enter* PRINCE OF WALES *and* SIR JOHN FALSTAFF *– central figures.*
(waking up after a heavy night in tavern)

FALSTAFF Now Hal, what time of day is it, lad?

102–3 we / Will hold at] *T. Johnson, Pope;* wil hold / At QqF Act 1, Scene 2 1.2] *Scæna Secunda.* F; *not in* Qq
0 SD] Qq; *Enter Henry Prince of Wales, Sir John Falstaffe, and Pointz* F

---

92 adventure a daring enterprise.

92 surprised captured (*OED* sv *v* 2b).

96 Malevolent . . . aspects Like a comet or meteor, 'malevolent' or unfavourable in all positions.

97 prune Worcester teaches Hotspur, as a hawk, to preen. The hawk trims his feathers for action; he *prunes* them with his beak.

97–8 bristle up . . . youth Carrying on the image of the bird of prey demonstrates its readiness for attack. The bird's aggression is especially clear when it raises the feathers on its head. 'Crest' may also suggest a helmet.

99–103 But I . . . lords The King exercises his power more forcefully than his opening lines would lead us to expect. In Holinshed's account, the Percys of their own accord arrive to challenge the King.

105–6 For . . . utterèd The King adapts a common proverb 'Nothing is well said or done in a passion' (Tilley N307).

Act 1, Scene 2

[1.2] The dialogue does not specify the location.

Most editors have assumed it to be the Prince's apartments in London, but some productions have erroneously treated this as the first of the tavern scenes. Both the general atmosphere and the predominant use of prose create strong contrasts with the opening scene.

0 SD The two characters may enter together or from opposite sides of the stage. Falstaff can be spruce and ready for action, or, in a staging popular since the early nineteenth century, he can be discovered asleep by the Prince. He may even sit down immediately on a vacant 'throne' and address the Prince in mimicry of Henry IV. To present a sleeping Falstaff ignores the stage direction but anticipates his nap behind the arras 2.4.443 ff.

1 Now . . . lad? A natural question, perhaps with the additional sense, 'What's up?' (if Falstaff is not discovered asleep). His tone can also suggest that he is thirsty, or hung over – or that, half-awake, he is reproving the Prince with mock seriousness. His nine monosyllables have a simplicity lacking in the Prince's first speech, a long aggressive response.

PRINCE Thou art so fat-witted with drinking of old sack, and unbutton-
ing thee after supper, and sleeping upon benches after noon, that
thou hast forgotten to demand that truly which thou wouldst truly
know. What a devil hast thou to do with the time of the day? Unless   5
hours were cups of sack, and minutes <u>capons</u>, and clocks the tongues
of bawds, and dials the signs of leaping-houses, and the blessed sun
himself a fair hot wench in flame-coloured taffeta, I see no reason
why thou shouldst be so superfluous to demand the time of the day.

FALSTAFF Indeed, you come near me now, Hal, for we that take purses   10
go by the moon and the seven stars, and not 'by Phoebus, he, that
wandering knight so fair'. And I prithee, sweet wag, when thou art
king, as God save thy grace – majesty, I should say, for grace thou
wilt have none –

11–12 'by . . . fair'] *Humphreys;* by . . . faire QqF   13 king] Qq2–5, F; a king Q1

2–9 **Thou art . . . day** 'This comic on-
slaught . . . with its tight logical framework and its
figures of climax . . . [is a] superlative instance of
high symmetricality combined with flexibility'
(Jonas Barish, 'Mixed verse and prose in Shakespearean comedy', *English Comedy*, ed. Michael
Cordner *et al.*, 1994, p. 66.) Many find in this
speech, however, a paradoxical effect of improvising, an apparent absence of order.

2 **fat-witted** thick-witted.

2 **sack** General name for white wines imported
from Spain and the Canary Islands. 1.2.92 indicates
that Falstaff adds sugar to his sack.

4 **forgotten** neglected, not bothered to (*OED*
Forget sv *v* 4).

5–9 **What a devil . . . time of the day** Hal
attacks Falstaff's supposed indifference to all clock
time.

6 **capons** castrated cocks, big and fat (like
Falstaff). The frequent association of Falstaff with
capons, his favourite food, emphasises his gluttony
and his size, and ironically glances at his alleged
lechery.

7 **dials** watches or clock faces; also sundials
which 'tell the hour of the day, by means of the
sun's shadow' (*OED* sb¹ 1).

7 **leaping-houses** brothels, clearly identified by
signs comparable to the signs of taverns or ale-
houses. Stow, *Survey*, describes the signs of the
former 'stewhouses' in Southwark as 'not hanged
out, but painted on the walles' (II, 55). Compare *Ado*
1.1.253–4, 'hang me up at the door of a brothel-
house for the sign of blind Cupid'.

8 **hot wench in flame-coloured taffeta** Taffeta is a silk fabric associated with dressing to attract
attention. Prostitutes might wear flame-coloured
taffeta for ostentatious petticoats or gowns (com-

pare *AWW* 2.2.22). The colour suggests passion,
but also hell, the punishment for lechery, and perhaps the torment of venereal disease. Hal's reference to 'the blessed sun himself' as an
exhibitionist 'wench' contrasts with his later appro-
priation of the sun/son analogy at 157.

9 **superfluous** needlessly concerned, with a pun
on self-indulgent, overflowing.

10 **come near me** A phrase borrowed from
fencing. Although it is often glossed as 'score a
point', it literally means 'just miss me' or 'almost hit
me' – an important distinction for Falstaff's first
line spoken in this duel of wits in which he proves so
elusive an opponent.

11 **go by** (1) are guided by the light of, (2) tell
time by.

11 **seven stars** constellation of the Pleiades and
perhaps the name of an inn.

11–12 **by Phoebus . . . fair** Warburton (1747)
thought this phrase might come from a lost ballad.
Steevens (1785) detected a possible allusion to the
wandering knight of the sun in *The Mirror of
Knighthood*, a romance translated in 1578 by
Margaret Tyler. Douce (*Illustrations of Shakespeare*,
1807) suggested a reference to *The Voyage of the
Wandering Knight*, translated in 1581 by William
Goodyear (cited by Hemingway).

11 **Phoebus** A name for Apollo, god of the sun.

12 **wag** Affectionate tag for a mischievous youth.
It shows the intimacy that the Prince allows Falstaff.

12–13 **when thou art king** The first of Falstaff's
many hopeful allusions to the future. The fact that
he so often refers to favours he will be granted when
Hal rules should refute the arguments of many critics that Falstaff cares only for the present.

13 **grace** A quibble which may well include four
meanings: (1) political majesty, (2) a state of spir-

PRINCE What, none?   15

FALSTAFF No, by my troth, not so much as will serve to be prologue to
an egg and butter.

PRINCE Well, how then? Come, roundly, roundly.

FALSTAFF Marry then, sweet wag, when thou art king let not us that are
squires of the night's body be called thieves of the day's beauty. Let   20
us be Diana's foresters, gentlemen of the shade, minions of the
moon. And let men say we be men of good government, being
governed as the sea is, by our noble and chaste mistress the moon,
under whose countenance we steal.

PRINCE Thou sayest well, and it holds well too, for the fortune of us   25
that are the moon's men doth ebb and flow like the sea, being
governed as the sea is, by the moon. As for proof now: a purse of
gold most resolutely snatched on Monday night, and most disso-
lutely spent on Tuesday morning, got with swearing 'Lay by!', and
spent with crying 'Bring in!', now in as low an ebb as the foot of the   30
ladder, and by and by in as high a flow as the ridge of the gallows.

27 proof now:] *Collier*; proofe. Now QQF; proof now, *Wilson*

itual grace, (3) refinement, and (4) the blessing before a meal, the meaning made explicit in Falstaff's
next speech.

17 an egg and butter a simple informal meal,
therefore not requiring that an elaborate grace be
said before it.

18 roundly plainly, without deception or cir-
cumlocution (*OED* 4); (the Prince may glance at
Falstaff's rotund shape).

19 Marry An oath (by the Virgin Mary), so mild
that it remained when others were deleted from F, in
response to the 1606 Act 'to Restraine Abuses of
Players', forbidding profanity onstage. See Textual
Analysis, pp. 199–200.

19–20 let not . . . beauty Falstaff absorbs Hal's
attack, rather than refuting it. Punning on night as
knight (a common pun even though the 'k' was
probably pronounced, Cercignani, 320), on body as
bawdy, and on beauty as booty, he asserts that those
who must serve at night should not be criticised for
wasting time during the day.

20–2 squires . . . moon Falstaff invents parodic
titles for officers in the government of the future
king.

20 squires of the night's body Squires of the
body were personal attendants to knights in great
medieval households. There is also a punning allusion to prostitutes whose bodies often are squired at
night.

21 Diana's foresters Servants to the goddess of
the moon, of the hunt, and (ironic in this context) of
chastity. For the bawdy sense, see *MM* 4.3.161–2,
'he's a better woodman than thou tak'st him for'.

21 gentlemen of the shade Suggesting shady
dealings, as in 'gentlemen of the road' for highwaymen. Wilson notes the title of members of the royal
household, 'Gentlemen of the Chamber', and
points out that in *FV*, the Prince promises an annual
pension to all highwaymen (469–74).

21 minions servants or lovers, compare 1.1.82.

22 government (1) discipline or conduct, (2) the
regime in which offices are held.

24 countenance A quibble: (1) face, (2) patronage or protection. Compare 126–7 below.

24 steal (1) rob, (2) go stealthily.

25 it holds well what you say is valid, it applies
(*OED* sv v 23c, citing this example).

29 Lay by The equivalent of 'Stand and
deliver' or 'Drop your weapons.'

30 Bring in Order for service in a tavern.

30–1 now . . . gallows According to the proverb, 'He that is at low ebb at Newgate may soon
be afloat at Tyburn' (Dent E56). Both low and high
tide, as metaphors for the fortunes of a thief, bring
disaster.

31 ladder At low tide it reaches down into the
water, at high, it leads up to the scaffold.

31 ridge the crossbar for the hangman's rope.

FALSTAFF By the Lord thou sayest true, lad – and is not my Hostess of
the tavern a most sweet wench?

PRINCE As the honey of Hybla, my old lad of the castle.
And is not a buff jerkin a most sweet robe of durance?   35

FALSTAFF How now, how now, mad wag? What, in thy quips and thy
quiddities? What a plague have I to do with a buff jerkin?

PRINCE Why, what a pox have I to do with my Hostess of the tavern?

FALSTAFF Well, thou hast called her to a reckoning many a time and
oft.   40

PRINCE Did I ever call for thee to pay thy part?

FALSTAFF No, I'll give thee thy due, thou hast paid all there.

PRINCE Yea, and elsewhere, so far as my coin would stretch, and where
it would not, I have used my credit.

FALSTAFF Yea, and so used it that were it not here apparent that thou   45
art heir apparent – but I prithee, sweet wag, shall there be gallows
standing in England when thou art king? And resolution thus

32 **thou sayest true, lad** Falstaff apparently accepts the Prince's insinuation, but quickly changes the subject.

34 **As the honey of Hybla** Hybla is a town in Sicily famous for its honey. The Prince adopts the common phrase 'as sweet as honey' (Dent H544) giving it more resonance through alliteration.

34 **my old lad of the castle** Echoing 'my Hostess of the tavern', with word-play on Sir John Oldcastle, the name given to the Falstaff character in the first version of the play. 'Old lad of the castle' was also a familiar phrase (Dent C124.1). Humphreys suggests an allusion to 'one of Southwark's principal brothels . . . called The Castle' (mentioned by Stow, *Survey*, II, 55), and cites G. R. Owst's observation that a tavern in homiletic works was often called 'the devil's castle' (*Literature and Pulpit in Medieval England*, 1961, p. 438.) On the change from 'Oldcastle' to Falstaff, see Introduction, pp. 5–6, 28–9 and Textual Analysis, p. 200.

35 **buff jerkin** close-fitting leather jacket worn by an arresting officer. Ian Donaldson, 'Falstaff's buff jerkin', *SQ* 37 (1986), 100–1, suggests that 'buff' may refer to human skin, initiating a sexual joke continued in 'sweet robe'. The Prince mocks Falstaff's praise for the Hostess by implying that she is a '*bona roba*' or prostitute.

35 **durance** (1) long wearing quality, (2) imprisonment (here for stealing), (3) sturdy fabric.

37 **quiddities** quibbles, subtleties (*OED* 2); literally 'subtle definitions', the 'what-ness of a thing'.

38 **what a pox** Echoes Falstaff's 'What a plague'. Because pocks/pox can mean 'plague' there is probably an allusion to venereal disease, prompted by insinuations about the Hostess.

39 **reckoning** (1) payment of the tavern bill, (2) an account for herself, and (3) by innuendo, sexual encounter. Bevington notes that this exchange continues to build through puns on payment and sexuality ('pay thy part', 41, 'paid all there', 42, 'coin would stretch', 43). Dent, p. xviii, uses this passage as a primary example of how recognising a proverb, 'Oft counting makes good friends' (C706) can throw new light on the text: 'For me, at least, this clarifies the jest in what has otherwise seemed a pointless line.'

44 **credit** (1) financial solvency, based on confidence that debts will be paid, as in 169, (2) good name (*OED* sv *sb* 5b).

45–9 **Yea . . . thief** Falstaff repeats for the third time 'when thou art king' and his anxiety about future legal consequences. In sharp contrast to Shakespeare's Prince Hal, the Prince in *FV* (455–6), claims, 'When I am King, we will have no such things' (as prisons).

45–6 **were . . . heir apparent** The obvious pun may cloak a warning against the loss of reputation.

47–8 **resolution thus fubbed** courage so cheated or robbed.

fubbed as it is with the rusty curb of old Father Antic the law? Do
not thou when thou art king hang a thief.

PRINCE No, thou shalt.   50

FALSTAFF Shall I? O rare! By the Lord, I'll be a brave judge!

PRINCE Thou judgest false already! I mean thou shalt have the hanging
of the thieves, and so become a rare hangman.

FALSTAFF Well, Hal, well! And in some sort it jumps with my humour
– as well as waiting in the court, I can tell you.   55

PRINCE For obtaining of suits?

FALSTAFF Yea, for obtaining of suits, whereof the hangman hath no
lean wardrobe. 'Sblood, I am as melancholy as a gib cat, or a lugged
bear.

PRINCE Or an old lion, or a lover's lute.   60

FALSTAFF Yea, or the drone of a Lincolnshire bagpipe.

PRINCE What sayest thou to a hare, or the melancholy of Moorditch?

FALSTAFF Thou hast the most unsavoury similes, and art indeed the
most comparative rascalliest sweet young prince. But Hal, I prithee

---

48 law?] F; law, Qq1, 2; law: Qq3–5   63 similes] Q5; smiles Qq1–4, F

---

48 **old Father Antic the law** Falstaff caricatures
authority as a grotesque old buffoon named for
Antic, a clown in earlier Tudor drama and a figure
for death in *R2* (3.2.162).

51 **brave** excellent, as well as courageous or
stylish.

52 **judgest** (1) pass sentence, (2) choose a
meaning.

52–3 **thou shalt . . . thieves** Proverbial: 'The
great thieves hang the little ones' (Dent T119). In
FV, the Prince promises to make his henchman Ned
Chief Justice (459–61).

54 **jumps with my humour** fits my temperament or mood. Compare 156.

55 **waiting in the court** 'Court' means royal
court as well as court of justice. Falstaff rejects the
role of petitioner or plaintiff waiting for his 'suit' or
plea to be dealt with.

57–8 **Yea . . . wardrobe** Public executioners received as perquisites the clothing ('suits') of those
they hanged.

58 **'Sblood** Literally, 'by Christ's blood', but
used loosely like 'zounds' ('God's wounds').

58–62 **melancholy . . . Moorditch** Falstaff
and Hal compete, returning, as if they were tennis
balls, similes of melancholy, a condition of gloom
which might be temporary or chronic.

58 **gib cat** A male or tom-cat, not necessarily
castrated (*OED sb¹* 2). Gib is a diminutive of
Gilbert, a common name for a cat.

58 **lugged** baited. A local allusion because bear-
baiting was a rival attraction to the theatre on
Bankside. The chained bear is a melancholy object.

60 **lover's lute** In *Ado*, Claudio contrasts the
sad pensive mood frequently connoted by lute
music to Benedick's earlier jesting humour (3.2.59–
60).

61 **drone . . . bagpipe** Davison suggests that
'Shakespeare has in mind the drone of a long-
winded speaker' or 'windbag', a meaning not recorded for 'bagpipe' until 1603. English bagpipes
were apparently linked in Elizabethan times to
Lancashire and Lincolnshire (Humphreys).

62 **hare** Dent (H151) cites the proverbial belief
that eating the hare's flesh caused melancholy. The
hare is commonly contrasted to the lion's active and
courageous temper. Turberville, *Booke of Hunting*,
1575, p. 160, says the hare is one of the 'moste
melancholike beastes that is'.

62 **Moorditch** A narrow, filthy ditch (remain-
ing from the moat around the walls) between
Bishopsgate and Moorgate, north of the City of
London. It had been widened and cleaned in 1595,
but was 'never the better' (Stow, *Survey*, I, 20). Its
proximity to Bedlam, the madhouse, would add to
its associations with melancholy (Sugden).

64 **comparative** one who makes witty comparisons. The King uses the word to describe trivial
mockers, 3.2.67.

64–9 **But Hal . . . too** Falstaff imitates 'the

trouble me no more with vanity. I would to God thou and I knew　65
where a commodity of good names were to be bought. An old lord
of the Council rated me the other day in the street about you, sir, but
I marked him not, and yet he talked very wisely, but I regarded him
not, and yet he talked wisely – and in the street too.

PRINCE　Thou didst well, for wisdom cries out in the streets and no man　70
regards it.

FALSTAFF　O, thou hast damnable iteration, and art indeed able to
corrupt a saint. Thou hast done much harm upon me, Hal, God
forgive thee for it. Before I knew thee, Hal, I knew nothing, and now
am I, if a man should speak truly, little better than one of the wicked.　75
I must give over this life, and I will give it over. By the Lord, an I do
not I am a villain. I'll be damned for never a king's son in Christendom.

PRINCE　Where shall we take a purse tomorrow, Jack?

FALSTAFF　Zounds, where thou wilt, lad, I'll make one; an I do not, call　80
me villain and baffle me.

PRINCE　I see a good amendment of life in thee, from praying to purse-
taking.

FALSTAFF　Why Hal, 'tis my vocation, Hal. 'Tis no sin for a man to
labour in his vocation.　85

---

70 wisdom . . . and] Qq; *not in* F　73 upon] Q1; unto Qq2–5, F　76 an] QqF (and), *Pope*

Scriptural style of the sanctimonious Puritan'
(Hemingway), initiating another serious concern,
repentance. Other examples include 'little better
than one of the wicked', 75, and 'I must give over
this life', 76. Hal takes up this theme in his soliloquy
that concludes this scene. Compare 76 and note.

65 trouble me no more with vanity Falstaff
pretends that he has been corrupted by the Prince's
frivolity. Bevington observes that the term 'vanity'
is 'repeatedly associated with Falstaff as Hal's
companion'.

66 commodity supply.

66 names reputations.

67 rated scolded.

70 wisdom . . . streets The Prince echoes
Proverbs 1.20: 'Wisdome cryeth without; she
uttereth her voyce in the stretes', and 1.24: 'Because
I have called, and ye refused: I have stretched
out mine hand, and none wolde regarde.' He
mocks Falstaff by implying that he is immune to
wisdom.

72 damnable iteration It was commonly
thought that the Devil was a sophisticated theolo-
gian and could glibly quote Scripture. Distorting
this sense, Falstaff jokingly accuses Hal of repeating

but twisting biblical allusion in order to lead him to
damnation.

73 corrupt a saint This self-praise is a comic
forerunner of the way the hypocrite Angelo identifies himself in *MM* 2.2.179–80: 'Oh cunning
enemy, that to catch a saint, / With saints dost bait
thy hook!'

76 I must give over this life A canting parody
in advance of Hal's programme for self-reform,
155 ff. The Wycliffites and Lollards, with whom the
historical Oldcastle was associated, anticipated the
Protestant Reformers in their emphasis on personal
faith and salvation.

76 an if.

77 villain one who (1) has no principles or honour, (2) is of low birth.

80 Zounds God's wounds; a particularly strong
oath. Compare ''Sblood', 58.

80 make one be one of the participants.

81 baffle Literally, to disgrace a perjured knight
who has lost his honour by hanging him – or his
shield – upside down. Compare Spenser, *The Faerie
Queene* VI, vii, 27.

82 amendment of life reformation.

84–5 'Tis no sin . . . vocation Alluding ironi-

Enter POINS   ~~save oge as Hal~~

POINS! Now shall we know if Gadshill have set a match. O, if men were to be saved by merit, what hole in hell were hot enough for him? This is the most omnipotent villain that ever cried 'Stand!' to a true man.

PRINCE   Good morrow, Ned.   90

POINS   Good morrow, sweet Hal. What says Monsieur Remorse? What says Sir John Sack, and Sugar Jack? How agrees the devil and thee about thy soul, that thou soldest him on Good Friday last, for a cup of Madeira and a cold capon's leg?

PRINCE   Sir John stands to his word, the devil shall have his bargain, for   95
he was never yet a breaker of proverbs. He will give the devil his due.

POINS   Then art thou damned for keeping thy word with the devil.

PRINCE   Else he had been damned for cozening the devil.

POINS   But my lads, my lads, tomorrow morning, by four o'clock early   100
at Gad's Hill, there are pilgrims going to Canterbury with rich

---

85 SD] Qq; *not in* F   86 Poins! Now] *Theobald;* Poynes nowe Q; Pointz. [*taken as a speech heading*] Now Qq4, 5, F   86 match]
Qq; Watch F   92 Sack, and Sugar Jack?] Qq1–4 *subst.;* Sacke and Sugar: Jacke? F; Sack-and-Sugar? Jack! *Rowe*

---

cally to 1 Cor. 7.20, 'Let every man abide in the same vocation wherein he is called.' This was a favourite text of Protestant preachers, urging hard work and conformity to the social order.

86 Poins See Collation for the confusion of speakers in Qq4, 5, F.

86 Gadshill See List of Characters for the confusion of the character and the location, Gad's Hill (101 below).

86 set a match thieves' cant, meaning 'plan a robbery'. In 2.2.40, Gadshill is 'our setter'.

87 by merit i.e. by good works, not faith alone. Falstaff finds it opportune here to side against Lutheran theology in the Reformation controversy over salvation. Luther maintained that man could only be saved by faith and God's grace.

88 omnipotent almighty, a comic exaggeration.

88 Stand The cry with which the highwayman stops his victim.

89 true honest.

91 Monsieur Remorse Continuing the mockery of Puritan piety. In giving Falstaff a fictive name, Poins shows familiarity with Falstaff's pretence of repentance.

92 Sir John Sack, and Sugar Jack 'Jack' is the familiar diminutive of John, while sack and sugar is Sir John's favourite drink. Poins' word-play

touches on 'jack' as a common term for 'knave' (i.e. a social inferior) and for a drinking vessel. 'Sack' may quibble on the sackcloth worn by a penitent (Monsieur Remorse). Q punctuation, followed here, creates a more balanced antithesis; if Poins pauses instead after 'John' or 'Sugar', he can alter the play of meaning within the line (i.e. 'after all, you are only Jack').

93 Good Friday The strictest fast-day.

95–9 Sir John . . . devil Promise-keeping was essential to the knightly code. Hal and Poins enjoy using it to trap Falstaff (if one accepts their logic) in hell.

96 breaker of proverbs A proverbial saying (Dent P615.1), applied to someone who breaks the rules taught by proverbs.

96 devil The insistent allusions to damnation keep an audience aware of the Morality-drama features of the play. See Introduction, pp. 10 ff.

99 cozening cheating.

101 Gad's Hill Two miles north-west of Rochester in Kent on the road to London. It was notorious for robberies.

101 pilgrims A major route for pilgrims going to the shrine of St Thomas at Canterbury crossed Gad's Hill. Those actually robbed in 2.2 are simply called Travellers.

offerings and traders riding to London with fat purses. I have
vizards for you all; you have horses for yourselves. Gadshill lies
tonight in Rochester. I have bespoke supper tomorrow night in
Eastcheap. We may do it as secure as sleep. If you will go, I will stuff   105
your purses full of crowns. If you will not, tarry at home and be
hanged.

FALSTAFF Hear ye, Yedward, if I tarry at home and go not, I'll hang
you for going.

POINS You will, chops?   110

FALSTAFF Hal, wilt thou make one?

PRINCE Who I? Rob? I, a thief? Not I, by my faith.

FALSTAFF There's neither honesty, manhood, nor good fellowship in
thee, nor thou camest not of the blood royal, if thou darest not stand
for ten shillings.   115

PRINCE Well then, once in my days I'll be a madcap.

FALSTAFF Why, that's well said.

PRINCE Well, come what will, I'll tarry at home.

FALSTAFF By the Lord, I'll be a traitor then, when thou art king.

PRINCE I care not.   120

POINS Sir John, I prithee leave the Prince and me alone. I will lay him
down such reasons for this adventure that he shall go.

FALSTAFF Well, God give thee the spirit of persuasion, and him the
ears of profiting, that what thou speakest may move, and what he
hears may be believed, that the true prince may – for recreation sake   125

---

110 chops ?] Q7; chops. QQ1–5, F, Q6   123 God give . . . him] Qq; maist thou have . . . he F

103 vizards masks.
104 bespoke ordered.
105 Eastcheap District of the City of London,
named after Great Eastcheap Street, and the setting
for the tavern scenes, 2.4 and 3.3. In *FV* the Prince
himself proposes a meeting there. Shakespeare
never names the tavern – traditionally called 'The
Boar's Head'. Compare 2.4.12.
106 crowns Coins valued at five shillings each.
Ironic parallels between stealing kingdoms and
stealing money, as well as between rulers and
coins, become more explicit at 114–15. Contrast the
plan of the Prince to reveal himself as 'bright metal',
172.
108 Yedward Dialect form of Edward.
108–9 hang you turn state's evidence and get
you hanged. Clearly a jest.
110 chops fat or bloated cheeks (*OED* sv *sb*² 3).
114 royal A quibble on the coin of that

name, then worth ten shillings. Compare *2H4*
1.2.23.
114–15 stand for (1) fight for, (2) be worth ten
shillings.
116 madcap reckless, wildly impulsive person
(*OED*), alluding to a proverb, Dent D121.1, 'to be
mad once in one's days'.
122 adventure daring feat. Compare 1.1.92 and
note.
123–7 Well . . . countenance. Falstaff parodies
the emphasis on inspiration and spiritual receptive-
ness in Puritan preaching. His speech takes the
form of a 'collect' or prayer used at the conclusion of
a service and aptly leads to his exit-line (Bevington,
citing Peter Milward, *Shakespeare's Religious Background*, 1973, pp. 107–8 on the prayer, and Rich-
mond Noble, *Shakespeare's Biblical Knowledge and
use of the Book of Common Prayer*, 1935, p. 171 on
the service).

– prove a false thief, for the poor abuses of the time want countenance. Farewell, you shall find me in Eastcheap.

PRINCE Farewell, the latter spring! Farewell, All-hallown summer!

[Exit Falstaff]

POINS Now my good sweet honey lord, ride with us tomorrow. I have
a jest to execute that I cannot manage alone. Falstaff, Peto,   130
Bardolph, and Gadshill shall rob those men that we have already
waylaid – yourself and I will not be there. And when they have the
booty, if you and I do not rob them – cut this head off from my
shoulders.

PRINCE How shall we part with them in setting forth?   135

POINS Why, we will set forth before or after them, and appoint them a
place of meeting – wherein it is at our pleasure to fail – and then will
they adventure upon the exploit themselves, which they shall have
no sooner achieved but we'll set upon them.

PRINCE Yea, but 'tis like that they will know us by our horses, by our   140
habits, and by every other appointment to be ourselves.

POINS Tut, our horses they shall not see, I'll tie them in the wood. Our
vizards we will change after we leave them. And, sirrah, I have cases
of buckram for the nonce, to immask our noted outward garments.

PRINCE Yea, but I doubt they will be too hard for us.   145

POINS Well, for two of them, I know them to be as true-bred cowards
as ever turned back, and for the third, if he fight longer than he sees
reason, I'll forswear arms. The virtue of this jest will be the incom-

128 the] QqF; thou *Pope*   128 SD *Exit Falstaff*] F2; *not in* QqF   130–1 Peto, Bardolph] *Bevington;* Harvey, Rossill QqF;
Bardolph, Peto *Theobald;* Harvey, Russell *Oxford*   135 How] Qq; But how F   140 Yea, but] Qq (Yea but)*;* I, but F
145 Yea, but] Qq; But F

126–7 **poor . . . countenance** Falstaff refers to
complaints that the nobility are not sufficiently
generous; he may also be asking them, perhaps
hypocritically, to prevent disorder by helping the
poor.

128 **All-hallown summer** Like 'latter spring',
referring to Falstaff's youthful behaviour in old
age, unseasonal warm weather sometimes occurring
about 1 November, All Hallows or All Saints'
Day.

129 **sweet honey** Terms of endearment addressed to both sexes. Compare 'Sugar Jack', 92
above.

130–1 **Peto, Bardolph** For a detailed analysis of
how the names of Falstaff's companions, Bardolph
and Peto, were presumably altered from Rossill and
Harvey when Oldcastle was changed to Falstaff, see
Melchiori p. 5 and pp. 9–15.

132 **waylaid** set an ambush for.

135–53 **How shall . . . Farewell** Hal plays
the straight man, thereby learning the details of
Poins's plan, but delaying our insight about his own
character.

137 **at our pleasure** our choice.

141 **habits** clothing.

141 **appointment** piece of equipment, accoutre-
ment.

143 **sirrah** A familiar form of 'sir', used when
addressing underlings and children, but also, as
here, comrades (Kittredge).

143–4 **cases . . . nonce** coarse cloth suits or
overalls for the occasion.

145 **doubt** fear.

148–9 **incomprehensible** (1) beyond limits or
bounds, (2) beyond understanding. The meaning
'uncatchable', not cited by *OED* before 1607, may
also be suggested; to 'comprehend' is to seize or
entrap (*OED v* 1).

prehensible lies that this same fat rogue will tell us when we meet at
supper. How thirty at least he fought with, what wards, what blows,   150
what extremities he endured, and in the reproof of this lives the jest.
PRINCE Well, I'll go with thee. Provide us all things necessary and meet
me tomorrow night in Eastcheap. There I'll sup. Farewell.
POINS Farewell, my lord.   *Exit Poins*

[margin handwriting: I know where / I am vis-à-vis you all]

PRINCE I know you all, and will a while uphold   *I know where*   155
    The unyoked humour of your idleness,   *— a tiny bit of duplicity*

[margin: S imbedded narrator in role]

    Yet herein will I imitate the sun,   *(Saturnalia — lord of misrule will have to be expelled)*
    Who doth permit the base contagious clouds
    To smother up his beauty from the world,
    That when he please again to be himself,   160
    Being wanted, he may be more wondered at
    By breaking through the foul and ugly mists   *clouds bring bad weather + disease*

[margin: cf 3.2]

    Of vapours that did seem to strangle him.
    If all the year were playing holidays,   *Winter — Saturnalia*
    To sport would be as tedious as to work;   165
    But when they seldom come, they wished-for come,
    And nothing pleaseth but rare accidents.
    So when this loose behaviour I throw off,
    And pay the debt I never promisèd,
    By how much better than my word I am,   170

[margin handwriting: Falstaff will be exorcised in future]

151 lives] Q1; lyes Qq2–5, F

---

149 **this same fat rogue** Falstaff. According to
OED, 'rogue' (sv *sb*) is one of 'the numerous canting
words introduced about the middle of the 16th cent.
to designate the various kinds of beggars and vaga-
bonds . . .'. Shakespeare uses 'rogue' fourteen times
in *1H4*, twice as often as in any other play except
2H4 (thirteen).
  150 **wards** stances for defence or methods of
parrying attack in fencing.
  151 **reproof** disproof, with the additional sense
'reprimand' perhaps implied (*OED* sv *sb*¹ 5 and 3).
Compare 3.2.23.
  153 **tomorrow night** They of course plan to
meet in the morning at Gad's Hill, but the mind and
tongue of the Prince (or of his creator) leap ahead to
the more exciting aftermath of the robbery.
  155 **I know you all** Although only Poins has
just departed, 'you all' refers generally to Prince
Hal's companions. Its sense may even extend to
all the people in the audience and in the realm.
Johnson comments on the Prince's speech here as 'a

natural picture of a great mind offering excuses to
itself and palliating those follies which it can neither
justify nor forsake' (*Johnson on Shakespeare*, The
Yale Edition, vol. VII ed. Arthur Sherbo, 1968, p.
458). For detailed discussion of this soliloquy, its
implications, and possible staging, see Introduction,
pp. 10–12, 211 and illustration 2.
  156 **unyoked humour** unrestrained inclination.
  157 **sun** Often used as a symbol for royalty.
  158 **contagious clouds** 'Pestilence was thought
to be generated in fog, mist, and cloud' (Kittredge).
  161 **Being wanted . . . more wondered at** For
strikingly similar cynicism about creating a reputation for virtue, compare Cressida's soliloquy, *Tro.*
1.2.282–95.
  161 **wanted** missed.
  163 **strangle** stifle or quench (a fire) (*OED* sv *v*
3a). Compare *Mac.* 'dark night strangles the travel-
ling lamp' (2.4.7).
  167 **rare accidents** exceptional events which are
also unexpected.

By so much shall I falsify men's hopes.
And like bright metal on a sullen ground,
My reformation, glitt'ring o'er my fault,
Shall show more goodly, and attract more eyes
Than that which hath no foil to set it off.   175
I'll so offend, to make offence a skill,
Redeeming time when men think least I will.   *Exit*

cf comedies

[**1.3**] *Enter the* KING, NORTHUMBERLAND, WORCESTER, HOTSPUR,
SIR WALTER BLUNT, *with others*

KING My blood hath been too cold and temperate,
Unapt to stir at these indignities,
And you have found me – for accordingly
You tread upon my patience. But be sure
I will from henceforth rather be myself,   5
Mighty, and to be feared, than my condition
Which hath been smooth as oil, soft as young down,
And therefore lost that title of respect,
Which the proud soul ne'er pays but to the proud.
WORCESTER Our house, my sovereign liege, little deserves   10

175 foil] Qq1–3 (foile); soile Qq4, 5; soyle F   177 SD] Qq; *not in* F   Act 1, Scene 3   1.3] *Scæna Tertia.* F; *not in* Qq

171 hopes expectations. 'Hope' for Elizabethans could be much more ambivalent than for the modern audience. In the primary meaning (*OED* sv *sb*[1] 1a), expectation and desire are combined; in a second sense, there is no implication of desire.

172 bright metal See 106 n. above.

172 sullen ground dark background serving as a foil (175), as on a damascened sword.

175 foil That which makes another thing look better by a contrast in colour or quality (*OED* sv *sb*[1] 6).

176 skill A piece of good strategy and an art (not a vice or crime).

177 Redeeming time (1) Paying back time, as in 'redeeming a debt', (2) Making amends for lost time, (3) Making the best use of time as in 'walke circumspectly, not as fooles, but as wise, / Redeeming the time: for the dayes are evil' (Eph. 5.15–16). Compare Col. 4.5.

Act 1, Scene 3
[**1.3**] No explicit time or place is designated in the

dialogue. The Council meeting was proposed at 1.1.102–3 for Windsor, where Holinshed also locates it. Some time must have passed after 1.1. This may now well be 'Wednesday next' (1.1.102).

0 SD In contrast to 1.1, where the King dominates his reliable followers, this second court scene gives prominence to three men whom the King distrusts.

1–9 My blood . . . to the proud Starting with his first word, using five first-person pronouns or adjectives, King Henry shows much greater confidence than he did in opening the play. No longer 'wan with care', he forcefully moves in five lines from past to present to future. See Introduction, p. 9.

3 found found me so.

5 myself my royal self.

6 condition natural disposition, as in 'blood', 1 above. Compare 3.1.175.

10 house An extended alliance of the Percy family with their followers.

> The scourge of greatness to be used on it,
> And that same greatness too which our own hands
> Have helped to make so portly.
> NORTHUMBERLAND   My lord –
> KING Worcester, get thee gone, for I do see
> Danger and disobedience in thine eye.   15
> O sir, your presence is too bold and peremptory,
> And majesty might never yet endure
> The moody frontier of a servant brow.
> You have good leave to leave us. When we need
> Your use and counsel we shall send for you.   20

>   *Exit Worcester*

> [*To Northumberland*] You were about to speak.
> NORTHUMBERLAND   Yea, my good lord.
> Those prisoners in your highness' name demanded,
> Which Harry Percy here at Holmedon took,
> Were, as he says, not with such strength denied
> As is delivered to your majesty.   25
> Either envy therefore, or misprision,
> Is guilty of this fault, and not my son.
> HOTSPUR My liege, I did deny no prisoners.
> But I remember when the fight was done,
> When I was dry with rage and extreme toil,   30
> Breathless and faint, leaning upon my sword,
> Came there a certain lord, neat and trimly dressed,
> Fresh as a bridegroom, and his chin new reaped
> Showed like a stubble-land at harvest-home.

---

13 helped] Qq (holpe)   20 SD *Exit Worcester*] Qq; *not in* F   21 SD *To Northumberland*] Rowe; *not in* QqF   22 name] Qq; *not in* F   25 is] Qq1–4; he Q5; was F   26 Either envy therefore] Qq; Who either through envy F   27 Is] Qq; Was F

---

11 **scourge** The action, agent, and instrument of extreme punishment. Compare 3.2.7 and n.

13 **portly** stately, imposing, (with a hint of criticism). In *R2*, Northumberland and Worcester were Henry's strongest supporters.

16 **peremptory** obstinate.

18 **moody . . . brow** frowning forehead of a servant. Henry compares the angry brows to a fort's rampart, objecting to such hostility from an ally. In calling Worcester 'servant', he exaggerates the inferior status of a subject.

19 **good leave** full permission.

25 **delivered** reported.

26 **envy** malice.

26 **misprision** misunderstanding.

32 **neat** foppish, exquisite.

33–4 **new reaped . . . harvest-home** His fresh shaved chin contrasts with the soldiers' rough beards, the image implying that their work, unlike the harvest, is not yet finished.

vivid, viral speech

He was perfumèd like a milliner,   35
And 'twixt his finger and his thumb he held
A pouncet-box, which ever and anon
He gave his nose, and took't away again –
Who therewith angry, when it next came there,
Took it in snuff. And still he smiled and talked;   40
And as the soldiers bore dead bodies by,
He called them untaught knaves, unmannerly,
To bring a slovenly unhandsome corpse
Betwixt the wind and his nobility.
With many holiday and lady terms   45
He questioned me, amongst the rest demanded
My prisoners in your majesty's behalf.
I then, all smarting with my wounds being cold,
To be so pestered with a popinjay,
Out of my grief and my impatience   50
Answered neglectingly, I know not what,
He should, or he should not, for he made me mad
To see him shine so brisk, and smell so sweet,
And talk so like a waiting-gentlewoman
Of guns, and drums, and wounds, God save the mark!   55
And telling me the sovereignest thing on earth
Was parmacity for an inward bruise,
And that it was great pity, so it was,
This villainous saltpetre should be digged
Out of the bowels of the harmless earth,   60

---

52 or he] Qq; or F   59 This] Qq; That F

---

35 milliner dealer in bonnets and gloves, often perfumed; an occupation for men in earlier times. The analogy suggests effeminacy, as at 45 and 54 below.

37 pouncet-box a small box with a perforated lid, which held aromatic herbs or snuff. The term is not recorded before this example (*OED*).

39 Who i.e. the nose, suggesting a personification, as of the sun at 1.2.158 and the river at 1.3.103.

40 Took it in snuff Inhaled, and (with a pun) took offence (*OED* Snuff *sb*¹ 4).

45 holiday and lady terms dainty, lady-like expressions, not workaday words.

46 questioned 'interrogated' and perhaps also insisted on talking.

49 popinjay parrot, a prattler with gaudy plumes

who only repeats imitatively. The explosive alliteration displays Hotspur's impatience.

50 grief pain (*OED* sv *sb* 6)

51 neglectingly negligently (first citation in *OED*).

55 God save the mark An expression of indignation, but normally (Dent G179.1) a common formula for apology and deprecation. 'Mark' probably refers to the sign of the cross, used to ward off evil. Hotspur may be parroting one of the messenger's 'lady terms'.

57 parmacity A variant form of spermaceti, fatty substance from the sperm whale used as medicine.

59 saltpetre Chief ingredient in gunpowder, also used as medicine.

Which many a good tall fellow had destroyed
So cowardly, and but for these vile guns
He would himself have been a soldier.
This bald unjointed chat of his, my lord,
I answered indirectly, as I said,   65
And I beseech you, let not his report
Come current for an accusation
Betwixt my love and your high majesty.

BLUNT The circumstance considered, good my lord,
Whate'er Lord Harry Percy then had said   70
To such a person, and in such a place,
At such a time, with all the rest retold,
May reasonably die, and never rise
To do him wrong, or any way impeach
What then he said, so he unsay it now.   75

KING Why, yet he doth deny his prisoners,
But with proviso and exception,
That we at our own charge shall ransom straight
His brother-in-law, the foolish Mortimer,
Who, on my soul, hath wilfully betrayed   80
The lives of those that he did lead to fight
Against that great magician, damned Glendower,
Whose daughter, as we hear, that Earl of March
Hath lately married. Shall our coffers then
Be emptied to redeem a traitor home?   85

---

61 **Which** The saltpetre, 59; gunpowder has destroyed many a brave man.

61 **tall** strong in combat.

64 **bald** empty, trivial.

65 **indirectly** without paying attention. Compare 'neglectingly', 51 and note.

67 **come current** (1) be accepted at face value, (2) rush in, like a flood.

70 **had said** may have said.

72 **retold** Compare 1.1.46, the only other use in the play.

74–5 **or . . . now** i.e. or provide legal grounds for accusation, unless he refuses to retract it now.

76 **yet** still (spoken emphatically).

77 **But . . . exception** i.e. except on the condition or stipulation ('proviso').

78 **ransom** The ruler had a duty to free his agents and officers.

78 **straight** at once, immediately.

79 **brother-in-law** The historical Hotspur married Elizabeth (called Kate by Shakespeare) who was elder sister to Lord Edmund Mortimer (1376–1409), Glendower's captive and son-in-law. See 2.3.75 and List of Characters.

82 **great magician, damned Glendower** The King is understandably angry at this Welshman who has defeated him personally three times and won over Mortimer, his representative. Compare 3.1.60–3. For a fuller discussion, see Appendix, pp. 210–11.

83 **Earl of March** i.e. Mortimer. Shakespeare confused this Edmund Mortimer with his brother Roger's son, Edmund, heir to the throne. The older Edmund Mortimer was in fact never Earl of March. See List of Characters.

85 **redeem** In association with 'coffers', the commercial sense 'buy back' applies. For the wide range of meanings crucial to the play, see 1.2.177 and note. As with 'ransom' 78 above, spiritual and financial meanings become ironically intertwined.

Shall we buy treason, and indent with fears
When they have lost and forfeited themselves?
No, on the barren mountains let him starve.
For I shall never hold that man my friend
Whose tongue shall ask me for one penny cost   90
To ransom home revolted Mortimer.

HOTSPUR   Revolted Mortimer!
He never did fall off, my sovereign liege,
But by the chance of war. To prove that true
Needs no more but one tongue for all those wounds,   95
Those mouthèd wounds, which valiantly he took,
When on the gentle Severn's sedgy bank,
In single opposition, hand to hand,
He did confound the best part of an hour
In changing hardiment with great Glendower.   100
Three times they breathed, and three times did they drink
Upon agreement of swift Severn's flood,
Who then affrighted with their bloody looks
Ran fearfully among the trembling reeds,
And hid his crisp head in the hollow bank   105
Bloodstained with these valiant combatants.
Never did bare and rotten policy
Colour her working with such deadly wounds,
Nor never could the noble Mortimer
Receive so many, and all willingly.   110

94 war.] Qq2–5, F; war, Q1   95 tongue for] *Hanmer;* tongue: for Qq; tongue. For F   107 bare] Qq; base F

86 **Shall . . . fears** Make a binding contract with those who (1) are cowards, (2) threaten us.

88 **No . . . starve** According to Thomas Phaer in *A Mirror for Magistrates*, the Prince of Wales chased Glendower 'to the mountaynes, where he miserably dyed for lacke of foode' (Bullough, p. 197). Shakespeare turns a probability into a wish and changes its human object.

93 **fall off** (1) leave our party, (2) change allegiance.

96 **mouthèd** gaping. See *JC* 3.1.259–60: 'wounds . . . / Which like dumb mouths do ope their ruby lips'. The association of wounds with mouths is conventional.

97 **Severn** A river which divides England from south-eastern Wales. See 3.1.70–1.

97 **sedgy** bordered with reeds and rushes.

98 **single opposition** man-to-man.

99 **confound** spend (*OED* sv *v* 1c, citing this line). For a vivid contrast, see 'fought a long hour', 5.4.140 and n.

100 **changing hardiment** exchanging hard and courageous blows.

101 **breathed** paused for breath.

102 **flood** river.

103 **Who** The river is personified in this rhetorically elaborate passage. Compare 39 above.

105 **crisp** Continuing the personification of the river, here seen as wavy-haired because of its rippled or curled surface.

107–8 **Never . . . wounds** i.e. these dreadful wounds prove that Mortimer was loyal, because a deceiver (the King's accusation) cannot counterfeit such wounds.

107 **bare** poor, beggarly. Compare 3.2.13 and note.

107 **policy** cunning, trickery, expedience.

108 **Colour** Disguise (and make coloured).

           Then let not him be slandered with revolt.
KING Thou dost belie him, Percy, thou dost belie him,
           He never did encounter with Glendower.
           I tell thee, he durst as well have met the devil alone
           As Owen Glendower for an enemy.   115
           Art thou not ashamed? But sirrah, henceforth
           Let me not hear you speak of Mortimer.
           Send me your prisoners with the speediest means –
           Or you shall hear in such a kind from me
           As will displease you. My Lord Northumberland: 120
           We license your departure with your son.
           Send us your prisoners, or you will hear of it.
                              Exit King [, with Blunt and train]
HOTSPUR And if the devil come and roar for them
           I will not send them. I will after straight
           And tell him so, for I will ease my heart,   125
           Albeit I make a hazard of my head.
NORTHUMBERLAND What? Drunk with choler? Stay, and pause a while,
           Here comes your uncle.

                      Enter WORCESTER

HOTSPUR   Speak of Mortimer?
           Zounds, I will speak of him, and let my soul
           Want mercy if I do not join with him.   130
           Yea, on his part I'll empty all these veins
           And shed my dear blood, drop by drop in the dust,
           But I will lift the down-trod Mortimer

---

114 I tell thee,] As QqF; *deleted by Pope; as a separate line, Steevens*   122 SD *with Blunt and train*] Capell subst.; *not in* QqF   126 Albeit I make a] Qq; Although it be with F   131 Yea, on his part] Qq; In his behalfe F   133 down-trod] Qq; downfall F

111 **slandered** accused or discredited. 'Slander' often connotes deliberate malice and falsehood in Shakespeare's plays. C. T. Onions' influential *A Shakespeare Glossary* (1911; enlarged edn 1966) misleadingly confines its senses to 'reproach' or 'bring disgrace upon'.
112–22 **Thou . . . it** Henry dishonours Hotspur by denying his word and by referring to him as 'thou', 'thee', 'sirrah', and 'your son'.
112 **belie** misrepresent.
114 **I . . . alone** QqF print these thirteen syllables as one line.
121 **We . . . son** A command thinly disguised as a permission.

123 **if the devil come and roar** This echoes 1 Pet. 5.8: 'Your adversarie the devil, as a roaring lyon walketh about, seeking whome he may devoure.'
124 **will after straight** will follow him at once.
126 **Albeit** Although (literally, 'although it be that'). Compare *Cym.* 2.3.55–6: 'A worthy fellow, / Albeit he comes on angry purpose now.'
127 **choler** anger, a humour or physical condition caused by excessive bile.
130 **Want mercy** Be damned.
133 **But** i.e. even if I have to bleed to death (131–2).

As high in the air as this unthankful King,
As this ingrate and cankered Bullingbrook.   135
NORTHUMBERLAND Brother, the King hath made your nephew mad.
WORCESTER Who struck this heat up after I was gone?
HOTSPUR He will forsooth have all my prisoners,
     And when I urged the ransom once again
     Of my wife's brother, then his cheek looked pale,   140
     And on my face he turned an eye of death,
     Trembling even at the name of Mortimer.
WORCESTER I cannot blame him. Was not he proclaimed,
     By Richard that dead is, the next of blood?
NORTHUMBERLAND He was, I heard the proclamation.   145
     And then it was, when the unhappy King –
     Whose wrongs in us God pardon! – did set forth
     Upon his Irish expedition;
     From whence he, intercepted, did return
     To be deposed, and shortly murderèd.   150
WORCESTER And for whose death we in the world's wide mouth
     Live scandalised and foully spoken of.
HOTSPUR But soft, I pray you, did King Richard then
     Proclaim my brother Edmund Mortimer
     Heir to the crown?
NORTHUMBERLAND   He did, myself did hear it.   155
HOTSPUR Nay then, I cannot blame his cousin King,
     That wished him on the barren mountains starve.
     But shall it be that you that set the crown
     Upon the head of this forgetful man,

---

135 Bullingbrook] QqF (Bullingbrooke); Bolingbroke, *Pope*   143 not he] Qq; he not F   157 starve] Qq; starv'd F

---

135 ingrate ungrateful.

135 cankered diseased, ulcerated, wormy. Hotspur may insinuate the King's inferior stock or lineage, as in his reference to the 'canker' or wild rose at 174 below.

135 Bullingbrook Hotspur rudely insists upon the name used before the King assumed the crown. See List of Characters.

138 forsooth 'truly' in normal usage, but here used to show impatience.

141 an eye of death a look (1) showing 'mortal fear' (Kittredge) as well as (2) 'menacing death' (Johnson).

143–4 Was not . . . blood? Worcester's question presents Henry's power as illegitimate. By inference this explains his hostility to Hotspur (and his fellow former main supporters) as characteristic

of his treacherous nature. For an analysis of how Shakespeare develops this sequence from Holinshed, see Introduction, p. 7 and Appendix, p. 211.

145 He Mortimer.

146 unhappy unlucky.

147 in us inflicted by us.

148 his Irish expedition While Richard suppressed a rebellion in Ireland, Bullingbrook returned from exile and seized power. See *R2* 2.3 and 3.1.

149 intercepted interrupted.

152 scandalised disgraced.

153 soft slow down.

154 brother brother-in-law. Compare 79 above and n.

And for his sake wear the detested blot 160
Of murderous subornation – shall it be
That you a world of curses undergo,
Being the agents, or base second means,
The cords, the ladder, or the hangman rather?
O pardon me, that I descend so low, 165
To show the line and the predicament
Wherein you range under this subtle King!
Shall it for shame be spoken in these days,
Or fill up chronicles in time to come,
That men of your nobility and power 170
Did gage them both in an unjust behalf –
As both of you, God pardon it, have done –
To put down Richard, that sweet lovely rose,
And plant this thorn, this canker Bullingbrook?
And shall it in more shame be further spoken, 175
That you are fooled, discarded, and shook off
By him for whom these shames ye underwent?
No, yet time serves wherein you may redeem
Your banished honours, and restore yourselves
Into the good thoughts of the world again: 180
Revenge the jeering and disdained contempt
Of this proud King, who studies day and night
To answer all the debt he owes to you,
Even with the bloody payment of your deaths.
Therefore, I say –
WORCESTER   Peace, cousin, say no more. 185
And now I will unclasp a secret book,
And to your quick-conceiving discontents

---

160 wear] Qq; wore F

160 **detested blot** hated stain or blemish, physical or moral.
161 **murderous subornation** aiding the killer.
163 **base second means** shameful instruments.
166 **the line and the predicament** Hotspur underscores the lowered status of his father and uncle. 'Line', signifying rank, status, is punningly related to 'cords' and the hangman's rope, 164. 'Predicament' means dangerous situation (*OED* 3).
167 **range** (1) are ranked, (2) are permitted to move (i.e. despite restriction).
167 **subtle** cunning.
171 **gage them** pledge their 'nobility and power' (170).

171 **behalf** interest, cause.
174 **canker** the dog-rose, an inferior category as opposed to 'that sweet lovely rose', Richard, in 173. Also, as canker worm, it recalls 135. Compare *Ham.* 5.2.69.
181 **disdained** disdainful. This grammatical form, '-ed' (compare 'hated'), is an alternative to the '-ful' form.
183 **answer** discharge.
183–4 **debt . . . deaths** Word-play, more forcefully used by Falstaff at 5.1.127.
186 **unclasp . . . book** Literally, 'reveal a plot'. Expensively produced Bibles and missals often had clasps.

> I'll read you matter deep and dangerous,
> As full of peril and adventurous spirit
> As to o'er-walk a current roaring loud   190
> On the unsteadfast footing of a spear.

HOTSPUR If he fall in, good night, or sink, or swim!   *vision of field of honor*
> Send danger from the east unto the west,
> So honour cross it from the north to south,
> And let them grapple. O, the blood more stirs   195
> To rouse a lion than to start a hare!

accomplishing a feat - gay to win

NORTHUMBERLAND Imagination of some great exploit
> Drives him beyond the bounds of patience.

[HOTSPUR] By heaven, methinks it were an easy leap   *romance being*
> To pluck bright honour from the pale-faced moon,   200
> Or dive into the bottom of the deep,
> Where fathom-line could never touch the ground,
> And pluck up drownèd honour by the locks,
> So he that doth redeem her thence might wear
> Without corrival all her dignities.   205
> But out upon this half-faced fellowship!

idealism

WORCESTER He apprehends a world of figures here,   *clever with language*

misses the pt of political manouvring - Hotspur just interested in honour in battle, grandeur

---

199 SH HOTSPUR] Q5, F; *not in* Qq0–4

191 **footing of a spear** Humphreys explains this as referring to the 'perilous bridge' or 'sword-bridge' of medieval romances such as the *Mabinogion* and *Erec and Enid*.

192 **If . . . swim** Hotspur's impetuousness is apparent in this outburst: 'good night' suggests 'that's the end of him, he's had it'.

192 **or sink, or swim** This ambiguous phrase may refer only to an adversary or to both the adversary and Hotspur. In the literal sense, 'he's doomed, whether he sinks quickly or delays it by swimming (and who cares?)'; alternatively, both the speaker and his opponent are stimulated by the challenge of 'danger', the 'footing of a spear'.

194 **So** Provided that.

196 **rouse . . . start** Hunting terms: 'to start' applies to small animals, 'to rouse', to bigger game. Hotspur's 'lion' is of course the King.

199 From this line to the end of 2.2, Q0 provides the primary text.

199 SH HOTSPUR Qq0–4 do not provide a new speaker here, but it is hard to imagine a reader who would not readily accept the emendation from Q5. Editors agree that Q0 simply omitted a speech heading.

199–206 **By heaven . . . fellowship** Hotspur

reveals both his commitment to honourable acts and his recklessness. The accelerated pace makes these heroic acts absurd. Hotspur's own splendid sense of humour perhaps contributes to the feeling that he mocks himself as well as others. Parody in this play is often linked to political subversion.

202 **fathom-line** Used to test the depth of the sea, measured in fathoms (*OED* Fathom sv *sb* 6). A fathom is roughly 6 feet or 1.9 metres.

204 **redeem** save, restore.

205 **Without corrival** i.e. without sharing. 'Corrival' can mean (1) a rival in loving honour, here personified as female, (2) a competitor whose claims are equal.

205 **dignities** favours of the rescued 'honour'; also titles, as in 5.4.78.

206 **half-faced** partial, imperfect. Usually said of a coin, having a profile stamped on it (*OED* a1). The term suggests that Hotspur must be the sole hero, shared honour being only a flat, partial glory.

207 **apprehends** perceives, recognises (*OED v* 8).

207 **figures** Both (1) the images in Hotspur's speech, and (2) appearances rather than 'form' (Johnson).

But not the form of what he should attend.
Good cousin, give me audience for a while.
HOTSPUR I cry you mercy.
WORCESTER   Those same noble Scots   210
That are your prisoners –
HOTSPUR   I'll keep them all!
By God he shall not have a scot of them,   *scotem – small.*
No, if a Scot would save his soul he shall not.
I'll keep them, by this hand!
WORCESTER   You start away,
And lend no ear unto my purposes.   215
Those prisoners you shall keep –
HOTSPUR   Nay, I will. That's flat!
He said he would not ransom Mortimer,
Forbade my tongue to speak of Mortimer,
But I will find him when he lies asleep,
And in his ear I'll holla 'Mortimer!'   220
Nay, I'll have a starling shall be taught to speak
Nothing but 'Mortimer', and give it him
To keep his anger still in motion.
WORCESTER Hear you, cousin, a word.
HOTSPUR All studies here I solemnly defy,   225
Save how to gall and pinch this Bullingbrook.
And that same sword-and-buckler Prince of Wales –
But that I think his father loves him not
And would be glad he met with some mischance –
I would have him poisoned with a pot of ale. –   230
WORCESTER Farewell, kinsman. I'll talk to you *scolding him*

209 a while.] Qq; a-while, / And list to me F   210–11 Those . . . Scots / That . . . prisoners] F; *as one line*, Qq   220 holla]
F; hollow Qq0–2; hollo Qq3–4; hallow Q5; holler *Bevington*

208 **form** principle or idea.
212 **a scot** a small payment.
214 **start** Compare 196 and n. above.
220 **holla** shout.
221–2 **Nay . . . 'Mortimer'** Compare Hotspur's
reference to the popinjay, 49 above, and Lady
Percy's 'paraquito' at 2.3.79. Humphreys notes that
'Elizabethan texts have many talking starlings', e.g.
Florio's *Montaigne* II, xii, 267 ('An Apologie of
Raymond Sebond'), 'We teache Blacke-birds,
Starlins . . . to chat'; and Drayton, *The Owle*, line
634, 'Like a *Starling*, that is taught to prate'.
223 **still** continually.
225 **studies** occupations.

225 **defy** renounce.
226 **gall and pinch** irritate, harass. These verbs
suggest that he does not take his foe very seriously.
227 **sword-and-buckler** Hotspur accuses Hal
of vulgarity. By 1590, the sword and small round
shield or buckler were left to servants and swagger-
ers. Gentlemen used the rapier and dagger. *OED*
(Sword sv *sb* 6d) cites this line and Porter, *Two
Angry Women of Abington*, 1599, p. 61, 'a good
sword and buckler man, will be spitted like a cat or
a conney'.
230 **pot of ale** Another slap at Hal's plebeian
tastes. By *2H4*, Hal is growing tired of small beer
(2.2.5–11).

When you are better tempered to attend.
NORTHUMBERLAND Why, what a wasp-stung and impatient fool
　　Art thou to break into this woman's mood,
　　Tying thine ear to no tongue but thine own!   235
HOTSPUR Why, look you, I am whipped and scourged with rods,
　　Nettled, and stung with pismires, when I hear
　　Of this vile politician Bullingbrook.
　　In Richard's time – what do you call the place?
　　A plague upon it, it is in Gloucestershire.   240
　　'Twas where the madcap Duke his uncle kept –
　　His uncle York – where I first bowed my knee
　　Unto this king of smiles, this Bullingbrook –
　　'Sblood, when you and he came back from Ravenspurgh –
NORTHUMBERLAND At Berkeley Castle.
HOTSPUR 　　　　　　　　　　　　　You say true.   245
　　Why, what a candy deal of courtesy
　　This fawning greyhound then did proffer me!
　　'Look when his infant fortune came to age',
　　And 'gentle Harry Percy', and 'kind cousin'.
　　O, the devil take such cozeners – God forgive me!   250
　　Good uncle, tell your tale. I have done.
WORCESTER Nay, if you have not, to it again,
　　We will stay your leisure.
HOTSPUR 　　　　　　　　　　　　　I have done, i'faith.

---

233 wasp-stung] Qq0–1; waspe-tongue Qq2–5; Waspe-tongu'd F   236 Why, look you,] Q1 (Why looke you,); Why looke you? Q0   236 whipped] Qq1–5, F (whipt); whip Q0

233 **wasp-stung** irritable, impatient.
234 **this woman's mood** In this play, women and most references to women occur in the worlds of the rebels and the tavern. Such references are strangely absent from the scenes at court. See Introduction, pp. 12, 15, 16.
237 **Nettled** Irritated, stung with nettles.
237 **pismires** ants.
238 **politician** A noun almost always contemptuous or sinister in Elizabethan usage. Compare *Lear* 4.6.171.
239–44 **In Richard's time . . . Ravenspurgh –** Q0's punctuation using commas suggests the startling breaks in the consciousness of the speaker.
241 **madcap Duke** Edmund Langley, Duke of York, as described in Holinshed. He does not show such a trait in *R2* or in *Woodstock*.
241 **kept** lived.
244 **'Sblood** This oath in the Q version lends an

extra syllable to Hotspur's otherwise regular line, thereby conveying his 'impatience with his faulty memory' (Bevington).
244 **Ravensburgh** In Yorkshire, where Bullingbrook landed in 1399 when he returned from exile.
245 **Berkeley Castle** In Gloucestershire northeast of Bristol; hundreds of miles to the south and west of Ravensburgh.
246 **candy deal** sugary or flattering lot.
247 **fawning greyhound** Shakespeare's clustered images of dogs, of licking candy, and of melting, are 'called up inevitably by the thought of false friends or flatterers' (Spurgeon, *Shakespeare's Imagery and What It Tells Us*, 1935, p. 195). Humphreys comments, 'The image-cluster may be Shakespearean, but its parts are popular tags.'
248 **Look when** When.
250 **cozeners** cheats (with a pun on cousins).
253 **stay** wait for.

WORCESTER Then once more to your Scottish prisoners.
          Deliver them up without their ransom straight,   255
          And make the Douglas' son your only mean
          For powers in Scotland, which, for divers reasons
          Which I shall send you written, be assured
          Will easily be granted. [*To Northumberland*] You my lord,
          Your son in Scotland being thus employed,   260
          Shall secretly into the bosom creep
          Of that same noble prelate well-beloved,
          The Archbishop.
HOTSPUR   Of York, is it not?
WORCESTER True, who bears hard
          His brother's death at Bristol, the Lord Scroop.   265
          I speak not this in estimation,
          As what I think might be, but what I know
          Is ruminated, plotted, and set down,
          And only stays but to behold the face
          Of that occasion that shall bring it on.   270
HOTSPUR I smell it! Upon my life it will do well!
NORTHUMBERLAND Before the game is afoot thou still let'st slip.
HOTSPUR Why, it cannot choose but be a noble plot;
          And then the power of Scotland, and of York,
          To join with Mortimer, ha?
WORCESTER   And so they shall.   275
HOTSPUR In faith it is exceedingly well aimed.
WORCESTER And 'tis no little reason bids us speed,
          To save our heads by raising of a head.
          For, bear ourselves as even as we can,

259 granted. You my lord] *Hanmer subst.;* granted you my lord QQ0, 1, 4; granted you, my Lord QQ2, 3, 5, F   259 SD *To Northumberland*] *Theobald; not in* QQF   271 I smell it! Upon . . . do well] QQ; I smell it: / Upon . . . do wondrous well F

255 **straight** immediately.

256 **the Douglas' son** The Earl of Fife, mistakenly called son of Douglas. The definite article used before 'Douglas' indicates the headship of a distinguished Scottish family (Humphreys).

256 **mean** means, instrument. Worcester takes it for granted that sons (including Hotspur) should be the instruments of feudal politics.

261 **into . . . creep** insinuate himself into the confidence.

264–5 **who . . . Scroop** William Scroop, Earl of Wiltshire and Lord Treasurer under Richard II, was executed by Bullingbrook at Bristol in 1399

with Richard's other favourites (*R2* 3.2.141–2). He was the cousin of the Archbishop of York, Richard Scroop, not his brother. Holinshed confuses the relationship.

266 **estimation** conjecture.

271 **smell** Like hounds finding the scent of a quarry in a hunt.

272 **thou still let'st slip** Northumberland, picking up the hunting metaphor in 'smell', scolds his son for releasing the dogs prematurely.

278 **head** army of family, retainers, and followers.

279 **even** (1) carefully, (2) justly.

  The King will always think him in our debt,   280
  And think we think ourselves unsatisfied,
  Till he hath found a time to pay us home.
  And see already how he doth begin
  To make us strangers to his looks of love.
HOTSPUR He does, he does, we'll be revenged on him.   285
WORCESTER Cousin, farewell. No further go in this
  Than I by letters shall direct your course.
  When time is ripe, which will be suddenly,
  I'll steal to Glendower and Lord Mortimer,
  Where you, and Douglas, and our powers at once,   290
  As I will fashion it, shall happily meet
  To bear our fortunes in our own strong arms,
  Which now we hold at much uncertainty.
NORTHUMBERLAND Farewell, good brother. We shall thrive, I trust.
HOTSPUR Uncle, adieu. O, let the hours be short,   295
  Till fields, and blows, and groans applaud our sport!

                 Exeunt

Different stratum
↓

[**2.1**] *Enter a* CARRIER *with a lantern in his hand*   *strands of social classes*

FIRST CARRIER Heigh-ho! An it be not four by the day I'll be hanged.
 Charles' Wain is over the new chimney, and yet our horse not
 packed. What, Ostler!

289 Lord] *Rowe;* Lo: Qq0, 1; loe Qq2–5, F   292 bear our] Qq1–5, F; beare out Qo   296 SD *Exeunt*] Qq; *exit* F   **Act 2, Scene**
1 2.1] *Actus Secundus. Scena Prima.* F; *not in* Qq

282 pay us home pay us back (with the punning implication 'give us a fatal blow').
288 suddenly at once.
290 at once altogether.
296 fields battlefields.
296 sport Hotspur treats battle as a diversion or amusement, like hunting. Compare the Prince's view of playing as strategic political work, 1.2.164 ff. Both young men have a sense of humour, in contrast to their fathers, who see playfulness as mere weakness.

Act 2, Scene 1
[**2.1**] In the fictional narrative, this scene is set at dawn in an innyard, presumably on the London–Canterbury road near Gad's Hill. The costumes and language immediately establish a contrast with the preceding court scene.

0 SD CARRIER Produce and goods were brought on pack-horses, 2–3, to London by the carriers in their panniers and baskets.
0 SD **lantern** The play would originally have been performed at an arena playhouse in daylight. The lantern conventionally signifies that the action takes place at night or near daybreak.
1 by the day towards morning.
2 Charles' Wain An old name, derived from Charlemagne's wagon, for the constellation known as the Plough.
2 horse horses. 'Horse' was used in both plural and singular forms.
3 packed loaded.
3 Ostler Groom, stable-boy.

Handy problems

OSTLER [*Within*] Anon, anon.

FIRST CARRIER I prithee, Tom, beat Cut's saddle, put a few flocks in   5
the point; poor jade is wrung in the withers, out of all cess.

Enter another CARRIER

SECOND CARRIER Peas and beans are as dank here as a dog, and that is
the next way to give poor jades the bots. This house is turned upside
down since Robin Ostler died.

FIRST CARRIER Poor fellow never joyed since the price of oats rose, it   10
was the death of him.

SECOND CARRIER I think this be the most villainous house in all
London road for fleas, I am stung like a tench.

FIRST CARRIER Like a tench! By the mass, there is ne'er a king Christian could be better bit than I have been since the first cock.   15

SECOND CARRIER Why, they will allow us ne'er a jordan, and then we
leak in your chimney, and your chamber-lye breeds fleas like a loach.

---

4 SD *Within*] *Theobald; not in* QqF   12 be] Qq0–4; *to be* Q5; *is* F   14 By the mass] Qq; *not in* F   14–15 Christian] Qq
(christen); *in* Christendome F   16 ne'er] Qq (nere); ne're F

---

4 **Anon** Just a minute.

5 **Tom** This seems to be the name of the Ostler.
The First Carrier is addressed at line 36 as Mugs,
which may be a nickname. On the variable identification of secondary characters, see Textual Analysis, pp. 201 ff.

5 **beat** smooth by beating to make it less lumpy
and more comfortable.

5 **Cut** The name of this horse. Cut was also
the common word for a work-horse, referring
either to its having a docked tail or to its being
gelded.

5–6 **put . . . point** stuff wool into the pommel of
the saddle.

6 **jade** nag, old horse.

6 **wrung . . . withers** rubbed or bruised on the
ridge between the shoulder-blades.

6 **out of all cess** excessively.

7 **Peas and beans are as dank here as a dog**
i.e. the horses' fodder is as 'damp as can be'
(Bevington). Compare Dent D433–41 for sayings
which use 'dog' to intensify conditions (such as 'sick
as a dog', 'dog-tired').

7 **dank** unwholesomely damp and cold.

8 **next** quickest.

8 **bots** parasitic maggots in horses' intestines.
These were 'little short wormes with great red
heads, and long small white Tailes', according to G.
Markham, *Maister-Peece of Farriery*, 1615, chap.
74, as noted by Humphreys who observes that they

are hatched from eggs on the leaves that the horse
eats.

8 **house** inn.

8–9 **turned upside down** badly run, disordered.

10 **price of oats rose** Because of many poor
harvests, the price almost tripled between 1593 and
1596, after which it fell. England experienced severe
periods of dearth in the last decade of the sixteenth
century. See D. M. Palliser, *The Age of Elizabeth*,
1983, chaps. 4 and 5.

13 **tench** fish, the spotted markings of which may
have suggested flea-bites. Humphreys suggests
that it was, like the loach, 17, thought to breed
parasites.

14 **By the mass** A gentle, old-fashioned oath,
nevertheless dropped in the Folio.

14–15 **king Christian** king in Christendom,
implying that kings 'have the best of everything'
(Kittredge).

15 **first cock** Conventionally midnight; the
second cock came at 3 a.m., the third, an hour
before dawn.

16 **jordan** chamber-pot.

17 **leak** urinate.

17 **your** Used to refer to something commonly
known, not necessarily possessed. See Abbott 221.

17 **chimney** fireplace.

17 **chamber-lye** urine.

17 **loach** A small freshwater fish, popularly
thought to breed lice.

FIRST CARRIER What, Ostler! Come away, and be hanged, come away!

SECOND CARRIER I have a gammon of bacon, and two races of ginger, to be delivered as far as Charing Cross.   20

FIRST CARRIER God's body! The turkeys in my pannier are quite starved. What, Ostler! A plague on thee, hast thou never an eye in thy head? Canst not hear? An 'twere not as good deed as drink to break the pate on thee, I am a very villain. Come and be hanged! Hast no faith in thee?   25

Enter GADSHILL

GADSHILL Good morrow, carriers, what's o'clock?

[FIRST] CARRIER I think it be two o'clock.

GADSHILL I prithee lend me thy lantern, to see my gelding in the stable.

FIRST CARRIER Nay, by God, soft! I know a trick worth two of that, i'faith.   30

GADSHILL I pray thee lend me thine.

SECOND CARRIER Ay, when? Canst tell? Lend me thy lantern, quoth he! Marry I'll see thee hanged first.

GADSHILL Sirrah carrier, what time do you mean to come to London?

SECOND CARRIER Time enough to go to bed with a candle, I warrant   35

---

27 SH FIRST] *Hanmer subst.; Car.* QqF   29 by God, soft!] Qq; soft I pray ye F   31 pray thee] Qq0–2; prethee Qq3–5, F

18 **Come . . . hanged** Come on, blast you (see Dent H130.1).

19 **gammon of bacon** ham.

19 **races** roots of ginger, used both medicinally and as a spice. They recall the complaint in *FV* by the carrier: he 'hath taken the great rase of ginger, that bouncing Bess with the jolly buttocks should have had' (302–4).

20 **Charing Cross** A familiar landmark between the City (London) and Westminster, located towards the west end of the Strand near its junction with Whitehall. The stone cross, erected in 1294 (to commemorate the last spot where the body of Eleanor, queen of Edward I, had rested on the way to Westminster) was in ruinous condition by 1596–7 (Sugden; compare Stow, *Survey*, II, 100–1).

21 **God's body** Another oath omitted from the Folio.

21 **pannier** Either of a pair of large baskets used to carry provisions.

22–3 **hast . . . head** Dent E248.1 lists this proverbial expression.

22 **never** not (intensified).

23 **as good deed as drink** Proverbial expression (Dent D183.1), playfully equating good deeds and self-indulgence. Falstaff repeats it at 2.2.18. See Dent's Introduction, p. xxiv, on how this phrase

helped establish his criteria for describing sayings as proverbial, '[even though] . . . there are no known instances outside Shakespeare until Sir Wilfull Witwood in Congreve [1700]. It is difficult otherwise to account for Falstaff's sharing the whole of an expression with the First Carrier, and the bulk of it with Sir Andrew Aguecheek [*TN* 2.3.126].'

24 **break . . . thee** i.e. 'crack your skull', an exaggerated threat referring to a blow that draws blood but need not actually cause a fracture.

24 **very** true.

25 **faith** trustworthiness.

27 **two o'clock** The Carrier, in the first line of this scene, declared that it was four o'clock. Unless there is a textual error, this reply indicates that he does not sufficiently trust Gadshill even to tell him the correct time, much less to lend him his lantern.

29 **soft** wait a minute.

29 **I know . . . that** i.e. 'You can't fool me', a familiar saying (Dent T518).

32 **Ay, when? Canst tell?** Proverbial denial (Dent T88), to the effect of 'You haven't got a hope!'

35 **Time . . . candle** Evasive and contemptuous reply.

35 **warrant** assure.

thee! Come, neighbour Mugs, we'll call up the gentlemen, they will
along with company, for they have great charge.

Exeunt [Carriers]

GADSHILL What ho! Chamberlain!

Enter CHAMBERLAIN

CHAMBERLAIN 'At hand, quoth pick-purse.'

GADSHILL That's even as fair as 'At hand, quoth the chamberlain', for   40
thou variest no more from picking of purses than giving direction
doth from labouring. Thou layest the plot how.

CHAMBERLAIN Good morrow, Master Gadshill. It holds current that I
told you yesternight. There's a franklin in the Weald of Kent hath
brought three hundred marks with him in gold – I heard him tell it   45
to one of his company last night at supper, a kind of auditor, one that
hath abundance of charge too, God knows what. They are up already, and call for eggs and butter. They will away presently.

GADSHILL Sirrah, if they meet not with Saint Nicholas' clerks, I'll give
thee this neck.   50

CHAMBERLAIN No, I'll none of it, I pray thee keep that for the hangman, for I know thou worshippest Saint Nicholas, as truly as a man
of falsehood may.

GADSHILL What talkest thou to me of the hangman? If I hang, I'll make

---

37 SD *Carriers*] *Rowe; not in* QqF   38 SD *Enter* CHAMBERLAIN] *Kittredge; after* 37, QqF   44 Weald] Q0 (wild); wilde Qq1–
5, F   51 pray thee] Qq; prythee F

36–7 will . . . charge prefer to travel with a
group because they have valuables or baggage.

38 Chamberlain Servant in charge of guests'
rooms at an inn. Harrison, *The Description of Britain*
(Holinshed, I, 414–15), criticises the dishonesty of
inn servants, who give 'warning to such od ghests as
hant the house and are of [their] confederacie, to the
utter undoing of manie an honest yeoman as he
iournieth by the waie'.

39 At hand, quoth pick-purse 'Here I am', a
popular tag, which is ironically apt from the
crooked Chamberlain to the thief Gadshill.

40 even as fair as 'as good as saying'.

41–2 thou variest . . . labouring you are no
more different from an actual pickpocket than is
an overseer from his labourers, i.e. you are both
responsible for the work.

42 Thou layest the plot how You supervise the
labour, plan the crime.

44 franklin A rich yeoman, one who holds his
own land and ranks just below the gentry.

44 Weald The area lying between the North and
South Downs, a rich agricultural district, formerly
wooded.

45 three hundred marks two hundred
pounds. A mark was worth 13s. 4d., or two-thirds of
a pound. It was not a coin.

46 auditor A royal officer who examined the
accounts of receivers, sheriffs, and other officers of
the crown.

48 eggs and butter see 1.2.17 and note.

48 presently at once.

49 Saint Nicholas' clerks Slang for highwaymen. St Nicholas, the popular patron saint of wandering scholars, travellers, and children, became,
probably through the suggestion of the popular
name 'Old Nick' for the Devil, the protector of
thieves and masterless men as well. In the legend
which is the subject of the miracle play *Ludus Super
Iconia Sancti Nicolai* (ed. Pollard, *English Miracle
Plays*, Appendix II), the saint causes robbers to
restore a treasure (cited by Hemingway). Compare
5.4.112 and n. on 'termagant'. The cant term 'nick'
meant cheat or defraud (*OED* sv v^2 11).

49–50 give . . . neck you can hang me, 'neck'
offering a pun on 'nick'.

54 What Why.

a fat pair of gallows. For if I hang, old Sir John hangs with me, and   55
thou knowest he is no starveling. Tut, there are other Troyans that
thou dreamest not of, the which for sport sake are content to do the
profession some grace, that would, if matters should be looked into,
for their own credit sake make all whole. I am joined with no foot-
landrakers, no long-staff sixpenny strikers, none of these mad   60
mustachio purple-hued maltworms, but with nobility and tranquillity, burgomasters and great oneyres, such as can hold in, such as
will strike sooner than speak, and speak sooner than drink, and drink
sooner than pray. And yet, zounds, I lie, for they pray continually to
their saint the commonwealth, or rather not pray to her, but prey on   65
her, for they ride up and down on her, and make her their boots.

---

62 oneyres] Qqo, 1; Oneyers Qq2–5, F; Oneraires *conj. Pope;* One-eyers *conj. Pope²;* Moneyers *Theobald;* owners *Hanmer;*
one-yers *Johnson*   **65 prey**] Q5, F; pray Qqo–4

---

56 starveling one emaciated from lack of food
(*OED* sv *sb* a).

56 Troyans Trojans, cant term for good companions, like Hal's 'Corinthian', 2.4.10, and the
Page's reference to 'Ephesians . . . of the old
church', *2H4* 2.2.150. In *Wiv.* 4.5.18, the tavern
host is termed an 'Ephesian'.

57 the which who.

57–8 do . . . grace favour the profession.

58 looked into subjected to criminal
investigation.

59 for . . . whole for the sake of their own reputation, make sure there was no trouble.

59–60 foot-landrakers wandering footpads,
who presumably cannot afford a horse. To 'rake' is
to wander (*OED v²* 1).

60 long-staff sixpenny strikers cut-price
thieves who will rob for a mere sixpence. They use
long poles with an iron hook on the end to pull men
from their horses. 'Strike' is a cant term for picking
pockets.

61 mustachio Fierce moustaches supposedly indicated valour.

61 purple-hued maltworms heavy drinkers
with purple faces. Compare Falstaff on Bardolph's
purple face, 3.3.23–5, and his description of
Bardolph's face in *2H4* 2.4.333–4: 'Lucifer's
privy-kitchen, where he doth nothing but roast
malt-worms'. These worms infest the malt used to
brew, and hence those who drink it. Compare allusions to other parasites in 'bots', 8, 'tench', 13,
'fleas', 13, 17, and 'loach', 17. Analogies between
animal and human parasites are latent throughout
the scene.

61–2 tranquillity An invented meaning which

may travesty pretentious diction. Compare *TN*
2.3.26, 'I did impeticos thy gratillity.'

62 burgomasters chief magistrates of a town.

62 oneyres 'honeyers', probably an invented
word. If 'honey' is spelled without an 'h' (*OED sb*
variant) like 'Ebrew' (2.4.152) and employed as a
verb meaning to use terms of endearment or to
flatter (*OED* sv *v* 2–3), it is possible to suppose
that Gadshill characterises as 'honeyers' the
Prince's followers, both for their flattery (i.e. 'good
sweet honey lord', 1.2.129) and for their wenching
(as in *Ham.* 3.4.93), with a glance at Falstaff's taste
for sugared sack. The King compares common
popularity to a surfeit of honey at 3.2.69–71. As
the Collation indicates, the word has been extensively discussed and amended. Johnson suggested
that Gadshill gives a 'cant termination' to 'great
ones' 'as we say privateer, auctioneer'. Malone
suggested 'onyers', derived from the abbreviation
'o.ni.' (*oneratur, nisi habeat sufficientem
exonerationem*), a term used by the royal treasury to
identify revenue collected by sheriffs but owed to
the crown. Other proposed emendations include
seigniors, junkers, mynheers, wonyers, one-ers.
Davison proposes 'Oyeas', Jowett (*Textual Companion*), 'Oiezres' or court officials, West, 'younker'
(compare 3.3.63).

62 hold in A multiple pun: (1) keep a secret, (2)
stick together, (3) continue to pursue a quarry.

63 strike . . . drink are as ready to knock down a
victim as to speak; 'sooner' implies preference or
choice (*OED Soon adv* 11b). 'To speak to or with a
victim was thieves' cant for holding him up'
(Humphreys).

66 make her their boots use her for their

CHAMBERLAIN What, the commonwealth their boots? Will she hold
   out water in foul way?

GADSHILL She will, she will, justice hath liquored her. We steal as
   in a castle, cock-sure. We have the receipt of fern-seed, we walk   70
   invisible.

CHAMBERLAIN Nay, by my faith, I think you are more beholding to the
   night than to fern-seed for your walking invisible.

GADSHILL Give me thy hand, thou shalt have a share in our purchase,
   as I am a true man.   75

CHAMBERLAIN Nay, rather let me have it as you are a false thief.

GADSHILL Go to, *homo* is a common name to all men. Bid the ostler
   bring my gelding out of the stable. Farewell, you muddy knave.

                                                             [Exeunt]

① MEDY - rediculars complication. - mood setting

[2.2] *Enter* PRINCE, POINS, *and* PETO [*with* BARDOLPH]

POINS Come, shelter, shelter! I have removed Falstaff's horse, and he
   frets like a gummed velvet.

74 purchase] Qq; purpose F   78 my] Qq; the F   78 SD *Exeunt*] F; *not in* Qq   Act 2, Scene 2   2.2] *Scæna Secunda.* F; *not in* Qq   0 SD *and* PETO *with* BARDOLPH] *Bevington subst.; and Peto Etc.* Qq0–5; *and Peto* F; *Bardolph and Peto, at some distance* / *Malone*

financial advantage, with a pun on booty and a sexual slur.

67–8 Will . . . way Literally, 'can she (like boots) keep your feet dry on a wet muddy road?', can she help you in need?

69 justice hath liquored her the authorities have (1) given her a protective coat to keep out legal prosecution (58–9 above and notes), (2) made her drunk.

70 in a castle in complete security, echoing the commonplace, 'as safe as in a castle' (Dent C122.1). Perhaps, in an earlier version of the text, this was a reference to Oldcastle (Kittredge).

70 receipt of fern-seed recipe for making oneself invisible. Small fern-seeds were believed to become visible only on St John's or Midsummer Eve, 23 June. Anyone who picked them then and carried them later on would also become invisible.

74 purchase plunder, a euphemism for booty.

75 true man one who keeps his word; taken by the Chamberlain, 76, as a claim to general honesty. Compare thieves 'true one to another', 2.2.22–3.

77 homo . . . all men The Latin word for 'man' includes all humanity; therefore, a thief must be 'a true man'. Gadshill's term may derive from

Lily and Colet's *Shorte Introduction of Grammar* (1549).

78 muddy dull-witted or muddled, with a suggestion of dishonesty (as in 'foul', 68).

Act 2, Scene 2
[2.2] The opening lines indicate a brief passage of time and a change of location, but closely follow the narrative thread of the last scene. It is still too dark for the thieves gathered at Gad's Hill to see one another clearly; Poins identifies the 'setter' by his voice, 40–1. Between the two robberies, 75 SD, the unlocalised Elizabethan stage makes possible the illusion of movement along a road.

0 SD *with* BARDOLPH Not named in stage directions of QqF, but Q0 and Q1 have '*&c*' which implies Bardolph because no other character becomes relevant in the ensuing sequence. Falstaff cries out to Bardolph and Peto at 17, as if they were both nearby. When they enter with the Prince and Poins, they are presumably aware of the first joke, that being played with Falstaff's horse.

2 frets like a gummed velvet is irritated, chafes. Proverbial (Dent T8); velvet wore quickly or 'fretted' when treated with gum to give it gloss or an appearance of firmness.

PRINCE Stand close!

[They retire]

Enter FALSTAFF

FALSTAFF Poins! Poins, and be hanged! Poins!
PRINCE [*Coming forward*] Peace, ye fat-kidneyed rascal, what a brawling   5
    dost thou keep!
FALSTAFF Where's Poins, Hal?
PRINCE He is walked up to the top of the hill. I'll go seek him.

[He steps to one side]

FALSTAFF I am accursed to rob in that thief's company. The rascal hath
    removed my horse and tied him I know not where. If I travel but   10
    four foot by the square further afoot, I shall break my wind. Well, I
    doubt not but to die a fair death for all this, if I scape hanging for
    killing that rogue. I have forsworn his company hourly any time this
    two-and-twenty years, and yet I am bewitched with the rogue's
    company. If the rascal have not given me medicines to make me love   15
    him, I'll be hanged. It could not be else. I have drunk medicines.
    Poins! Hal! A plague upon you both! Bardolph! Peto! I'll starve ere
    I'll rob a foot further – an 'twere not as good a deed as drink to turn
    true man, and to leave these rogues, I am the veriest varlet that ever
    chewed with a tooth. Eight yards of uneven ground is threescore-   20

---

3 SD.1 *They retire*] *Dyce; not in* QqF   5 SD *Coming forward*] *Dyce; not in* QqF   8 SD *He steps to one side*] *Bevington subst.; not in* QqF   11 square] QqF (squire)   14 two-and-twenty] F; *xxii* Qq0–4; 22 Q5   17 Bardolph] F; *Bardol* Q0; *Bardoll* Qq1–5 (*throughout, with variation of spelling*)

---

3 **Stand close** Hide

3 SD.1 *They retire* The fluid staging of the jokes in this scene calls for several conjectured directions not provided by QqF. With a platform stage, the audience (unlike Falstaff) may be able to see the characters who hide. See Textual Analysis, pp. 201–2, on how stage directions and dialogue leave open options for several entrances and exits.

5 **fat-kidneyed** fat-gutted.

5 **rascal** knave. As a term for lean young deer that are unsuitable for hunting, 'rascal' may suggest that a fat old man makes an absurd highway robber.

5 **brawling** clamour.

6 **keep** make.

10–11 **but . . . square** exactly four feet. A square (variant spelling for obsolete 'squire') is a measuring instrument. Humphreys cites Spenser, *The Faerie Queene*, II, i, 57, 'Temperance . . . with golden squire / . . . can measure out a meane.'

11 **break my wind** (1) pant or wheeze, (2) fart.

11–12 **I doubt not but to** I expect to.

12 **die . . . this** die honourably, in spite of all this torment.

13 **I have . . . company** Falstaff at first may refer here to Poins, but the next four lines are taken by many to refer to the Prince. See Introduction, p. 33.

15 **medicines** love potions. Compare *Oth.* 1.3.60–1: 'She is abus'd, stol'n from me, and corrupted / By spells and medicines bought of mountebanks.'

17 **starve** die (the original sense), but almost certainly suggesting death by hunger (*OED* sv *v* 4a).

18 **as good . . . drink** On this proverbial phrase, compare 2.1.23 and n.

18–19 **turn true man** reform. Falstaff puns on the paradoxes of truth among false men that were initiated in 2.1.

19 **veriest** truest, most authentic.

19 **varlet** servant or groom; in chivalry, the attendant on a knight.

and-ten miles afoot with me, and the stony-hearted villains know it
well enough. A plague upon it when thieves cannot be true one to
another!

They whistle

Whew! A plague upon you all. Give me my horse you rogues, give
me my horse and be hanged!   25

PRINCE [*Coming forward*] Peace, ye fat-guts, lie down, lay thine ear
close to the ground and list if thou canst hear the tread of travellers.

FALSTAFF Have you any levers to lift me up again, being down?
'Sblood, I'll not bear my own flesh so far afoot again for all the coin
in thy father's exchequer. What a plague mean ye to colt me thus?   30

PRINCE Thou liest, thou art not colted, thou art uncolted.

FALSTAFF I prithee good Prince, help me to my horse, good king's son.

PRINCE Out ye rogue, shall I be your ostler?

FALSTAFF Hang thyself in thine own heir-apparent garters! If I be
taken, I'll peach for this. An I have not ballads made on you all, and 35
sung to filthy tunes, let a cup of sack be my poison. When a jest is so
forward – and afoot too – I hate it!

Enter GADSHILL

GADSHILL Stand!

FALSTAFF So I do, against my will.

POINS [*Coming forward with Bardolph and Peto*] O, 'tis our setter, I know 40
his voice. Bardolph, what news?

---

26 SD *Coming forward*] Dyce; *not in* QQF   29 my own] QO (*my owne*); *mine owne* QQI–5, F   40 SD *Coming forward with
Bardolph and Peto*] Dyce; *not in* QQF   41 Bardolph, what news?] QQF *subst.; Bardolph. What news? Var. 1773, conj. Johnson,
Bevington* (*taking Bardolph as a speech heading*)

22–3 **A plague . . . another** The proverb,
'Thieves are never rogues among themselves' (Dent
T121a) is revised in order to proclaim that thieves
should be more loyal than honest men.

24 **Whew** Perhaps a comic response to the preceding stage direction. Wilson thinks Falstaff may
mock the whistling of the others, while Davison
infers that Falstaff, out of breath, is laughable in his
attempts to whistle. Alternatively, he expresses disgust or makes a noise indicating that he pauses for
breath – a repeated motif.

30 **exchequer** treasury; it holds funds collected
by sheriffs and other royal officers (*OED* sv *sb* 4).

30 **colt** trick, cheat.

33 **shall . . . ostler** For the sake of a pun, Hal
mistakes Falstaff's meaning, interpreting his 'help
me' as a request for aid to mount, rather than to
find, his horse. In a literal sense, Hal suggests that
he would help, but only as a servant, not as a friend
or companion.

34 **Hang . . . garters** As heir apparent, the
Prince of Wales belonged to the Order of the Gar-
ter. Falstaff answers Hal with another outrageous
pun, based on a proverbial saying (Dent G42).

35 **peach** inform against an accomplice (*OED* sv
v 2, citing this example).

35 **ballads . . . all** It was a common practice to
shame or mock one's enemies by hiring a writer
whose verses would be set to familiar music. In *Ant.*
Cleopatra fears that 'scald rhymers [will] / Ballad's
out a' tune' (5.2.215–16).

37 **forward** (1) presumptuous, insulting his dignity, (2) advanced (i.e. the plot to rob the travellers).

37 SD Some editions bring Bardolph and Peto on
here with Gadshill rather than at the beginning of
the scene, but see 0 SD n. above.

40 **setter** Thieves' term for one who sets up the
victim or who gathers information (*OED* sv *sb*¹ 7a).

41–3 **Bardolph, what . . . exchequer** There is
nothing improbable in QO's giving to Poins,

BARDOLPH Case ye, case ye, on with your vizards, there's money of the
    King's coming down the hill. 'Tis going to the King's exchequer.
                      [*They put on visors*]

FALSTAFF You lie, ye rogue, 'tis going to the King's tavern.

GADSHILL There's enough to make us all –   45

FALSTAFF To be hanged.

PRINCE Sirs, you four shall front them in the narrow lane. Ned Poins
    and I will walk lower – if they scape from your encounter, then they
    light on us.

PETO How many be there of them?   50

GADSHILL Some eight or ten.

FALSTAFF Zounds, will they not rob us?

PRINCE What, a coward, Sir John Paunch?

FALSTAFF Indeed, I am not John of Gaunt your grandfather, but yet no
    coward, Hal.   55

PRINCE Well, we leave that to the proof.

POINS Sirrah Jack, thy horse stands behind the hedge. When thou
    need'st him, there thou shalt find him. Farewell, and stand fast!

FALSTAFF Now cannot I strike him, if I should be hanged.

PRINCE [*Aside to Poins*] Ned, where are our disguises?   60

POINS Here, hard by, stand close.

                    [*Exeunt Prince and Poins*]

FALSTAFF Now, my masters, happy man be his dole, say I. Every man
    to his business.

Enter the TRAVELLERS

---

42 SH BARDOLPH] QqF; Gadshill *Johnson, Bevington*   47 Poins] Qq; *not in* F   60 SD *Aside to Poins*] *Collier; not in* QqF
61 SD *Exeunt Prince and Poins*] *Malone; not in* QqF

'Bardoll, what news?' and the following lines 'Case
ye . . . exchequer' to Bardolph, who can have been
lurking observantly to the side or just offstage.
Bevington, however, assigns 'What news?' to
Bardolph and the reply 'Case . . . exchequer' to
Gadshill. He argues that the Q0 compositor mistook
'Bardoll', intended as a speech heading before 'what
news', and wrongly attributed to Poins as a speech,
'Bardoll [F: Bardolfe], what newes'. See Textual
Analysis, p. 202.

    42 **Case ye** Put on your masks.

    42 **vizards** masks.

    51 **eight or ten** See 63 SD and n. below.

    54 **John of Gaunt** A quick countering of 'Sir
John Paunch', with a pun on the name of the

Prince's grandfather, implying as an insult that Hal
inherits his thinness. Compare the exchange between the Prince and Falstaff at 2.4.201–6.

    61 SD *Exeunt Prince and Poins* QqF give no
'*Exeunt*' but specify at 75 that they '*Enter*'. Here
they may simply stand aside.

    62 **happy . . . dole** A familiar expression (Dent
M158), with the basic sense, 'may happiness be our
lot'.

    63 SD TRAVELLERS QqF do not indicate any
specific number. Hal later says that he saw 'you four
set on four' (2.4.210). Mahood, *Bit Parts*, shows
that playtexts frequently leave indeterminate the
precise numbers of 'nonentities', depending upon
the supernumeraries available (pp. 8–11).

[FIRST] TRAVELLER Come, neighbour, the boy shall lead our horses
    down the hill. We'll walk afoot a while and ease our legs.   65
THIEVES Stand!
[SECOND] TRAVELLER Jesus bless us!
FALSTAFF Strike, down with them, cut the villains' throats! Ah,
    whoreson caterpillars, bacon-fed knaves, they hate us youth! Down
    with them, fleece them!   70
[FIRST] TRAVELLER O, we are undone, both we and ours for ever!
FALSTAFF Hang ye, gorbellied knaves, are ye undone? No, ye fat chuffs,
    I would your store were here! On, bacons, on! What, ye knaves,
    young men must live! You are grandjurors, are ye? We'll jure ye,
    faith.   75

Here they rob them and bind them

Exeunt

Enter the PRINCE *and* POINS [, *disguised*]

PRINCE The thieves have bound the true men. Now, could thou and I
    rob the thieves, and go merrily to London, it would be argument for
    a week, laughter for a month, and a good jest for ever.
POINS Stand close, I hear them coming.

[They retire]

Enter the thieves again

FALSTAFF Come, my masters, let us share, and then to horse before   80
    day. An the Prince and Poins be not two arrant cowards there's no
    equity stirring. There's no more valour in that Poins than in a wild
    duck.

As they are sharing the PRINCE *and* POINS *set upon them*

64 SH FIRST] *Capell; not in* QQF   67 SECOND] *Dyce²; not in* QQF   67 Jesus] Qq; Jesu F   71 SH FIRST] *Capell; not in* QQF   75
SD.3 *disguised*] *Cam.; not in* QQF   79 SD.1 *They retire*] *Dyce; not in* QQF   83 SD *As . . . them*] QQF *subst.* (Qqo, 1 *print with 85
SD in four lines to the right of 84–5*)

69 **whoreson** vile, wretched.

69 **caterpillars** extortioners who prey upon the
commonwealth like parasitic worms. Compare
2.1.64–6. Bullingbrook describes the King's coun-
cillors as caterpillars in *R2* 2.3.166; the allegation
occurs frequently in feudal justifications of
rebellion. Falstaff deflects his own failings onto his
opponents.

69 **bacon-fed knaves** overfed bumpkins.

69 **us youth** A deliberate comic absurdity, at
least for Falstaff; strife between generations is often
treated seriously in other contexts.

72 **gorbellied** pot-bellied, corpulent (*OED*).

72 **chuffs** wealthy miserly yeomen or citizens.

73 **your store** 'all you possess' (Kittredge).

74 **grandjurors** Only men of standing or wealth,
normally landowners, could serve on a grand jury
(*OED* Jury sv *sb* 2 b).

74 **jure ye** A pun on 'jury' used as a threat: 'We'll
dose you with your own medicine!'

77 **argument** subject-matter of discussion or
discourse (*OED* sv *sb* 6).

81–2 **no equity stirring** no measure of justice in
the world.

PRINCE Your money!

POINS Villains!   85

They all run away, and Falstaff after a blow or two runs away too,
leaving the booty behind them

PRINCE Got with much ease. Now merrily to horse.
The thieves are all scattered and possessed with fear
So strongly that they dare not meet each other.
Each takes his fellow for an officer!
Away, good Ned! Falstaff sweats to death,   90
And lards the lean earth as he walks along.
Were it not for laughing I should pity him.

POINS How the fat rogue roared!

Exeunt

[**2.3**] *Enter* HOTSPUR [*alone,*] *reading a letter*

[HOTSPUR] '*But for mine own part, my lord, I could be well contented to be*
there, in respect of the love I bear your house.'
He could be contented! Why is he not then? In respect of the love he
bears our house. He shows in this he loves his own barn better than
he loves our house. Let me see some more.   5
'*The purpose you undertake is dangerous,*'
Why, that's certain. 'Tis dangerous to take a cold, to sleep, to drink.
But I tell you, my lord fool, out of this nettle, danger, we pluck this
flower, safety.

---

85 SD.1 *and Falstaff... too*] Qq; *not in* F   **86–92** Got ... him] *As verse, Pope; as prose,* QqF   **93** fat] Q0; *not in* Qq1–5, F
Act 2, Scene 3   2.3] *Scæna Tertia.* F; *not in* Qq   0 SD *alone*] *solus* QqF   1 SH HOTSPUR] *Capell; not in* QqF   3 respect of]
F; *the respect of* Qq1–5

86–92 Got ... him Printed as prose in QqF but
most editors follow Pope in having Hal implicitly
assert his royal stature by returning to verse. Compare 1.2.155–77, 3.3.162–71, and 5.3.38–52.

89 takes ... officer mistakes for a constable. In
a familiar proverb, 'The thief does fear each bush an
officer' (Dent T112).

91 lards fattens (*OED* sv *v* 2, this example), as if
Falstaff were sweating his own fat rather than drops
of water. The verb suggests meat cooking on a spit.

Act 2, Scene 3
[**2.3**] The Percy plot is now well advanced. The
letter that Hotspur reads is a response to 'certeine
articles' (Holinshed) and letters circulated by the
conspirators. It reflects, but modifies, Holinshed's
report that 'when the matter came to triall, the most
part of the confederates abandoned them' (III, 23).

In the Elizabethan theatre, audiences first see a
single actor in an unlocalised setting. The entries
of Lady Percy and the servants create a domestic
atmosphere.

The text of this edition from the beginning of this
scene to the end of the play is based upon Q1. See
Textual Analysis, pp. 199–201.

0 SD The scene begins in mid-argument between
Hotspur and the absent, never to be identified
writer of the letter.

2 *house* family. Compare 1.3.10 and n.

7 'Tis ... drink Hotspur mocks what he considers the writer's great timidity.

7 take a cold catch a cold.

8–9 out ... safety An adaptation of the proverbs, 'Danger itself the best remedy for danger'
(Dent D30) and 'To pluck a flower from among
nettles' (Dent F388.1).

'*The purpose you undertake is dangerous, the friends you have named*　　10
uncertain, the time itself unsorted, and your whole plot too light, for the
counterpoise of so great an opposition.'
Say you so, say you so? I say unto you again, you are a shallow
cowardly hind, and you lie. What a lack-brain is this! By the Lord,
our plot is a good plot, as ever was laid, our friends true and　　15
constant. A good plot, good friends, and full of expectation. An
excellent plot, very good friends. What a frosty-spirited rogue is
this! Why, my Lord of York commends the plot, and the general
course of the action. Zounds, an I were now by this rascal I could
brain him with his lady's fan. Is there not my father, my uncle, and　　20
myself? Lord Edmund Mortimer, my Lord of York, and Owen
Glendower? Is there not besides the Douglas? Have I not all their
letters to meet me in arms by the ninth of the next month, and are
they not some of them set forward already? What a pagan rascal is
this, an infidel! Ha! You shall see now in very sincerity of fear and　　25
cold heart will he to the King, and lay open all our proceedings! O,
I could divide myself, and go to buffets, for moving such a dish of
skim milk with so honourable an action! Hang him, let him tell the
King, we are prepared. I will set forward tonight.

Enter his LADY

How now, Kate? I must leave you within these two hours.　　30
LADY PERCY　O my good lord, why are you thus alone?
　　　For what offence have I this fortnight been
　　　A banished woman from my Harry's bed?

14 By the Lord] Qq; I protest F　19 Zounds, an] Qq (Zoundes and); By this hand if F

11 *unsorted* not well chosen.
12 *counterpoise* a balancing force or weight (*OED* sv sb 1).
14 **hind** (1) menial servant (*OED* sv sb² 1), (2) rustic or boor (*OED* sv sb² 3).
14–17 **By . . . friends** Hotspur's misguided enthusiasm mounts despite the reasonable objections that have been raised.
15 **friends** allies, supporters.
16 **full of expectation** extremely promising.
18–19 **my Lord . . . action** In Holinshed, Richard Scroop, Archbishop of York, is said to have written the 'articles' that attempt to justify the Percy cause.
20 **brain . . . lady's fan** Hotspur follows up his claim that the writer is a lack-brain, 14, by this threat to use an almost weightless weapon.
24 **pagan** Like 'infidel', 25, one who resists the established faith.

26 **will he** he will go.
27 **divide . . . buffets** split into two parts and set each to cuffing the other. Hotspur anticipates Lady Percy's diagnosis of his condition, 50 below.
27 **moving** urging.
30 **Kate** See List of Characters and 1.3.79.
31–58 **O my . . . loves me not** Kate's long first speech and the following dialogue are often compared to the exchanges between Portia and Brutus, *JC* 2.1.233 ff. Both women are shrewd observers of their husbands, but Kate communicates her anxiety in a jesting manner. Hotspur does not respond to her direct questions, perhaps because he wishes to tease her, perhaps because he is too preoccupied.
33 **banished woman** Sexual activity supposedly diminished a man's energy and physical strength – a notion still current among some sports managers and journalists.

Something
warped

Tell me, sweet lord, what is't that takes from thee
Thy stomach, pleasure, and thy golden sleep?   35
Why dost thou bend thine eyes upon the earth,
And start so often when thou sittest alone?
Why hast thou lost the fresh blood in thy cheeks,
And given my treasures and my rights of thee
To thick-eyed musing, and curst melancholy?   40
In thy faint slumbers I by thee have watched
And heard thee murmur tales of iron wars,
Speak terms of manage to thy bounding steed,
Cry 'Courage! To the field!' and thou hast talked
Of sallies, and retires, of trenches, tents,   45

Anafra

Of palisadoes, frontiers, parapets,
Of basilisks, of cannon, culverin,
Of prisoners' ransom, and of soldiers slain,
And all the currents of a heady fight.
Thy spirit within thee hath been so at war,   50
And thus hath so bestirred thee in thy sleep,
That beads of sweat have stood upon thy brow
Like bubbles in a late-disturbèd stream,
And in thy face strange motions have appeared,
Such as we see when men restrain their breath   55
On some great sudden hest. O, what portents are these?
Some heavy business hath my lord in hand,
And I must know it, else he loves me not.

41 thy] QQ1–3; my QQ4–5, F   42 thee] QQ2–5, F; the Q1   48 ransom] QQF (ransome); ransom'd *Dyce²*, *conj. Capell*

35 **stomach** appetite.
35 **golden** precious (*OED* sv *a* 4a).
39 **my treasures and my rights** Kate expresses how much pleasure she has taken in the exercise of the more formal 'rights' that are owed to a wife.
40 **thick-eyed** dim-sighted, related to 'bend thine eyes upon the earth', 36. These acute observations create an image that contrasts sharply with her husband's confident rhetoric.
40 **curst** waspish, cross, bad-tempered.
41 **faint** light.
41 **watched** (1) kept awake (*OED* sv *v* 1b), (2) been on the lookout.
42 **iron wars** Figurative description of battle.
43 **manage** The art of training and managing horses (*OED* sv *sb* 1).
45 **sallies** sudden rushes towards an enemy from a besieged position.
45 **retires** retreats.

46 **palisadoes** Variant of palisades, fences made out of stakes and used for enclosure or defence.
46 **frontiers** ramparts. Compare 1.3.18.
46 **parapets** defences made of earth or stone, raised on the ground or on a rampart, literally breast-high (*OED* 1).
47 **basilisks** The largest cannons, named for a fabulous monster, the basilisk or cockatrice, which was hatched by a serpent from a cock's egg. Its breath or gaze was supposedly fatal.
47 **culverin** A small cannon originally used as a handgun. Its name derives from French '*couleuvre*', snake. 'Names of reptiles were frequently applied to early cannon' (*OED* 1).
49 **currents** movements.
49 **heady** violent.
54 **motions** (1) commotions, (2) expressions.
56 **hest** behest, injunction.
57 **heavy** grave.

HOTSPUR What ho!

[*Enter a* SERVANT]

Is Gillams with the packet gone?
SERVANT He is, my lord, an hour ago.   60
HOTSPUR Hath Butler brought those horses from the sheriff?
SERVANT One horse, my lord, he brought even now.
HOTSPUR What horse? A roan, a crop-ear is it not?
SERVANT It is, my lord.
HOTSPUR   That roan shall be my throne.
Well, I will back him straight. O Esperance!   65
Bid Butler lead him forth into the park.

[*Exit Servant*]

LADY PERCY But hear you, my lord.
HOTSPUR What sayest thou, my lady?
LADY PERCY What is it carries you away?   } teasing him
HOTSPUR Why, my horse, my love, my horse.   }   70
LADY PERCY Out, you mad-headed ape!
A weasel hath not such a deal of spleen
As you are tossed with. In faith,
I'll know your business, Harry, that I will.
I fear my brother Mortimer doth stir   75

---

59 SD *Enter a* SERVANT] *Capell; after 58, Dering MS.; not in* QQF   63 A roan] Qq3–5, F; Roane Qq1, 2   65–6 Well . . . park] *As verse, Pope; as prose,* QQF   66 SD *Exit Servant*] *Dering MS., Hanmer; not in* QQF   71–7 Out . . . go] *As verse, Capell; as prose,* QQF   73 In faith] Qq; In sooth F

59 packet dispatch or message (about the conspiracy, we infer).

59, 61 Gillams, Butler Why Shakespeare chooses to name these servants who never appear has not received clear explanation. The names may provide evidence of the closeness of Q1 to an unrevised authorial manuscript. Compare the use of names: Tom, Cut, Robin Ostler, and Mugs in the short sequence 2.1.5–36.

61 sheriff high officer in a shire who represents the king. This sheriff apparently supports the locally powerful Percy family.

63 A roan A horse either named for or described by its colours, reddish brown mottled with white or grey. Hal mocks Hotspur's preference for this horse at 2.4.92.

64–82 That roan . . . true Editors generally follow Pope in arranging the lines as verse; QQF print this passage as prose. With the emendation from Q3, 'A roan', verse can begin one line earlier at 63.

65 back him mount him.

65 Esperance 'Esperance' or 'Esperance ma comforte' (Hope, my comfort) was the Percy motto. Compare 5.2.96.

67–71 But . . . ape Five consecutive short lines, mostly in monosyllables, capture the quick repartee of Hotspur and Kate.

69 What . . . away (1) Why are you going? (2) What (passion) sweeps you away?

72 weasel 'As angry as a weasel' (Dent W211.1) was a common comparison.

72 spleen a capricious humour, marked by sudden, contradictory emotions and thought to be caused, like more violent tempers, by the organ of the body called the spleen. Compare 3.2.125 and 5.2.19, 'A hare-brained Hotspur, governed by a spleen'.

75 my brother Mortimer Historically, Lord Edmund Mortimer, captured by Glendower, was her younger brother; the heir presumptive was her nephew. See 1.3.79 n. and List of Characters for Shakespeare's conflation of the two.

About his title, and hath sent for you
To line his enterprise. But if you go –
HOTSPUR So far afoot I shall be weary, love.
LADY PERCY Come, come, you paraquito, answer me
Directly unto this question that I ask.   80
In faith, I'll break thy little finger, Harry,
And if thou wilt not tell me all things true.
HOTSPUR Away,
Away you trifler! Love! I love thee not,
I care not for thee, Kate; this is no world   85
To play with mammets, and to tilt with lips.
We must have bloody noses, and cracked crowns,
And pass them current too. God's me! My horse!
What say'st thou, Kate? What wouldst thou have with me?
LADY PERCY Do you not love me? Do you not indeed?   90
Well, do not then, for since you love me not
I will not love myself. Do you not love me?
Nay, tell me if you speak in jest or no?
HOTSPUR Come, wilt thou see me ride?
And when I am a-horseback I will swear   95
I love thee infinitely. But hark you, Kate,
I must not have you henceforth question me
Whither I go, nor reason whereabout.
Whither I must, I must. And, to conclude,
This evening must I leave you, gentle Kate.   100
I know you wise, but yet no farther wise

79–82 Come . . . true] *As verse, Pope; as prose,* QqF   81 In faith] Qq; Indeede F   93 you speak] Qq; thou speak'st F   98, 99 Whither] Qq; Whether F

---

76 title claim to the crown.

77 line strengthen, reinforce (as in lining a garment).

79 paraquito A small parrot, used as a term of endearment, but also suggesting excessive talk. Compare 'popinjay' 1.3.49 and n.

83–4 Away . . . not Hotspur facetiously replies to Kate's demand at 58: because he cannot tell her his business, it follows that he does not love her.

86 mammets dolls or puppets, and, by implication, his wife as a sexual partner. The original meaning, idols or false gods, (from Mahomet or Mohammed) tinges Hotspur's gibe with a charge of false belief. Compare 'pagan' and 'infidel', 24–5.

86 tilt with lips Literally, to joust with lips. This may imply that (1) both tournaments and kissing are idle sports or games in time of war, (2) only sexual play is inappropriate.

87 crowns (1) heads, (2) coins, valued at five shillings, still used in sixteenth-century England.

88 pass them current (1) use them as valid currency despite their being cracked, (2) use them frequently, i.e. crack many heads.

88 God's me God save me, an oath that escaped purging in the Folio.

98 reason whereabout examine my purpose.

Than Harry Percy's wife. Constant you are,
But yet a woman. And for secrecy,
No lady closer, for I well believe
Thou wilt not utter what thou dost not know.   *cf. macbeth* 105
And so far will I trust thee, gentle Kate.
LADY PERCY How? So far?
HOTSPUR Not an inch further. But hark you, Kate,
Whither I go, thither shall you go too.   *echo - Book of Ruth*
                                          Union stable - healthy
Today will I set forth, tomorrow you.   110
Will this content you, Kate?
LADY PERCY   It must, of force.

                                        Exeunt

[2.4] *Enter* PRINCE *and* POINS

PRINCE Ned, prithee come out of that fat room, and lend me thy hand
    to laugh a little.
POINS Where hast been, Hal?
PRINCE With three or four loggerheads, amongst three or fourscore
    hogsheads. I have sounded the very base string of humility. Sirrah,   5
    I am sworn brother to a leash of drawers, and can call them all by

---

104 well] Qq1–3; wil Q4; will Q5, F   106 far will] Qq1–4; farewill Q5; farre wilt F   Act 2, Scene 4 2.4] *Scena quarta.* F; *not in* Qq

103 But yet a woman Hotspur's unwillingness to trust his wife balances his misplaced confidence in 'a dish of skim milk', 27–8 above.

105 Thou . . . know Humphreys traces this 'venerable jest' back to Seneca, *Controversiae*, II, xiii, 12. Compare Dent w649, s196, w706.1.

109 Whither . . . too An echo of Ruth's refusal to abandon Naomi, in Ruth 1.16 (Davison).

111 of force of necessity.

Act 2, Scene 4

[2.4] This first tavern scene, as it is conventionally and accurately known, takes place in Eastcheap, 12 below. The inn, never explicitly named in the text, has traditionally been identified as the Boar's Head, which stood on the north side of Great Eastcheap. This street, noted for its meat-markets, provides an appropriate background for numerous references to food and feasting. Both neighbourhood and tavern are closely associated with Falstaff. In *2H4* 2.2.146–7, Prince Hal asks, 'Doth the old boar feed in the old frank?'

Tables, chairs, and drinking vessels provide the only props needed.

1 fat (1) filled with dense, cloying air (*OED* sv *a* 7c), (2) vat, a large cask in which to ferment or store beer or cider; distinct from the 'hogsheads' among which Hal has been drinking, 5 below.

1 lend . . . hand give me your support, i.e. lend a helping hand (*OED* sv *v*[2] 2e).

4 loggerheads blockheads, the drawers, 6, who invite some of the guests into their cellar to drink among the casks.

4–5 amongst . . . hogsheads i.e. in the cellar. Dekker in *Guls Horne-booke* (1609), ed. Grosart, II, 260, advises gallants 'to accept of the courtesie of the Cellar when tis offered you by the drawers' (cited by Humphreys).

5 humility (1) 'freedom from pride or arrogance' (Hemingway), (2) humble or low condition (*OED* 2).

6 leash set of three; a hunting term, often used for dogs.

6 drawers tapsters.

their Christian names, as Tom, Dick, and Francis. They take it
already upon their salvation that though I be but Prince of Wales yet
I am the king of courtesy, and tell me flatly I am no proud Jack like
Falstaff, but a Corinthian, a lad of mettle, a good boy – by the Lord,   10
so they call me! – and when I am King of England I shall command
all the good lads in Eastcheap. They call drinking deep 'dyeing
scarlet', and when you breathe in your watering they cry 'Hem!' and
bid you 'Play it off!' To conclude, I am so good a proficient in one
quarter of an hour that I can drink with any tinker in his own   15
language during my life. I tell thee, Ned, thou hast lost much
honour that thou wert not with me in this action. But, sweet Ned –
to sweeten which name of Ned I give thee this pennyworth of sugar,
clapped even now into my hand by an underskinker, one that never
spake other English in his life than 'Eight shillings and sixpence',   20
and 'You are welcome', with this shrill addition, 'Anon, anon, sir!
Score a pint of bastard in the Half-moon!', or so. But Ned, to drive
away the time till Falstaff come – I prithee do thou stand in some by-
room while I question my puny drawer to what end he gave me the
sugar. And do thou never leave calling 'Francis!', that his tale to   25

---

7 Christian] Q5; christen Qq1–4; *not in* F   8 salvation] Qq; confidence F   10–11 by . . . me] Qq; *not in* F

---

7 Christian names Dekker, *Guls Horne-booke*,
II, 256, mockingly recommends, 'Your first comple-
ment shall be to grow most inwardly acquainted
with the drawers, to learne their names, as *Jack*, and
Will, and *Tom*' (Humphreys).

9 king best example (Dent K65.1).

9 Jack Fellow or knave, as well as Falstaff's nickname.

10 Corinthian Drinking companion; the
ancient Greek city of Corinth was notorious for
dissipation and wenching. Compare 'Troyans'
2.1.56 and n.

10 mettle courageous temperament (*OED* sv *sb*
3, this example); originally a figurative use of
'metal'. Compare 290.

12–13 dyeing scarlet What happens to the com-
plexions of deep drinkers; compare 'purple-hued
malt worms' 2.1.61. The phrase derives from the
practice of mixing urine into dyes, thereby making
them colour-fast on fabric. 'Topers' urine was supposed to make the best scarlet dye' (Wilson).

13 breathe in your watering pause for breath
while drinking, a sign of inexperience. 'Breathe' is
used repeatedly in *1H4* to signal pauses in vigorous
combat; see 1.3.101 and 207 below.

13 Hem 'Clear your throat' (Wilson) and keep on
drinking.

14 Play it off 'Finish up'.

15–16 tinker . . . language These craftsmen,
often itinerant menders of metal utensils, were
known as great drinkers who often used a canting
language. For an account of how the Prince masters
the languages of England, see Joan Webber, 'The
renewal of the king's symbolic role from *Richard II*
to *Henry V*', *TSLL* 4 (1963), 530–8.

17 action military venture, as at 2.3.19 and 28,
but said in jest.

18 to sweeten . . . sugar i.e. to compliment you
by making your (plain) name more appetising.

19 clapped pressed.

19 underskinker subordinate tapster.

21 Anon, anon (1) 'Right away' (2) 'In a minute'.

22 Score Charge to a bill, reckon up.

22 bastard Sweet Spanish wine, often
adulterated.

22 Half-moon A room in the tavern, like
'Pomgarnet', 31.

23–4 by-room side room.

24 puny (1) junior or inferior in rank, like an
'underskinker', 19, (2) raw, inexperienced (not
necessarily small or thin).

me may be nothing but 'Anon'. Step aside, and I'll show thee a
precedent.

                                            [Poins withdraws]

POINS [*Within*] Francis!
PRINCE Thou art perfect.
POINS [*Within*] Francis!   30

                     Enter [FRANCIS, *a*] *Drawer*

FRANCIS Anon, anon, sir. Look down into the Pomgarnet, Ralph!
PRINCE Come hither, Francis.
FRANCIS My lord?
PRINCE How long hast thou to serve, Francis?
FRANCIS Forsooth, five years, and as much as to –   35
POINS [*Within*] Francis!
FRANCIS Anon, anon, sir.
PRINCE Five year! By'r lady, a long lease for the clinking of pewter. But
    Francis, darest thou be so valiant as to play the coward with thy
    indenture, and show it a fair pair of heels, and run from it?   40
FRANCIS O Lord, sir, I'll be sworn upon all the books in England, I
    could find in my heart –
POINS [*Within*] Francis!
FRANCIS Anon, sir.
PRINCE How old art thou, Francis?   45
FRANCIS Let me see, about Michaelmas next I shall be –
POINS [*Within*] Francis!

27 precedent] F (President), *Pope;* present Qq   27 SD *Poins withdraws*] *Theobald subst.; not in* QqF   28 SD, 30 SD.1 *Within*]
Dyce; not in QqF   30 SH POINS] Qq4, 5, F; *Prin.* Qq1–3 *subst.*   30 SD.2 FRANCIS, a] *Rowe; not in* QqF   36, 43, 47, 54, 68
SD *Within*] *Capell; not in* QqF

27 precedent example (of how the drawer
speaks English). This reading from F appears to
correct the Qq version, 'present'; it could be an
editorial intervention, rather than evidence that F
relies on the authority of a manuscript or prompt-
book. See Textual Analysis, p. 206.

27 SD *Poins withdraws* Poins has no exit in QqF,
but he enters at line 74. He may simply retire to the
rear or to the side of the stage.

31 Look down into Go down and look into.

31 Pomgarnet Pomegranate. Another tavern
room given a name, like the Bunch of Grapes in
MM 2.1.128–9.

34 to serve i.e. as an apprentice; the normal
length of service was seven years. Francis would
probably be fourteen to sixteen if he has served for
two years.

38 By'r lady By Our Lady (the Virgin Mary).

38 lease term.

40 indenture contract; compare 1.3.86, where
'indent' is used figuratively. The rebels draw up
'indentures' at 3.1.76, 135, and 253.

40 show . . . heels A common saying (Dent
P31). The Prince may be going on to tempt Francis
with employment in his own household (Wilson);
compare Gobbo's decision to serve a new master in
MV 2.2.1–32.

41 books Bibles or prayer-books.

46 Michaelmas 29 September, the feast of
Michael the Archangel; also a quarter-day (annual
dates, on which quarterly charges fall due).

FRANCIS Anon, sir – pray stay a little, my lord.

PRINCE Nay but hark you, Francis, for the sugar thou gavest me, 'twas
a pennyworth, was't not?   50

FRANCIS O Lord, I would it had been two!

PRINCE I will give thee for it a thousand pound – ask me when thou wilt,
and thou shalt have it.

POINS [*Within*] Francis!

FRANCIS Anon, anon.   55

PRINCE Anon, Francis? No, Francis, but tomorrow, Francis. Or
Francis, a-Thursday. Or indeed Francis, when thou wilt. But
Francis!

FRANCIS My lord?

PRINCE Wilt thou rob this leathern-jerkin, crystal-button, not-pated,   60
agate-ring, puke-stocking, caddis-garter, smooth-tongue Spanish
pouch?

FRANCIS O Lord, sir, who do you mean?

PRINCE Why then your brown bastard is your only drink. For look you,
Francis, your white canvas doublet will sully. In Barbary, sir, it   65
cannot come to so much.

FRANCIS What, sir?

POINS [*Within*] Francis!

PRINCE Away, you rogue, dost thou not hear them call?
           Here they both call him; the Drawer stands amazed,
                  not knowing which way to go

48 **stay a little** wait for a moment.

60 **rob** i.e. steal your own services, which belong
to your master, by running away.

60–2 **leathern-jerkin ... Spanish pouch** Hal
reels off this burlesque of the vintner and his apparel in order to confuse Francis and to satirise
innkeepers.

60 **not-pated** with close-cropped hair (*OED* Not
sv *a* 1), as worn by Chaucer's Yeoman (Prologue,
Canterbury Tales, 109). It was a common style for
lower and middle classes.

61 **agate-ring** Probably a seal-ring (and status-
symbol) carved from an agate. Compare 3.3.64.

61 **puke-** of dark grey or blue-black wool.
Gentlemen wore light-coloured silk stockings.

61 **caddis-garter** gartered with coarse worsted
tape or yarn.

61 **smooth-tongue** flattering, but also articulate
speaker, (which Francis might resent). This suggestion of glibness provides a jolting break in a series of
sharply visualised traits.

61–2 **Spanish pouch** Vintners commonly wore
pouches of Spanish leather (Humphreys).

62 To replace this QqF punctuation with a dash,
as do many editors, suggests that Francis, in the
next line, interrupts his Prince. That seems unlikely, however befuddled the drawer might be.

64–6 **Why ... much** The Prince's 'humbug
style' (Gentleman, 1773) serves to baffle Francis.
Hal may imply that he has offered Francis adventure in Barbary, as well as a new position in his own
household, 38–40; because Francis has not seized
this chance, he may be better off in the tavern than
seeking his fortune. Heroic apprentices would soon
be celebrated in Thomas Deloney's tales of shoe-
makers in *The Gentle Craft* (1598). Compare the
questing heroes of Thomas Heywood's *The Four
Prentices of London* (1615, but probably written by
1594).

65 **Barbary** Northern Africa.

Enter VINTNER

VINTNER　What, standest thou still and hearest such a calling? Look to　　70
the guests within.

[*Exit Francis*]

My lord, old Sir John with half-a-dozen more are at the door. Shall
I let them in?

PRINCE　Let them alone a while, and then open the door.

[*Exit Vintner*]

Enter POINS

Poins!　　　　　　　　　　　　　　　　　　　　　　　　　　　　75

POINS　Anon, anon, sir.

PRINCE　Sirrah, Falstaff and the rest of the thieves are at the door. Shall
we be merry?

POINS　As merry as crickets, my lad. But hark ye, what cunning match
have you made with this jest of the drawer? Come, what's the issue?　　80

PRINCE　I am now of all humours that have showed themselves humours
since the old days of goodman Adam to the pupil age of this present
twelve o'clock at midnight.

[*Enter* FRANCIS]

What's o'clock, Francis?

FRANCIS　Anon, anon, sir.　　　　　　　　　　　　　　[*Exit*]　　85

PRINCE　That ever this fellow should have fewer words than a parrot,
and yet the son of a woman! His industry is up-stairs and down-
stairs, his eloquence the parcel of a reckoning. I am not yet of

71 SD *Exit Francis*] Johnson (*Exit Drawer); not in* QQF　74 SD.1 *Exit Vintner*] Theobald (*after 75); not in* QQF　74 SD.2 *Enter*
POINS] QQF (*after 76*)　83 SD *Enter* FRANCIS] Malone (*Re-enter Francis, with wine); not in* QQF　84 o'] QQF (a)　85 SD *Exit*]
Collier; *not in* QQF

69 SD.3 VINTNER Innkeeper, literally wine-
merchant.

74 Let . . . door Hal shows his eagerness to
stage-manage the situation by controlling its timing.

74 SD.2 *Enter* POINS Compare 27 SD above. If he
has left the stage, Poins can enter by one door as the
Vintner leaves by the other.

79 my lad Poins, like Falstaff, feels free to address the Prince informally. Because the Prince
does not object, one might infer that he takes such
playful intimacy for granted.

79–80 what cunning . . . drawer? i.e. what sort
of witty contest have you turned this joke into?
Poins may be tactfully calling attention to the energy that Hal is expending on so easy a trick. He
invokes the model of winning and losing in a con-

text where battles of wits seem irrelevant.

80 what's the issue? (1) what's the outcome? (2)
what's your purpose?

81–3 I am . . . midnight 'I am in the mood to
indulge any fancy that any man has ever had since
the creation' (Kittredge). Hal either evades Poins'
question or suggests that he is now too 'humorous'
to worry about 'issues'.

82 goodman Title given to a yeoman or a
farmer. The Prince speaks of Adam as if he were a
neighbour.

82 pupil A minor or a ward. Midnight is treated
as the beginning (youth) of a new day.

88 parcel of a reckoning item in a bill.

88–9 I am . . . mind This sudden shift of subject in mid-speech alerts the actor to the instability

[handwritten: close to fecundity of Shakespeare – have diff players play parts]

[handwritten: Trying to appreciate Percy]

Percy's mind, the Hotspur of the north, he that kills me some six or
seven dozen of Scots at a breakfast, washes his hands, and says to his   90
wife, 'Fie upon this quiet life, I want work.' 'O my sweet Harry',
says she, 'how many hast thou killed today?' 'Give my roan horse a
drench', says he, and answers, 'Some fourteen', an hour after, 'a
trifle, a trifle'. I prithee, call in Falstaff. I'll play Percy, and that
damned brawn shall play Dame Mortimer his wife. 'Rivo!' says the   95
drunkard. Call in Ribs, call in Tallow!

[handwritten: Falstaff – great at improvisation]

Enter FALSTAFF [, GADSHILL, BARDOLPH, *and* PETO;
        followed by FRANCIS, *with wine*]

POINS Welcome, Jack, where hast thou been?
FALSTAFF A plague of all cowards, I say, and a vengeance too, marry
and amen! Give me a cup of sack, boy. Ere I lead this life long, I'll
sew nether-stocks, and mend them and foot them too. A plague of   100
all cowards! Give me a cup of sack, rogue. Is there no virtue extant?

He drinks

PRINCE Didst thou never see Titan kiss a dish of butter – pitiful-

---

96 SD.1 GADSHILL . . . PETO] *Theobald; not in* QQF   96 SD.2 *followed . . . wine*] *Dering MS., Dyce; not in* QQF   100 and foot
them] Qq; *not in* F   102 Titan!] *Warburton;* Titan QQF

---

of the Prince's mood. He mocks Hotspur's single-
minded attitude as opposed to his own 'all humours'. The leap with no transition from Francis to
Hotspur (in this, the Prince's first explicit reference
to his rival) may suggest an undercurrent that unex-
pectedly links the tapster and the rebel.

89 **kills me** kills. The ethical dative 'me' makes
the slaughter of Scots sound absurdly practical.

91–4 **Fie . . . trifle** A shrewd imitation of
Hotspur's style, capturing his long-delayed responses and his exasperated understatements.

93 **drench** (1) drink, (2) dose of medicine.

94 **I'll play Percy** An intriguing promise never
enacted.

95 **brawn** (1) the meat of the boar, (2) the flesh
most suitable for roasting.

95 **Rivo** A cry of uncertain origin used in drinking bouts; perhaps from Italian '*riviva*', meaning
'Another toast!' (Davison).

96 **Ribs . . . Tallow** Meat (on bones) . . .
coarse, hard fat, dripping, or gravy. Wilson, *Fortunes*, p. 27, notes that these terms 'recall the chief
stock-in-trade of the victuallers and butchers of
Eastcheap'.

98 **of** on.

100 **nether-stocks** stockings or hose. Falstaff

pretends to humble virtue, like that of the honest
citizen in Jonson's *The Alchemist* who 'sate up a
mending my wifes stockings' (5.1.35).

100 **foot** make feet for. Bevington links this
vision of tedious labour to Falstaff's discomfort
'afoot'.

102–4 **Didst . . . compound** The Prince invents
a riddle which refers to Falstaff's excessive drinking
and/or to his sweating. It further hints at his contradictory nature. The sun (Titan) overpowers and
melts the dish of butter, which may (to ludicrous
effect) identify with butter the helpless mortals
loved by the gods of classical myths. Within this
scenario, there are several possible meanings: (1)
Falstaff is the sun, the cup of sack, his butter; (2)
Falstaff, incongruously, is both sun and butter,
huge and red-faced (the Titans were rebellious
giants), but in process of dissolution; (3) The Prince
is the sun, perpetrator of the joke that has caused
Falstaff (the butter) to sweat his own fat (2.2.90–1)
or 'Tallow' (96 above). 'To melt like butter before
the sun' was a common saying (Dent B780).

The second 'Titan' has been considered by some
editors to be a printer's error; Theobald proposed
'butter'. 'Pitiful' could mean compassionate or
tender.

hearted Titan! – that melted at the sweet tale of the sun's? If thou
didst, then behold that compound.

FALSTAFF You rogue, here's lime in this sack too. There is nothing but   105
roguery to be found in villainous man, yet a coward is worse than a
cup of sack with lime in it. A villainous coward! Go thy ways, old
Jack, die when thou wilt. If manhood, good manhood, be not forgot
upon the face of the earth, then am I a shotten herring. There lives
not three good men unhanged in England, and one of them is fat,   110
and grows old. God help the while, a bad world I say. I would I were
a weaver: I could sing psalms – or anything. A plague of all cowards,
I say still.

PRINCE How now, woolsack, what mutter you?

FALSTAFF A king's son! If I do not beat thee out of thy kingdom with a   115
dagger of lath, and drive all thy subjects afore thee like a flock of
wild geese, I'll never wear hair on my face more. You, Prince of
Wales!

PRINCE Why, you whoreson round man, what's the matter?

FALSTAFF Are not you a coward? Answer me to that – and Poins there?   120

---

103 sun's] *Cam.*; soanes Qq1, 2; sunne Qq3–5, F   112 psalms – or anything] Qq; all manner of songs F

---

104 compound (1) mixture, (2) a substance in which the elements composing it retain their distinctive (and in this case mismatched) qualities. Both meanings antedate *OED*'s earliest examples.

105 lime Alkaline substance (i.e. calcium oxide, not lime juice), used by vintners to make wine dry and sparkling. Humphreys cites Elyot's *Ortho-epia Gallica* II, 40 on this practice, regarded as worse than watering the wine: 'nothing is more hurtfull to mens bodies . . . for thence proceed infinit maladies, and specially the goutes'.

105–6 There . . . man Adapting a proverbial saying, 'There is no faith (trust, honesty) in man' (Dent F34), Falstaff returns to his theme of truth among thieves. Compare 2.2.18 ff.

109 shotten herring one thin and emaciated because it had shot or spawned its roe. Falstaff, the festive, meaty, carnival figure, contrasts his bulk with that of a popular Lenten food, simultaneously mocking the thin Prince Hal. Compare 'soused gurnet' 4.2.11.

110 good (1) brave, (2) virtuous.

111 the while these bad times.

111–12 I would . . . psalms Weavers were noted for singing at work; they may often have been pious immigrants from the Low Countries to East

Anglia. (See Peter Milward, *Shakespeare's Religious Background*, 1973, p. 153). Compare *TN* 2.3.58–9: 'a catch that will draw three souls out of one weaver'.

112 or anything i.e. as if weaving or sewing, too, were the most extreme renunciations imaginable.

114 woolsack (1) a large bale or bag made of wool, (2) an incongruous 'compound' (104) of stuffing and wine.

114 mutter An implicit stage direction: Falstaff may be talking to himself.

116 dagger of lath A stage property of the Morality-play Vice, a role attributed to Falstaff at 375 below. For the absurd uproar associated with the Vice, compare *TN* 'the old Vice . . . / Who with dagger of lath / In his rage and his wrath / Cries, ah, ha! to the devil' (4.2.124–8). On uses of Morality-play conventions in *1H4*, see Introduction, p. 10 ff. Falstaff's weapon may be 'a traditional apprentice's play-sword made of wood', i.e. 'a false staff', according to David Wiles, *Shakespeare's Clown*, 1987, pp. 121–2.

117 I'll . . . more Perhaps a 'gibe at Hal's hairless chin' (Wilson).

POINS Zounds, ye fat paunch, an ye call me coward by the Lord I'll stab thee.

FALSTAFF I call thee coward? I'll see thee damned ere I call thee coward, but I would give a thousand pound I could run as fast as thou canst. You are straight enough in the shoulders, you care not who   125
sees your back. Call you that backing of your friends? A plague upon such backing, give me them that will face me! Give me a cup of sack! I am a rogue if I drunk today.

PRINCE O, villain! Thy lips are scarce wiped since thou drunk'st last.

FALSTAFF All is one for that. (*He drinks.*) A plague of all cowards, still   130
say I.

PRINCE What's the matter?

FALSTAFF What's the matter? There be four of us here have taken a thousand pound this day morning.

PRINCE Where is it, Jack, where is it?   135

FALSTAFF Where is it? Taken from us it is. A hundred upon poor four of us.

PRINCE What, a hundred, man?

FALSTAFF I am a rogue if I were not at half-sword with a dozen of them two hours together. I have scaped by miracle. I am eight times   140
thrust through the doublet, four through the hose, my buckler cut through and through, my sword hacked like a handsaw – *ecce signum*! I never dealt better since I was a man. All would not do. A plague of all cowards! Let them speak. If they speak more or less than truth, they are villains and the sons of darkness.   145

[PRINCE] Speak, sirs, how was it?

---

121 SH POINS] QQ1–4; *Prin.* Q5, F   130 All is] QQ1, 2; *All's* QQ3–5, F   146 SH PRINCE] *Prince Henry* F, *Dering MS.; Gad* QQ

---

126 **backing** (1) supporting, (2) turning to flee.

129 **O, villain . . . last** A particularly apposite twist to the saying, 'You licked not your lips since you lied last' (Dent L329, Appendix C).

133–4 **a thousand pound** Perhaps an echo of *FV*, 86; Shakespeare's robbers have stolen only 300 marks (436), or a mere 200 pounds. For use of the phrase as hyperbole, compare 52 and 124 above. The sum is repeatedly associated with Falstaff and his expenses in this play, in *2H4* and in *Wiv.*

139 **at half-sword** (1) fighting at close quarters (*OED* 2), (2) fighting with short swords (*OED* 1).

141 **buckler** A small round shield, in Shakespeare's day considered more suitable for servants and rowdies. Falstaff's 'claim to sturdy old-

fashioned manhood . . . extends also to his choice of weapons' (Humphreys). Compare Hotspur's remark at 1.3.227 and n.

142–3 *ecce signum* behold the proof (or sign); an implied stage direction using a familiar saying (Dent S443), perhaps suggested by 'miracle' in 140. Falstaff supports his pose as a virtuous outlaw by alluding to the Catholic mass.

143 **All would not do** Even my bravery was not enough.

145 **sons of darkness** A biblical echo, 1 Thess. 5.5: 'Ye are all the children of light . . . we are not of the night nether of darkenes.'

146, 147, 149, 153 SHS Q gives 146 to 'Gad', and the other three lines to 'Ross.' (for Rossill), as Bardolph was originally called. For an account of

[BARDOLPH] We four set upon some dozen –
FALSTAFF Sixteen at least, my lord.
[BARDOLPH] And bound them.
PETO No, no, they were not bound.   150
FALSTAFF You rogue, they were bound, every man of them, or I am a
    Jew else: an Ebrew Jew.
[BARDOLPH] As we were sharing, some six or seven fresh men set upon
    us –
FALSTAFF And unbound the rest, and then come in the other.   155
PRINCE What, fought you with them all?
FALSTAFF All? I know not what you call all, but if I fought not with fifty
    of them I am a bunch of radish. If there were not two or three and
    fifty upon poor old Jack, then am I no two-legg'd creature.
PRINCE Pray God you have not murdered some of them.   160
FALSTAFF Nay, that's past praying for, I have peppered two of them.
    Two I am sure I have paid, two rogues in buckram suits. I tell thee
    what, Hal, if I tell thee a lie, spit in my face, call me horse. Thou
    knowest my old ward – here I lay, and thus I bore my point. Four
    rogues in buckram let drive at me –   165
PRINCE What, four? Thou saidst but two even now.
FALSTAFF Four, Hal, I told thee four.
POINS Ay, ay, he said four.
FALSTAFF These four came all afront, and mainly thrust at me. I made
    me no more ado, but took all their seven points in my target, thus! 170
PRINCE Seven? Why, there were but four even now.

147, 149, 153 SH BARDOLPH] *Dering MS., Collier (Bard.); Ross.* Qq; *Gad.* F   150 SH PETO] QqF; *Bard./ Dering MS.*
160 SH PRINCE] Qq1–4 *subst.; Poines.* Q5, F

the textual confusion surrounding the robbery and
its aftermath, see Textual Analysis, p. 203.
   152 Ebrew Jew i.e. an authentic one (compare
'the veriest varlet' 2.2.19); perhaps also a clumsily
comic repetition or intensifier. At a time when no
Jews could publicly practise their religion in England, casual equations of Jews with knaves, though
indefensible, were common. Compare Benedick's
vow (*Ado* 2.3.263).
   155 other all the others.
   158 a bunch of radish Radishes could signify
excessive leanness. See 'shotten herring' 109 and
note. In *2H4* Falstaff compares Shallow to a 'fork'd
redish' (3.2.311). According to Elyot, *Castle of
Health*, 1539, p. 35, 'Radyshe rootes have the vertu
to extenuate or make thin' (Wilson).
   158–9 three and fifty Many editors consider

this an allusion to the fifty-three Spanish ships that
opposed the *Revenge* in 1591.
   161 peppered trounced, severely injured.
   162 paid killed, settled with.
   163 call me horse A common expression of contempt; compare *TN* 2.3.186–7, 'If thou hast her not
i'th'end, call me cut' (i.e. horse, with a docked tail).
Falstaff also plays on 'no two-legg'd creature', 159.
   164 ward position of defence.
   164 here . . . point this is how I stood and how I
pointed my sword. Falstaff acts out his words.
   169 afront abreast.
   169 mainly mightily.
   170 target light shield (the 'buckler', 141). It
would be quite a feat for seven armed men abreast to
strike it at once.

FALSTAFF In buckram?

POINS Aye, four, in buckram suits.

FALSTAFF Seven, by these hilts, or I am a villain else.

PRINCE Prithee let him alone, we shall have more anon.　　　　175

FALSTAFF Dost thou hear me, Hal?

PRINCE Ay, and mark thee too, Jack.

FALSTAFF Do so, for it is worth the listening to. These nine in buckram
　　　that I told thee of –

PRINCE So, two more already.　　　　180

FALSTAFF Their points being broken –

POINS Down fell their hose.

FALSTAFF – began to give me ground. But I followed me close, came in,
　　　foot and hand, and, with a thought, seven of the eleven I paid.

PRINCE O monstrous! Eleven buckram men grown out of two!　　　　185

FALSTAFF But as the devil would have it, three misbegotten knaves in
　　　Kendal green came at my back and let drive at me, for it was so dark,
　　　Hal, that thou couldst not see thy hand.

PRINCE These lies are like their father that begets them, gross as a
　　　mountain, open, palpable. Why, thou clay-brained guts, thou　　　190
　　　knotty-pated fool, thou whoreson obscene greasy tallow-catch –

FALSTAFF What, art thou mad? Art thou mad? Is not the truth the truth?

---

177 too, Jack] Qq2–5, F *subst.;* to iacke Q1　191 -catch] QqF; chest *Dering MS.* (*orig.* catch, *then altered*); ketch *Hanmer;*
keech *Var. 1778;* cake *Cowl and Morgan*

---

174 hilts sword handle. Because it had three
parts – a knob on the end, a handle, and a hand-
guard – the 'hilt' could be referred to as both
singular and plural. Its cross-like shape made it
appropriate for swearing an oath on. Compare *Ham.*
1.5.147.

177 mark (1) pay attention to, (2) keep count
(Wilson).

181–2 Their points . . . hose An aggressive
quibble on points as (1) swords (or their sharp
ends), (2) the laces used to attach stockings to the
doublet.

183 followed me followed; ('me' is an ethical
dative, as in 89).

183–4 came . . . hand pursued closely. Here the
common phrase expresses the lunging of sword-
play; it may also suggest 'in close attendance', as if
ready to 'wait upon one hand and foot' (*OED* Foot
sv *sb* 30b).

184 with a thought as quick as thought.

186 misbegotten illegally engendered. Falstaff
is prompted by the Prince's exclamation, 185.

187 Kendal green Cloth associated with Kendal

in Westmoreland (now Cumbria), commonly worn
by foresters, servants, country people, and thieves
in disguise. Compare Robert Armin's *Nest of Nin-
nies* (1608, probably echoing Falstaff), ed. Collier,
p. xvi: 'Truth, in plaine attire, is the easier knowne:
let fixion [fiction] maske in Kendall greene' (cited
by Humphreys).

189 father Falstaff. The Prince alludes to the
saying that the Devil is the father of lies (Dent
D241.1 and F92).

190 clay-brained dull-witted.

191 knotty-pated block-headed; compare loggerheads, 4.

191 obscene disgusting.

191 tallow-catch A pan or tub to catch the fat
which drips from roasting meat. This QqF reading
echoes references to 'lard', 'tallow', and 'butter'.
The emendation 'keech', adopted by many editors,
does correspond to the Prince's adjectives. A
'keech' is the fat of a slaughtered animal, rolled up
by the butcher into a lump (*OED* sv *sb* 1).

192 Is not . . . truth? A proverbial expression
(Dent T581).

PRINCE Why, how couldst thou know these men in Kendal green when
it was so dark thou couldst not see thy hand? Come, tell us your
reason. What sayest thou to this?   195
POINS Come, your reason, Jack, your reason!   *[handwritten: God's wounds, God's blood – not quite swearing]*
FALSTAFF What, upon compulsion? Zounds, an I were at the strappado,
or all the racks in the world, I would not tell you on compulsion.
Give you a reason on compulsion? If reasons were as plentiful as
blackberries, I would give no man a reason upon compulsion, I.   200
PRINCE I'll be no longer guilty of this sin. This sanguine coward, this
bed-presser, this horse-back-breaker, this huge hill of flesh –
FALSTAFF 'Sblood, you starveling, you elf-skin, you dried neat's-
tongue, you bull's-pizzle, you stock-fish! O for breath to utter what
is like thee! You tailor's-yard, you sheath, you bow-case, you vile 205
standing tuck!

---

203 elf-skin] QQ1, 2 (elʃskin); elfskin QQ3–5; elfe-skin F; eel-skin *Hanmer*

197 strappado A kind of torture in which the victim was lifted, then let down by ropes that tied his hands behind his back, often dislocating his shoulders. He could also be dropped suddenly, fracturing many other bones.

198 racks Instruments of torture consisting of a frame, with rollers at each end, on which the victim was stretched.

199 reason on compulsion Wilson notes that 'reasons' or opinions were at that time often 'extracted by the "compulsion" of torture'.

199–200 If reasons . . . blackberries As cheap as blackberries was a common saying (Dent B442). Falstaff puns on 'raisins', pronounced much like 'reasons' (Cercignani, 235).

201 this sin i.e. failing to challenge Falstaff's lies.

201 sanguine coward 'A comic contradiction in terms' (Davison). Because of his red face and robust size, Falstaff looks like a man of sanguine temperament, which is normally associated with courage.

203 starveling emaciated person, in contrast to Falstaff.

203 elf-skin Falstaff compares the thin Prince 'to the thinnest thing he could think of . . . a fairy's skin' (Wright, ed. 1897). QQ1, 2 read 'elʃskin'. Wilson, Humphreys, and Bevington follow Hanmer by emending to 'eel-skin', which anticipates three more comparisons to fish or flesh (Hemingway) and appears in other work by Shakespeare, notably in *2H4* 3.2.325–6 when Falstaff says of the 'starved justice' Shallow, 'you might have thrust him and all his apparel into an eel-skin'. The emendation pro-

posed by Evans to 'elshin' or 'elsin' – a shoemaker's awl – would apply more to a tall than a thin man. Davison convincingly suggests that a compositor could easily mistake part of a ligatured long 's' (ʃ) for an 'f', producing elʃskin; if 'eelskin' were intended, however, the compositor has made a 'complex sequence of errors'.

203–4 neat's-tongue ox's tongue.

204 bull's-pizzle penis, dried (like the tongue) for use as a whip.

204 stock-fish dried cod. Falstaff ascribes to the Prince a dryness and sexual inadequacy more common to old age. Compare *MM* 3.2.109: 'he was begot between two stock-fishes'. Coleman, p. 216, refers to the statement by Lechery in Marlowe, *Doctor Faustus*, 2.2.708–9, 'I am one that loves an inch of raw Mutton, better than an ell of fryde Stockfish.'

205 tailor's yard yard-stick, again suggesting thinness and perhaps a lack of virility.

205 sheath empty case or cover, a retort to Hal's many gibes about Falstaff's weight, and possibly an allusion to female genitals.

205 bow-case Long thin case for unstrung bows; perhaps a figure for sexual impotence.

206 standing tuck A very small dagger that has gone stiff, losing its temper and resilience (*OED* Standing *ppl a* 8). Falstaff's sexual slur is both devastating and unusual, when he twists the more conventional bawdy sense of 'stand' from the desirable (male erection) to the undesirable (military unreadiness).

PRINCE Well, breathe a while, and then to it again, and when thou hast
tired thyself in base comparisons hear me speak but this.

POINS Mark, Jack!

PRINCE We two saw you four set on four, and bound them and were   210
masters of their wealth – mark now how a plain tale shall put you
down. Then did we two set on you four, and, with a word, out-faced
you from your prize, and have it, yea, and can show it you here in
the house. And Falstaff, you carried your guts away as nimbly, with
as quick dexterity, and roared for mercy, and still run and roared, as   215
ever I heard bull-calf. What a slave art thou to hack thy sword as
thou hast done, and then say it was in fight! What trick, what device,
what starting-hole canst thou now find out, to hide thee from this
open and apparent shame?

POINS Come, let's hear Jack, what trick hast thou now?   220

FALSTAFF By the Lord, I knew ye as well as he that made ye. Why, hear
you, my masters, was it for me to kill the heir apparent? Should I
turn upon the true prince? Why, thou knowest I am as valiant as
Hercules. But beware instinct. The lion will not touch the true
prince. Instinct is a great matter. I was now a coward on instinct. I   225
shall think the better of myself, and thee, during my life – I for a
valiant lion, and thou for a true prince. But by the Lord, lads, I am
glad you have the money! Hostess, clap to the doors! Watch tonight,
pray tomorrow! Gallants, lads, boys, hearts of gold, all the titles of
good fellowship come to you! What, shall we be merry? Shall we   230
have a play extempore?

---

215 run] Qq; ranne F   225 now] Q1; *not in* Qq2–5, F

210 set . . . bound The shift in mood to the
indicative past is a common usage.
  212 with a word (1) with only a word, quickly,
(2) with a brief shout.
  218 starting-hole bolt-hole, a hiding place for a
hunted animal, criminal, or enemy (*OED*).
  219 apparent clear, undeniable.
  221 I . . . ye A forceful use of a familiar expression (Dent K170.1). In addition to providing a climactic escape for Falstaff from a long sequence of
traps, it may ironically glance at how little the
Prince's biological father does know him.
  222 my masters gentlemen (*OED* sv sb¹ 21), a
courteous address that need not imply superiority.
  224 Hercules One of the most familiar heroes or
demigods from Greek mythology, noted for his extraordinary strength and courage.
  224–5 The lion . . . prince A belief expressed in
many Elizabethan texts, which can be traced back to
Pliny. Topsell's *Historie of Foure-footed beastes* men-

tions an English lion 'which by evident token was
able to distinguish betwixt the King, Nobles, and
vulgar sort of people' (1658 edn, p. 370, cited by
Humphreys).
  225–7 I shall . . . true prince Falstaff continues
to quibble on different meanings of 'true'.
  228 clap to shut noisily or slam (*OED* sv v¹ 4b).
  228 Watch (1) Keep guard, (2) Carouse. An
ironic echo of Lady Percy, 2.3.41, as well as of Matt.
26.41, 'Watch, and pray, that ye enter not into
tentation.' Compare Mark 14.38.
  229 pray The pun on 'prey' repeats Gadshill's
joke about predators at 2.1.64–6.
  231 play extempore Professional theatre was
prohibited at this time in inns under jurisdiction of
the City of London; scenes without written texts
often served as substitutes. See Glynne Wickham,
Early English Stages 1300–1660, vol. II, *1576–1660*,
Part II, 1972, pp. 22, 99.

PRINCE Content, and the argument shall be thy running away.

FALSTAFF Ah, no more of that Hal, an thou lovest me.

Enter HOSTESS

HOSTESS O Jesu, my lord the Prince!

PRINCE How now, my lady the Hostess, what sayest thou to me?   235

HOSTESS Marry my lord, there is a nobleman of the court at door would
    speak with you. He says he comes from your father.

PRINCE Give him as much as will make him a royal man and send him
    back again to my mother.

FALSTAFF What manner of man is he?   240

HOSTESS An old man.

FALSTAFF What doth gravity out of his bed at midnight? Shall I give
    him his answer?

PRINCE Prithee do, Jack.

FALSTAFF Faith, and I'll send him packing.   *Exit* 245

PRINCE Now sirs, by'r lady, you fought fair, so did you, Peto, so did
    you, Bardolph. You are lions too, you ran away upon instinct, you
    will not touch the true prince, no, fie!

BARDOLPH Faith, I ran when I saw others run.

PRINCE Faith, tell me now in earnest, how came Falstaff's sword so   250
    hacked?

PETO Why, he hacked it with his dagger, and said he would swear truth
    out of England but he would make you believe it was done in fight,
    and persuaded us to do the like.

BARDOLPH Yea, and to tickle our noses with spear-grass, to make them   255
    bleed, and then to beslubber our garments with it, and swear it was
    the blood of true men. I did that I did not this seven year before: I
    blushed to hear his monstrous devices.

---

246 by'r lady] Qq (birlady), *Pope;* not in F   **247** lions too,] Q1 *corr.* (lions to,) *Huntington Library copy;* lions, to Q1 *uncorr.*
British Museum and Trinity College Cambridge copies   **255** SH BARDOLPH] Q1, F (*Bar.*); *Car.* Qq2–5

232 argument plot of the story.

233 no more . . . an thou lovest me Many actors playing Falstaff assume, despite the literal
sense of 'an' as 'if', that Hal does love him, while
others convey doubt. On the varied feelings of the
Prince for Falstaff in recent productions, see Introduction, pp. 55, 58, 60; on their 'friendship', see
Introduction, pp. 31–3. Falstaff's evocative line
employs a familiar saying (Dent M1154.1).

233 SD HOSTESS See List of Characters for some
of the variations in her later parts in *2H4*, *H5*, and
Wiv.

236, 238 nobleman, royal man Hal puns on the
value of coins and on social rank. See 1.2.114–15.

242 gravity Falstaff seems to invent a Morality-
play character, one of over-earnest age.

252–3 swear . . . England 'swear so many false
oaths that Truth would flee the country . . . in horror' (Kittredge).

253 but he would i.e. if that is what he must do
to.

255–7 tickle . . . men An echo of *FV* 1426–30,
where Dericke tells how he made himself appear to
be wounded in Henry V's French campaign so that
he would not have to fight in battle.

257 that something.

PRINCE O villain, thou stolest a cup of sack eighteen years ago, and wert
taken with the manner, and ever since thou hast blushed extempore.   260
Thou hadst fire and sword on thy side, and yet thou ran'st away.
What instinct hadst thou for it?

BARDOLPH My lord, do you see these meteors? Do you behold these
exhalations?

PRINCE I do.   265

BARDOLPH What think you they portend?

PRINCE Hot livers, and cold purses.

BARDOLPH Choler, my lord, if rightly taken.

PRINCE No, if rightly taken, halter.

Enter FALSTAFF

Here comes lean Jack, here comes bare-bone. How now my sweet   270
creature of bombast, how long is't ago, Jack, since thou sawest thine
own knee?

FALSTAFF My own knee? When I was about thy years, Hal, I was not an
eagle's talon in the waist – I could have crept into any alderman's
thumb-ring. A plague of sighing and grief, it blows a man up like a   275

---

269 SD *Enter* FALSTAFF] F; *after 268*, Qq   274 talon] QqF (talent)

---

260 taken with the manner A common legal
expression (Dent M633) meaning caught in the act.
By turning Bardolph's face red, the sack has betrayed his crime.

260 blushed extempore All blushing is
unplanned or spontaneous. The Prince mocks
Bardolph's pretence of sincerity, 257–8, by jesting
that he has been turning on this blush for eighteen
years.

261 fire and sword i.e. invincible military
might. The fire comes from Bardolph's complexion.

264 exhalations fiery meteors, as in *Rom.* 3.5.13,
'It is some meteor that the sun [exhal'd]'. In some
productions, Bardolph points to his face to signify
ominous portents in the heavens.

267 Hot livers, and cold purses Drink will heat
the liver, i.e. (1) the seat in the body of courage and
love, (2) one who lives. Paying for the drink will
empty the purse.

268 Choler A temperament dominated by anger.
Bardolph tries to pretend that his face shows his
wrathful nature.

268 rightly taken correctly interpreted.

269 No . . . halter The Prince manages to pun
on three of his five words: rightly (justly), taken
(arrested), and halter (choler, collar, the hangman's
noose).

269 SD In some productions, Bardolph leaves
when Falstaff enters. QqF provide no exits for
Bardolph, the Hostess or Francis – none of whom
speaks until Bardolph enters 'running' at 399 below,
soon followed by the Hostess, 403. Although confused and informal movement seems appropriate
for a tavern late at night, Shakespeare probably left
the movements of these two actors to be worked out
in rehearsal. They might have remained visible to
the audience while they listened to Hal and Falstaff.

271 bombast (1) cotton stuffing (*OED* sv *sb* 2b),
(2) inflated language (*OED* sv *sb* 3).

274 talon claw. The QqF spelling 'talent' was one
of several variants. Compare, 'If a talent be a claw',
LLL 4.2.63.

274–5 alderman's thumb-ring Worn on the
thumb, it might be decorated with a seal and used to
stamp documents. (First reference in *OED*). An
alderman was the chief officer of a London ward.

275–6 it . . . bladder i.e. it turns a man into a
windbag. Animal bladders, used as containers,
floats, or in bagpipes (see 1.2.61 and *OED* 3), could
signify frivolity; compare *H8* 3.2.359, 'little wanton
boys that swim on bladders' (as in Brueghel's
carnivalesque painting *Children's Games*). This
parody of renunciation, Bevington notes, distorts
the received belief that grief, by making the heart

bladder. There's villainous news abroad. Here was Sir John Bracy
from your father. You must to the court in the morning. That same
mad fellow of the north, Percy, and he of Wales that gave Amamon
the bastinado, and made Lucifer cuckold, and swore the devil his
true liegeman upon the cross of a Welsh hook – what a plague call   280
you him?

POINS   O, Glendower.

FALSTAFF   Owen, Owen, the same. And his son-in-law Mortimer, and
old Northumberland, and that sprightly Scot of Scots, Douglas,
that runs a-horseback up a hill perpendicular –   285

PRINCE   He that rides at high speed, and with his pistol kills a sparrow
flying.

FALSTAFF   You have hit it.

PRINCE   So did he never the sparrow.

FALSTAFF   Well, that rascal hath good mettle in him, he will not run.   290

PRINCE   Why, what a rascal art thou then, to praise him so for running!

FALSTAFF   A-horseback, ye cuckoo, but afoot he will not budge a foot.

PRINCE   Yes, Jack, upon instinct.

FALSTAFF   I grant ye, upon instinct. Well, he is there too, and one
Mordake, and a thousand blue-caps more. Worcester is stolen away   295
tonight. Thy father's beard is turned white with the news. You may
buy land now as cheap as stinking mackerel.

PRINCE   Why then, it is like if there come a hot June, and this civil

292 afoot] Qq2, 3; a foote Qq1, 4, 5, F

contract, withdraws heat, blood, and colour from
the body.

276 Bracy The chronicles and other sources do
not mention this name.

278 Amamon A major devil. Reginald Scot, *Discovery of Witchcraft* (1584), identifies him as 'king of
the east' (xv, 3) and 'king Baell' or Amoiman (xv,
19) (cited by Humphreys).

279 bastinado A blow with a stick or club, especially on the soles of the feet (*OED* sv *sb* 1).

279 made . . . cuckold gave him his horns by
seducing his wife.

279–80 swore . . . Welsh hook made him swear
allegiance as a vassal upon a billhook, a hooked staff
used as a rustic weapon which had no hilt, and
therefore no cross upon which to swear. Falstaff
travesties Glendower's reputation for supernatural
powers.

290 mettle . . . run Pun on mettle as (1) courageous temperament, (2) metal which dissolves if
poorly made. 'Mettle', like QqF 'mettall', is a variant
spelling of 'metal'. Compare 10 above.

292 cuckoo witless repeater, who misses the
figurative sense of 'run', 290, and remembers the
literal one, 285. Compare 'ape', 2.3.71, and
'paraquito', 2.3.79.

292 afoot in hand-to-hand combat (Bevington).
Compare 'foot and hand', 184 above.

295 Mordake Earl of Fife. For Shakespeare's
misidentification of him as Douglas' son, see 1.1.71
and n.

295 blue-caps Scottish soldiers wearing blue
hats.

297 as cheap . . . mackerel extremely inexpensive, almost for nothing. This fish has gone bad, but
it cost very little even when fresh.

298–9 it is . . . hob-nails 'Given the heat of
summer, and the excitements of civil war, the girls
won't resist us at all' (Humphreys). This reading
omits the dark weight of 'hob-nails', used to protect
heavy boots (*OED* sv *sb* 1). As 'booty', the Prince
implies, the maidens will have no power to resist
attack. Compare 2.1.66 and n.

298 like likely, probable.

buffeting hold, we shall buy maidenheads as they buy hob-nails, by
the hundreds.   300

FALSTAFF By the mass, lad, thou sayest true, it is like we shall have
good trading that way. But tell me, Hal, art not thou horrible
afeard? Thou being heir apparent, could the world pick thee out
three such enemies again, as that fiend Douglas, that spirit Percy,
and that devil Glendower? Art thou not horribly afraid? Doth not   305
thy blood thrill at it?

PRINCE Not a whit, i'faith, I lack some of thy instinct.

FALSTAFF Well, thou wilt be horribly chid tomorrow when thou
comest to thy father. If thou love me, practise an answer.

PRINCE Do thou stand for my father and examine me upon the particu-   310
lars of my life.

FALSTAFF Shall I? Content! This chair shall be my state, this dagger my
sceptre, and this cushion my crown.

PRINCE Thy state is taken for a joint-stool, thy golden sceptre for a
leaden dagger, and thy precious rich crown for a pitiful bald crown.   315

FALSTAFF Well, an the fire of grace be not quite out of thee, now shalt
thou be moved. Give me a cup of sack to make my eyes look red,
that it may be thought I have wept, for I must speak in passion, and
I will do it in King Cambyses' vein.

PRINCE Well, here is my leg.   320

FALSTAFF And here is my speech. Stand aside, nobility.

HOSTESS O Jesu, this is excellent sport, i'faith.

---

299 buffeting fighting, with a sense of blows struck in hand-to-hand combat.

299 hold takes place.

304 spirit devil, as well as the embodiment of courage.

306 thrill shiver as if cold.

310–11 Do thou . . . life Perhaps suggested by *FV* 386–416 where Dericke the clown pretends to be the Prince and John Cobler, the Lord Chief Justice.

312 state royal throne, a basic prop on the Elizabethan stage.

314–15 Thy state . . . crown The Prince playfully reverses the process of theatrical illusion (in which a 'stool' would normally be 'taken for', or believed to be, a throne) both to mock the power of illusion and to imply its fragility.

314 joint-stool stool well made by a joiner or skilled craftsman, but still the most ordinary and movable of furnishings. Compare *Shr.* 2.1.198–9.

315 leaden dagger knife made of a baser metal,

too heavy to be useful. Compare 'dagger of lath', 116, and n.

315 pitiful bald crown This surprising substitution for 'cushion' may suggest that as the eye of the subject moves from the bottom (the well-made joint stool) to the top of this monarch, expectations of majesty are increasingly frustrated.

318 in passion with deep emotion. Compare 344 and n.

319 King Cambyses' vein The style of Thomas Preston's *Lamentable Tragedie, mixed full of plesant mirth, containing the Life of Cambises King of Persia* (1569). Both its style and its title were parodied in the entertainment staged by the craftsmen in *MND* called 'A tedious brief scene of young Pyramus / And his love Thisby; very tragical mirth' (5.1.56–7). Falstaff's 'vein' combines extravagant analogies modelled on John Lyly's 'euphuism' with more parody of Puritan sermons.

320 here . . . leg A stage direction: Hal bows to Falstaff as he speaks. Courtiers drew back one leg while bending the other.

FALSTAFF Weep not, sweet Queen, for trickling tears are vain.

HOSTESS O the Father, how he holds his countenance!

FALSTAFF For God's sake, lords, convey my tristful Queen,   325
For tears do stop the floodgates of her eyes.

HOSTESS O Jesu, he doth it as like one of these harlotry players as ever
I see!

FALSTAFF Peace, good pint-pot, peace, good tickle-brain. Harry, I do
not only marvel where thou spendest thy time, but also how thou   330
art accompanied. For though the camomile, the more it is trodden
on the faster it grows, yet youth, the more it is wasted the sooner it
wears. That thou art my son I have partly thy mother's word, partly
my own opinion, but chiefly a villainous trick of thine eye, and a
foolish hanging of thy nether lip, that doth warrant me. If then thou 335
be son to me – here lies the point – why, being son to me, art thou
so pointed at? Shall the blessed sun of heaven prove a micher, and
eat blackberries? A question not to be asked. Shall the son of England prove a thief, and take purses? A question to be asked. There
is a thing, Harry, which thou hast often heard of, and it is known to   340
many in our land by the name of pitch. This pitch – as ancient

---

324 Father] F; father Qq   325 tristful] *Dering MS., Rowe;* trustfull QqF   327 Jesu] Qq; rare F   332 yet] Qq3–5, F;
so Qq1, 2   337 sun] Q1 (sunne); sonne Qq2–5, F

---

323 **Weep not . . . vain** Weeping queens and
paramours were common in early plays about ty-
rants and conquerors. 'Then, daintie damsell, stint
these trickling teares' from Greene's *Alphonsus,
King of Aragon*, ed. Grosart (1881–6), line 1825, is
the closest of many analogues that have been proposed. Greene probably parodied Tamburlaine's
high-flying response to Zenocrate's wet 'passion'
(Marlowe, *1 Tamburlaine* 5.135 ff.).

325 **tristful** sorrowful (*OED* sv *a*²). This emendation (Dering *MS.*) has been generally preferred to
'trustfull' in QqF. Because 'tristful' could also mean
'trustworthy' (*OED* sv *a*¹), the emendation retains
Falstaff's frequent word-play on loyalty and truth.

327 **harlotry** knavish, worthless; here and at
3.1.192 used with affection.

329 **pint-pot, tickle-brain** Names suggesting
the hostess' trade; 'tickle-brain' was 'slang for a kind
of strong liquor' (Humphreys).

331–3 **camomile . . . wears** An aromatic plant
with white leaves which proverbially grew faster the
more it was stepped on (Dent C34). Shakespeare
closely parodies Lyly's *Euphues* (ed. Bond, I, 196).
This ludicrous contrast between camomile, a creep-
ing ground-cover, and the Prince's prodigality,
launches Falstaff. 'His sustained speech and labori-

ous working out of rhetorical propositions and
questions establish his pretended authority; and at
the same time, sexual innuendoes, everyday comparisons, triteness, and near-nonsense, all mock that
authority' (John Russell Brown, ed., *Shakespeare in
Performance*, 1976, p. 151).

333 **thy mother's word** Compare the familiar
expression, 'Ask the mother if the child be like his
father' (Dent M1193). Only in this scene (239 above
and here) and only in jest are there references to the
mother of the Prince.

334 **trick** characteristic. Compare 5.2.11.

335 **foolish** ridiculous, wanting in judgement.

337–8 **Shall . . . blackberries** An echo of Lyly's
Campaspe, pointed out by Arnold Davenport, *N&Q*
199 (1954), 19. Hephaestion, the emperor, rebukes
Alexander for desiring the beautiful slave girl,
Campaspe, alleging that 'Bewty is like the black-
berry, which seemeth red when it is not ripe' (Bond,
ed., 2.2.48, noted by Bevington).

337 **micher** truant (*OED* sv *sb* 3).

341–2 **This pitch . . . defile** A pious allusion to
Eccles. 13.1: 'He that toucheth pitch, shalbe defiled
with it.' Lyly alludes to this text in *Euphues to
Philautus*, ed. Bond, I, 250 and in *Euphues to his
Friend Livia*, I, 320.

writers do report – doth defile, so doth the company thou keepest. For, Harry, now I do not speak to thee in drink, but in tears; not in pleasure, but in passion; not in words only, but in woes also. And yet there is a virtuous man whom I have often noted in thy com-   345
pany, but I know not his name.

PRINCE What manner of man, an it like your majesty?

FALSTAFF A goodly portly man, i'faith, and a corpulent; of a cheerful look, a pleasing eye, and a most noble carriage; and, as I think, his age some fifty, or by'r lady, inclining to three score. And now I   350
remember me, his name is Falstaff. If that man should be lewdly given, he deceiveth me, for, Harry, I see virtue in his looks. If then the tree may be known by the fruit, as the fruit by the tree, then peremptorily I speak it, there is virtue in that Falstaff. Him keep with, the rest banish. And tell me now, thou naughty varlet, tell me   355
where hast thou been this month?

PRINCE Dost thou speak like a king? Do thou stand for me, and I'll play my father.

FALSTAFF Depose me? If thou dost it half so gravely, so majestically, both in word and matter, hang me up by the heels for a rabbit-   360
sucker, or a poulter's hare.

PRINCE Well, here I am set.

FALSTAFF And here I stand. Judge, my masters.

PRINCE Now, Harry, whence come you?

FALSTAFF My noble lord, from Eastcheap.   365

343 Harry, now] Q1 *corr.* (Harrie, now) *Huntington Library copy;* Harrie now Q1 *uncorr. British Museum and Trinity College Cambridge copies*

343–4 **For, Harry . . . also** The excessive balance and antithesis of these phrases typifies euphuism; it also resonates with the repeated use of 'no more' by King Henry in the first speech of the play.

343 **not . . . in drink** Like Falstaff, Cambyses loved to drink.

344 **passion** suffering, but also a tragic performance, as in Thisbe's concluding 'passion' (*MND* 5.1.315).

348 **portly** stately, majestic; compare 1.3.13 and n.

348 **corpulent** 'full-bodied – not in the modern sense of "extremely stout"' (Kittredge). Falstaff flatters himself through understatement.

351–2 **lewdly given** disposed to act wickedly or lasciviously.

352–3 **If . . . tree** A popular saying from Matt. 12.33, 'the tre is knowen by the frute'; compare Luke 6.44 and Dent T497. Lyly alludes to this say-

ing in *Euphues – The Anatomy of Wit*, ed. Bond, I, 207): 'No, no, ye tree is knowen by his fruite, the golde by his touch, the sonne by the sire.'

354 **peremptorily** decisively.

355–6 **And . . . month** Falstaff suddenly changes the subject and adopts the tone of a normal father scolding his young son. The Prince responds to his question by proposing that they exchange roles.

360–1 **rabbit-sucker** baby rabbit, extremely lean.

361 **poulter's hare** one hanging in a poulterer's shop.

362 **Well . . . set** The Prince takes his place rapidly, omitting elaborate business with props. For examples of the extreme variety of attitudes and responses possible for both Hal and Falstaff in this sequence, see Introduction, pp. 14, 49, 55 and illustration 7.

[handwritten: Falstaff trying to be Henry IV in a euphuism play]

PRINCE The complaints I hear of thee are grievous.

FALSTAFF 'Sblood, my lord, they are false! Nay, I'll tickle ye for a
young prince, i'faith.

PRINCE Swearest thou, ungracious boy? Henceforth ne'er look on me.
Thou art violently carried away from grace. There is a devil haunts   370
thee in the likeness of an old fat man, a tun of man is thy companion.
Why dost thou converse with that trunk of humours, that bolting-
hutch of beastliness, that swollen parcel of dropsies, that huge
bombard of sack, that stuffed cloak-bag of guts, that roasted
Manningtree ox with the pudding in his belly, that reverend Vice,   375
that grey Iniquity, that Father Ruffian, that Vanity in years?
Wherein is he good, but to taste sack and drink it? Wherein neat and
cleanly, but to carve a capon and eat it? Wherein cunning, but in
craft? Wherein crafty, but in villainy? Wherein villainous, but in all
things? Wherein worthy, but in nothing?   380

FALSTAFF I would your grace would take me with you. Whom means
your grace?

PRINCE That villainous abominable misleader of youth, Falstaff, that
old white-bearded Satan.

FALSTAFF My lord, the man I know.   385

PRINCE I know thou dost.

FALSTAFF But to say I know more harm in him than in myself were to

[right margin handwritten: cf HIV & what HV will become]

---

367 tickle ye for please you as; perhaps an aside
to the onstage audience.

369 ungracious profane, in response to
Falstaff's ''Sblood'.

369 Henceforth . . . me In retrospect, we can
observe that this statement will apply to Falstaff,
but not to the Prince, whose father will never give
such a command.

371 tun (1) large barrel for wine or beer, (2) ton.

372 converse keep company with (*OED* sv *v* 2).

372 trunk large chest, with a pun on Falstaff's
torso.

372 humours The four bodily fluids: blood,
phlegm, choler, and melancholy. In balanced pro-
portions, they maintain health. Here they are mor-
bid and excessive, producing disease.

372–3 bolting-hutch bin used to sift impurities
from grain. The hutch retains only those coarse
impurities.

373 dropsies diseased condition caused by fluids
accumulating in body cavities.

374 bombard large leather vessel for wine.

374 cloak-bag bag used to carry any clothing.
The figurative sense of pretence (*OED* Cloak sv *v*
3a) may slip in.

374–5 that . . . belly A roasted ox, its own guts
replaced with a bag-pudding or a stuffing of grain or
minced meat (vs 'rabbit-sucker', 360–1). In *Christes
Teares Over Jerusalem*, 1593 (ed. McKerrow, II,
180), Nashe wrote, 'All the rest of his invention is
nothing but an oxe with a pudding in his bellie'
(Wilson). Manningtree, a small town near the estuary of the River Stour in Essex, seems to have been
noted for Morality plays, probably performed at a
fair (Humphreys).

375–6 reverend Vice . . . Vanity in years
Morality plays and Interludes portrayed characters
known as Vice, Iniquity, and Vanity. Ruffian was a
name for the Devil. The Prince plays upon the
incongruity between Falstaff's age and behaviour.

378 cleanly adroit or clever in action (*OED* sv *a*
5).

378 cunning skilful.

381 take me with you (1) let me catch up with
your meaning or (2) slow down for me. Compare
Dent T28.1.

383–4 That . . . Satan The crucial Morality-
play role of tempter was frequently taken by evil
companions and Vices rather than by the Devil
himself.

say more than I know. That he is old, the more the pity, his white
hairs do witness it, but that he is, saving your reverence, a
whoremaster, that I utterly deny. If sack and sugar be a fault, God 390
help the wicked! If to be old and merry be a sin, then many an old
host that I know is damned. If to be fat be to be hated, then
Pharaoh's lean kine are to be loved. No, my good lord! Banish Peto,
banish Bardolph, banish Poins – but for sweet Jack Falstaff, kind
Jack Falstaff, true Jack Falstaff, valiant Jack Falstaff – and therefore 395
more valiant, being as he is old Jack Falstaff – banish not him thy
Harry's company, banish not him thy Harry's company. Banish
plump Jack, and banish all the world.
PRINCE   I do, I will.

[*A knocking heard*]
[*Exeunt Hostess, Francis, and Bardolph*]

Enter BARDOLPH *running*

BARDOLPH   O my lord, my lord, the Sheriff with a most monstrous 400
watch is at the door.
FALSTAFF   Out, ye rogue! Play out the play! I have much to say in the
behalf of that Falstaff.

Enter the HOSTESS

HOSTESS   O Jesu, my lord, my lord!
PRINCE   Heigh, heigh, the devil rides upon a fiddle-stick. What's the 405
matter?

393 lean] QQ2–5, F; lane Q1   399 SD. 1, 2 *A knocking . . . and Bardolph*] Malone; *not in* QQF   405 SH PRINCE] QQ1–3; *Fal.*
QQ4, 5, F *subst.;* Poyn./ Dering MS.

389 saving your reverence A polite expression
used to introduce disagreement. See Dent R93.
393 Pharaoh's lean kine In Gen. 41 Joseph
interprets the Pharaoh's dream, in which seven
'evilfavoured and leane fleshed' cattle devour seven
fat ones, by predicting seven years of famine.
399 I do, I will Clearly distinguished in tone and
syntax from the earlier verbal attack in which the
Prince plays his father, this short line provokes conspicuous, if widely divergent responses from stage
Falstaffs. Falstaff may clearly hear the four words or
he may not; he may believe the Prince or think he
merely jests. There may be a long pause or immediate commotion with the knocking. Some of these
choices, even with the same actor, may well vary
from day to day. The line offers a timely reminder
of the Prince's soliloquy in 1.2. See Introduction,
pp. 49, 53–4.

399 SDS *A knocking . . . running* Most editions
and many productions welcome this series of directions proposed by Malone. The knocking can
'ensure that an even keel is restored' (Davison) or
replace an intensely personal confrontation with an
alarming reminder of the outside world. QQF simply
give 'Enter Bardoll running' and at 403 below,
'Enter the hostesse'. Compare 269 SD and n.
401 watch A group of citizens chosen to keep
order in the streets, especially at night. In *FV*, the
Mayor tells King Henry that the Prince was arrested because, when brawling with his companions
outside the 'Eastcheape' tavern, 'neither watchmen
nor any other could stay them' (248).
405 devil . . . fiddle-stick A saying or pseudo-proverb possibly invented by Hal (Dent D263). Its
nonsense heightens his practical question.

HOSTESS The Sheriff and all the watch are at the door. They are come
to search the house. Shall I let them in?

FALSTAFF Dost thou hear, Hal? Never call a true piece of gold a counterfeit. Thou art essentially made without seeming so.   410

PRINCE And thou a natural coward without instinct.

FALSTAFF I deny your major. If you will deny the Sheriff, so; if not, let
him enter. If I become not a cart as well as another man, a plague on
my bringing up! I hope I shall as soon be strangled with a halter as
another.   415

PRINCE Go hide thee behind the arras, the rest walk up above. Now, my
masters, for a true face, and good conscience.

FALSTAFF Both which I have had, but their date is out, and therefore
I'll hide me.

[Exeunt all but the Prince and Peto]

PRINCE Call in the Sheriff.   420

Enter SHERIFF *and the* CARRIER

---

410 made] Qq, F1, F2; mad F3, F4   419 SD *Exeunt . . . Peto*] Collier; *Exit* F; *not in* Qq

409–10 Never . . . so These two short sentences
have become one of the most disputed passages in
1H4. The general import of the first sentence,
'Never call . . . counterfeit', seems unexception-
able. The validity of the application of 'true gold' to
Falstaff himself may be uncertain, but it does continue arguments and images he has repeatedly used.
The relation of this first sentence to the second,
however, raises difficulties. Of three problematic
words in the second sentence, 'Thou . . . so', two –
'essentially' and 'seeming' – develop from 'true' and
'counterfeit' in the preceding statement. The third
word, 'made' or 'mad', has become a difficult crux.
410 Thou . . . so Perhaps meaning 'You are basi-
cally true/loyal to your friends even if your last
speeches do not show this.' In this second statement, Falstaff abruptly changes the subject from
himself to the Prince, and attributes to Hal his own
paradoxical sense of truth.

By reading 'made' as 'mad', F3 (followed by
Malone, Wilson, and many other editors) not only
introduced a spelling variant, but suggested other
possibilities for interpretation. Falstaff could be
calling the Prince a madcap who is only playing
games no matter how well he acts (compare 192
above). But the earlier Qq reading 'made', although
more difficult at first for modern audiences, has a
stronger case. It would apply the preceding metaphors of 'true gold' and 'counterfeit', which echo

earlier word-play on debased metals (290, 315).
Falstaff would again be insinuating that he has true
and real value, developing his 'Banish plump Jack
and banish all the world.'

411 And . . . instinct By echoing Falstaff's syntax, the Prince yokes 'instinct' with 'seeming', again
rejecting as pretence Falstaff's claim that he ran
away because he recognised the Prince.

412 your major i.e. your fundamental premise
(that I am an 'essential' or natural coward).

412 deny the Sheriff Falstaff quibbles on three
senses: (1) prevent him from entering, (2) reject his
authority, (3) contradict him (as in 'deny your
major').

413 become not do not behave suitably.

413 cart wagon used to expose disgraced crimi-
nals while carrying them to the gallows.

414 bringing up (1) breeding or raising, (2) being summoned before a law court or taken physically to the gallows.

416 arras curtain or tapestry, possibly hanging
from projecting frames on the back wall of the stage.

418 date is out lease has expired (compare Dent
D42.1).

419 SD *Exeunt . . . Peto* There has been editorial
controversy about whether Peto or Poins should
remain, but Peto is identified three times below as
speaker by QqF. F additionally attributes 448–52 below to Peto.

Now, master Sheriff, what is your will with me?
SHERIFF First, pardon me, my lord. A hue and cry
Hath followed certain men unto this house.
PRINCE What men?
SHERIFF One of them is well known, my gracious lord,   425
A gross fat man.
CARRIER As fat as butter.
PRINCE The man I do assure you is not here,
For I myself at this time have employed him.
And Sheriff, I will engage my word to thee,   430
That I will by tomorrow dinner-time
Send him to answer thee, or any man,
For anything he shall be charged withal.
And so let me entreat you leave the house.
SHERIFF I will, my lord. There are two gentlemen   435
Have in this robbery lost three hundred marks.
PRINCE It may be so. If he have robbed these men
He shall be answerable. And so, farewell.
SHERIFF Good night, my noble lord.
PRINCE I think it is good morrow, is it not?   440
SHERIFF Indeed, my lord, I think it be two o'clock.

Exit [with Carrier]

PRINCE This oily rascal is known as well as Paul's. Go call him forth.
PETO Falstaff! Fast asleep behind the arras, and snorting like a horse.
PRINCE Hark how hard he fetches breath. Search his pockets.

[Peto] searches his pockets, and finds certain papers

What hast thou found?   445
PETO Nothing but papers, my lord.
PRINCE Let's see what they be, read them.

[handwritten margin note beside lines 429–433:] indicative of what he is about to become

---

421–7 Now . . . butter] *As verse*, Pope; *as prose*, QqF   441 SD *with Carrier*] Hanmer *subst.; not in* QqF   443, 446, 461 SH
PETO] QqF; *Poins/ Dering MS., Var. 1773, conj. Johnson*   444 SD *Peto*] *He* QqF

422 hue and cry citizens banded in pursuit of a criminal.

428 not here True of course only in a literal sense because Falstaff is behind the arras. The actor might emphasise 'here', thereby equivocating to avoid a direct lie.

430 engage pledge.

431–2 I will . . . answer thee This forceful, unambiguous lie may create insecurity for audiences (in deciding when to believe the promises of the Prince).

431 dinner-time Usually about noon.

433 withal with (*OED prep.*)

436 three hundred marks Compare 133–4 and n.

442 Paul's The gothic cathedral of St Paul's, later (like the Boar's Head tavern) destroyed in the London fire of 1666. It towers over the City in drawings and prints contemporary with Shakespeare.

[PETO] [*Reads*] *Item a capon*   *2s. 2d.*
    Item sauce   *4d.*
    Item sack two gallons   *5s. 8d.*   450
    Item anchovies and sack after supper *2s. 6d.*
    Item bread   *ob.*

[PRINCE] O monstrous! But one half-pennyworth of bread to this intolerable deal of sack? What there is else keep close, we'll read it at
more advantage. There let him sleep till day. I'll to the court in the   455
morning. We must all to the wars, and thy place shall be honourable. I'll procure this fat rogue a charge of foot, and I know his death
will be a march of twelve score. The money shall be paid back again
with advantage. Be with me betimes in the morning, and so, good
morrow, Peto.   460

PETO Good morrow, good my lord.

                                                                  Exeunt

[3.1] *Enter* HOTSPUR, WORCESTER, LORD MORTIMER, OWEN
GLENDOWER

MORTIMER These promises are fair, the parties sure,
    And our induction full of prosperous hope.
HOTSPUR Lord Mortimer, and cousin Glendower, will you sit down?
    And uncle Worcester. A plague upon it!

---

448 SH PETO] F; *not in* Qq; *Poin.*/ *Dering MS., Var. 1773, conj. Johnson*   448 SD *Reads*] *Capell; not in* QqF   453 SH PRINCE]
F; *not in* Qq   **Act 3, Scene 1**   3.1] *Actus Tertius. Scena Prima.* F; *not in* Qq   3–9 Lord . . . heaven] *As verse, Humphreys,*
F *subst., printing line 3 as* Lord . . . Glendower / Will . . . downe?; *as prose,* Qq

451 anchovies Often eaten to increase thirst and
to improve the taste of wine; first use recorded in
OED.

452 ob. obolus or halfpenny.

453–4 intolerable exceedingly great (*OED* 1c,
this example).

454 deal portion.

454 close secret, hidden.

454–5 at more advantage at a better time.

457 charge of foot company of infantry.

458–9 The money . . . advantage For this detail, Shakespeare may be indebted to Stow's *Chronicles* (Bullough, p. 219). In *FV*, the Prince protects
the thieves without repaying the stolen money.

459 advantage interest.

459 betimes early.

Act 3, Scene 1
[3.1] The basis of this unhistorical scene is
Holinshed's brief reference (III, 22) to the 'tripartite

indenture' sealed by 'deputies' of the lords at the
house of the archdeacon of Bangor in Wales. Shakespeare brings together the Percys, Mortimer, and
Glendower, apparently in Glendower's home.

2 induction beginning, as in a brief scene before
the main action of a play.

3–10 Lord . . . spoke of Printed as eight lines of
prose by Qq, probably in order to save space; the F
compositor stretched the passage into eleven lines
of text, nine in verse, but printed Hotspur's reply,
'And . . . of', 9–10, as prose. This edition follows
Humphreys' lineation as irregular verse because
lines 3 and 7 'cannot be reduced to decasyllables
without producing surplus words which improperly
halt the rhythm'.

3 cousin Compare 1.1.31 and n.

I have forgot the map.
GLENDOWER   No, here it is.   5
Sit, cousin Percy, sit, good cousin Hotspur;
For by that name as oft as Lancaster doth speak of you
His cheek looks pale, and with a rising sigh
He wisheth you in heaven.
HOTSPUR   And you in hell,
As oft as he hears Owen Glendower spoke of.   10
GLENDOWER I cannot blame him. At my nativity
The front of heaven was full of fiery shapes,
Of burning cressets, and at my birth
The frame and huge foundation of the earth
Shaked like a coward.
HOTSPUR   Why, so it would have done   15
At the same season if your mother's cat
Had but kittened, though yourself had never been born.
GLENDOWER I say the earth did shake when I was born.
HOTSPUR And I say the earth was not of my mind,
If you suppose as fearing you, it shook.   20
GLENDOWER The heavens were all on fire, the earth did tremble –
HOTSPUR O, then the earth shook to see the heavens on fire,
And not in fear of your nativity.
Diseasèd nature oftentimes breaks forth
In strange eruptions, oft the teeming earth   25
Is with a kind of colic pinched and vexed
By the imprisoning of unruly wind
Within her womb, which for enlargement striving

9–10 And . . . of] *As verse, Collier; as prose,* QqF   15–17 Why . . . born] *As verse, Pope; as prose,* QqF

7 **Lancaster** The King, referred to by his former title as a duke. See 60 below, where Glendower again implicitly denies the King's legitimacy by calling him Henry Bullingbrook.

11–15 **At my nativity . . . coward** Shakespeare expands upon Holinshed's suggestion that 'strange wonders happened (as men reported) at the nativitie of this man' (III, 21). Holinshed's preceding syntax makes it possible to interpret 'this man' as Mortimer rather than Glendower.

12 **front** The sky personified as having a face or forehead.

13 **cressets** torches (*OED* 2). Glendower refers to an astonishing display of comets or to lights which may have ominous significance; compare the beacon in *Per.* 1.4.87.

24–30 **Diseasèd . . . towers** This explanation

of earthquakes may be traced back to Aristotle, *Meteorologica* and Pliny, *Natural History*. Gabriel Harvey, *Pleasant . . . Discourse of the Earthquake in Aprill Last*, 1580 (ed. Grosart, I, 52) describes the 'Materiall Cause' as 'great aboundance of wynde, or stoare of grosse and drye vapors, and spirites fast shut up, & as a man would saye, emprysoned in the Caues, and Dungeons of the Earth: which winde or vapors, seeking to be set at libertie . . . violently rush out' (cited by Humphreys).

25 **eruptions** (1) the bursting out of powerful natural forces, (2) outbreaks of disease.

25 **teeming** bearing offspring.

28 **enlargement** release from confinement (*OED* 5a). Hotspur's metaphors associate the earth's symptoms, and indirectly Glendower, with flatulence as well as childbirth.

Shakes the old beldam earth, and topples down
Steeples and moss-grown towers. At your birth   30
Our grandam earth, having this distemperature,
In passion shook.
GLENDOWER   Cousin, of many men
I do not bear these crossings. Give me leave
To tell you once again that at my birth
The front of heaven was full of fiery shapes,   35
The goats ran from the mountains, and the herds
Were strangely clamorous to the frighted fields.
These signs have marked me extraordinary,
And all the courses of my life do show
I am not in the roll of common men.   40
Where is he living, clipped in with the sea
That chides the banks of England, Scotland, Wales,
Which calls me pupil or hath read to me?
And bring him out that is but woman's son
Can trace me in the tedious ways of art,   45
And hold me pace in deep experiments.
HOTSPUR   I think there's no man speaks better Welsh.
    I'll to dinner.
MORTIMER   Peace, cousin Percy, you will make him mad.
GLENDOWER   I can call spirits from the vasty deep.   50
HOTSPUR   Why, so can I, or so can any man,
    But will they come when you do call for them?
GLENDOWER   Why, I can teach you, cousin, to command the devil.

---

44 son] Q1 *corr.* (sonne) *British Museum copy,* F; sonne? Q1 *uncorr. Huntington Library and Trinity College Cambridge copies*

---

29 beldam Synonymous with grandam or grandmother, as at 31.

31 distemperature disorder of the body (*OED* 2), as in 'colic' (26); compare *Err.* 5.1.81–2, 'At her heeles a huge infectious troop / Of pale distemperatures'.

32 passion fit of suffering.

32 of from.

33 crossings thwartings, contradictions.

37 frighted terrified.

41 clipped in surrounded by.

42 chides chafes with a rough, brawling sound.

43 Which Who.

43 read to instructed.

45 trace . . . art follow my tracks in the demanding discipline of magic.

46 hold me pace keep up with me.

47 no man speaks better Welsh i.e. the lan-guage I cannot understand is better than his Eng-lish. Hotspur rudely implies that Glendower (1) only boasts, (2) talks too much. The transparent 'compliment' insults all speakers of Welsh.

50 call summon, convene (using my art).

50 vasty deep huge abyss (*OED* sv *sb* 3c, this example); perhaps also a transposition of 'the depths of vastness', suggesting an unfathomable immensity.

52 call for Hotspur twists 'call', 50, which im-plied success through magic art, into a simple do-mestic cry, one that may well be futile.

53–4 teach you, cousin . . . teach thee, coz Hotspur reduces Glendower's 'you' to 'thee' and 'cousin' to 'coz', giving additional signs of his lack of respect for his older host. These words may im-ply that Hotspur tries to assume the role of com-manding officer. His thrice-repeated 'tell truth' and

HOTSPUR   And I can teach thee, coz, to shame the devil
      By telling truth. Tell truth, and shame the devil.   55
      If thou have power to raise him, bring him hither,
      And I'll be sworn I have power to shame him hence.
      O, while you live, tell truth, and shame the devil!
MORTIMER   Come, come, no more of this unprofitable chat.
GLENDOWER   Three times hath Henry Bullingbrook made head   60
      Against my power, thrice from the banks of Wye
      And sandy-bottomed Severn have I sent him
      Bootless home, and weather-beaten back.
HOTSPUR   Home without boots, and in foul weather too!
      How scapes he agues, in the devil's name?   65
GLENDOWER   Come, here is the map, shall we divide our right
      According to our threefold order taken?
MORTIMER   The Archdeacon hath divided it
      Into three limits very equally.
      England, from Trent and Severn hitherto,   70
      By south and east is to my part assigned.
      All westward, Wales beyond the Severn shore,
      And all the fertile land within that bound,

---

54 coz] Q1 (coose); Cousin F

'shame the devil' in this short speech suggest how coherent argument is giving way to 'unprofitable chat', 59.

55 Tell . . . devil Proverbial saying (Dent T566). Hotspur continues to treat Glendower like a childish 'pupil', despite the older man's objections that no living man can instruct him, 41–3 above.

60–3 Three times . . . back Hardyng's *Chronicle[s]* (1812 edn, p. 358) say that Henry went three times to Wales in the harvest season and was repeatedly hindered by 'mystes & tempestes'. Holinshed describes the King's successful raid on Wales in 1400 (III, 17), the defeated expedition led by Mortimer in 1402 (20), the King's vain pursuit of Glendower in 1402 (20), a more successful skirmish fought by 'the princes companie' in 1405 (33–4), and a frustrating raid, again led by the King, in 1405 (39–40). Compare 1.3.114–15 and Appendix, p. ••.

60 made head raised an army.

61 my power my forces.

61–2 Wye . . . Severn Both rivers wind from the Cambrian mountains of Wales towards the Severn estuary. The Severn to the north, and the Wye, farther south, serve in places as the border between Wales and England. In Holinshed, the King penetrates more deeply into Wales (III, 17, 20, 39–40).

63 Bootless (1) Having failed, (2) Empty-handed. In 1400, according to Holinshed, Henry returned to England 'with a great bootie of beasts and cattell' (III, 17). In a reversal of Holinshed's viewpoint, Shakespeare's Glendower speaks of Henry as if he were the 'irregular and wild' marauder. Compare 1.1.40.

63 weather-beaten back In Holinshed, Glendower was said to have escaped from the King in 1402 by causing extraordinary 'foule weather' (III, 20).

65 scapes escapes.

66 our right the land we are entitled to.

67 threefold order taken three-way agreement (the 'indentures tripartite', 76 below).

68 Archdeacon The archdeacon of Bangor. See headnote.

69 limits territories (*OED* sv *sb* 3a, this example).

70 Trent The River Trent flows south-east through the Midlands, but turns sharply north-east beyond Burton-on-Trent, through Nottinghamshire and Lincolnshire, entering the estuary of the Humber.

70 hitherto thus far (*OED* 3, this example). Mortimer points out his boundary line.

To Owen Glendower. And, dear coz, to you
The remnant northward lying off from Trent.   75
And our indentures tripartite are drawn,
Which being sealèd interchangeably –
A business that this night may execute –
Tomorrow, cousin Percy, you and I
And my good Lord of Worcester will set forth   80
To meet your father and the Scottish power,
As is appointed us, at Shrewsbury.
My father Glendower is not ready yet,
Nor shall we need his help these fourteen days.
[*To Glendower*] Within that space you may have drawn together 85
Your tenants, friends, and neighbouring gentlemen.

GLENDOWER A shorter time shall send me to you, lords,
And in my conduct shall your ladies come,
From whom you now must steal and take no leave,
For there will be a world of water shed   90
Upon the parting of your wives and you.

HOTSPUR Methinks my moiety, north from Burton here,
In quantity equals not one of yours.
See how this river comes me cranking in,
And cuts me from the best of all my land   95
A huge half-moon, a monstrous scantle out.
I'll have the current in this place dammed up,
And here the smug and silver Trent shall run
In a new channel fair and evenly.
It shall not wind with such a deep indent,   100
To rob me of so rich a bottom here.

---

85 SD *To Glendower*] *Capell; not in* QQF   96 scantle] Qq; cantle F

76 **indentures tripartite** contracts drawn up in triplicate.

77 **interchangeably** so that each seals all three copies.

78 **this . . . execute** i.e. we can finish tonight.

82 **Shrewsbury** Town strategically located on the Severn River, not far from Glendower's residence by the River Dee.

83 **father** father-in-law.

86 **tenants** those who hold land on condition they provide military support when required.

88 **in my conduct** escorted by me.

92 **moiety** share or portion.

92 **Burton** present-day Burton-on-Trent.

94 **cranking in** winding sharply, zigzagging.

96 **monstrous scantle** large portion. Qq's 'scantle', a small portion or 'scantling', contradicts 'monstrous', thereby implying that Hotspur's objection is part bluff. F's 'cantle' (a projecting corner or angle, *OED* sv *sb* 1b) appears in *Ant.*: 'The greater cantle of the world is lost' (3.10.6). The Folio editors or revisers may have discarded the initial 's' on the assumption that it was picked up from the last letter of the preceding word.

98 **smug** smooth, neat (the earliest example of this sense, *OED* sv *a* 3).

101 **bottom** river-valley.

GLENDOWER Not wind? It shall, it must – you see it doth.
MORTIMER Yea,
　　　　But mark how he bears his course, and runs me up
　　　　With like advantage on the other side,   105
　　　　Gelding the opposèd continent as much
　　　　As on the other side it takes from you.
WORCESTER Yea, but a little charge will trench him here,
　　　　And on this north side win this cape of land,
　　　　And then he runs straight and even.   110
HOTSPUR I'll have it so, a little charge will do it.
GLENDOWER I'll not have it altered.
HOTSPUR   Will not you?
GLENDOWER No, nor you shall not.
HOTSPUR   Who shall say me nay?
GLENDOWER Why, that will I.
HOTSPUR Let me not understand you then, speak it in Welsh.   115
GLENDOWER I can speak English, lord, as well as you,
　　　　For I was trained up in the English court,
　　　　Where, being but young, I framèd to the harp
　　　　Many an English ditty lovely well,
　　　　And gave the tongue a helpful ornament –   120
　　　　A virtue that was never seen in you.
HOTSPUR Marry and I am glad of it with all my heart!
　　　　I had rather be a kitten and cry 'mew'
　　　　Than one of these same metre ballad-mongers.

---

102 wind?] Qq2–5, F; wind Q1   103–7 Yea . . . you] *As verse, Steevens, followed by Humphreys; as verse* Yea . . . course /
And . . . side, / Gelding . . . much / As . . . you F; *as prose* Qq   124 ballad-mongers] QqF (balletmongers)

103–7 Yea . . . you Printed by Qq as three lines
of prose. This edition follows Humphreys and
Davison in using lineation to separate Mortimer's
diplomatic 'Yea' from his thoughtful 'But'. Compare the irregularity in 103–4 with the short lines at
110 and 112–14 below. From Mortimer's 'Yea' to
Glendower's 'will I', 103–14, the three speakers
employ frequent short or split lines, each of which
can be effective onstage. F, in contrast, prints
103–7 as four irregular verse lines; the second,
'And . . . side' with its fourteen feet, is unconvincing. See Textual Analysis, pp. 208–9.
　104 he the Trent.
　106 Gelding . . . continent Cutting off from the
opposite bank.
　108 charge cost.
　108 trench divert by creating a new channel.
　117 For . . . court Suggesting that he had been
a page or body-squire. Holinshed reports that

Glendower had been 'an apprentise of the
law . . . and served king Richard at Flint castell,
when he was taken by Henrie duke of Lancaster,
though other have written that he served this king
Henrie the fourth, before he came to atteine the
crowne, in roome of an esquier' (III, 17). See also
List of Characters.
　119 ditty the words of a song, without the
music.
　120 gave the tongue a helpful ornament used
music and poetry to adorn and enhance the English
language.
　121 virtue accomplishment (*OED sv sb* 5b).
'Virtue' may also refer to a power or energy that
Hotspur, being no poet, cannot share.
　124 ballad-mongers street pedlars who traffic
in ballads. Hotspur travesties Glendower's belief
that poetry is an art (as he had magic). He eliminates
any sense of the poet's creativity.

I had rather hear a brazen canstick turned,   125
Or a dry wheel grate on the axle-tree,
And that would set my teeth nothing on edge,
Nothing so much as mincing poetry.
'Tis like the forced gait of a shuffling nag.
GLENDOWER Come, you shall have Trent turned.   130
HOTSPUR I do not care, I'll give thrice so much land
    To any well-deserving friend.
    But in the way of bargain, mark ye me,
    I'll cavil on the ninth part of a hair.
    Are the indentures drawn? Shall we be gone?   135
GLENDOWER The moon shines fair, you may away by night.
    I'll haste the writer, and withal
    Break with your wives of your departure hence.
    I am afraid my daughter will run mad,
    So much she doteth on her Mortimer.   *Exit*   140
MORTIMER Fie, cousin Percy, how you cross my father!
HOTSPUR I cannot choose. Sometime he angers me
    With telling me of the moldwarp and the ant,
    Of the dreamer Merlin and his prophecies,
    And of a dragon and a finless fish,   145
    A clip-winged griffin and a moulten raven,
    A couching lion and a ramping cat,

---

125 canstick] Qq; Candlestick F   127 on] Qq3, 4; an Qq1, 2, 5, F

---

125 **brazen canstick turned** The loathsome noise produced by metal-workers as they turned candlesticks on their lathes 'to make them smooth and bright' was mentioned by Stow in his description of Loth ('Lath' or 'Load') berie Street, *Survey*, I, 277.

126 **dry wheel** Another source of excruciating sound. According to a proverb, 'A dry cart-wheel cries the loudest' (Dent C109.1).

128 **mincing** tripping along in an affectation of elegance (*OED* sv *ppl.* a2). Compare *MV* 3.4.67–8: 'and turn two mincing steps / Into a manly stride'.

129 **forced . . . nag** Hotspur demonstrates his contempt for 'metre' ballads, 124, through this caricature of metrical regularity.

134 **cavil on** wrangle.

135 **drawn** drawn up, prepared.

137 **haste the writer** make the scrivener (of the indentures) go faster.

138 **Break with** Disclose information to.

141 **cross** contradict; compare 'crossings', 33, and ''cross', 166.

142–9 **Sometime . . . faith** The so-called

'prophecies of Merlin', with their cast of monstrous creatures, flourished whenever the royal succession was in question. Hall and Holinshed scorned the 'blind and fantasticall dreames of the Welsh prophesiers' (III, 23). But in *The Faerie Queene* III (1590), Spenser made Merlin a magus and treated him as a wise and accurate prophet of the Tudor dynasty.

143 **moldwarp** a mole, which casts up or 'warps' the earth or 'mold'.

144 **Merlin** The greatest wizard in Arthurian legends, as well as the young Arthur's protector and mentor.

145 **dragon** The historical Glendower adopted this crest, traditionally associated, according to Geoffrey of Monmouth, with King Arthur and with the last of the British kings, Cadwallader.

146 **griffin** Fabulous beast with the head and wings of an eagle, the body and hind legs of a lion.

147 **couching . . . ramping** lying down with head erect (couchant) and rearing on hind legs (rampant). Hotspur burlesques heraldic symbols. Bevington notes that the 'finless', 'clip-winged', and

And such a deal of skimble-skamble stuff
As puts me from my faith. I tell you what –
He held me last night at least nine hours   150
In reckoning up the several devils' names
That were his lackeys. I cried 'Hum', and 'Well, go to!'
But marked him not a word. O, he is as tedious
As a tired horse, a railing wife,
Worse than a smoky house. I had rather live   155
With cheese and garlic in a windmill, far,
Than feed on cates and have him talk to me
In any summer house in Christendom.
MORTIMER In faith, he is a worthy gentleman,
Exceedingly well read, and profited   160
In strange concealments, valiant as a lion,
And wondrous affable, and as bountiful
As mines of India. Shall I tell you, cousin?
He holds your temper in a high respect
And curbs himself even of his natural scope   165
When you come 'cross his humour, faith he does.
I warrant you that man is not alive
Might so have tempted him as you have done
Without the taste of danger and reproof.

---

166 come 'cross] Qq (come crosse); doe crosse F

'moulten' (featherless) creatures of 145–6 are 'deprived of locomotion'.

148–9 And ... faith Keith Thomas uses this passage as epigraph for his chapter on 'Ancient prophecies', which like Merlin's were rarely believed, he maintains, after the seventeenth century (*Religion and the Decline of Magic*, 1971).

148 skimble-skamble stuff No synonyms can match this exasperated summary of prophetic nonsense.

149 puts ... faith makes me forget (or deny) my religious belief.

152 lackeys footmen, servile attendants.

152 Well, go to An expression of derisive incredulity (*OED* sv v 93b).

154–5 railing ... house Both make a man want to rush outside. Similar are Prov. 27.15: 'A continual dropping in the day of raine, and a contencious woman are a like' and Dent H781.

156 cheese ... windmill i.e. the least desirable food and the noisiest residence. Garlic often stands for foul breath; the windmill, besides its incessant

sound, may suggest that Glendower's monologues get nowhere.

157 cates delicacies.

158 summer house An elegant and courtly pavilion in the grounds of a country house or palace. Compare Stowe on the structures springing up in the gardens beyond London's walls: 'fayre summer houses ... like Midsommer Pageantes, with Towers, Turrets, and Chimney tops', *Survey*, II, 78.

160–1 profited ... concealments adept at magic or occult arts.

162 wondrous affable remarkably courteous, especially in conversation. Possibly echoing this scene, the Welsh Captain, Fluellen, in *H5*, 3.2.127, complains that he has not been used with 'affability' by the hot-tempered Irishman, MacMorris.

163 mines of India Legendary source of wealth since the conquests of Alexander the Great. Compare Marlowe, *1 Tamburlaine* 3.3.263–4.

164 temper disposition; compare *John* 5.2.40: 'A noble temper dost thou show in this.'

165 scope liberty to act.

But do not use it oft, let me entreat you.   170
WORCESTER In faith, my lord, you are too wilful-blame,
And since your coming hither have done enough
To put him quite besides his patience.
You must needs learn, lord, to amend this fault.
Though sometimes it show greatness, courage, blood –   175
And that's the dearest grace it renders you –
Yet oftentimes it doth present harsh rage,
Defect of manners, want of government,
Pride, haughtiness, opinion, and disdain,
The least of which haunting a nobleman   180
Loseth men's hearts and leaves behind a stain
Upon the beauty of all parts besides,
Beguiling them of commendation.
HOTSPUR Well, I am schooled – good manners be your speed!
Here come our wives, and let us take our leave.   185

Enter GLENDOWER *with the* LADIES

MORTIMER This is the deadly spite that angers me,
My wife can speak no English, I no Welsh.
GLENDOWER My daughter weeps, she'll not part with you,
She'll be a soldier too, she'll to the wars.
MORTIMER Good father, tell her that she and my aunt Percy   190
Shall follow in your conduct speedily.
Glendower speaks to her in Welsh, and she answers him in the same

---

171 **too wilful-blame** (1) to be blamed for excessive wilfulness, (2) deliberately blameworthy. 'To' was often mistaken as 'too'; blame could be understood as an adjective (*OED* Blame sv *v* 6). Humphreys cites, as one of many examples, *2H4* 2.4.361: 'I feele me much too blame'(Q) and 'to blame'(F).
173 **besides** out of.
175 **blood** high spirit.
176 **dearest grace** noblest honour.
177 **present** show, as in 175.
178 **government** self-control.
179 **opinion** arrogance or conceit (*OED* sv *sb* 5c).
180–3 **The least ... commendation** A reminder that the medieval baron's power depended on the trust and support of a personal alliance.
181 **stain** indelible blot. Worcester, like King Henry, argues that dishonour causes an almost physical change in appearance. Compare 1.1.84 and n.

183 **Beguiling** Cheating out of (*OED* Beguile sv *v* 2).
184 **be your speed** give you success or good luck. Hotspur may speak ironically, thinking of a battlefield.
185 **and** Elizabethans could use 'and' to join an affirmation and a command. Compare 5.4.33, 'I will assay thee, and defend thyself.'
186 **spite** vexation.
190 **aunt Percy** Hotspur's wife was in fact sister to the Mortimer who married Glendower's daughter, aunt to the younger Mortimer designated by Richard II as his heir. See 2.3.75 n., and List of Characters.
191 SD Glendower and his daughter may have been played by Welsh actors; perhaps Shakespeare left the selection of Welsh speeches and music to them. W. J. Lawrence (*Welsh Song*, 1922) argues that Shakespeare's lines for Lady Mortimer show he had a boy-actor who could sing well in Welsh.

GLENDOWER She is desperate here, a peevish, self-willed harlotry, one
    that no persuasion can do good upon.
                 The lady speaks in Welsh
MORTIMER I understand thy looks, that pretty Welsh
    Which thou pourest down from these swelling heavens   195
    I am too perfect in, and but for shame
    In such a parley should I answer thee.
             The lady [speaks] again in Welsh
    I understand thy kisses, and thou mine,
    And that's a feeling disputation,
    But I will never be a truant, love,   200
    Till I have learnt thy language, for thy tongue
    Makes Welsh as sweet as ditties highly penned,
    Sung by a fair queen in a summer's bower
    With ravishing division to her lute.
GLENDOWER Nay, if you melt, then will she run mad.   205
             The lady speaks again in Welsh
MORTIMER O, I am ignorance itself in this!
GLENDOWER She bids you on the wanton rushes lay you down,
    And rest your gentle head upon her lap,
    And she will sing the song that pleaseth you,
    And on your eyelids crown the god of sleep,   210
    Charming your blood with pleasing heaviness,
    Making such difference 'twixt wake and sleep
    As is the difference betwixt day and night,
    The hour before the heavenly-harnessed team

192–3 She . . . upon] *As prose,* Cam., *followed by Humphreys; one line of verse* She . . . here, *the remainder as prose* Qq; *as verse* Shee . . . heere: / A . . . Harlotry, / One . . . upon F   **197** SD *speaks*] *Malone subst.; not in* QqF

---

192 desperate determined.

192 harlotry woman. Glendower uses the term with more compassion than scorn, unlike Capulet, *Rom.* 4.2.14, 'A peevish self [-willed] harlotry it is.'

195 swelling heavens tear-filled eyes.

196 too perfect in understand only too well.

197 parley (1) argument, (2) conference with a military adversary (suggested by 'soldier', 189).

197 answer i.e. reply with tears.

199 feeling disputation Argument carried on through emotions, rather than words.

202 highly penned Written in an exquisite or elegant style.

204 division Musical term referring to 'a bril-liant passage, of short notes, which is founded essentially on a much simpler passage of longer notes' (Edward W. Naylor, *Shakespeare and Music*, 1931, p. 28.)

205 melt weep.

207 wanton profuse, luxuriant (*OED* sv *a* 7a), as in *MND* 2.1.99: 'quaint mazes in the wanton green'.

207 rushes Fresh green rushes were used as floor-covering in homes and theatres.

210 And . . . sleep give sleep absolute power over you.

211 Charming Enchanting.

214 heavenly-harnessed team horses which pull the chariot, an image that symbolises the sun.

Begins his golden progress in the east.   215
MORTIMER With all my heart I'll sit and hear her sing,
    By that time will our book, I think, be drawn.
GLENDOWER Do so, and those musicians that shall play to you
    Hang in the air a thousand leagues from hence,
    And straight they shall be here. Sit, and attend.   220
HOTSPUR Come, Kate, thou art perfect in lying down.
    Come, quick, quick, that I may lay my head in thy lap.
LADY PERCY Go, ye giddy goose.

The music plays

HOTSPUR Now I perceive the devil understands Welsh,
    And 'tis no marvel he is so humorous,   225
    By'r lady, he is a good musician.
LADY PERCY Then should you be nothing but musical,
    For you are altogether governed by humours.
    Lie still, ye thief, and hear the lady sing in Welsh.
HOTSPUR I had rather hear Lady my brach howl in Irish.   230
LADY PERCY Wouldst thou have thy head broken?
HOTSPUR No.
LADY PERCY Then be still.
HOTSPUR Neither, 'tis a woman's fault.
LADY PERCY Now, God help thee!   235
HOTSPUR To the Welsh lady's bed.
LADY PERCY What's that?
HOTSPUR Peace, she sings.

---

215 progress journey or tour made by a king or queen, usually ceremonial and spectacular.

217 book the indentures tripartite or documents, 76 above.

218–20 those musicians . . . here How their performance is represented can support or undermine Glendower's claim to control spirits, 50. Zitner suggests two demystified stagings: (1) by a playful gesture, Glendower indicates the musicians visible in the third gallery, the highest tier above the tiring-house; (2) as suggested by Hotspur's response at 224–6, music comes from an invisible source 'below the stage, whence the Devil's infernal music issued in old plays' ('Staging the occult in *1 Henry IV*', in *Mirror up to Shakespeare: Essays in Honour of G. R. Hibbard*, ed. J. C. Gray, 1984, pp. 138–48).

221–43 Come . . . day An uncertain mixture of verse and prose in both Qq and F. The lineation in Q has been followed here, 221–40. See Textual Analysis, pp. 208–9.

225 humorous capricious, implying that the temperament in question has physiological causes. Compare 30–2 above. Q's comma after 'humorous' makes it possible to read the syntax backwards or forwards, applying 'humorous' to 'Welsh' or to 'musician'. On the 'syntactical looseness of English' in the late sixteenth century, see Anne Ferry, *The Art of Naming*, 1988, pp. 63–4.

229 thief A mock-serious charge.

230 brach bitch, hunting dog.

230 I . . . Irish Hotspur ridicules the Welsh lady's allegedly uncouth language and discredits her skill.

233 still silent.

234 Neither . . . fault A punning reply to both of Lady Percy's threats. 'A woman's fault' quibbles upon 'head broken' as 'broken maidenhead'. He also mistakes her meaning of 'still', 233, as sexual passivity.

235 God help thee i.e. no one else can manage you.

Here the lady sings a Welsh song

Come, Kate, I'll have your song too.

LADY PERCY Not mine, in good sooth.   240

HOTSPUR Not yours, in good sooth! Heart, you swear like a comfit-
maker's wife – 'Not you, in good sooth!' and 'As true as I live!'
and 'As God shall mend me!', and 'As sure as day!' –
      And givest such sarcenet surety for thy oaths
      As if thou never walk'st further than Finsbury.   245
      Swear me, Kate, like a lady as thou art,
      A good mouth-filling oath, and leave 'In sooth',
      And such protest of pepper-gingerbread,
      To velvet-guards, and Sunday citizens.
      Come, sing.   250

LADY PERCY I will not sing.

HOTSPUR 'Tis the next way to turn tailor, or be redbreast teacher. An
the indentures be drawn I'll away within these two hours. And so,
come in when ye will.   *Exit*

GLENDOWER Come, come, Lord Mortimer, you are as slow   255
      As hot Lord Percy is on fire to go.
      By this our book is drawn – we'll but seal,
      And then to horse immediately.

MORTIMER With all my heart.

Exeunt

241–3 Not ... day] Qq; *as verse* Not ... sooth? / You ... Wife: / Not ... live; / And ... day: F, *omitting* Heart   256 hot]
F; Hot. Qq1–3; Hot, Q4; *Hot* Q5

---

240 in good sooth in truth, a mild oath used to
strengthen an exclamation, as opposed to 'Heart'
('Christ's heart'), 241.

241–3 Not ... day Hotspur parrots the sober
oaths of pious London citizens, who are often
mocked in later plays of the period. In *2H4*, Falstaff
snobbishly refers to an obsequious tradesman who
refuses to sell him cloth on credit as a 'yea-forsooth
knave' (1.2.36).

241–2 comfit-maker candy-maker, suggesting
that her oath is (1) insubstantial, (2) beneath her
rank.

244 sarcenet surety a guarantee of certainty
(*OED* Surety *sb* 6), which is no stronger than
sarcenet, a soft, fine silk (*OED* Sarsenet 2b).

245 Finsbury Finsbury Fields, north of London
beyond Moorfields, popular with citizens as a place
for recreation. It was close to the Curtain theatre
where *1H4* may have been staged. Stow mentions

the traditional archery competitions held on this site
(*Survey*, I, 104; II, 77).

248 protest of pepper-gingerbread oaths that,
like hot spiced gingerbread, nip the mouth instead
of filling it.

249 velvet-guards Equated with the citizens
who wear trimmings or facings of velvet on their
Sunday clothes.

252 'Tis ... teacher Another mockery of singing, as at 230. 'Tailors', like weavers, were noted for
singing; they are further disdained by Hotspur
through association with citizens who wear pretentious clothes ('velvet-guards', 249). 'Redbreast
teacher' scoffs at the idiocy of valuing as art that
which robins do better than people.

252 next easiest.

257 seal To ratify their agreement or 'book' by
affixing their individual seals. Compare 2.4.274–5
and n.

[**3.2**] *Enter the* KING, PRINCE OF WALES, *and others*

KING Lords, give us leave. The Prince of Wales and I
      Must have some private conference – but be near at hand,
      For we shall presently have need of you.

                                       Exeunt Lords
      I know not whether God will have it so
      For some displeasing service I have done,   5
      That in his secret doom out of my blood
      He'll breed revengement and a scourge for me.
      But thou dost in thy passages of life
      Make me believe that thou art only marked
      For the hot vengeance and the rod of heaven,   10
      To punish my mistreadings. Tell me else,
      Could such inordinate and low desires,
      Such poor, such bare, such lewd, such mean attempts,
      Such barren pleasures, rude society,
      As thou art matched withal, and grafted to,   15

Act 3, Scene 2   3.2] *Scæna Secunda.* F; *not in* Qq

Act 3, Scene 2

[**3.2**] According to Holinshed, Stow, and other chroniclers, late in the reign of Henry IV (1412) the Prince discovered that he was suspected of planning to usurp the throne. He therefore took the initiative for a meeting with the King and led a group of his followers to the court at Westminster. He reassured his father, professing his loyalty and dismissing his train. The interview in this scene takes place before the battle of Shrewsbury (1403). Without specific historical source, it has been influenced by accounts of the reconciliation in 1412 that *FV* and *2H4* dramatised. It takes place at an unlocalised court, following the summons the Prince received in 2.4.

The entry of these lords (unnamed, of unspecified number, and given no lines), draws attention to the King's suspicion of the Prince and emphasises the intimacy of their meeting.

1 give us leave A polite request for privacy (Dent L167.1).

2–3 but . . . you This command may suggest that the King anticipates physical violence from his son.

4–17 I know . . . heart The King begins with an indirect reference to his own guilt, but quickly focuses on shaming the Prince. In a second reconciliation scene preceding his death in *2H4* 4.2.311 ff., he will acknowledge more openly by 'what by-paths and indirect crooked ways / I met this crown.'

5 some displeasing service A probable allusion to his responsibility for the death of Richard II.

6 doom judgement.

6 blood children, 'my own flesh and blood'.

7 scourge The human instrument through whom divine punishment functions. Scourges were believed to experience as well as to inflict God's wrath. Compare 8–11 below and *Ham.* 3.4.173–5: 'Heaven hath pleas'd it so / To punish me with this, and this with me, / That I must be their scourge and minister.'

8 thy passages of life your way of living.

11 else i.e. if what I have said is not true.

12 inordinate disorderly and intemperate (another of the King's latinate terms).

13 bare (1) worthless (*OED* sv *a* 10), (2) exposed. Compare *R2* 'detested sins . . . / Stand bare and naked, trembling at themselves' (3.2.44–6).

13 lewd vulgar, base.

13 attempts escapades.

14 rude uncivil, and perhaps violent, barbarous, as in 1.1.41, 'the rude hands of that Welshman'.

15 grafted to joined to. In grafting, a shoot from one tree is literally inserted into another so that the sap can flow into it. The metaphor emphasises the Prince's alienation from his own 'blood' and lineage, 16.

Accompany the greatness of thy blood
And hold their level with thy princely heart?
PRINCE So please your majesty, I would I could
        Quit all offences with as clear excuse
        As well as I am doubtless I can purge   20
        Myself of many I am charged withal.
        Yet such extenuation let me beg
        As, in reproof of many tales devised,
        Which oft the ear of greatness needs must hear,
        By smiling pickthanks, and base newsmongers,   25
        I may for some things true, wherein my youth
        Hath faulty wandered and irregular,
        Find pardon on my true submission.
KING   God pardon thee! Yet let me wonder, Harry,
        At thy affections, which do hold a wing   *fallen away from*   30
        Quite from the flight of all thy ancestors.   *your kind.*
        Thy place in Council thou hast rudely lost,
        Which by thy younger brother is supplied,   *John of Lancaster*
        And art almost an alien to the hearts
        Of all the court and princes of my blood.   35
        The hope and expectation of thy time
        Is ruined, and the soul of every man
        Prophetically do forethink thy fall.

17 **hold their level** be in an equal position with (*OED* Level sv *sb* 3c).

18–28 **So please . . . submission** The Prince apologises without explaining himself clearly. He may kneel to his father, as he does in Holinshed (III, 54), but his lines here do not require so literal or so penitent a gesture. He maintains that many of the stories about him are lies and that he should be pardoned even for those others that he readily admits are true.

19 **Quit** Acquit myself of.

23 **in reproof** upon disproof.

25 **pickthanks** 'officious parasites' (Steevens, 1778); those who gain favour or gifts through flattery or by telling tales. Holinshed mentions that servants had tried to create 'discord' between father and son by insinuating that the Prince intended to seize power (III, 53).

25 **newsmongers** tale-bearers like 'pickthanks'; literally, sellers of news.

28 **submission** admission or confession. Compare *Wiv.* 4.4.11: 'Be not as extreme in submission as in offence.'

29–91 **God . . . tenderness** In this sixty-three-line speech, the longest in the play, the King in effect refuses the Prince's request for 'extenuation' of his offences, 22, and judges them in the bleak light of his own political experience.

30 **affections** inclinations.

30–1 **hold . . . flight** i.e. take a course quite different from that; the metaphor derives from falconry.

32 **Thy place . . . lost** The King may allude to a notorious episode in the legend of the wild Prince: reprimanded for drunken brawling, he had cuffed the Lord Chief Justice. In consequence, he was expelled by the King from the Privy Council. The story had been told by Elyot, *The Governor* (1531), and made familiar to audiences through *FV*. On Shakespeare's revision of tales about the Prince, see Introduction, pp. 2, 25–6.

34 **art** thou art.

36 **The hope . . . time** 'Your hopeful and promising youth' (Wilson).

37–8 **the soul . . . fall** The King's statement, if true, confirms the Prince's success in his plan to 'falsify men's hopes', 1.2.171.

Had I so lavish of my presence been,
So common-hackneyed in the eyes of men,　　　　　　40
So stale and cheap to vulgar company,
Opinion, that did help me to the crown,
Had still kept loyal to possession,
And left me in reputeless banishment,
A fellow of no mark nor likelihood.　　　　　　　45
By being seldom seen, I could not stir
But like a comet I was wondered at,
That men would tell their children, 'This is he!'
Others would say, 'Where, which is Bullingbrook?'
And then I stole all courtesy from heaven,　　　　50
And dressed myself in such humility
That I did pluck allegiance from men's hearts,
Loud shouts and salutations from their mouths,
Even in the presence of the crownèd King.
Thus did I keep my person fresh and new,　　　　55
My presence, like a robe pontifical,
Ne'er seen but wondered at, and so my state,
Seldom, but sumptuous, showed like a feast,
And won by rareness such solemnity.
The skipping King, he ambled up and down,　　　60

59 won] Q1 (wan); wonne F

39 **lavish** (1) prodigal in spending, (2) wild, as in *Mac.* 1.2.57, 'Curbing his lavish spirit'.
40 **common-hackneyed** commonplace or vulgar. The sense of 'hackney' as an ordinary horse (*OED* sv *sb* 1) may also suggest some recollection of the effect Bullingbrook produced by entering London on Richard II's horse, roan Barbary. Compare *R2* 5.2.7–11 and 5.5.76–80. Henry contrasts himself with Richard at 54 and 60 below.
42 **Opinion** Public opinion.
43 **to possession** i.e. to the possessor, King Richard II.
44 **reputeless banishment** dishonourable exile. Bullingbrook was literally banished by Richard II for challenging his authority (*R2* 1.3.139–43). The King implies that public 'opinion' ended his exile although, in fact, he created this opinion by returning illegally to England.
45 **mark** reputation, notice.
47 **comet** a meteor or shooting star, often viewed as prophetic of disorder on earth. Compare references to meteors by the King, 1.1.10, and by Glendower, 3.1.11–13.

50 **And ... heaven** 'Courtesy' refers to (1) the charming humble manner adopted by Bullingbrook, 51–3, and (2) his calculated acquisition of power through courtship, modelled on 'heaven' only insofar as he imitates a comet, 47. Compare the Prince's 'Yet herein will I imitate the sun', 1.2.157. The metaphors chosen by father and son expose striking similarities and differences in their characters and in their conceptions of power.
56–7 **My presence ... wondered at** A variation on the saying that 'A Maid oft seen, a gown oft worn, are disesteemed and held in scorn' (Dent, M20, Appendix C).
56 **robe pontifical** ceremonial vestment of a Pope or high priest. The reference might remind Shakespeare's predominantly Protestant audience that kings, like Catholic priests, could be accused of fostering idolatry.
57 **state** magnificence (*OED* sv *sb* 17a).
59 **solemnity** the grandeur characteristic of a great public ceremony.
60 **skipping** flighty (Wilson).

With shallow jesters, and rash bavin wits,
Soon kindled and soon burnt, carded his state,
Mingled his royalty with capering fools,   *in the pub*
Had his great name profanèd with their scorns,
And gave his countenance against his name   65
To laugh at gibing boys, and stand the push
Of every beardless vain comparative,
Grew a companion to the common streets,
Enfeoffed himself to popularity,
That, being daily swallowed by men's eyes,   70
They surfeited with honey, and began
To loathe the taste of sweetness, whereof a little
More than a little is by much too much.
So, when he had occasion to be seen,
He was but as the cuckoo is in June,   75
Heard, not regarded; seen, but with such eyes
As, sick and blunted with community,
Afford no extraordinary gaze,
Such as is bent on sun-like majesty

*Image of
Sun*

When it shines seldom in admiring eyes,   80
But rather drowsed and hung their eyelids down,
Slept in his face, and rendered such aspect
As cloudy men use to their adversaries,

---

63 capering] Q1 (capring); Carping QQ2–5, F   71–2 began / To loathe the] *As T. Johnson, Pope;* began to loathe / The QQF

61 rash bavin quickly lighted kindling, soon burnt out.

62 carded his state contaminated his display of power (by mingling with fools, 63). The expression here twists one sense of 'card': to comb impurities from wool or flax; it joins this to a second: to stir or mix (*OED* sv *v*[1] 1 and 2).

65 countenance royal authority. Compare 1.2.24 and note.

65 against his name to the prejudice of his reputation or title.

66 stand the push be prepared to take the thrust. Compare *2H4* 2.2.37, and *Tro.* 2.2.137. The King ironically implies that Richard lacked valour.

67 beardless vain comparative youth who makes trivial jokes. Compare 1.2.64.

69 Enfeoffed . . . popularity Made himself dependent upon the favour and power of the people. A king or lord enfeoffed a vassal by granting him land in return for support. In effect, Richard made himself the vassal.

71 surfeited with honey A familiar expression, as in Proverbs 25.16 and 27 and Dent H560. Compare the contemptuous references to honey at 1.2.34 and 2.1.62.

75–6 the cuckoo . . . regarded Compare Dent c894, 'No one regards the June (summer) cuckoo's song.' The King here relies on popular expressions to repudiate Hal's association with the common people.

77 community commonness (*OED* 5a), i.e. the experience of seeing the king as an ordinary familiar figure.

78 Afford Bestow, Grant (*OED* 5).

82 in his face in his presence. This affront to the dignity of a ruler is compared to the natural effect of getting too much sun.

83 cloudy Sullen or darkened because no longer reflecting the king's light as do obedient subjects. Compare 'moody', 1.3.18, and 'fair and natural light', 5.1.18.

Being with his presence glutted, gorged, and full.
And in that very line, Harry, standest thou,   85
For thou hast lost thy princely privilege
With vile participation. Not an eye
But is a-weary of thy common sight,
Save mine, which hath desired to see thee more,
Which now doth that I would not have it do,   90
Make blind itself with foolish tenderness.

PRINCE I shall hereafter, my thrice-gracious lord,
Be more myself.

KING   For all the world
As thou art to this hour was Richard then
When I from France set foot at Ravenspurgh,
And even as I was then is Percy now.   95
Now by my sceptre, and my soul to boot,
He hath more worthy interest to the state
Than thou the shadow of succession.
For of no right, nor colour like to right,   100
He doth fill fields with harness in the realm,
Turns head against the lion's armèd jaws,
And being no more in debt to years than thou
Leads ancient lords and reverend bishops on
To bloody battles, and to bruising arms.   105

---

85 line category, degree. Compare 1.3.166 and n.

87 vile participation fellowship with vile people. The King's abstractions keep the Prince's friends at a distance.

90 that that which.

91 blind itself i.e. by filling with tears, an implicit and self-conscious stage direction. Both in *FV* and in Holinshed, the King weeps sincerely during his reconciliation with the Prince.

92–3 I shall ... myself The Prince unknowingly repeats his father's self-assertion to the Percys at 1.3.5.

93–128 For all ... degenerate The King overwhelms the Prince's forceful interjection (92–3) with an apparently premeditated discourse on how history is repeating itself. For a more detailed discussion of the rhythms of this scene, see Introduction, p. 15.

95 Ravenspurgh Former seaport (later submerged by the sea) in Yorkshire where Bullingbrook landed upon his return from exile. Compare 1.3.244 and n.

97 to boot as well.

98–9 He ... succession i.e. his claim, based on

his intrinsic worth, betters yours, based only on inherited right.

100 colour like to semblance of.

101–2 He ... jaws The King's figures of speech, metonymy (the harness as part of the armour of many men) and heraldic emblem (the lion's jaws symbolising his own power) resemble those which he uses in 1.1.1–33. There they distract attention from personal responsibility for disruption. Here, however, such figures glorify the process controlled by one agent, Hotspur.

102 Turns head Leads a rebel army (*OED* head sv *sb*¹ 29).

103 no ... thou no older than you are. The historical Hotspur, born in 1364, was really several years older than the King himself, as well as twenty-three years older than the Prince. See List of Characters and Introduction, p. 23.

104 bishops An indication that the King is already aware of the Archbishop of York's confederacy with the rebels. See 4.4.38.

105 bruising crushing. Compare 5.1.13, 'crush our old limbs in ungentle steel'.

What never-dying honour hath he got
Against renownèd Douglas! Whose high deeds,
Whose hot incursions and great name in arms,
Holds from all soldiers chief majority
And military title capital   110
Through all the kingdoms that acknowledge Christ.
Thrice hath this Hotspur, Mars in swaddling clothes, *baby Mars*.
This infant warrior, in his enterprises
Discomfited great Douglas, taken him once,
Enlargèd him, and made a friend of him,   115
To fill the mouth of deep defiance up,
And shake the peace and safety of our throne.
And what say you to this? Percy, Northumberland,
The Archbishop's Grace of York, Douglas, Mortimer,
Capitulate against us and are up.   120
But wherefore do I tell these news to thee?
Why, Harry, do I tell thee of my foes,   *you are chief*
Which art my nearest and dearest enemy?   *of my enemies*
Thou that art like enough, through vassal fear,
Base inclination, and the start of spleen,   125
To fight against me under Percy's pay,
To dog his heels, and curtsy at his frowns,   *might as well be*
To show how much thou art degenerate.   *his dog*
PRINCE Do not think it so, you shall not find it so; *stunned by father's speech*
And God forgive them that so much have swayed — *now*   130
                                                 responding

---

107 renownèd] Qq4, 5, F; renowmed Qq1–3   112 swaddling] Qq1–3 (swathling); swathing Qq4, 5, F

107 Whose Hotspur's.
108 hot incursions sudden attacks, raids, as in 'sallies', 2.3.45.
109–10 Holds ... capital Holds the reputation of pre-eminent soldier. 'Majority' carries a secondary sense, 'of full age', suggesting that Hotspur has proved his manhood.
112–15 Thrice ... him Historically Hotspur engaged in three battles against the Douglas family or their representatives: Otterburn (1385) in which the then head of the family was killed and Hotspur himself captured, Nesbit (22 June 1402), and Holmedon (14 September 1402). Shakespeare seems to invent the capturing and releasing of Douglas, a pattern which the Prince follows at 5.5.27–8.
115 Enlargèd Freed.
116 To ... up The figure of the mouth filled

with a war-cry (another metonymy) conveys Hotspur's readiness to attack.
120 Capitulate Draw up articles (literally 'chapters') of agreement. These articles, circulated by the Percys (5.1.72–4 below and Holinshed III, 23), contained their grievances.
120 up up in arms.
123 dearest Both most cherished and most bitter, as in *Ham.* 1.2.182, 'my dearest foe'.
124 vassal Normally a term for a dependent member of a feudal alliance, but used by the King to suggest social debasement, slavishness. Compare 'Enfeoffed', 69.
125 start of spleen fit of ill humour. Compare 2.3.72 and n.
130 them the 'pickthanks' and 'newsmongers', 25.

Your majesty's good thoughts away from me!
I will redeem all this on Percy's head,
And in the closing of some glorious day
Be bold to tell you that I am your son,
When I will wear a garment all of blood,   135
And stain my favours in a bloody mask,
Which, washed away, shall scour my shame with it.
And that shall be the day, whene'er it lights,
That this same child of honour and renown,
This gallant Hotspur, this all-praisèd knight,   140
And your unthought-of Harry chance to meet.
For every honour sitting on his helm,
Would they were multitudes, and on my head
My shames redoubled. For the time will come   *coming to this from Act I*
That I shall make this northern youth exchange   145
His glorious deeds for my indignities.
Percy is but my factor, good my lord,   *factor* - agent ("my rep") ("do-er")
To engross up glorious deeds on my behalf,
And I will call him to so strict account
That he shall render every glory up,   150
Yea, even the slightest worship of his time,
Or I will tear the reckoning from his heart.
This in the name of God I promise here,
The which if He be pleased I shall perform,
I do beseech your majesty may salve   155
The long-grown wounds of my intemperance.

---

154 He . . . perform] Qq; I performe, and doe survive F   156 intemperance] Qq; intemperature F, *Bevington*

132 I will . . . head I will (1) make Percy pay for all this, (2) shift the blame for all this to Percy, (3) use Percy's head to make up for all this. The complex metaphor figuring redemption runs through this crucial promise. See 1.2.177 and n.

135 all of blood Compare the apocalyptic vision of Pyrrhus in *Ham.* 2.2.456–8: 'head to foot / Now is he total gules, horridly trick'd / With blood'. Bevington points out how the image picks up on the sunset of 133, 'reinforcing' a pun upon 'son', 134.

136 favours features, as well as chivalric tokens worn to symbolise great deeds and honours.

137 washed away Like a baptism, immersion in blood may transform character.

138 lights dawns.

139 child youth of gentle birth. Compare 'infant', 113.

141 unthought-of One for whom there are no

expectations. This echoes 131 and contrasts with the 'all-praisèd' Hotspur, 140.

142 every . . . helm all the honours that decorate his helmet, like 'favours', 136.

147 factor agent, especially in a commercial transaction.

148 engross up buy up, monopolise.

151 slightest . . . time the least of the honours ('worship') he has earned.

152 reckoning the account prepared and kept by the factor of the wealth belonging to his master.

155 salve heal.

156 intemperance disorderly behaviour. F substitutes 'intemperature', which emphasises the suggestion of disease in 'salve' and 'wounds'. Although this revision is attractive, we retain the copy-text reading.

If not, the end of life cancels all bands,
And I will die a hundred thousand deaths
Ere break the smallest parcel of this vow.
KING A hundred thousand rebels die in this.   160
Thou shalt have charge and sovereign trust herein.

[handwritten: Thatz the oath I wanted to hear from you]

[handwritten left margin: perfidy / situation reversed / family/nation are one]

Enter BLUNT

How now, good Blunt? Thy looks are full of speed.
BLUNT So hath the business that I come to speak of.
Lord Mortimer of Scotland hath sent word
That Douglas and the English rebels met   165
The eleventh of this month at Shrewsbury.
A mighty and a fearful head they are,
If promises be kept on every hand,
As ever offered foul play in a state.
KING The Earl of Westmoreland set forth today,   170
With him my son, Lord John of Lancaster,
For this advertisement is five days old.
On Wednesday next, Harry, you shall set forward.
On Thursday we ourselves will march.
Our meeting is Bridgnorth, and, Harry, you   175
Shall march through Gloucestershire, by which account,
Our business valuèd, some twelve days hence
Our general forces at Bridgnorth shall meet.
Our hands are full of business, let's away,
Advantage feeds him fat while men delay.   180

[handwritten left margin: Now sounds more like the King — military planner]

Exeunt

[handwritten: H IV humanized in this scene —]

161 SD *Enter* BLUNT] F; *after* 162 Qq   174–5 march. / Our meeting is] F; march. Our meeting / Is Qq   175–6 you / Shall
march through] T. Johnson, Capell; you shall march / Through QqF

159 **parcel** portion.
161 **charge** leadership.
161 **sovereign trust** (1) supreme responsibility,
(2) my confidence.
164 **Mortimer** Shakespeare assumes mistakenly
that the Scottish Earls of March were Mortimers,
like the English Earls of March.
166 **the eleventh . . . Shrewsbury** This rendezvous, only just planned during the immediately preceding scene, 3.1.82, may suggest the uncanny
independence of Welsh from English time – or simply a careless error by the dramatist.
167 **head** army.
172 **advertisement** information.
173–8 **On Wednesday . . . meet** The King

sends the Prince by a roundabout route through
Gloucestershire to Bridgnorth in Shropshire. But in
4.2, Hal meets Falstaff near Coventry, suggesting
that he may have travelled on a direct course towards the rendezvous. Wilson suggests that the repetition of 'Bridgnorth', 'march', and 'business' (179)
indicates imperfect revision of this passage.
176–7 **by . . . valuèd** according to the calculation
of the time that our purposes require.
180 **Advantage . . . delay** Compare the proverb, 'Delay breeds danger' (Dent D195). For discussion of the vivid contrast between the final line of
this scene and the first of the next, see Introduction,
p. 16 and 3.3.2. n. below.
180 **him** himself.

[3.3] *Enter* FALSTAFF *and* BARDOLPH

of 2.4 Hal says will banish

FALSTAFF Bardolph, am I not fallen away vilely since this last action?
Do I not bate? Do I not dwindle? Why, my skin hangs about me like
an old lady's loose gown. I am withered like an old apple-john. Well,
I'll repent, and that suddenly, while I am in some liking. I shall be
out of heart shortly, and then I shall have no strength to repent. And   5
I have not forgotten what the inside of a church is made of, I am a
peppercorn, a brewer's horse. The inside of a church! Company,
villainous company, hath been the spoil of me.

BARDOLPH Sir John, you are so fretful you cannot live long.

FALSTAFF Why, there is it. Come, sing me a bawdy song, make me   10
merry. I was as virtuously given as a gentleman need to be. Virtuous
enough. Swore little. Diced not above seven times – a week. Went
to a bawdy-house not above once in a quarter – of an hour. Paid
money that I borrowed – three or four times. Lived well, and in
good compass: and now I live out of all order, out of all compass.   15

Act 3, Scene 3   3.3] *Scena Tertia.* F; *not in* Qq   12 times –] *Staunton;* times QqF   13 quarter –] *Hanmer;* quarter QqF   14 borrowed –] *Hanmer;* borrowed Qq; borrowed, F

Act 3, Scene 3

[3.3] The entry of the Hostess after 39 below
indicates that the scene takes place at the tavern
in Eastcheap. It has traditionally been called the
second tavern scene.

1 last action the robbery at Gad's Hill, with the
consequent battle of wits of 2.4. Like the Prince at
2.4.17, Falstaff refers to jest or sport as a serious
military engagement.

2 bate i.e. abate, decrease in size or bulk (*OED* sv
v^2 4b). Falstaff's first lines counter the King's last
line in 3.2: 'Advantage feeds him fat while men
delay.' For discussion of the changes in the play
which are introduced in this scene and further developed in *Part Two*, see Introduction, pp. 16–18.
Falstaff initiates here the more self-conscious satiric
anatomy or exploration of bodily analogues for general disorder and death which will be sustained
throughout *2H4*.

3 apple-john A kind of apple picked around
St John's Day, 24 June (Midsummer), but eaten
long afterwards, and therefore shrivelled. In *2H4*,
Francis the drawer declares that 'Sir John cannot
endure an apple-john' (2.4.2–3).

4 suddenly immediately.

4 am in some liking (1) feel like it, (2) am in
fairly good condition. Falstaff plays upon this pun
as he continues.

5 out of heart (1) disheartened, (2) in poor
condition.

5 strength both (1) of intention, and (2) of body.

5 And If.

7 peppercorn An absurd comparison because
unground pepper is hard, dry, and tiny. Compare
'shotten herring', 2.4.109.

7 brewer's horse one on its last legs. Compare Dekker, *If This be not a good Play, the Devil
is in It* (1611): 'as noble-men use their great
horses, when they are past service: sell 'em to
brewers and make 'em drey-horses' (cited by
Humphreys).

9 fretful (1) emotionally anxious, (2) physically
fretted or worn down (like the gummed velvet,
2.2.2). Bardolph answers Falstaff with another
quibble.

10 there is it that's the point.

11 given disposed.

12–14 Diced . . . times By pausing before 'a
week', 'of an hour', and 'three or four times', stage
Falstaffs often emphasise their self-mockery.

14–15 in good compass within reasonable
bounds, a proverbial phrase (Dent c577).

15 out of all compass A quibble: (1) without
any order, (2) too large in girth for belts or girdles,
124–5 below (Dent c577.1).

BARDOLPH Why, you are so fat, Sir John, that you must needs be out
of all compass, out of all reasonable compass, Sir John.

FALSTAFF Do thou amend thy face, and I'll amend my life. Thou art
our admiral, thou bearest the lantern in the poop, but 'tis in the nose
of thee. Thou art the Knight of the Burning Lamp.   20

BARDOLPH Why, Sir John, my face does you no harm.

FALSTAFF No, I'll be sworn, I make as good use of it as many a man
doth of a death's-head, or a *memento mori*. I never see thy face but I
see below   think upon hell-fire, and Dives that lived in purple: for there he is
in his robes, burning, burning. If thou wert any way given to virtue,   25
I would swear by thy face. My oath should be 'By this fire, that's
God's angel!' But thou art altogether given over, and wert indeed,
but for the light in thy face, the son of utter darkness. When thou
ran'st up Gad's Hill in the night to catch my horse, if I did not think
thou hadst been an *ignis fatuus*, or a ball of wildfire, there's no   30
purchase in money. O, thou art a perpetual triumph, an everlasting

display of creativity   by Falstaff   &   use of metaphor

26–7 that's God's angel!] QQ3–5; that Gods Angell Qq1, 2; *not in* F

---

19 **admiral** flagship.

19 **lantern** Bardolph's red nose; the jest is
echoed in *2H4* 1.2.48 (Melchiori). A lantern was
hung in the poop of the flagship to guide the fleet.

20 **Knight of the Burning Lamp** A parody of
the Knight of the Burning Sword, Amadis.
Beaumont and Fletcher's later farce, *The Knight of
the Burning Pestle* (c. 1607), also mocks the titles
given to the heroes of popular romances. Compare
Falstaff's reference to 'Phoebus', 'that wandering
knight', 1.2.11–12 and n.

23 **death's-head** a human skull or the representation of one.

23 **memento mori** an object used to symbolise
death. Compare *2H4* 2.4.234–5: 'do not speak like
a death's-head, do not bid me remember mine
end'.

24 **hell-fire . . . Dives** An allusion to Christ's
parable of the rich man, Dives, and the beggar,
Lazarus. The rich man who 'fared wel and deli-
cately' allowed the beggar to starve at his gate. Later
Dives learned, too late, that he would burn eternally
in Hell, while Lazarus rested in the bosom of
Abraham (Luke 16.19–31). Falstaff refers to
'Lazarus in the painted cloth', 4.2.22. He associates
Bardolph's nose with the fires of hell in *2H4*
2.4.329–34; and in *H5* 2.3.40–2, he is said to joke on
his death-bed about a flea upon Bardolph's nose as a
'black soul burning in hell'.

26–7 **By . . . angel** A proverbial oath omitted
from F as profane. It may refer to the episode of

Moses and the Burning Bush in which 'the Angel of
the Lord appeared unto him in a flame of fyre'
(Exodus 3.2) or to Psalm 104.4 : 'a flaming fyre his
ministers'.

28 **the son of utter darkness** Falstaff repeats
'son(s) of darkness', his transformation at 2.4.145,
of 1 Thess. 5.5, and combines it with the 'utter'
darkness of Matt. 8.12, 22.13, and 25.30. 'Utter'
means 'indefinitely remote' (*OED* sv *a* 1); the King
James version substitutes 'outer'.

30 **ignis fatuus** Latin for 'foolish fire', will o' the
wisp, a light that appears to glimmer over marshes
and swamps and leads travellers fatally astray.

30 **ball of wildfire** (1) Translation of *ignis fatuus*,
(2) a flaming ball of gunpowder, used both for fire-
works and for naval battles, (3) a skin disease, ery-
sipelas (Wilson). In Marlowe, *Dido Queene of
Carthage*, Pirrhus is said to be followed by 'his band
of Mirmidons, / With balles of wilde fire in their
murdering pawes', 2.1.216–17.

31 **purchase** value.

31 **triumph** Either a procession celebrating victory or a great public festival, illuminated by the
bonfires and torches to which Bardolph's nose is
compared, 32 and 33.

31–2 **everlasting bonfire-light** Bonfires were
lit for St John's or Midsummer Eve; compare 'fern-
seed', 2.1.70, and 'apple-john', 3 above, and nn. An
allusion to hell-fire may be suggested, through
'everlasting' and 'bone-fire', which was a current
spelling, as well as a word for: (1) the burning of

bonfire-light! Thou hast saved me a thousand marks in links and
torches, walking with thee in the night betwixt tavern and tavern.
But the sack that thou hast drunk me would have bought me lights
as good cheap at the dearest chandler's in Europe. I have main-   35
tained that salamander of yours with fire any time this two-and-
thirty years, God reward me for it!

BARDOLPH 'Sblood, I would my face were in your belly!

FALSTAFF God-a-mercy! So should I be sure to be heart-burnt.

Enter HOSTESS

How now, dame Partlet the hen, have you enquired yet who picked   40
my pocket?

HOSTESS Why, Sir John, what do you think, Sir John, do you think I
keep thieves in my house? I have searched, I have enquired, so has
my husband, man by man, boy by boy, servant by servant – the tithe
of a hair was never lost in my house before.   45

FALSTAFF Ye lie, Hostess. Bardolph was shaved and lost many a hair,
and I'll be sworn my pocket was picked. Go to, you are a woman, go!

HOSTESS Who, I? No, I defy thee! God's light, I was never called so in
mine own house before.

FALSTAFF Go to, I know you well enough.   50

---

39 SD *Enter* HOSTESS] F; *after 40* (enquird) QQ1, 2; *after 41* QQ3–5   44 tithe] *Theobald;* tight QQF

heretics' bones or of proscribed books, (2) a funeral
pyre (*OED* sv *sb* 2, 3).

32 marks Each mark is worth two-thirds of a
pound.

32 links flares or torches.

34 me at my expense.

35 as good cheap as a good bargain (but costly
under the circumstances) (*OED* sv *sb* 5).

35 dearest most expensive.

35 chandler maker or seller of candles.

36 salamander nose. The belief that this lizard
could live in fire because it was cold-blooded derived from Pliny, *Natural History* (cited by
Humphreys).

36–7 two-and-thirty years No special significance has been found for the exact length of this
remarkably long relationship. In *2H4* the Hostess
claims to have known Falstaff for twenty-nine
years, Justice Shallow for approximately fifty-five
(2.4.382–3, 3.2.210).

38 I . . . belly A proverbial retort, inviting a
speaker to 'eat' his words: 'I wish it were in your
belly (for me)' (Dent B299). Falstaff plays upon the
literal meaning in his response below.

40 dame Partlet A traditional name for a hen,
commonly used to designate a scolding woman. In
WT, Leontes calls Paulina 'Dame Partlet' (2.3.76).
The name derived from folktales of Reynard the
Fox; 'Dame Pertelote' was the rooster's favourite
hen in Chaucer's *Nun's Priest's Tale*.

44 tithe tenth part, the traditional assessment
for contributions to the church or to charity.
Theobald's emendation from QQF 'tight' is made
more probable by 'denier' (the tenth of a penny), 62
below.

46 shaved . . . hair A quibble on 'tithe of a hair',
44–5. Three more puns on 'shaved' are latent: (1)
robbed or cheated, (2) deprived of hair because of
venereal disease ('The suggestion of the tavern as a
bawdy-house, where customers might suffer this
customary double consequence of lechery, is echoed
repeatedly in the double entendres of this scene',
Bevington); (3) treated in order to eliminate lice.
Prisoners in jails traditionally have been shaved.

47, 50 you are a woman, . . . I know you Using
derogatory connotations of 'woman' and 'know',
Falstaff implies that the Hostess is both deceitful
and sexually promiscuous.

HOSTESS No, Sir John, you do not know me, Sir John. I know you, Sir
John. You owe me money, Sir John, and now you pick a quarrel to
beguile me of it. I bought you a dozen of shirts to your back.

FALSTAFF Dowlas, filthy dowlas. I have given them away to bakers'
wives. They have made bolters of them.   55

HOSTESS Now as I am a true woman, holland of eight shillings an ell!
You owe money here besides, Sir John, for your diet, and by-
drinkings, and money lent you, four-and-twenty pound.

FALSTAFF He had his part of it, let him pay.

HOSTESS He? Alas, he is poor, he hath nothing.   60

FALSTAFF How? Poor? Look upon his face. What call you rich? Let
them coin his nose, let them coin his cheeks, I'll not pay a denier.
What, will you make a younker of me? Shall I not take mine ease in
mine inn but I shall have my pocket picked? I have lost a seal-ring
of my grandfather's worth forty mark.   65

HOSTESS O Jesu, I have heard the Prince tell him I know not how oft,
that that ring was copper.

FALSTAFF How? The Prince is a Jack, a sneak-up. 'Sblood, an he were
here I would cudgel him like a dog if he would say so.

Enter the PRINCE *marching* [*with* PETO], *and Falstaff meets him,
playing upon his truncheon like a fife*

How now, lad? Is the wind in that door, i'faith, must we all march?   70

---

68 sneak-up] Qq1, 2 (sneakeup); sneak-cup Qq3–5, F   69 SD.1 *with* PETO] *Theobald subst., not in* QQF   70 How] *Dyce; Falst.*
How QqF

---

53 to your back for you to wear.

54 Dowlas coarse linen, named after Doulas in
Brittany.

55 bolters cloths used for sifting meal, i.e. unsuitable for wearing.

56 holland fine linen fabric, lawn, originally
from the province of Holland in the Netherlands.

56 ell 45 inches or 1.1 metres.

57–8 diet . . . by-drinkings board (*OED* sv *sb*[1]
5b), and the frequent drinks between meals recorded by Falstaff's IOUs, 2.4.448 ff.

62 denier small coin worth one-tenth of a penny;
Falstaff may remember the Hostess' 'tithe of a hair'
44–5 above.

63 younker a free-spending and gullible young
nobleman, eager to be fashionable, but often ruined
by bad company. Compare *MV* 2.6.14: 'How like a
younger or a prodigal'.

63–4 Shall . . . inn Proverbial expression (Dent
E 42). Cowl and Morgan cite Harrison, *The Description of England*, 1587, Bk III, chap. 16, on the English

innkeeper who 'does not challenge a lordlie
authoritie over his guests . . . sith everie man may
use his inne as his owne house in England'.

64 seal-ring One decorated with a signet or seal.
The sentimental value of such an heirloom is suggested in Sir Thomas Overbury's 'character' of an
'Elder Brother': 'His pedigree and his fathers seale-
ring, are the stilts of his crazed disposition' (cited by
Humphreys). Compare the agate-ring, 2.4.61, and
the alderman's thumb-ring, 2.4.274–5.

68 a Jack, a sneak-up a knave, possibly referring to servile and potentially disloyal pages and
serving-men. Compare 2.4.9 and *R3* 1.3.53: 'silken,
sly, insinuating Jacks'.

69 SD.1 *with* PETO QQF omit, and some editors
follow Johnson in substituting Poins, but the Prince
addresses Peto at 164.

69 SD.2 *truncheon* a short thick staff, implied by
Falstaff's threat, 69, to cudgel the Prince.

70 Is . . . door? Is that (i.e. war) what will
happen? A familiar phrase (Dent W419).

Prince - not radically changed - man for all seasons.

BARDOLPH Yea, two and two, Newgate fashion.

HOSTESS My lord, I pray you hear me.

PRINCE What sayest thou, Mistress Quickly? How doth thy husband?
I love him well, he is an honest man.

HOSTESS Good my lord, hear me.   75

FALSTAFF Prithee let her alone, and list to me.

PRINCE What sayest thou, Jack?

FALSTAFF The other night I fell asleep here, behind the arras, and had
my pocket picked. This house is turned bawdy-house, they pick
pockets.   80

PRINCE What didst thou lose, Jack?

FALSTAFF Wilt thou believe me, Hal, three or four bonds of forty
pound apiece, and a seal-ring of my grandfather's.

PRINCE A trifle, some eight-penny matter.

HOSTESS So I told him, my lord, and I said I heard your grace say so.   85
And, my lord, he speaks most vilely of you, like a foul-mouthed
man as he is, and said he would cudgel you.

PRINCE What! He did not?

HOSTESS There's neither faith, truth, nor womanhood in me else.

FALSTAFF There's no more faith in thee than in a stewed prune, nor no   90
more truth in thee than in a drawn fox – and for womanhood, Maid
Marian may be the deputy's wife of the ward to thee. Go, you thing,
go!

HOSTESS Say, what thing, what thing?

FALSTAFF What thing? Why, a thing to thank God on.   95

HOSTESS I am no thing to thank God on, I would thou shouldst know
it, I am an honest man's wife, and setting thy knighthood aside,
thou art a knave to call me so.

73 doth] Qq1–4 *subst.;* does F   92 thing] Qq; nothing F   96 no thing] Q5, F; nothing Qq1–4

71 **Newgate fashion** Prisoners were led in pairs to the City prison, Newgate, or conducted from prison to trial.

82 bonds deeds entitling the holder to payment.

90 stewed prune Either a prostitute or someone closely linked with prostitution. Stewed prunes were served in brothels or 'stews'; compare *2H4* 2.4.146–7 and *MM* 2.1.90. Like the 'apple-john', 3, the prune may suggest old age.

91 drawn fox hunted (drawn from cover), and relying on its cunning to escape. Falstaff, an escape-artist himself, may mix some compliment with his ridicule.

91–2 Maid Marian . . . to thee i.e. Compared to you, Maid Marian may be a model of respectabil-ity. As a character in morris dances generally per-formed by a boy or man, Maid Marian became a symbol of grotesque disguise and foppish male dress. But her name was also used as that of the 'loved one', who was given presents in May Day games (Laroque, *Shakespeare's Festive World*, 1993, pp. 124–5). The deputy of a ward would be one of its most respectable citizens.

95 What thing . . . God on Having provoked her suspicion that he denies her gender and her morality, Falstaff can slip in an ambiguous compli-ment which the Hostess takes as a bawdy insult.

97 setting . . . aside A polite formula, meaning 'with all due respect to your knighthood'. Falstaff seizes on its literal meanings, 99.

FALSTAFF Setting thy womanhood aside, thou art a beast to say otherwise.   100

HOSTESS Say, what beast, thou knave, thou?

FALSTAFF What beast? Why – an otter.

PRINCE An otter, Sir John? Why an otter?

FALSTAFF Why? She's neither fish nor flesh, a man knows not where to
have her.   105

HOSTESS Thou art an unjust man in saying so, thou or any man knows
where to have me, thou knave, thou.

PRINCE Thou sayest true, Hostess, and he slanders thee most grossly.

HOSTESS So he doth you, my lord, and said this other day you owed
him a thousand pound.   110

PRINCE Sirrah, do I owe you a thousand pound?

FALSTAFF A thousand pound, Hal? A million, thy love is worth a
million, thou owest me thy love.

HOSTESS Nay my lord, he called you Jack, and said he would cudgel
you.   115

FALSTAFF Did I, Bardolph?

BARDOLPH Indeed, Sir John, you said so.

FALSTAFF Yea, if he said my ring was copper.

PRINCE I say 'tis copper, darest thou be as good as thy word now?

FALSTAFF Why Hal, thou knowest as thou art but man I dare, but as   120
thou art prince, I fear thee as I fear the roaring of the lion's whelp.

PRINCE And why not as the lion?

FALSTAFF The King himself is to be feared as the lion. Dost thou think
I'll fear thee as I fear thy father? Nay, an I do, I pray God my girdle
break.   125

PRINCE O, if it should, how would thy guts fall about thy knees! But

---

109 owed] QqF (ought)   121 prince] Qq; a Prince F   124 an] Qq (and); if F   124 I pray God] Qq; let F

103–4 **An otter . . . flesh** Humphreys cites Izaak
Walton, *Compleat Angler* (1653) 1, 2, on the inconclusive debate among 'great clerks' over the nature
of otters. Compare the popular saying, 'neither fish
nor flesh (nor good red herring)' (Dent F319).
Falstaff has led his listeners to expect a much more
monstrous 'beast', 99.

104–5 **a man . . . her** Understood by the Hostess in the most literal, sexual sense, 106–7, but perhaps, in addition, another back-handed compliment
(compare 90–1 and 95 above): 'She isn't easy to take
advantage of.' The innocent popular saying, in
which 'where to have' means 'how to understand'

(*Oxford Dictionary of Proverbs*, p. 438), suggests
how far both characters have travelled from any
simple comprehension.

110 **a thousand pound** Compare 2.4.134 and n.

121–3 **I fear thee . . . lion** Compare Prov. 19.12:
'The King's wrath is like the roaring of a lyon', and
Prov. 20.2. On the association of royalty with lions,
see 2.4.224–5 and n., and 3.2.102.

124–5 **I pray . . . break** Falstaff's surprising
prayer reworks both Bardolph's 'compass' joke, 16–
17 above, and the proverbial saying 'ungirt,
unblessed' (Tilley U10).

sirrah, there's no room for faith, truth, nor honesty in this bosom of thine. It is all filled up with guts and midriff. Charge an honest woman with picking thy pocket? Why, thou whoreson impudent embossed rascal, if there were anything in thy pocket but tavern   130 reckonings, memorandums of bawdy-houses, and one poor penny-worth of sugar-candy to make thee long-winded, if thy pocket were enriched with any other injuries but these, I am a villain. And yet you will stand to it, you will not pocket up wrong! Art thou not ashamed?   135

FALSTAFF Dost thou hear, Hal? Thou knowest in the state of innocency Adam fell, and what should poor Jack Falstaff do in the days of villainy? Thou seest I have more flesh than another man, and there-fore more frailty. You confess then, you picked my pocket?

PRINCE It appears so by the story.   140

FALSTAFF Hostess, I forgive thee, go make ready breakfast, love thy husband, look to thy servants, cherish thy guests, thou shalt find me tractable to any honest reason, thou seest I am pacified still – nay prithee be gone.

Exit Hostess

Now, Hal, to the news at court: for the robbery, lad, how is that   145 answered?

PRINCE O my sweet beef, I must still be good angel to thee – the money is paid back again.

FALSTAFF O, I do not like that paying back, 'tis a double labour.

PRINCE I am good friends with my father and may do anything.   150

141–4 Hostess . . . gone] Qq; *As verse* Hostesse . . . thee: / Go . . . Husband, / Looke . . . Guests: / Thou . . . reason: / Thou . . . still. / Nay . . . gone F   142 guests] Qq2–5, F *subst.*; ghesse Q1   145 court:] *Theobald;* court for QqF 147–8 O my . . . again] Qq; *as verse* O . . . Beefe: / I . . . thee. / The . . . againe F

127 bosom The figurative location of the qualities which have been crowded out ('chest' not 'breast').

128 midriff diaphragm (*OED* 1a, this example); what normally separates 'bosom' from 'guts'.

130 embossed (1) bulging (*OED ppl. a*[1] 4), (2) foaming at the mouth (like a hunted animal, driven to extremity (*OED v*[2] 4).

130 rascal (1) knave, (2) young male deer, unfit for the hunt (and therefore 'embossed'). Compare 2.2.5.

132 sugar-candy . . . long-winded A common prescription to improve stamina, especially of fighting cocks (Wright).

133 injuries i.e. the items Falstaff pretends were stolen.

134 pocket up submit to. In his word-play upon

a familiar phrase (Dent 170), the Prince mocks Falstaff's pretence of being wronged, puns on his picked 'pocket', and implies, 'You won't even try to hide the injury you have done.'

138–9 Thou seest . . . frailty A distortion of the proverbial saying, 'the flesh is frail', Bishops' Bible version of Matt. 26.41 and Mark 14.38; Geneva has 'weake'. Falstaff turns a condemnation of human depravity, symbolised by the body or 'flesh', into a justification.

140 by according to.

143 still as usual.

146 answered taken care of, dealt with.

147 sweet beef 'a fattened beast, or its carcass' (*OED* Beef sv *sb* 3) which is still fresh, i.e. not yet preserved with salt. There are many references to Falstaff as meat, living or dead.

FALSTAFF Rob me the exchequer the first thing thou dost, and do it
with unwashed hands too.

BARDOLPH Do, my lord.

PRINCE I have procured thee, Jack, a charge of foot.

FALSTAFF I would it had been of horse. Where shall I find one that can   155
steal well? O for a fine thief of the age of two-and-twenty or there-
abouts! I am heinously unprovided. Well, God be thanked for these
rebels, they offend none but the virtuous. I laud them, I praise
them.

PRINCE Bardolph!   160

BARDOLPH My lord?

PRINCE Go bear this letter to Lord John of Lancaster,
To my brother John, this to my Lord of Westmoreland.
                                                   [*Exit Bardolph*]

Go, Peto, to horse, to horse, for thou and I
Have thirty miles to ride yet ere dinner-time.   165
                                                        [*Exit Peto*]

Jack, meet me tomorrow in the Temple hall
At two o'clock in the afternoon.
There shalt thou know thy charge, and there receive
Money and order for their furniture.
The land is burning, Percy stands on high,   170
And either we or they must lower lie.   [*Exit*]

FALSTAFF Rare words! Brave world! Hostess, my breakfast, come!
O, I could wish this tavern were my drum.   [*Exit*]

156 the age of] Qq; *not in* F   163 SD *Exit Bardolph*] Dyce; *not in* QqF   164 Peto] QqF; Poins *Dering MS., Var. 1773, conj.*
Johnson   165 SD *Exit Peto*] Cam.; Exit Pointz / Dyce; *not in* QqF   167 o'] Qq2–5, F (a); of Q1   171 SD *Exit*] Dyce; *not in*
QqF   173 SD *Exit*] Capell; *not in* Q1; Exeunt Qq2–5; Exeunt omnes F

152 **with unwashed hands** with no scruples
(Dent H125).

157 **heinously unprovided** infamously ill-
equipped. Falstaff blames his poverty, as if it were a
crime in itself, on 'paying back', 149, and on the
Prince's failure as a thief, 156–7.

157–8 **God . . . virtuous** Falstaff praises the
rebels for giving him a timely chance to make
money. He suggests that there is little moral distinction between the rebels and those in power who
pretend to 'virtue'. Humphreys summarises
Wilson, *Fortunes*, p. 84: 'Falstaff's attitude to war is
blatantly, and indeed blasphemously, predatory.'
But in recent productions, Falstaff's complex
attitude is often close to that of Brecht's Mother
Courage.

163 SD, 165 SD *Exit Bardolph, Exit Peto* Q pro-

vides no exits and entrances separating this from the
following scene, while Qq2–5, F have only a group
exit at the end. Adding these exits for Bardolph and
Peto enhances the urgency of the action and leaves
the Prince and Falstaff together for the last time
until 5.1.121 ff. See Textual Analysis, pp. 201–2.

165 **thirty . . . dinner-time** 'This fixes the time
of the scene as early morning' (Wilson).

166 **Temple hall** The hall of the Inner Temple,
one of the Inns of Court where students prepared
for careers in law.

169 **furniture** equipment.

173 **I . . . drum** Hemingway suggests that
Falstaff 'may refer to the drum, in its literal sense,
as he pounds on the table for his breakfast'. The
drum called soldiers into battle.

[4.1] [*Enter* HOTSPUR, WORCESTER, *and* DOUGLAS]

HOTSPUR Well said, my noble Scot! If speaking truth
           In this fine age were not thought flattery,
           Such attribution should the Douglas have
           As not a soldier of this season's stamp
           Should go so general current through the world.   5
           By God, I cannot flatter. I do defy
           The tongues of soothers, but a braver place
           In my heart's love hath no man than yourself.
           Nay, task me to my word, approve me, lord.
DOUGLAS Thou art the king of honour.   10
           No man so potent breathes upon the ground
           But I will beard him.
HOTSPUR   Do so, and 'tis well.

                Enter [MESSENGER] *with letters*   not good news

           What letters hast thou there? – I can but thank you.
MESSENGER These letters come from your father.
HOTSPUR Letters from him? Why comes he not himself?   15
MESSENGER He cannot come, my lord, he is grievous sick.
HOTSPUR Zounds, how has he the leisure to be sick
           In such a jostling time? Who leads his power?

Act 4, Scene 1   4.1] *Actus Quartus. Scæna Prima.* F; *not in* Qq   0 SD *Enter* HOTSPUR, WORCESTER, *and* DOUGLAS] Qq2–
5, F *subst.; not in* Q1   1 SH HOTSPUR] Qq2–5, F; *Per.* (*to line 90*) Q1   12–13 But . . . you] *Capell, followed by Humphreys;*
But . . . him. / Do . . . there? / I . . . you Qq1, 2, F; *one line of verse* But . . . him, *the remainder as prose* Qq3–5   12 SD *Enter*
MESSENGER *with letters*] *Malone subst.; Enter one with letters,* Qq (*after* beard him); *Enter a Messenger* F (*after* beard
him)

9 **task** test.
9 **approve me** put my feeling to the proof.
11 **No man** No other man.
12 **beard** challenge or defy. The possible deriva-
tion of this sense from seizing the 'beard' of a lion
(*OED sv v* 3) is apposite.
16 **grievous sick** By delaying this sickness
which, according to Holinshed, came at an earlier
stage of the conspiracy, Shakespeare can emphasise
the divergent responses of the rebel leaders. The
chronicle narrative implies that Northumberland's
forces would have arrived in time to support his
relatives or 'procure a peace', had the King not
marched to Shrewsbury so swiftly (III, 24, 26). In
2H4 'Rumour' reports that Northumberland 'Lies
crafty-sick' (Induction, 37).
18 **jostling time** a time of great contention, of
clashing (as in a joust).

Act 4, Scene 1
  [4.1] The characters enter from the same door,
because Hotspur's first words respond to a speech
that he, unlike the audience, has just heard. The
scene takes place in the rebel camp.
  2 **fine** refined (spoken in a sarcastic tone).
  3 **attribution** praise, acclaim.
  4–5 **As . . . world** As no other soldier deserves.
Hotspur uses the metaphor of current coins to
emphasise the universal value of Douglas' heroic
conduct. Compare 2.3.87–8.
  4 **stamp** The design (a soldier) stamped on each
coin (*OED sv sb³* 12b).
  5 **general current** widely acceptable.
  6 **defy** distrust, as well as denounce.
  7 **soothers** flatterers.
  7 **braver** more worthy.

Under whose government come they along?
MESSENGER His letters bear his mind, not I, my lord.   20
WORCESTER I prithee tell me, doth he keep his bed?
MESSENGER He did, my lord, four days ere I set forth,
          And at the time of my departure thence
          He was much feared by his physicians.
WORCESTER I would the state of time had first been whole   25
          Ere he by sickness had been visited.
          His health was never better worth than now.
HOTSPUR Sick now? Droop now? This sickness doth infect
          The very life-blood of our enterprise.
          'Tis catching hither, even to our camp.   30
          He writes me here that inward sickness –
          And that his friends by deputation could not
          So soon be drawn, nor did he think it meet
          To lay so dangerous and dear a trust
          On any soul removed but on his own.   35
          Yet doth he give us bold advertisement
          That with our small conjunction we should on,
          To see how fortune is disposed to us.
          For, as he writes, there is no quailing now,
          Because the King is certainly possessed   40
          Of all our purposes. What say you to it?
WORCESTER Your father's sickness is a maim to us.
HOTSPUR A perilous gash, a very limb lopped off –
          And yet, in faith, it is not! His present want

---

20 bear] Q7; beares QQF   20 lord] *Capell;* mind QQF   31 sickness –] *Rowe;* sicknesse Q1; Sickness holds him *Capell*
32–3 deputation could not / So] *Capell;* deputation / Could not so QQF

19 government command.
20 bear . . . lord QQF 'beares' is probably a compositor's error. Although 'letters' is at times used as a singular noun by Shakespeare, the presence of 'I', governing the same verb, makes that usage unlikely here. Capell's emendation has been generally accepted.
24 He . . . feared His life was feared for.
31 sickness – The unfinished line in QQF has been thought defective, but may instead express a pause (perhaps staged with a gesture signifying 'you already know about his sickness'). Hotspur, typically impatient, then continues with a hasty but coherent third-person paraphrase of the letter. Proposed completions of the line include 'holds him' (Capell) and 'stays him' (Oxford).

32 by deputation by agents acting in his place.
33 drawn gathered together.
33 meet appropriate, just.
35 On . . . own On anyone less vitally concerned than he (the rallying of 'friends' or allies being a sensitive matter).
36 give . . . advertisement (1) instruct us to be resolute, (2) boldly instruct us.
37 conjunction combination of powers.
37 on i.e. march forward.
40–1 King . . . purposes In Holinshed (III, 23), the King writes an answer to the articles and letters in which the Percys justify their rebellion.
44 want absence.

Seems more than we shall find it. Were it good   45
To set the exact wealth of all our states
All at one cast? To set so rich a main
On the nice hazard of one doubtful hour?
It were not good, for therein should we read
The very bottom and the soul of hope,   50
The very list, the very utmost bound
Of all our fortunes.

DOUGLAS Faith, and so we should. Where now remains
A sweet reversion – we may boldly spend
Upon the hope of what is to come in.   55
A comfort of retirement lives in this.

HOTSPUR A rendezvous, a home to fly unto,
If that the devil and mischance look big
Upon the maidenhead of our affairs.

WORCESTER But yet I would your father had been here.   60
The quality and hair of our attempt
Brooks no division. It will be thought,
By some that know not why he is away,
That wisdom, loyalty, and mere dislike
Of our proceedings kept the Earl from hence.   65
And think how such an apprehension

53–5 Faith . . . in] *Collier*[1], *conj. Walker;* Faith . . . should, / Where . . . reversion, / We . . . in, Qq; Faith . . . should, / Where . . . reversion. / We . . . hope / Of . . . in: F; *Cam. conjectures a missing line after* reversion   55 is] F; 'tis Qq *subst.*

46–7 To set . . . cast To stake the total value of our combined powers on one throw of the dice.
47 main total power (with a serious pun on a stake in gambling).
48 nice precarious.
48 hazard (1) venture, fortune, (2) dice-game.
49–52 for therein . . . fortunes i.e. for we should regard such an action as signifying that we lacked any other source of confidence and had used up any luck we might have.
50 bottom bed of the sea, as in 1.3.201, 'bottom of the deep'.
50 soul essence, exposed or concentrated at the 'bottom'. Wilson notes a quibble on 'sole'.
51 list Synonymous with 'bound', an extreme limit or boundary (*OED sv sb*[3] 8a). Humphreys suggests two puns: a schedule and the selvedge of a cloth.
51 bound This term concludes a series which Mahood, *Wordplay*, 23, recognises as suggesting a naval venture: 'cast' and 'main' (47), 'hazard' (48), 'bottom' (50), 'list' and 'bound' (51).
53–5 Faith . . . in The lineation adopted here

avoids irregularities which become inevitable when Douglas' first sentence is either used to complete line 52 or given a line by itself. Qq punctuation by commas throughout is attractive in suggesting the speaker's relief and quick apprehension.
54 reversion possession or wealth that one expects to obtain in the future (*OED* 2a, this example).
56 retirement retreating, as in 5.4.5 (first recorded use in *OED*).
58 look big look threateningly (a common expression).
59 maidenhead of our affairs precarious beginning of our enterprise.
61 hair distinctive character, as in the saying 'of one hair' (*OED* Hair sv *sb* 6).
62 Brooks Tolerates or allows.
64 loyalty By implication, to the King, not to the rebels.
64 mere downright.
66 apprehension conception or idea (*OED* 10), perhaps shading towards the modern sense of uneasy or fearful anticipation.

May turn the tide of fearful faction,
And breed a kind of question in our cause.
For well you know we of the off'ring side
Must keep aloof from strict arbitrement,   70
And stop all sight-holes, every loop from whence
The eye of reason may pry in upon us.
This absence of your father's draws a curtain
That shows the ignorant a kind of fear
Before not dreamt of.

HOTSPUR   You strain too far.   75
I rather of his absence make this use.
It lends a lustre and more great opinion,
A larger dare to our great enterprise,
Than if the Earl were here. For men must think
If we without his help can make a head   80
To push against a kingdom, with his help
We shall o'erturn it topsy-turvy down.
Yet all goes well, yet all our joints are whole.

DOUGLAS As heart can think. There is not such a word
Spoke of in Scotland as this term of fear.   85

Enter SIR RICHARD VERNON

HOTSPUR My cousin Vernon! Welcome, by my soul!
VERNON Pray God my news be worth a welcome, lord.
The Earl of Westmoreland seven thousand strong
Is marching hitherwards, with him Prince John.
HOTSPUR No harm, what more?
VERNON   And further, I have learned,   90
The King himself in person is set forth,
Or hitherwards intended speedily,
With strong and mighty preparation.

85 term] QQ1–4 (tearme); deame Q5; Dreame F   85 SD RICHARD] F; *Ri*: QQ1–4; *Rih* Q5

67 **fearful faction** conspiracy which causes fear
(*OED* Fearful 1).
69 **off'ring** challenging, aggressive.
70 **strict arbitrement** rigorous and impartial
scrutiny.
71 **loop** loop-hole, window.
73 **draws** opens.
74 **a kind of fear** a doubt, based on 'reason', 72,
concerning our cause.

75 **strain too far** go out of your way to imagine
how people will think.
77 **opinion** prestige.
80 **make a head** (1) gather our supporters (compare 1.3.278 and note), (2) advance aggressively.
83 **joints** limbs.
84 **As heart can think** A familiar saying (Dent
H300.1).
92 **intended** (is) on the point of departure.

HOTSPUR He shall be welcome too. Where is his son
            The nimble-footed madcap Prince of Wales,   *skipping king* 95
            And his comrades that daft the world aside
            And bid it pass?
VERNON   All furnished, all in arms,   *Don't kid yourself*
            All plumed like estridges that with the wind   *— this is quite a foe*
         ✳ Bated, like eagles having lately bath'd,
            Glittering in golden coats like images,   100
            As full of spirit as the month of May,
            And gorgeous as the sun at midsummer,   *sun image again*
ready to go Wanton as youthful goats, wild as young bulls.
            I saw young Harry with his beaver on,   *2 greek gods*
            His cushes on his thighs, gallantly armed,   *Mercury vs Mars* 105
            Rise from the ground like feathered Mercury,
            And vaulted with such ease into his seat   *phoenix raising*

✳ Eagles rising - rebirth - burning old scales of eyes

98 with] QQF; wing *Rowe*   98–9 wind / Bated] QQF *subst.; Oxford, Oxford OS, and Bevington conjecture an omission after*
wind   99 Bated] QQ1–4 (Baited); Bayted Q5, F; Baiting *Oxford, Oxford OS;* Bating *Bevington*

95 **nimble-footed** Hotspur speaks condescend-ingly, suggesting cowardice and frivolity, but Shakespeare perhaps noticed praise for the Prince's swiftness in several chronicles (e.g. Holinshed: 'In strength and nimblenesse of bodie from his youth, few to him comparable', III, 133).

96 **daft** toss(ed) aside carelessly. Humphreys argues that 'bid', 97, it may be understood as either present or past in tense.

97–110 **All furnished . . . horsemanship** This choric speech is all the more effective because a rebel leader is so impressed, quite against his own partisan interest, by the Prince's dazzling transformation.

98–9 **All plumed . . . bath'd** Because of doubt-ful spelling and punctuation, this splendid passage remains a textual crux.

98 **estridges** ostriches, referring to the plumes of their crested helmets. Shakespeare probably read the description in Nashe, *The Unfortunate Traveller* (1594), II, 272, of a horse decked out as an ostrich for a ceremonial tilt, with wings which made him as proud 'as he had been some other Pegasus', i.e. the mythical flying horse mentioned in 109 below. Nashe also compared the sound of these artificial wings to that made by 'Eagles . . . pursuing their praie in the ayre'. (G. R. Coffman, *MLN* 13 (1927), 318, cited by Wilson.) 'Estridge' has also been glossed 'goshawk' or 'falcon' (as in Douce, *Illustra-tions of Shakespeare*, 1807), but such feathers could not have served as plumes.

98–9 **that . . . Bated** that beat their wings with the wind. 'Bate' is a term from falconry meaning 'to beat the wings impatiently' (*OED* sv v¹ 2). Spelled 'Baited' in QQ1–4, it can also, Wilson argues, sug-gest refreshment, as in Sidney's *Astrophel and Stella* (1598), 39: 'Come sleep . . . , / The baiting-place of wit, the balme of woe' (1–2). Such word-play may anticipate 'bath'd' by implying that the wind invig-orated the flying birds. Bevington prefers 'Bating' because 'Baited' may have been contaminated by 'bath'd' in the same line.

99 **like . . . bath'd** A passage frequently sug-gested as a source or analogue occurs in Spenser's *Faerie Queene* I, xi, 34 where the Red Crosse Knight (St George), reviving after his first battle with the dragon, is compared to an 'Eagle fresh out of the ocean wave' who tries his 'newly budded pinions'.

100 **golden coats** shining armour.

100 **images** gilded effigies of warriors or illumi-nated figures in paintings. They may also anticipate the winged deities in 106 and 108 below.

104 **beaver** helmet, or, strictly, its face-guard.

105 **cushes** thigh armour, cuisses.

106 **feathered Mercury** the messenger of the gods in Roman mythology. He was usually repre-sented with wings on heels and cap.

107 **vaulted with such ease** 'Vaulting fully-armed needed uncommon strength' (Humphreys).

As if an angel dropped down from the clouds
To turn and wind a fiery Pegasus,
And witch the world with noble horsemanship.   110
HOTSPUR No more, no more! Worse than the sun in March,
dazzling
repense
– twas over
speech
around.
This praise doth nourish agues. Let them come!
They come like sacrifices in their trim,   *guzzied up ready*
And to the fire-eyed maid of smoky war   *for sacrifice*
All hot and bleeding will we offer them.   115
The mailèd Mars shall on his altar sit
Up to the ears in blood. I am on fire
To hear this rich reprisal is so nigh,
And yet not ours! Come, let me taste my horse,
Who is to bear me like a thunderbolt   120
Against the bosom of the Prince of Wales.
Harry to Harry shall, hot horse to horse,   *panting – interrupts*
Meet and ne'er part till one drop down a corpse.   *speech.*
O that Glendower were come!
VERNON   There is more news.
I learned in Worcester as I rode along   125
He cannot draw his power this fourteen days.
DOUGLAS That's the worst tidings that I hear of yet.   *grave news.*
WORCESTER Ay, by my faith, that bears a frosty sound.   *– does not like*
HOTSPUR What may the King's whole battle reach unto?
VERNON To thirty thousand.
HOTSPUR   Forty let it be.   130

of bag/play – fancy fellow who didnt like smell of flesh

108 dropped] Qq2–5, F *subst.*; drop Q1   116 altar] Qq4, 5, F; altars Qq1–3   119 taste] Qq1, 2; take Qq3–5, F   123 ne'er]
Qq2–5, F (ne're); neare Q1   123 corpse] QqF (coarse)   126 cannot] Q5 *corr.*, F; can Qq1–4, Q5 *uncorr.*   127 yet] Q5, F; it
Qq1–4

109 wind turn. The expert horseman can make
his mount wheel around.
109 Pegasus winged horse in Greek and Roman
mythology ridden by the hero Perseus.
110 witch bewitch.
111–12 Worse . . . agues The early spring sun
was considered strong enough to help breed fevers,
by drawing up vapours from undrained marshes
(Kittredge).
113 sacrifices . . . trim animals garlanded in
preparation for sacrifice. Hotspur continues the
classical, heroic idiom of Vernon's speech.
114 fire-eyed . . . war Bellona, Roman goddess
of war.
116 mailèd Mars the god of war himself, in
armour. Hotspur magnifies Vernon's 'golden coats
like images', 100 above.
118 reprisal prize, booty.

119 taste put to the proof, test (*OED* sv v 2).
123 corpse QqF's 'coarse' indicates Elizabethan
pronunciation.
126 He . . . days Shakespeare follows Daniel,
Civile Wars III, st. 99, rather than Holinshed in de-
priving Hotspur of Welsh support. Compare 3.1.84
where Mortimer intimates that Glendower will not
be ready for fourteen days.
129 battle army.
130 To thirty . . . be Hotspur's reply indicates
both that success need not be based on numbers (as
the later English victory at Agincourt will prove)
and that numbers are difficult to establish.
Holinshed gives the Percys 14,000 men (III, 24) but
provides no figure for the King's side. Humphreys
cites Wyntoun's *Cronykil of Scotland* which gives
30,000 for the King, and Hall who says that over
40,000 were engaged on both sides.

My father and Glendower being both away,
The powers of us may serve so great a day.
Come, let us take a muster speedily.
Doomsday is near. Die all, die merrily.
DOUGLAS Talk not of dying, I am out of fear   135
Of death or death's hand for this one half year.

Exeunt

[4.2] *Enter* FALSTAFF [*and*] BARDOLPH

FALSTAFF Bardolph, get thee before to Coventry. Fill me a bottle of
  sack. Our soldiers shall march through. We'll to Sutton Coldfield
  tonight.
BARDOLPH Will you give me money, captain?
FALSTAFF Lay out, lay out.   5
BARDOLPH This bottle makes an angel.
FALSTAFF And if it do, take it for thy labour – and if it make twenty,
  take them all, I'll answer the coinage. Bid my lieutenant Peto meet
  me at town's end.
BARDOLPH I will, captain. Farewell.   *Exit*   10
FALSTAFF If I be not ashamed of my soldiers, I am a soused gurnet. I

134 merrily] Qq2–5, F; merely Q1   Act 4, Scene 2   4.2] *Scæna Secunda.* F; *not in* Qq   0 SD *and*] Qq2–5, F; *not in* Q1
2 Coldfield] *Johnson;* cop-hill Qq 1–5, F *subst.;* Co'fil *Cam.*   11 soused] Qq (souct)

132 serve be adequate for.
136 this one half year a little while longer.
Douglas attempts to modify the tone of Hotspur's
fatalistic last line.

Act 4, Scene 2
[4.2] The first three lines locate the scene by or on
the road to Coventry, along the route from London
to Shrewsbury.
2 Sutton Coldfield A town in Warwickshire 20
miles beyond Coventry, well off the direct route to
Shrewsbury and consequently a long march for
Falstaff with his foot soldiers. This has caused
much discussion about whether Shakespeare
wanted Falstaff to avoid Stratford-upon-Avon.
Hemingway's practical suggestion would resolve
the problem of why Falstaff and, perhaps, the
Prince may travel by roundabout routes: 'the coun-
tryside had to be combed for recruits'. Coldfield was
probably pronounced 'Cofil'.
5 Lay out Spend your own money.
6 makes an angel brings expenses to the value
of the gold coin worth between 6s. 8d., and 10s. It
was stamped with the archangel Michael killing a

dragon. 11 or 12s. was a typical weekly wage for a
journeyman (Davison).
7–8 and if . . . coinage Falstaff puns on 'makes'
above; by somehow raising (coining) money
Bardolph will profit rather than 'lay out'.
8 Peto Because Hal at 3.3.164–5 tells Peto to ride
with him, Johnson and other editors have assumed
that he cannot serve Falstaff here unless they replace him with Poins in 3.3. But Peto never reappears. Shakespeare and his characters seem to
have changed their minds; the Prince enters at 40
below, surprising Falstaff, and there is no further
mention of Peto in the play. Shakespeare individu-
alises attendants and companions, but uses them
with great flexibility. See Textual Analysis, pp.
203–4.
11 soused gurnet pickled gurnet (gurnard), a
small fish with a large spiny head, regarded as a
delicacy. This, with its size and shape, makes
Falstaff's comparison incongruous, like 'poulter's
hare' 2.4.361. After *1H4*, 'soused gurnet' became a
term of contempt (*OED* Gurnard 1b).
11–13 I have . . . pounds As a captain, Falstaff
has the power to impress forcibly (or draft) civilians

have misused the King's press damnably. I have got in exchange of
a hundred-and-fifty soldiers three hundred and odd pounds. I press
me none but good householders, yeomen's sons, enquire me out
contracted bachelors, such as had been asked twice on the banns,   15
such a commodity of warm slaves as had as lief hear the devil as a
drum, such as fear the report of a caliver worse than a struck fowl or
a hurt wild duck. I pressed me none but such toasts-and-butter,
with hearts in their bellies no bigger than pins' heads, and they have
bought out their services. And now my whole charge consists of   20
ancients, corporals, lieutenants, gentlemen of companies – slaves as
ragged as Lazarus in the painted cloth, where the glutton's dogs
licked his sores. And such as indeed were never soldiers, but discarded unjust serving-men, younger sons to younger brothers, re-

other half
of Divos

---

13 a hundred-and-fifty] Qq (150)   13 three hundred] Qq (300)   17 fowl] *Rowe;* foule Qq 1–3; foole Qq4, 5, F

---

into the army. His actions reflect current abuse of
these practices. See Introduction, pp. 30–1.

14 good wealthy, substantial.

14 yeomen small land-holders rich enough to
purchase their sons' freedom from military service.

15 contracted engaged to be married.

15 banns announcements of couples intending
to marry, read out in the established church on
three successive Sundays. QqF 'banes' is a spelling
variant.

16 commodity parcel or 'lot' of wares (*OED* 7a).

16 warm slaves contemptible, comfort-loving
civilians (*OED* Warm sv *a* 8).

17 caliver firearm, light enough to fire without a
rest or support.

17 struck wounded, a hunting term normally
applied to deer. Compare 5.4.106. Johnson suggested that Shakespeare might have written 'struck
sorel' (a young deer), avoiding duplication by 'hurt
wild duck'.

18 toasts-and-butter milk-toasts, continuing
the satire on civilians. Fynes Morrison's *Itinerary*,
1617, Bk 1, chap. 3, 53, first cited by Malone,
reports that 'Londiners, and all within the sound of
Bow-Bell, are in reproch called Cocknies, and eaters
of buttered tostes' (Kittredge).

20 bought out their services bribed Falstaff
(or, as in *2H4* 3.2.220–33, perhaps Bardolph) to
release them from the 'press', 12. Steevens (1793)
quotes *The Voyage to Cadiz* (1597) (Hakluyt Soc.) I,
607: 'A certaine Lieutenant was degraded and
cashiered, &c., for the taking of money by the way
of corruption of certaine prest souldiers in the
countrey, and for placing of others in their roomes,
more unfit for service and of less sufficiency and
abilitie' (cited by Humphreys).

20 charge company.

21 ancients (1) The next in command under a
lieutenant, (2) ensigns, standard-bearers. The 'ensign or ancient of a company was an officer of the
highest responsibility and trust' (T. R. Henn, *The
Living Image*, 1972, p. 107).

21 gentlemen of companies They held a rank
between ordinary soldiers and officers. Usually they
were exempt from sentinel duty. In *H5* the disguised King identifies himself as 'a gentleman of a
company' after Pistol challenges him: 'art thou officer, / Or art thou base, common, and popular?'
(4.1.37–9).

22–3 Lazarus . . . sores Falstaff refers again to
the parable of the beggar Lazarus and the rich man;
compare 3.3.24 and n. Cowl and Morgan suggested
that pictures painted on cloth were an inexpensive
substitute for tapestry. In *2H4* 2.1.144–5, Falstaff
suggests that the Hostess can pawn her tapestry and
replace it with 'a pretty slight drollery, or the story
of the Prodigal, or the German hunting in water
work' (i.e. water colour, perhaps on paper).

23–4 discarded unjust discharged for dishonesty. *Sir Thomas More* (1593), 5.2.39 ff., makes it
clear that all discharged servants, even those not at
fault, could be in dire straits.

24 younger sons to younger brothers They
were doubly removed from any prospect of inheritance which, under the law of primogeniture, only
the eldest living son could claim. Poins says, 'The
worst that they can say of me is that I am a second
brother', in *2H4* 2.2.66–7.

24–5 revolted tapsters drawers who have run
away from their masters; a reminder of the Prince
and Francis in 2.4.38–40.

volted tapsters, and ostlers trade-fallen, the cankers of a calm world   25
and a long peace, ten times more dishonourable-ragged than an
old fazed ancient. And such have I to fill up the rooms of them as
have bought out their services, that you would think that I had a
hundred-and-fifty tattered prodigals lately come from swine-
keeping, from eating draff and husks. A mad fellow met me on the   30
way, and told me I had unloaded all the gibbets and pressed the
dead bodies. No eye hath seen such scarecrows. I'll not march
through Coventry with them, that's flat. Nay, and the villains
march wide betwixt the legs as if they had gyves on, for indeed I had
the most of them out of prison. There's not a shirt and a half in all   35
my company, and the half shirt is two napkins tacked together and
thrown over the shoulders like a herald's coat without sleeves. And
the shirt, to say the truth, stolen from my host at Saint Albans, or
the red-nose innkeeper of Daventry. But that's all one, they'll find
linen enough on every hedge.   40

Enter the PRINCE, *[and the]* LORD OF WESTMORELAND

PRINCE How now, blown Jack? How now, quilt?

27 old fazed] Q1 (olde fazd); old-fac'd F   29 tattered] QqF *subst.* (tottered)   40 SD *and the*] Qq2–5, F; *not in* Q1

25 ostlers stable-men.
25 trade-fallen whose business has fallen off.
25 cankers (1) worms which destroy leaves and
buds, (2) cancers like the 'sores', 23, that consume
bodies and societies. Compare 1.3.174 and n.
26 long peace Often considered unhealthy, as if
society were an organism requiring occasional drastic cures. Hamlet refers to 'th'impostume of much
wealth and peace', / That inward breaks', 4.4.27–8.
26 dishonourable-ragged i.e. dishonourable
because ragged.
27 fazed ancient worn out, fraying ensign
or military banner (*OED* Feaze sv *v*[1] 1a). The F 'old-
fac'd Ancient' suggests that the compositor misread
the phrase to mean an elderly officer.
29 prodigals Alluding to the parable of the
prodigal son, Luke 15.11–31. Falstaff associates this
story with wall decoration in *2H4* 2.1.144–5. In
Wiv. 4.5.7–8, the Hostess describes Falstaff's
chamber as 'painted about with the story of the
Prodigal'. On the importance of the story of the
prodigal son as one model for understanding the
Prince's career, see Introduction, p. 10.
30 draff swill fed to swine.
30 husks a recollection of Luke 15.16 in the
Geneva Bible; the Bishops' and Great Bibles give
'coddes'.

31 gibbets gallows.
33 that's flat that's for sure.
34 gyves leg irons or shackles.
35 out of prison Possibly one of the few specific
references in this play to a current event or circumstance: 'The Privy Council emptied the London
prisons in 1596 to furnish recruits for the Cadiz
expedition' (Wilson).
37 herald's ... sleeves A tabard, open at the
sides and emblazoned with the sovereign's coat of
arms. The napkin-shirts resemble the wretched
'tabarte' in Berners, *Froissart* (1523) I, xii, 12: 'a
tabarte, suche as traytours and theves were wont to
were' (*OED* Tabard 1).
38–9 Saint Albans ... Daventry Towns between London and Coventry.
39–40 they'll find ... hedge Clothes and sheets
drying on hedges were frequently snatched by
thieves. The song of Autolycus *WT* 4.3.5 ff. shows
how familiar this practice would be to the audience.
41 blown (1) swollen, (2) short-winded; compare
'embossed', 3.3.130.
41 quilt 'fat man', with a pun on 'Jack', a sleeveless padded tunic worn with or as a substitute for
armour (*OED* Jack sv *sb*[2] 1b; compare Quilt sv *sb*[1] 2).

FALSTAFF What, Hal! How now, mad wag? What a devil dost thou in
Warwickshire? My good Lord of Westmoreland, I cry you mercy, I
thought your honour had already been at Shrewsbury.

WESTMORELAND Faith, Sir John, 'tis more than time that I were there,   45
and you too, but my powers are there already. The King I can tell
you looks for us all, we must away all night.

FALSTAFF Tut, never fear me, I am as vigilant as a cat to steal cream.

PRINCE I think, to steal cream indeed, for thy theft hath already made
thee butter. But tell me, Jack, whose fellows are these that come   50
after?

FALSTAFF Mine, Hal, mine.

PRINCE I did never see such pitiful rascals.

FALSTAFF Tut, tut, good enough to toss, food for powder, food for
powder, they'll fill a pit as well as better. Tush, man, mortal men,   55
mortal men.

WESTMORELAND Ay, but Sir John, methinks they are exceeding poor
and bare, too beggarly.

FALSTAFF Faith, for their poverty I know not where they had that. And
for their bareness I am sure they never learned that of me.   60

PRINCE No, I'll be sworn, unless you call three fingers in the ribs bare.
But sirrah, make haste. Percy is already in the field.   *Exit*

FALSTAFF What, is the King encamped?

WESTMORELAND He is, Sir John, I fear we shall stay too long. [*Exit*]

FALSTAFF Well,   65

---

62 SD *Exit*] Qq; *not in* F   64 SD *Exit*] Capell; *not in* QqF   65–7 Well . . . guest] *As verse*, Pope; *as prose*, QqF

42–3 What . . . Warwickshire? Falstaff's question may provoke laughter (has the Prince lost his way?) and enhance a mood of confusion caused by the swift, uncertain movement of troops. On the Prince's plans and journey in relation to Falstaff's, see 2 and 8 above and nn.
43 I cry you mercy I beg your pardon.
47 must away must (march) away. The use of 'away' as a verb-substitute adds urgency, as in *R2* 5.1.54, 'With all swift speed you must away to France'; compare *MV* 3.2.304.
48 fear doubt.
48 vigilant wakeful and watchful.
49–50 made thee butter (1) made butter for you (out of cream), (2) made you fat. Compare the melting of butter at 2.4.102–4 and n., and the turning of a bottle into 'angels', 6–8 above. The Prince may hint that Falstaff functions as and looks like a churn.
54 toss toss on a pike.

54 food for powder cannon fodder, something for the enemy to shoot at.
55 pit mass grave on a battlefield.
60 bareness Falstaff ignores many possible meanings of 'bare', 58 (uncovered, threadbare, destitute, unarmed). He echoes instead the sense of Hal's earlier joke ('Here comes lean Jack, here comes bare-bone', 2.4.270).
61 three fingers A measure of how fat Falstaff is. A finger is three-quarters of an inch, or a little less than 2 centimetres.
64 SD, 67 SD *Exit* Q gives *Exeunt* at the end of the scene. Falstaff's final speech, however, stands independent of Westmoreland's and has the qualities of a terminal soliloquy.
65–7 Well . . . guest Verse presents more graphically the oppositions included in this proverbial saying (Dent C547).

To the latter end of a fray, and the beginning of a feast
Fits a dull fighter and a keen guest.   [*Exit*]

[4.3] *Enter* HOTSPUR, WORCESTER, DOUGLAS, [*and*] VERNON

HOTSPUR We'll fight with him tonight.
WORCESTER   It may not be.
DOUGLAS You give him then advantage.
VERNON   Not a whit.
HOTSPUR Why say you so, looks he not for supply?
VERNON So do we.
HOTSPUR   His is certain, ours is doubtful.
WORCESTER Good cousin, be advised, stir not tonight.   5
VERNON Do not, my lord.
DOUGLAS   You do not counsel well.
    You speak it out of fear and cold heart.
VERNON Do me no slander, Douglas. By my life,
    And I dare well maintain it with my life,
    If well-respected honour bid me on,   10
    I hold as little counsel with weak fear
    As you, my lord, or any Scot that this day lives.
    Let it be seen tomorrow in the battle
    Which of us fears.
DOUGLAS   Yea, or tonight.
VERNON   Content.
HOTSPUR Tonight, say I.   15
VERNON Come, come, it may not be. I wonder much,
    Being men of such great leading as you are,
    That you foresee not what impediments

---

67 SD *Exit*] Capell; *Exeunt* QqF   Act 4, Scene 3   4.3] *Scæna Tertia.* F; *not in* Qq   0 SD DOUGLAS, *and*] Qq2–5, F; *Doug:*
Q1   13–14 Let . . . battle / Which . . . fears] F; *as one line* Qq   16–17 Come . . . much / Being . . . are] *As* T. *Johnson,*
Pope; Come . . . be. / I . . . are QqF *subst.*

Act 4, Scene 3
    [4.3] The unlocalised stage makes possible a
rapid juxtaposition of Falstaff's preparations for
battle with those of the rebels.
    1 him the King, whose forces have arrived. In
Holinshed's account, his speed takes the Percys by
surprise, distracting them from a planned attack
on Shrewsbury and compelling Hotspur to exhort

his forces to prepare for battle (III, 24). Compare
Daniel, *Civile Wars*, III, st. 99–100.
    2 then i.e. if you don't fight him tonight. Douglas
agrees with Hotspur.
    3 supply reinforcements.
    10 well-respected well-considered (*OED* Re-
spect sv *v* 2).
    11 hold . . . with am as little moved by.
    17 leading experience in military command.

Drag back our expedition. Certain horse
Of my cousin Vernon's are not yet come up,   20
Your uncle Worcester's horse came but today,
And now their pride and mettle is asleep,
Their courage with hard labour tame and dull,
That not a horse is half the half of himself.
HOTSPUR   So are the horses of the enemy   25
In general journey-bated and brought low.
The better part of ours are full of rest.
WORCESTER   The number of the King exceedeth ours.
For God's sake, cousin, stay till all come in.
                 The trumpet sounds a parley

                 Enter SIR WALTER BLUNT

BLUNT   I come with gracious offers from the King,   30
If you vouchsafe me hearing and respect.
HOTSPUR   Welcome, Sir Walter Blunt: and would to God
You were of our determination!
Some of us love you well, and even those some
Envy your great deservings and good name,   35
Because you are not of our quality,
But stand against us like an enemy.
BLUNT   And God defend but still I should stand so,
So long as out of limit and true rule
You stand against anointed majesty.   40
But to my charge. The King hath sent to know

---

21 horse] Q5, F; horses Qq1–4   28 ours] F; our Qq1–5

19 **horse** companies of cavalry.
22 **pride and mettle** natural spirit; the terms are synonyms.
26 **journey-bated** exhausted or 'abated' by their journey.
29 SD.1 *parley* a trumpet-call offstage to announce that the other side desires a conference.
29 SD.2 BLUNT Shakespeare builds up the role of Blunt, respected by the rebels as well as by the King. See Margaret B. Bryan, '"Sir Walter Blunt: There's honor for you"', *SQ* 26 (1975), 292–8. In Holinshed, the Abbot of Shrewsbury and a clerk of the privy seal carry the King's offer of pardon (III, 25).
31 **respect** consideration. See 10 above.
33 **determination** settled purpose or resolve (*OED* 10).
34 **those some** those persons.

35 **Envy** Begrudge.
36 **quality** party or side (*OED* sv *sb* 5c).
38 **defend but still I should** prevent my ever failing to.
39 **out of limit** beyond a limit or boundary, as in 5.4.89: 'A kingdom for it was too small a bound.' Blunt means that the rebels are not behaving as obedient subjects; they are 'out of place'.
39 **true rule** (1) the established political order, (2) the legitimate authority of the King.
41–2 **The King . . . griefs** That the King already knows the grievances proclaimed by the rebels becomes clear at 5.1.72–3. In Holinshed, he reads a final set of rebel 'articles' the day before his offer of pardon, which he makes only once (III, 25). Compare 4.1.40–1 and n. for his earlier responses to the rebels.

The nature of your griefs, and whereupon
You conjure from the breast of civil peace
Such bold hostility, teaching his duteous land
Audacious cruelty. If that the King   45
Have any way your good deserts forgot,
Which he confesseth to be manifold,
He bids you name your griefs, and with all speed
You shall have your desires with interest
And pardon absolute for yourself, and these   50
Herein misled by your suggestion.
HOTSPUR The King is kind, and well we know the King
Knows at what time to promise, when to pay.
My father, and my uncle, and myself
Did give him that same royalty he wears,   55
And when he was not six-and-twenty strong,
Sick in the world's regard, wretched and low,
A poor unminded outlaw sneaking home,
My father gave him welcome to the shore.
And when he heard him swear and vow to God   60
He came but to be Duke of Lancaster,
To sue his livery, and beg his peace
With tears of innocency and terms of zeal,
My father, in kind heart and pity moved,
Swore him assistance, and performed it too.   65

42 **whereupon** on what ground.

43 **conjure** summon up.

45 **Audacious** Probably daring, but also shameless. Blunt's language begins to resemble the King's weighty and latinate idiom.

45 **If that** If.

51 **suggestion** sinister instigation or temptation.

54–105 **My father . . . continuance** Hotspur requires 52 lines to express his 'griefs', punctuated with one short, almost rude, interruption by Blunt. Hotspur's survey of recent history may be compared with the representation of events in *R2*. Only his final 13 lines focus on those in *1H4*. Blunt's interruption, 89, implies that the methods by which the King gained power are now beside the point. On the subjective interpretation of their past by different characters, see Introduction, p. 27.

56 **six-and-twenty strong** Holinshed, II, 853, says 'not past three score persons'. But in *R2*, Northumberland shares intelligence that Bullingbrook is approaching with 8 noblemen and 3,000 men of war (2.1.279–88).

58 **unminded** disregarded. In *R2*, several lords eagerly rush to support Bullingbrook (2.2.53–5).

59–61 **My father . . . Lancaster** In *R2*, Northumberland assists and flatters Bullingbrook before acting as his spokesman. He then uses this vow as a means of reassuring York and King Richard (*R2* 2.3.148–51; 3.3.105–13). Holinshed describes the oath sworn by Bullingbrook at Doncaster at II, 853.

62 **sue his livery** make legal suit in the Court of Wards for his dukedom, which had reverted to King Richard upon the death of Bullingbrook's father, John of Gaunt.

62 **beg his peace** seek reconciliation with the King by confirming mutual obligations (*OED* Peace sv *sb* 1c, cited by Humphreys). In *R2*, York accuses Richard of injustice, both in denying Bullingbrook the right to sue his livery and in repudiating his proffered homage (2.1.201–4).

63 **terms of zeal** professions of allegiance.

Now, when the lords and barons of the realm
Perceived Northumberland did lean to him,
The more and less came in with cap and knee,
Met him in boroughs, cities, villages,
Attended him on bridges, stood in lanes,   70
Laid gifts before him, proffered him their oaths,
Gave him their heirs as pages, followed him
Even at the heels in golden multitudes.
He presently, as greatness knows itself,
Steps me a little higher than his vow   75
Made to my father while his blood was poor
Upon the naked shore at Ravenspurgh;
And now forsooth takes on him to reform
Some certain edicts and some strait decrees
That lie too heavy on the commonwealth,   80
Cries out upon abuses, seems to weep
Over his country's wrongs – and by this face,
This seeming brow of justice, did he win
The hearts of all that he did angle for.
Proceeded further – cut me off the heads   85
Of all the favourites that the absent King
In deputation left behind him here,
When he was personal in the Irish war.

---

72 heirs as pages, followed] F4 (Heires, as Pages, followed), *conj. Malone;* heires, as Pages followed QqF *subst.;* heires, as Pagesfollowed Q1 *uncorr. Huntington Library copy*   79 strait] Q1 (streight)   82 country's] *Rowe;* Countrey Q1

68 The more . . . knee Both higher and lower social orders conventionally offered allegiance with hat (or cap) in hand, bending their knees. That Bullingbrook received nearly universal support is emphasised in *R2* 3.2.112–20. The emphasis on 'more and less' seems to eliminate here any class distinction between those who wore hats and those who wore caps.

70 Attended Waited for.

70 lanes files or rows.

72 Gave . . . pages Bevington follows Wilson in arguing that the pages serve as hostages to secure their fathers' loyalty. But the practice of placing children in affiliated households was widespread throughout the middle ages and early renaissance. Here it is meant to indicate the confidence, since lost, of the fathers in Bullingbrook's integrity. Malone's emendation, moving the comma which follows 'heirs' in QqF to follow 'pages', has been widely accepted.

73 golden (1) triumphant, (2) resplendent.

74 as . . . itself i.e. as he realises how to use the power he has acquired. Hotspur's explanation of

how Bullingbrook's ambition escalated may be compared with those of Worcester, 5.1.48 ff., and of the King in *2H4* 4.5.183–5.

75 his vow his promise to seek no more than his inheritance, 60–2 above.

76 his . . . poor (1) his temper was humble, (2) his nature was not royal.

78–80 takes . . . commonwealth Mentioned in Holinshed II, 853, but omitted in *R2*. By claiming to protect the commonwealth, feudal rebels tried to avoid seeming to attack its ruler.

79 strait harsh.

82–3 this face . . . justice Synonyms for hypocrisy.

85–6 cut . . . favourites In *R2* Northumberland silently and willingly carries out Bullingbrook's order to kill the 'favourites' (3.1.35).

87 In deputation As his deputies. King Richard had 'deputed' Bullingbrook's uncle York as lord governor (2.1.220) while Worcester served as steward of the household.

88 was personal in went in person to.

BLUNT Tut, I came not to hear this.
HOTSPUR   Then to the point.
    In short time after he deposed the King,   90
    Soon after that deprived him of his life,
    And in the neck of that tasked the whole state.
    To make that worse, suffered his kinsman March –
    Who is, if every owner were well placed,
    Indeed his King – to be engaged in Wales,   95
    There without ransom to lie forfeited.
    Disgraced me in my happy victories,
    Sought to entrap me by intelligence,
    Rated mine uncle from the Council-board,
    In rage dismissed my father from the court,   100
    Broke oath on oath, committed wrong on wrong,
    And in conclusion drove us to seek out
    This head of safety, and withal to pry
    Into his title, the which we find
    Too indirect for long continuance.   105
BLUNT Shall I return this answer to the King?
HOTSPUR Not so, Sir Walter. We'll withdraw a while.
    Go to the King, and let there be impawned
    Some surety for a safe return again,
    And in the morning early shall mine uncle   110
    Bring him our purposes – and so, farewell.
BLUNT I would you would accept of grace and love.
HOTSPUR And may be so we shall.
BLUNT   Pray God you do.

                                     [*Exeunt*]

113 SD *Exeunt*] F; *not in* Qq

90–1 In . . . life A swift summation of a crisis, dramatised in the final two acts in *R2*. Henry's responsibility for Richard's murder was indirect; compare *R2* 5.4.1–11, 5.6.30–52.

92 in the neck of immediately after.

92 tasked taxed, technically the term for a levy of a 'fifteenth', authorised by the Magna Carta (Humphreys).

93–5 suffered . . . Wales Even Holinshed does not suggest that Henry sent Mortimer to Wales to get rid of him. For Shakespeare's re-fashioning of his source and, consequently, of the King's motivation, see Appendix, pp. 201–11.

94 owner . . . placed i.e. if those entitled to positions always held them.

95 engaged held as hostage. Compare 'impawned' 108 below.

96 lie forfeited remain unreclaimed like a pawned article that has not been redeemed.

98 intelligence The use of spies. 'Perhaps the popinjay (1.3.49 ff.) is meant' (Wilson).

99 Rated Dismissed by berating, recalling the treatment of Worcester, 1.3.14–20.

103 head of safety army for self-defence.

103 withal in addition.

105 indirect (1) acquired by devious means, (2) not in the direct line of succession.

108 impawned pledged as security. Westmoreland will be so 'engaged' (5.2.43).

111 purposes proposals.

113 And . . . shall According to Holinshed, Hotspur 'began to give eare unto the kings offers' (III, 25).

[4.4] *Enter* [*the*] ARCHBISHOP OF YORK [*and*] SIR MICHAEL

ARCHBISHOP Hie, good Sir Michael, bear this sealèd brief
    With wingèd haste to the Lord Marshal,
    This to my cousin Scroop, and all the rest
    To whom they are directed. If you knew
    How much they do import, you would make haste.   5
SIR MICHAEL My good lord,
    I guess their tenor.
ARCHBISHOP   Like enough you do.
    Tomorrow, good Sir Michael, is a day
    Wherein the fortune of ten thousand men
    Must bide the touch. For, sir, at Shrewsbury,   10
    As I am truly given to understand,
    The King with mighty and quick-raisèd power
    Meets with Lord Harry, and I fear, Sir Michael,
    What with the sickness of Northumberland,
    Whose power was in the first proportion,   15
    And what with Owen Glendower's absence thence,
    Who with them was a rated sinew too,
    And comes not in, o'er-ruled by prophecies,
    I fear the power of Percy is too weak
    To wage an instant trial with the King.   20
SIR MICHAEL Why, my good lord, you need not fear,
    There is Douglas, and Lord Mortimer.

Act 4, Scene 4   4.4] *Scena Quarta.* F; *not in* Qq   0 SD *the*] F; *not in* Qq   0 SD *and*] Qq2–5, F; *not in* Q1   0 SD MICHAEL]
Q1 (Mighell) (*and through the scene*)   6–7 My ... do] *As Var. 1773;* My ... tenor / Arch. Like ... do QqF *subst.*

Act 4, Scene 4
  [4.4] Often cut in performance, this brief scene anticipates the continuation of the rebellion in *2H4*. In the Elizabethan theatre, its location need not be fixed, but it is clearly set some distance from the battleground.

  0 SD ARCHBISHOP OF YORK See List of Characters.

  0 SD SIR MICHAEL A member of the Archbishop's household, possibly a knight or priest, who serves as a messenger; he is not a historical figure.

  1 brief letter, dispatch (*OED* sv *sb* 4a, citing this line).

  2 Lord Marshal Thomas Mowbray, Duke of Norfolk, a leader of the rebels in *2H4*.

  3 my cousin Scroop Possibly (1) Sir Stephen Scroop who tells King Richard that his brother

William, the Earl of Wiltshire, has been executed, *R2* 3.2.141–2, or (2) his son Sir Henry, a traitor in *H5* 2.2. On the Archbishop's motives for opposing the King, see 1.3.264–5 and n.

  7 tenor drift, general meaning.

  10 bide the touch be put to the test, as gold is tested with a touchstone (*OED* sv *sb* 5a).

  15 in the first proportion 'the largest of all' (Wilson).

  17 rated sinew reckoned to be a mainstay (*OED* Sinew sv *sb* 4).

  18 o'er-ruled by prophecies This new motive for Glendower's absence (compare 4.1.126) was invented by Shakespeare. According to Holinshed, Glendower was absent from Shrewsbury, but Welsh fighters did assist the Percys. Daniel says there were no Welshmen present.

ARCHBISHOP No, Mortimer is not there.

SIR MICHAEL But there is Mordake, Vernon, Lord Harry Percy,
    And there is my Lord of Worcester, and a head   25
    Of gallant warriors, noble gentlemen.

ARCHBISHOP And so there is. But yet the King hath drawn
    The special head of all the land together.
    The Prince of Wales, Lord John of Lancaster,
    The noble Westmoreland, and warlike Blunt,   30
    And many more corrivals and dear men
    Of estimation and command in arms.

SIR MICHAEL Doubt not, my lord, they shall be well opposed.

ARCHBISHOP I hope no less, yet needful 'tis to fear,
    And to prevent the worst, Sir Michael, speed.   35
    For if Lord Percy thrive not, ere the King
    Dismiss his power he means to visit us,
    For he hath heard of our confederacy,
    And 'tis but wisdom to make strong against him.
    Therefore make haste – I must go write again   40
    To other friends. And so, farewell, Sir Michael.

                                         Exeunt

[**5.1**] *Enter the* KING, PRINCE OF WALES, LORD JOHN OF LANCASTER,
SIR WALTER BLUNT, [*and*] FALSTAFF

KING How bloodily the sun begins to peer
    Above yon bulky hill. The day looks pale

---

31 more] QqF *subst.* (mo)   36 not,] Qq2, 3, F; not Qq1, 4, 5   **Act 5, Scene 1** 5.1] *Actus Quintus. Scena Prima.* F; *not in* Qq   0 SD.1–2 LANCASTER, SIR] *Hanmer; Lancaster, Earle of Westmerland, Sir* QqF   0 SD.2 *and*] Qq2–5, F; *not in* Q1   2 bulky] Q1; busky Qq2–5, F, Wilson

---

28 **special head** pre-eminent warriors.

31 **more** Arguments for QqF 'mo' as meaning 'number' while 'more' means 'quantity' rest on an unconvincing distinction. Bevington points out that Shakespeare uses 'more' sixty-one times in *1H4*.

31 **corrivals** associates.

31 **dear** worthy, honourable.

32 **estimation** value.

35 **prevent** forestall.

37 **he means ... us** This prediction is confirmed at 5.5.34–8.

Act 5, Scene 1

[**5.1**] The action in this and the following scenes moves through the battlefield at Shrewsbury. These scenes rely on a combination of intimate dialogue and violent combat to suggest the battle between large forces. The King's party, in contrast to 1.1 and 1.3, now includes the Prince and Falstaff.

1 **How ... peer** A red morning proverbially promises bad weather.

2 **bulky** large, looming. Humphreys points out that a great 'hump-like mound' represents 'Wrekin hill' on Saxton's 1577 map of Shropshire. Compare 'gross as a mountain', 2.4.189–90. The 'l' of 'bulky' in Q1, although erased at the top, is clearly distinct from the thicker 'ſ' character. 'Busky' (bosky), meaning 'bushy', (illustrated by *OED*, using this reference), preferred by Wilson and Bevington, is a picturesque, less weighty term.

                    At his distemperature.
PRINCE   The southern wind
          Doth play the trumpet to his purposes,
          And by his hollow whistling in the leaves   5
          Foretells a tempest and a blust'ring day.
KING   Then with the losers let it sympathise,
          For nothing can seem foul to those that win.
                              The trumpet sounds

                    Enter WORCESTER [*and* VERNON]

          How now, my Lord of Worcester! 'Tis not well
          That you and I should meet upon such terms   10
          As now we meet. You have deceived our trust,
          And made us doff our easy robes of peace
          To crush our old limbs in ungentle steel.
          This is not well, my lord, this is not well.
          What say you to it? Will you again unknit   15
          The churlish knot of all-abhorrèd war,
          And move in that obedient orb again
          Where you did give a fair and natural light,
          And be no more an exhal'd meteor,
          A prodigy of fear, and a portent   20

---

8 SD.2 *and* VERNON] *Theobald; not in* QQF

3 **his distemperature** the physical disorder of
the sun. The King's use of personification to suggest that earth and sky may mirror political disorder, as at 7 below, recalls his speech opening the
play.
4 **Doth . . . purposes** Like a herald, announces
the intentions of the sun.
8 **nothing . . . win** An echo of the proverb, 'He
laughs that wins' (Dent L93).
8 SD.2 *and* VERNON Although he neither speaks
nor is spoken to (or even mentioned) in this scene,
Vernon's presence here, made probable by his argument with Worcester, 5.2.1–27, is confirmed by his
report of the Prince's challenge, 5.2.51–68. Most
editors follow Theobald by adding his entry at this
point.
12 **easy** comfortable.
13 **crush . . . steel** An implicit stage direction,
indicating that all the King's party and their opponents probably now wear armour. In actual history,
the King in 1403 was only thirty-six years old.
Compare Marlowe, *Edward II*, where an accelera-
tion of the King's age is made to suggest drastic
personal and political disruption.

17–18 **And . . . light** An analogy to the
Ptolemaic cosmos – stars and planets revolving in
fixed orbits or spheres around the earth, the centre
of the cosmic system – is used to define the obedience of a mighty subject to the King. Compare *Tro.*
1.3.89–94, where 'the glorious planet Sol / In noble
eminence enthron'd and spher'd' is imagined to
correct and control the other planets.
19 **exhal'd meteor** An omen or portent, as at
1.1.10 and 3.1.11–15; 'exhal'd' can suggest: (1) the
process of the sun's heat drawing a vapour out of the
earth and turning it into a meteor, (2) being dragged
out or away, i.e. from a proper celestial orbit (*OED*
sv *v²*), (3) being breathed out or extruded by the
earth, anticipating the latent birth metaphors in
'prodigy' and 'broachèd . . . unborn', 20 and 21
below (*OED* sv *v¹* 5). Compare Bardolph's similar
pairing of these terms at 2.4.263–4 (the only other
such pairing in *1H4*) and Hotspur's explanation of
earthquakes, 3.1.24–30.
20 **prodigy of fear** omen of evil, synonymous
with 'portent', but also a monster or freak of nature
(*OED* 2b). Compare *R2* 2.2.64, 'Now hath my soul
brought forth her prodigy.'

Of broachèd mischief to the unborn times?
WORCESTER Hear me, my liege.
    For mine own part I could be well content
    To entertain the lag end of my life
    With quiet hours. For I protest   25
    I have not sought the day of this dislike.
KING You have not sought it? How comes it, then?
FALSTAFF Rebellion lay in his way, and he found it.
PRINCE Peace, chewet, peace!
WORCESTER It pleased your majesty to turn your looks   30
    Of favour from myself, and all our house,
    And yet I must remember you, my lord,
    We were the first and dearest of your friends.
    For you my staff of office did I break
    In Richard's time, and posted day and night   35
    To meet you on the way, and kiss your hand,
    When yet you were in place and in account
    Nothing so strong and fortunate as I.
    It was myself, my brother, and his son,
    That brought you home, and boldly did outdare   40
    The dangers of the time. You swore to us,
    And you did swear that oath at Doncaster,
    That you did nothing purpose 'gainst the state,
    Nor claim no further than your new-fallen right,
    The seat of Gaunt, dukedom of Lancaster.   45
    To this we swore our aid. But in short space
    It rained down fortune showering on your head,
    And such a flood of greatness fell on you,

---

21 broachèd . . . times a calamity released, as by piercing a cask (*OED* Broach *v*¹ 4).

21 mischief evil plight, calamity.

24 entertain occupy, while away; compare *The Rape of Lucrece* 1361: 'The weary time she cannot entertain.'

29 chewet A pun on (1) chough or jackdaw (i.e. a chattering bird), (2) minced-meat pie. Hal's tone may express some pleasure in Falstaff's put-down of Worcester or it may show annoyance at his intrusion. A comparable interruption by Enobarbus (*Ant.* 2.2.103–6) provokes irritation onstage, but laughter followed by some discomfort in the audience.

32–71 And . . . enterprise Worcester's memory of events in which he was more active than Hotspur can be compared with Hotspur's account (4.3.54–

105), with pertinent scenes in *R2*, and with the versions of Daniel and the chroniclers.

32 remember remind.

34–5 For you . . . time Mentioned by Holinshed (II, 855), and emphasised in *R2* 2.2.58–9 and 2.3.26–8.

35 posted travelled in haste, possibly with relays of horses.

38 Nothing Nowhere near (adverb).

42 that oath Compare 4.3.62 and note. The articles sent by the Percys to the King at Shrewsbury charged him with 'manifest perjurie' in violating this vow (Holinshed, III, 25).

44 new-fallen right Inheritance through the recent death of his father, John of Gaunt.

45 seat estate.

What with our help, what with the absent King,
What with the injuries of a wanton time,   50
The seeming sufferances that you had borne,
And the contrarious winds that held the King
So long in his unlucky Irish wars
That all in England did repute him dead.
And from this swarm of fair advantages   55
You took occasion to be quickly wooed
To gripe the general sway into your hand,
Forgot your oath to us at Doncaster,
And being fed by us, you used us so
As that ungentle gull the cuckoo's bird   60
Useth the sparrow – did oppress our nest,
Grew by our feeding to so great a bulk
That even our love durst not come near your sight
For fear of swallowing. But with nimble wing
We were enforced for safety's sake to fly   65
Out of your sight, and raise this present head,
Whereby we stand opposèd, by such means
As you yourself have forged against yourself,
By unkind usage, dangerous countenance,
And violation of all faith and troth   70
Sworn to us in your younger enterprise.
KING   These things indeed you have articulate,
Proclaimed at market crosses, read in churches,
To face the garment of rebellion

---

65 safety's] QqF (safety)   72 articulate] Qq; articulated F

---

50 injuries abuses.
50 wanton anarchic, badly managed.
51 sufferances wrongs.
56 occasion opportunity.
60–4 ungentle . . . swallowing The cuckoo lays its eggs in the nests of other smaller birds; when hatched, the aggressive and ungrateful young cuckoo crowds out or even eats up the host family. Compare *Lear* 1.4.215–16.
60 ungentle . . . bird i.e. that rough nestling, the cuckoo's offspring. Both 'gull' (*OED* sv *sb²*, citing this passage) and 'bird' (*OED* sv *sb* 1a) refer to unfledged or very young birds.
64 swallowing being swallowed.
65–8 to fly . . . against yourself Most editions omit Q's comma after 'means', 67. The addition of a comma after 'opposèd' clarifies the passage in link-

ing 'by such means' to 'fly' and 'raise', thus emphasising that the Percys are not merely provoked by the King; they have been driven to use his own methods.
69 unkind (1) 'ungentle' (60), (2) unfamilial or unnatural.
69 dangerous countenance menacing attitude and appearance. Worcester returns the King's charge against him at 1.3.18.
70 troth vow or plighted word.
71 younger earlier, referring to his initial claim, 44.
72 articulate set forth, item by item, in articles.
74 face trim or decorate to disguise the nature of the 'garment' underneath. Compare 'velvet-guards', 3.1.249.

With some fine colour that may please the eye   75
Of fickle changelings and poor discontents,
Which gape and rub the elbow at the news
Of hurly-burly innovation.
And never yet did insurrection want
Such water-colours to impaint his cause,   80
Nor moody beggars starving for a time
Of pell-mell havoc and confusion.

PRINCE In both your armies there is many a soul
Shall pay full dearly for this encounter
If once they join in trial. Tell your nephew,   85
The Prince of Wales doth join with all the world
In praise of Henry Percy. By my hopes,
This present enterprise set off his head,
I do not think a braver gentleman,
More active-valiant or more valiant-young,   90
More daring or more bold, is now alive
To grace this latter age with noble deeds.
For my part, I may speak it to my shame,
I have a truant been to chivalry,
And so I hear he doth account me too.   95
Yet this before my father's majesty –
I am content that he shall take the odds
Of his great name and estimation,
And will, to save the blood on either side,
Try fortune with him in a single fight.   100

---

83 your] Qq; our F 88 off] F; of Qq 90 active-valiant . . . valiant-young] *Theobald;* active, valiant . . . valiant yong QqF *subst.*

75 colour A quibble on (1) outward pretence, (2) the literal colour of the fabric used as trim.

76 fickle changelings and poor discontents unpredictable persons inclined to change their masters or abandon their lords and leaders.

77 gape gaze foolishly, with open mouth.

77 rub the elbow 'hug themselves (with pleasure), arms crossed and hands on elbows. Joy supposedly made the elbows itch' (Humphreys).

78 hurly-burly innovation violent commotion and change, 'turning the world upside down'.

79 want lack.

80 water-colours i.e. deceptions. Like thin or cheap paints, they hide nothing from judicious observers and are easily washed off.

81 moody sullen.

81–2 beggars . . . confusion The 'changelings' and 'discontents' (76) have come down in the world. Compare their alleged hunger for an insurrection which will feed them with Falstaff's enthusiasm for war, 3.3.157–9.

82 havoc general devastation, originally from the military order to pillage or plunder (*OED* sv *sb* 1).

83–100 In . . . fight This chivalric speech ending in a challenge seems to be Shakespeare's invention, perhaps suggested partly by Hotspur's speech in Daniel, III, st. 101–2. See Introduction, pp. 16–17.

83 your i.e. the King's and the rebels'. Some editions adopt 'our' from F.

88 set off his head not counted against him. Compare 3.2.132.

92 latter later, more recent.

KING And, Prince of Wales, so dare we venture thee,
　　　　Albeit considerations infinite
　　　　Do make against it. No, good Worcester, no,
　　　　We love our people well, even those we love
　　　　That are misled upon your cousin's part,　　　　　　　　　　105
　　　　And will they take the offer of our grace,
　　　　Both he, and they, and you, yea, every man
　　　　Shall be my friend again, and I'll be his.
　　　　So tell your cousin, and bring me word
　　　　What he will do. But if he will not yield,　　　　　　　　110
　　　　Rebuke and dread correction wait on us,
　　　　And they shall do their office. So, be gone.
　　　　We will not now be troubled with reply.
　　　　We offer fair, take it advisedly.

　　　　　　　　　　　　　　Exeunt Worcester [and Vernon]

PRINCE It will not be accepted, on my life.　　　　　　　　　　115
　　　　The Douglas and the Hotspur both together
　　　　Are confident against the world in arms.

KING Hence, therefore, every leader to his charge,
　　　　For on their answer will we set on them,
　　　　And God befriend us as our cause is just!　　　　　　　　120

　　　　　　　　　Exeunt; the Prince and Falstaff remain

FALSTAFF Hal, if thou see me down in the battle and bestride me so, 'tis
　　　　a point of friendship.

PRINCE Nothing but a Colossus can do thee that friendship.
　　　　Say thy prayers, and farewell.

FALSTAFF I would 'twere bed-time, Hal, and all well.　　　　　125

---

114 SD *and Vernon*] *Theobald subst.; not in* QQF 120 SD *the Prince and Falstaff remain*] QQF *subst.* (*manent Prince,
Falst.*) 121–4 Hal . . . farewell] *As prose, Pope; as verse,* Hal . . . battel / And . . . friendship. / *Prin.* Nothing . . .
friendship, / Say . . . farewell QQF *subst.*

102 Albeit Although. Compare 1.3.126 and n.
105 cousin kinsman, meaning his nephew,
Hotspur.
106 grace pardon.
111 wait on us attend me, await my (royal) command.
112–14 So . . . advisedly The King briefly combines royal dignity and generosity with an assertion
of power and, perhaps informally, a threat: 'If you
know what's good for you, take my offer.'
119 on their answer i.e. 'as soon as they refuse',
almost certainly not 'whatever they reply'. The
King's conciliatory language and twice-proffered
pardon to the rebels make his desire here for peace

seem unequivocal. Some recent productions, however, treat this line as evidence of bad faith.
121 bestride me stand over me in order to protect me. Compare *Err.* 5.1.191–2: 'the service that
long since I did thee, / When I bestrid thee in the
wars'.
123 Colossus A giant or a gigantic statue of a
man. The statue of Apollo at Rhodes, one of the
seven wonders of the ancient world, was reputed to
have stood astride the harbour entrance.
125 bed-time An exceptionally simple and
straightforward moment. Falstaff, in response to
'Say thy prayers', here speaks as if he were still a
small child.

PRINCE Why, thou owest God a death.   [*Exit*]

FALSTAFF 'Tis not due yet – I would be loath to pay him before his day.
What need I be so forward with him that calls not on me? Well, 'tis
no matter, honour pricks me on. Yea, but how if honour prick me
off when I come on, how then? Can honour set to a leg? No. Or an   130
arm? No. Or take away the grief of a wound? No. Honour hath no
skill in surgery then? No. What is honour? A word. What is in that
word honour? What is that honour? Air. A trim reckoning! Who
hath it? He that died a' Wednesday. Doth he feel it? No. Doth he
hear it? No. 'Tis insensible, then? Yea, to the dead. But will it not   135
live with the living? No. Why? Detraction will not suffer it. Therefore I'll none of it. Honour is a mere scutcheon – and so ends my
catechism.   *Exit*

[**5.2**] *Enter* WORCESTER, [*and*] SIR RICHARD VERNON   *worst behaviour in play*

WORCESTER O no, my nephew must not know, Sir Richard,
    The liberal and kind offer of the King.
VERNON 'Twere best he did.
WORCESTER   Then are we all undone.
    It is not possible, it cannot be,

---

126 SD *Exit*] *Hanmer; not in* QQF   129 Yea, but] Qq; But F   130 then? Can] Qq2, 3, F; then can Qq1, 4, 5   135 will it] Qq2–
5, F; wil Q1   Act 5, Scene 2   5.2] *Scena Secunda.* F; *not in* Qq   0 SD *and*] Qq2–5, F; *not in* Q1   3 undone] Q5, F; under
one Qq1–4

126 **thou . . . a death** Proverbial saying (Dent
G237), with a quibble on 'debt'.
126 SD **Exit** QQF provide no exit for the Prince.
After his 'farewell', 124, Hal is in a hurry to be off;
clearly, by 128 Falstaff is talking to himself and
to the theatre audience. The opening lines of his
soliloquy might be addressed to the departing
Prince.
129 **pricks me on** spurs me on.
129–30 **prick me off** mark me down for death.
Falstaff's pun refers to the practice of making holes
as marks on a list of names. Compare *JC* 4.1.1:
'These many then, shall die; their names are
prick'd.' In *2H4* 3.2.110–78, the repeated 'pricking'
of recruits turns into farce.
130 **set to a leg** set a broken or disjointed leg.
131 **grief** pain.
133 **trim reckoning** fine account (ironic).
135 **insensible** not perceptible to the senses (and
perhaps senseless).
136 **Detraction** Slander.

136 **suffer** permit.
137 **scutcheon** The most humble of heraldic devices, a tablet or canvas panel representing a coat of
arms which could be carried in a funeral procession
or hung in a church to honour the dead. It is comparable to the 'hatchment' mentioned by Laertes in
Ham. 4.5.215: 'No trophy, sword, nor hatchment
o'er his bones'.
138 **catechism** A common method of religious
instruction which uses an established question-and-
answer format.

Act 5, Scene 2
1–2 **O . . . King** Worcester's treachery is based
on Holinshed (III, 25), but Shakespeare invents his
motives and self-justification, 4–25 below.
3 **undone** ruined. This Q5, F reading has been
widely accepted. Wilson follows Pollard in suggesting that Shakespeare may have written 'und one',
which the Q printer mistakenly 'corrected'.

The King should keep his word in loving us.   5
He will suspect us still, and find a time
To punish this offence in other faults.
Supposition all our lives shall be stuck full of eyes,
For treason is but trusted like the fox,
Who, never so tame, so cherished and locked up,   10
Will have a wild trick of his ancestors.
Look how we can, or sad or merrily,
Interpretation will misquote our looks,
And we shall feed like oxen at a stall,
The better cherished still the nearer death.   15
My nephew's trespass may be well forgot,
It hath the excuse of youth and heat of blood,
And an adopted name of privilege –
A hare-brained Hotspur, governed by a spleen.
All his offences live upon my head   20
And on his father's. We did train him on,
And, his corruption being ta'en from us,
We as the spring of all shall pay for all.
Therefore, good cousin, let not Harry know
In any case the offer of the King.   25

Enter [HOTSPUR *and* DOUGLAS]

VERNON Deliver what you will; I'll say 'tis so.   *Vernon agrees to deceipt.*
Here comes your cousin.

HOTSPUR   My uncle is returned;

8 Supposition] QQF; Suspicion *Rowe, Bevington*   12 merrily] Q1 (merely)   25 SD *Enter* HOTSPUR *and* DOUGLAS] *Rowe (after* cousin *line 27);* Enter Percy Q1; *Enter* Hotspurre F *(after* Cosin *line 27)*

6 **still** always.
7 **in** when he punishes.
8 **Supposition** Following Rowe, many editors have emended the QQF reading to 'Suspicion'; the line will be hypermetric in either case. 'Supposition' is more consistent with Worcester's own readiness to formulate the mistaken thoughts and inferences of others at 1.3.281 and 4.1.62–75.
8 **stuck full of eyes** The notion of an allegorical figure 'full of eyes' probably derives from the 'Fama' (Rumour) of Virgil's *Aeneid* (IV. 181–3), a monster covered with as many eyes, tongues, mouths, and ears as she has feathers. Gibbons comments on *MM* 4.1.56 'millions of false eyes' that they suggest 'artificial eyes on the robes of a pageant or emblem figure'.

10 **never so** no matter how.
11 **trick** trait.
12 **or . . . or** whether . . . or.
13 **misquote** misconstrue.
18 **an adopted . . . privilege** a nickname that gives him a special licence.
19 **spleen** rash impulse. Compare 2.3.72, 3.2.125 and nn.
21 **train** draw on by art or allure (*OED* sv *v*[1]).
23 **spring** source.
25 SD Many editors follow F in placing this entrance after 27; directors must decide the exact timing. A larger group of rebels should be onstage for Hotspur's exhortations at 75, 81, and 92 below.

Deliver up my Lord of Westmoreland.
Uncle, what news?
WORCESTER The King will bid you battle presently.   30
DOUGLAS Defy him by the Lord of Westmoreland.
HOTSPUR Lord Douglas, go you and tell him so.
DOUGLAS Marry, and shall, and very willingly.   *Exit*
WORCESTER There is no seeming mercy in the King.
HOTSPUR Did you beg any? God forbid!   35
WORCESTER I told him gently of our grievances,
Of his oath-breaking – which he mended thus,
By now forswearing that he is forsworn.
He calls us rebels, traitors, and will scourge
With haughty arms this hateful name in us.   40

Enter DOUGLAS

DOUGLAS Arm, gentlemen, to arms! For I have thrown
A brave defiance in King Henry's teeth,
And Westmoreland that was engaged did bear it,
Which cannot choose but bring him quickly on.
WORCESTER The Prince of Wales stepped forth before the King,   45
And, nephew, challenged you to single fight.
HOTSPUR O, would the quarrel lay upon our heads,
And that no man might draw short breath today
But I and Harry Monmouth! Tell me, tell me,
How showed his tasking? Seemed it in contempt?   50
VERNON No, by my soul, I never in my life   progressive build up
Did hear a challenge urged more modestly,   of Hal
Unless a brother should a brother dare
To gentle exercise and proof of arms.
He gave you all the duties of a man,   55
Trimmed up your praises with a princely tongue,
Spoke your deservings like a chronicle,

50 tasking] Q1; Talking Qq2–5, F

28 **Deliver ... Westmoreland** The identity, not heretofore important, of the 'surety' required at 4.3.109.
31 **Defy ... Westmoreland** i.e. Have Westmoreland carry your defiance to the King.
33 **Marry, and shall** Yes, I will.
34 **no seeming** no appearance of.
38 **forswearing** denying with a false oath.
42 **brave** bold.

43 **engaged** held as hostage.
44 **cannot choose but** must of necessity.
49 **Harry Monmouth** i.e. the Prince of Wales. Monmouth, the Welsh town where the Prince was born, is sometimes used as his name.
52 **urged** proposed.
54 **proof** test or trial.
55 **duties of a man** marks of respect owed to true manhood.

Making you ever better than his praise
By still dispraising praise valued with you,
And, which became him like a prince indeed,   60
He made a blushing cital of himself,
And chid his truant youth with such a grace
As if he mastered there a double spirit
Of teaching and of learning instantly.
There did he pause. But let me tell the world –   65
If he outlive the envy of this day,
England did never owe so sweet a hope
So much misconstrued in his wantonness.
HOTSPUR Cousin, I think thou art enamoured
On his follies! Never did I hear   70
Of any prince so wild a liberty.
But be he as he will, yet once ere night
I will embrace him with a soldier's arm,
That he shall shrink under my courtesy.
Arm, arm with speed! And fellows, soldiers, friends,   75
Better consider what you have to do
Than I that have not well the gift of tongue
Can lift your blood up with persuasion.

Enter a MESSENGER

[FIRST] MESSENGER My lord, here are letters for you.
HOTSPUR I cannot read them now.   80
    O gentlemen, the time of life is short!   – *rep. in death speech*
    To spend that shortness basely were too long
    If life did ride upon a dial's point,   *apart from treachery of elder*
    Still ending at the arrival of an hour.

71 a liberty] QQ1–4 (a libertie), at libertie Q5, F *subst.*, a libertine *Capell*   79 SH FIRST] *This edn; not in* QQF

59 dispraising ... you (1) making you the standard of what is worth praising, (2) valuing you more than words can express.
61 blushing modest (probably not meant literally).
61 cital reproof or impeachment (*OED* 2, this example).
64 instantly simultaneously.
66 envy malice.
67 owe own.
68 wantonness unruliness.
71 liberty lawlessness, licence.
73–4 I will embrace ... courtesy This con-temptuous response to the Prince's challenge parodies its chivalric, fraternal spirit by promising a brutal encounter.
74 shrink (1) cower, (2) shrivel up.
76–8 Better ... persuasion i.e. reflect well, yourselves, and you will act better than I, with my weak skills in argument, can persuade you to do by raising your spirits.
82–4 To spend ... hour i.e. a base life would be too long if it lasted only an hour.
83 If Even if.
83 dial's point the pointed hand of a clock.

And if we live, we live to tread on kings,   85
If die, brave death when princes die with us!
Now, for our consciences, the arms are fair
When the intent of bearing them is just.

Enter another [MESSENGER]

[SECOND] MESSENGER My lord, prepare, the King comes on apace.
HOTSPUR I thank him that he cuts me from my tale,   90
    For I profess not talking. Only this —
    Let each man do his best. And here draw I
    A sword whose temper I intend to stain
    With the best blood that I can meet withal
    In the adventure of this perilous day.   95
    Now, Esperance! Percy! and set on!
    Sound all the lofty instruments of war,
    And by that music let us all embrace,
    For, heaven to earth, some of us never shall
    A second time do such a courtesy.   100
    Here they embrace, the trumpets sound

                  [*Exeunt*]

[5.3] *The* KING *enters with his power. Alarum to the battle. Then enter*
DOUGLAS *and* SIR WALTER BLUNT [*disguised as the King*]

BLUNT What is thy name that in [the] battle thus

---

88 SD MESSENGER] F; *not in* Qq   89 SH SECOND] *Capell; not in* QqF   92–3 Let . . . stain] *As Pope;* Let . . . sword, /
Whose . . . staine QqF   100 SD.1 *Here . . . sound*] QqF (*not separated from opening* SD *of 5.3*)   100 SD.2 *Exeunt*] Rowe; *not in*
QqF   Act 5, Scene 3   5.3] *Capell; not in* QqF   0 SD.2 *disguised as the King*] Wilson *subst.; not in* QqF   1–3 What . . . head?]
As Hanmer; What . . . me, / What . . . head? QqF   1 the] T. Johnson, Hanmer; *not in* QqF

---

87 **for** as regards.

87 **fair** justifiable.

90 **cuts . . . tale** stops me telling my story.

91 **I profess not** I claim no skill at.

93–4 **A sword . . . blood** The idea of augment-
ing the 'temper' or hard metallic composition of a
sword by blood occurs in *Beowulf*, 1460, and is an
epic commonplace.

95 **adventure** chance, but as weighted here with
the sense of a chivalric enterprise, extremely challenging and hazardous.

96 **Esperance** The Percy battle-cry, meaning
'Hope, my comfort.' Compare 2.3.65 and n.

99 **heaven to earth** i.e. I'll wager heaven against
earth, or 'the odds are as heaven is to earth'
(Humphreys).

Act 5, Scene 3

0 SD The action is continuous in QqF and stage
directions run on (i.e. combine directions for the
exiting party with those for the entering). These
give no '*Exeunt*' or any other break between the
sounding of trumpets (5.2.100 SD) and the King's
entry. The scene change, first suggested by Capell,
has been retained here only for convenience of reference. Onstage, the foregrounding of an individual
can be emphasised both through contrast with
group fighting and through battle sounds; compare
Falstaff's solitary entry following '*Alarum*' at 29 SD
below.

0 SD.1 *Alarum* A call to battle by drums or trumpets. In the theatre, this usually preceded the entry
of groups of soldiers.

Thou crossest me? What honour dost thou seek
Upon my head?
DOUGLAS   Know then my name is Douglas,
And I do haunt thee in the battle thus
Because some tell me that thou art a king.   5
BLUNT   They tell thee true.
DOUGLAS   The Lord of Stafford dear today hath bought
Thy likeness, for instead of thee, King Harry,
This sword hath ended him: so shall it thee
Unless thou yield thee as my prisoner.   10
BLUNT   I was not born a yielder, thou proud Scot,
And thou shalt find a king that will revenge
Lord Stafford's death.
                    They fight; Douglas kills Blunt

                    Then enter HOTSPUR

HOTSPUR   O Douglas, hadst thou fought at Holmedon thus
I never had triumphed upon a Scot.   15
DOUGLAS   All's done, all's won. Here breathless lies the King.
HOTSPUR   Where?
DOUGLAS   Here.
HOTSPUR   This, Douglas? No, I know this face full well.
A gallant knight he was, his name was Blunt,   20
Semblably furnished like the King himself.
DOUGLAS   A fool go with thy soul, whither it goes!
A borrowed title hast thou bought too dear.
Why didst thou tell me that thou wert a king?
HOTSPUR   The King hath many marching in his coats.   25
DOUGLAS   Now, by my sword, I will kill all his coats!

16 won. Here] Qq2, 3 (won: here); won here, Q1; won, here Qq4, 5, F   22 A fool go] *Capell;* ah foole, goe Qq; Ah foole:
go F

7–9 **The Lord . . . him** Shakespeare synthesises
distinct bits of information from Holinshed (III, 25–
6): (1) that Blunt, the standard-bearer, and Stafford
were both killed when Hotspur and Douglas tried to
slay the King himself in a 'violent onset', (2) that
when the King later broke through enemy ranks,
Douglas struck him down and killed 'Sir Walter
Blunt, and three other, apparelled in the kings sute
and clothing'. Daniel, III, st. 111–12, makes it explicit that historically there were two Blunts. Compare *2H4* 1.1.16–17: 'both the Blunts / Kill'd by the
hand of Douglas'.

7–8 **bought thy likeness** paid for his similarity
to you.
16 **breathless** dead.
21 **Semblably furnished like** Dressed and
armed to resemble.
22 **A fool . . . soul** i.e. 'You are a fool', a common
gibe. Compare Dent G150.1 and Jonson, *Volpone*,
'Rooke goe with you, raven' (1.4.124). Capell's
emendation of QqF's 'Ah' makes the idiomatic expression recognisable and has been widely accepted.
25 **coats** sleeveless surcoats bearing heraldic
devices, worn over armour. Compare 4.2.37 and n.

I'll murder all his wardrobe, piece by piece,
Until I meet the King.
HOTSPUR   Up and away!
Our soldiers stand full fairly for the day.

                                               [*Exeunt*]

            Alarum. Enter FALSTAFF *alone*

FALSTAFF Though I could scape shot-free at London, I fear the shot   30
here, here's no scoring but upon the pate. Soft! Who are you? Sir
Walter Blunt – there's honour for you! Here's no vanity! I am as hot
as molten lead, and as heavy too. God keep lead out of me, I need no
more weight than mine own bowels. I have led my ragamuffins
where they are peppered. There's not three of my hundred-and-   35
fifty left alive – and they are for the town's end, to beg during life.
But who comes here?

                    Enter the PRINCE

PRINCE What, stand'st thou idle here? Lend me thy sword.
Many a nobleman lies stark and stiff
Under the hoofs of vaunting enemies,   40
Whose deaths are yet unrevenged. I prithee
Lend me thy sword.
FALSTAFF O Hal, I prithee give me leave to breathe a while. Turk

---

29 SD.1 *Exeunt*] F; *not in* Qq   29 SD.2 *Enter* FALSTAFF *alone*] Qq (*Enter Falstaffe solus*); *and enter Falstaffe solus* F
34 ragamuffins] *Capell*; *rag of Muffins* QQF   35–6 hundred-and-fifty] QQF (150)   38 stand'st] Qq2–5, F *subst.*; stands
Q1   39 nobleman] F; *noble man* Qq   41 I prithee] Qq (*preethe*); *Prethy* F

---

29 **stand . . . day** are well on their way to
victory.

30 shot-free A quibble: (1) without being
wounded or shot at, (2) without paying the tavern
reckoning or 'shot', by making a mark or notching a
tally stick.

31 scoring charging to a tavern account. In
battle, the word refers to slashing or notching the
head or 'pate'.

32 Here's no vanity! The actor can speak ironically, in the manner of his 'catechism' (5.1.127–38),
implying that death for honour is the ultimate folly
('If this isn't futile, what is?'). Or he can recognise
the battlefield reality of sudden death, far from the
'vanity' of 'shot-free' London.

34–5 I have led . . . peppered 'Falstaff leads his
"charge" to a hot corner, and then himself takes
cover, in order that he may pocket the pay of those
killed' (Wilson). Humphreys cites contemporary
attacks upon this common form of military
corruption.

36 town's end outskirts of a town where rubbish
was dumped and beggars gathered.

41–52 I prithee . . . dally now A 'mixture of
prosy verse and versy prose' (Humphreys). Hal
breaks the regular cadence of his verse, while
Falstaff speaks rhythmical, orderly prose.

43–4 Turk Gregory 'Turk' could be a synonym
for an outrageously violent man. Two different
Popes have been identified as this 'Gregory': (1)
Hildebrand, who became Gregory VII (1073–85),
and was denounced for his fury by Protestant writers, especially John Foxe in *Acts and Monuments*,
1563, p. 14 (cited by Humphreys), or (2) Gregory
XIII (1572–85) who 'blessed if he did not instigate
the Massacre of St Bartholomew, and promised ple-
nary indulgence to anyone who would murder
Elizabeth' (Wilson). See also Henry IV's letter of
1408 to Gregory XII (1406–15), complaining of
policies prolonging schism in the church
(Holinshed, III, 47).

Gregory never did such deeds in arms as I have done this day. I
have paid Percy, I have made him sure.   45
PRINCE He is indeed, and living to kill thee.
   I prithee lend me thy sword.
FALSTAFF Nay, before God, Hal, if Percy be alive thou gets not my
sword, but take my pistol if thou wilt.
PRINCE Give it me. What, is it in the case?   50
FALSTAFF Aye, Hal, 'tis hot, 'tis hot. There's that will sack a city.
   The Prince draws it out, and finds it to be a bottle of sack
PRINCE What, is it a time to jest and dally now?
                   He throws the bottle at him   *Exit*
FALSTAFF Well, if Percy be alive, I'll pierce him. If he do come in my
way, so. If he do not, if I come in his willingly, let him make a
carbonado of me. I like not such grinning honour as Sir Walter   55
hath. Give me life, which if I can save, so. If not, honour comes
unlooked for, and there's an end.   [*Exit*]

[**5.4**] *Alarum. Excursions. Enter the* KING, *the* PRINCE, LORD JOHN OF
LANCASTER, [*and*] EARL OF WESTMORELAND

KING I prithee, Harry, withdraw thyself, thou bleedest too much.
   Lord John of Lancaster, go you with him.
LANCASTER Not I, my lord, unless I did bleed too.
PRINCE I beseech your majesty, make up,
   Lest your retirement do amaze your friends.   5

---

57 SD *Exit*] F; *not in* Qq   **Act 5, Scene 4**   5.4] *Capell; Scena Tertia* F; *not in* Qq   0 SD.2 *and*] F; *not in* Qq

45 paid killed, with a pun on 'settled his score'.

45 made him sure (1) got rid of him, (2) made
him secure. The Prince picks up the second
meaning.

51 'tis hot i.e. from repeated firing.

51 sack destroy, with a pun on the contents of his
case.

53 pierce Pronounced 'perse' and allowing a pun
on 'Percy', as an instrument of violence.

55 carbonado a piece of fish or flesh scored
across, ready for grilling (*OED* sv *sb*¹). Compare
Marlowe, *1 Tamburlaine* 4.4.43–4: 'I will make thee
slice the brawnes of thy armes into carbonadoes,
and eat them.'

57 there's an end (1) to life, (2) to my speech, as
in 'so ends my catechism' 5.1.137–8.

57 SD Q provides no exit for Falstaff, and there is
no evidence whether the corpse of Blunt is removed
or remains onstage.

Act 5, Scene 4

0 SD.1 *Excursions* Raids. The exchange between
two characters gives way to the busy movement of
unidentified soldiers and the noise of battle before
the King and his leaders enter.

1 I prithee . . . much This extra-metrical line
(Q1) may convey a sense of haste.

1 thou bleedest too much Holinshed describes
how the Prince, hurt in the face by an arrow, refused to leave the field when several nobles tried to
escort him off (III, 26).

4 make up bring your forces forward, as at 57
below.

5 retirement falling back.

5 amaze alarm, fill with consternation (*OED* sv *v*
3).

KING I will do so. My Lord of Westmoreland,
     Lead him to his tent.
WESTMORELAND Come, my lord, I'll lead you to your tent.
PRINCE Lead me, my lord? I do not need your help,   *acting as Prince now*
     And God forbid a shallow scratch should drive   10
     The Prince of Wales from such a field as this,
     Where stained nobility lies trodden on,
     And rebels' arms triumph in massacres!
LANCASTER We breathe too long: come, cousin Westmoreland,
     Our duty this way lies: for God's sake, come.   15
                    [*Exeunt Lancaster and Westmoreland*]
PRINCE By God, thou hast deceived me, Lancaster,
     I did not think thee lord of such a spirit:
     Before, I loved thee as a brother, John,   *salute to brother*
     But now I do respect thee as my soul.
KING I saw him hold Lord Percy at the point   20
     With lustier maintenance than I did look for
     Of such an ungrown warrior.
PRINCE O, this boy lends mettle to us all!   *Exit*

                    [*Enter* DOUGLAS]

DOUGLAS Another king! They grow like Hydra's heads.
     I am the Douglas, fatal to all those   25
     That wear those colours on them. What art thou
     That counterfeitest the person of a king?
KING The King himself, who, Douglas, grieves at heart
     So many of his shadows thou hast met,

6–7 I . . . tent] *As Capell; as one line* Qq; *I . . . so: / My . . . Tent* F   15 SD *Exeunt Lancaster and Westmoreland*] *Capell subst.; not in* QqF   22–3 Of . . . all] QqF; *Of . . . warrior. Prince. O . . . boy (as one line) /* Lends . . . all *Pope, followed by Humphreys*   23 SD.2 *Enter* DOUGLAS] F; *not in* Qq

6–7 I . . . tent Printed as a single line in Qq; compare 1 above.
12 stained i.e. by blood and dirt. The Prince wants to belittle his scratch by comparison with the blood of those massacred, 13, not suggest that they are dishonoured. Compare 'stain my favours in a bloody mask', 3.2.136.
14 breathe pause for breath.
15 SD This '*Exeunt*', not given in QqF, could be delayed until 19 or until the Prince leaves at line 23. The praise from the Prince and the King, 16–23, would then become direct compliment to Lancaster.
21 lustier maintenance more energetic bearing (*OED* Maintenance *sb* 1, this example).
23 mettle spirit, courage.

24 Another king Compare 5.3.7–9 and n. In Holinshed (III, 26) Douglas strikes down the King and his decoys when the King is in the van of battle; here he finds Henry retired.
24 Hydra's heads The many heads of Hydra grew back as soon as Hercules cut them off. This analogy is commonly used to characterise evil when it spreads as fast as it is destroyed.
26 colours the colours of the 'coats' Douglas vowed to kill, 5.3.26.
29 shadows (1) delusive semblances, (2) reflections or mirror images, (3) those who play or act the King. Because many of these 'shadows' have been slain, the grieving King may also suggest that they are phantoms or shades.

And not the very King. I have two boys   30
Seek Percy and thyself about the field,
But seeing thou fallest on me so luckily
I will assay thee, and defend thyself.

DOUGLAS I fear thou art another counterfeit,
And yet, in faith, thou bearest thee like a king –   35
But mine I am sure thou art, whoe'er thou be,
And thus I win thee.

They fight, the King being in danger

Enter PRINCE OF WALES

PRINCE Hold up thy head, vile Scot, or thou art like
Never to hold it up again! The spirits
Of valiant Shirley, Stafford, Blunt are in my arms.   40
It is the Prince of Wales that threatens thee,
Who never promiseth but he means to pay.

They fight; Douglas flieth   (middle english)

Cheerly, my lord, how fares your grace?
Sir Nicholas Gawsey hath for succour sent,
And so hath Clifton – I'll to Clifton straight.   R-evaluato|woke new) 45

KING Stay and breathe a while.   1 · | 177

✻ Thou hast redeemed thy lost opinion,

And showed thou mak'st some tender of my life
In this fair rescue thou hast brought to me.

PRINCE O God, they did me too much injury   50
That ever said I hearkened for your death.

---

33 thee, and] Qq2–5; thee and Q1; thee: so F

30 very true, real.

33 assay test.

36 mine my conquest.

37 SDS Daniel credits the Prince with saving his father's life from Douglas: 'Hadst thou not there lent present speedy ayd / To thy indaungerde father nerely tyrde, / Whom fierce incountring *Dowglas* overlaid, / That day had there his troublous life expirde' (III, st. III).

40 Shirley Listed ('Shorlie') among the slain by Holinshed (III, 26), along with Gawsey (Gausell) and Clifton, who are fighting fiercely at 44 and 45 below.

42 Who . . . pay i.e. Who keeps his word. The Prince's assertion resonates with many different expressions of obligation and redemption in the play, including his own vow to 'pay the debt I never

promisèd' (1.2.169), Hotspur's allegation that 'the King / Knows at what time to promise, when to pay' (4.3.52–3), and Falstaff's grim puns on death as a final reckoning or payment (5.1.127, 5.3.30–1).

43 Cheerly A terse encouraging shout.

47 opinion reputation. Compare 3.2.42: 'Opinion, that did help me to the crown'.

48 thou mak'st some tender of i.e. you care to preserve from harm (*OED* sv *sb* 3).

50–1 they . . . your death There are echoes of such slander at 3.2.25 and 124–26 but no support for it in *1H4*. In *FV*, however, the Prince frankly hopes for his father's death, 93–4, 455–7, and 479–81.

51 hearkened for lay eagerly in wait for. Compare *Shr.* 1.2.258: 'The youngest daughter, whom you hearken for'.

If it were so, I might have let alone
The insulting hand of Douglas over you,
Which would have been as speedy in your end
As all the poisonous potions in the world,   55
And saved the treacherous labour of your son.
KING Make up to Clifton, I'll to Sir Nicholas Gawsey.   *Exit*

Enter HOTSPUR

HOTSPUR If I mistake not, thou art Harry Monmouth.
PRINCE Thou speakest as if I would deny my name.
HOTSPUR My name is Harry Percy.
PRINCE   Why then I see   60
A very valiant rebel of the name.
I am the Prince of Wales, and think not, Percy,
To share with me in glory any more.
Two stars keep not their motion in one sphere,
Nor can one England brook a double reign   65
Of Harry Percy and the Prince of Wales.
HOTSPUR Nor shall it, Harry, for the hour is come
To end the one of us; and would to God
Thy name in arms were now as great as mine.
PRINCE I'll make it greater ere I part from thee,   70
And all the budding honours on thy crest
I'll crop to make a garland for my head.
HOTSPUR I can no longer brook thy vanities.
                    They fight

Enter FALSTAFF

FALSTAFF Well said, Hal! To it, Hal! Nay, you shall find no
boy's play here, I can tell you.   75

60–1 My . . . name] *As Rowe³; My . . . Percy. / Why . . . name QqF (subst.)*   **67 Nor**] F; *Now* Qq

---

53 insulting scornfully triumphant.
57 Make up Move your forces forward.
64 Two stars . . . sphere In the Ptolemaic system, each star kept within its own orbit. Compare the King's use of this analogy at 5.1.17 and Dent s992: 'Two suns cannot shine in one sphere.'
65 brook endure. Hotspur repeats the word at 73 and 77 below.
67 Nor Qq's 'Now' would be an error easily made by a printer and is clearly wrong.
71 honours on thy crest Literally, the chivalric favours decorating Hotspur's helmet; figuratively,

his glorious reputation, as in 'proud titles', 78 below.

73 vanities vain boasts.
74 Well said Well done.

Enter DOUGLAS; *he fighteth with Falstaff,* [*who*] *falls down as if he were dead*

[*Exit Douglas*]

The Prince killeth Percy   *ef sonnet Shakespear (No)*
loves not tries
fool

HOTSPUR O Harry, thou hast robbed me of my youth!

Death
speech   I better brook the loss of brittle life
Than those proud titles thou hast won of me.
They wound my thoughts worse than thy sword my flesh.
But thoughts, the slaves of life, and life, time's fool,   80
And time, that takes survey of all the world,
Must have a stop. O, I could prophesy,
But that the earthy and cold hand of death
Lies on my tongue. No, Percy, thou art dust,
And food for –   85

aposiopesis   [*He dies*]

↓
new speech
iched up
by aditor

PRINCE For worms, brave Percy. Fare thee well, great heart!
Ill-weaved ambition, how much art thou shrunk.
When that this body did contain a spirit,
A kingdom for it was too small a bound.
But now two paces of the vilest earth   90
Is room enough. This earth that bears thee dead
Bears not alive so stout a gentleman.
If thou wert sensible of courtesy
I should not make so dear a show of zeal,
But let my favours hide thy mangled face,   95

---

75 SD.1 *who*] F; *he* Qq   75 SD.2 *Exit Douglas*] Capell; not in QqF   75 SD.3 *killeth Percy*] QqF; *mortally wounds Hotspur /
Humphreys*   80 thoughts,] Q1; *thought's* Qq2–5, F   85 for –] F; *for.* Qq1, 2; *for* Qq3–5   85 SD *He dies*] Rowe; not in
QqF   91 thee] Q7; *the* Qq1–5, F, Q6

75 SD.2 *Exit Douglas* Not indicated by QqF. The
later report by the Prince that Douglas 'saw . . .
The noble Percy slain' means that he understood
this death to be part of his bad fortune, 5.5.17–20,
not that he felled Falstaff, then stayed onstage as a
mere by-stander while the Prince killed Hotspur.

75 SD.3 *The Prince killeth Percy* The Prince
gives a mortal wound to Hotspur, who does not die
until 85 below. QqF use 'Percy' *subst.* here, but
'Hotspur' in all other stage directions and speech
headings of 5.4. In Holinshed, the King is responsible, but only indirectly, for Hotspur's death: 'The
other on his part [i.e. the other warriors on the
King's side] incouraged by his doing, fought
valiantlie and slue the lord Persie, called Sir Henrie
Hotspurre' (III, 26). For stagings of this combat and
its aftermath, see Introduction, pp. 47, 51, 58.

80 thoughts The Q1 reading is preferable to
Qq2–5,F 'thought's' because it links 'thoughts'

grammatically with 'life' 80, and 'time' 81, as subjects of 'Must have a stop' (i.e. Come to an end), 82.

82 prophesy On the proverbial ability of dying
men to develop foresight, compare Dent M514,
'Dying men speak true', and *R2* 2.1.5–16 and 31–9.

85 SD *He dies* QqF give no explicit direction.

87 Ill-weaved (1) loosely or poorly woven and
therefore apt to shrink, (2) woven with evil purpose.

92 stout valiant.

93 sensible of able to recognise.

94 so . . . zeal so heartfelt a display of admiration.

95 favours tokens of honour or personal favour
worn on the helmet. Herbert Hartman, 'Prince
Hal's "shew of zeale"', *PMLA* 46 (1931), 720–3,
suggests that the Prince lays his plumes (4.1.98)
upon Hotspur's face. C. W. Scott-Giles, *Shakespeare's Heraldry*, 1950, p. 91, proposes 'a torse of
silk of his own colours, white and blue, which he
unbound from his helm for the purpose'.

And even in thy behalf I'll thank myself
For doing these fair rites of tenderness.
Adieu, and take thy praise with thee to heaven!
Thy ignominy sleep with thee in the grave,
But not remembered in thy epitaph.   100
              He spieth Falstaff on the ground
What, old acquaintance, could not all this flesh
Keep in a little life? Poor Jack, farewell!
I could have better spared a better man.
O, I should have a heavy miss of thee
If I were much in love with vanity.   105
Death hath not struck so fat a deer today,
Though many dearer, in this bloody fray.
Embowelled will I see thee by and by,
Till then in blood by noble Percy lie.   *Exit*
              Falstaff riseth up

FALSTAFF Embowelled? If thou embowel me today, I'll give you leave   110
to powder me and eat me too tomorrow. 'Sblood, 'twas time to
counterfeit, or that hot termagant Scot had paid me, scot and lot
too. Counterfeit? I lie, I am no counterfeit. To die is to be a counterfeit, for he is but the counterfeit of a man who hath not the life of
a man. But to counterfeit dying, when a man thereby liveth, is to be   115
no counterfeit, but the true and perfect image of life indeed. The

---

97 rites] Qq2–5, F; rights Q1   106 fat] Q1, F; faire Qq2–5

---

104 heavy sorrowful, with a faint pun on the notion of weight.

107 dearer (1) more valiant, (2) more truly admired. The Prince puns on 'deer', 106, and ironically echoes his praise of Hotspur, 94 above. Compare Antony's metaphor for the murdered Caesar, *JC* 3.1.204 : 'Here wast thou bay'd, brave hart.'

108 Embowelled Disembowelled, in preparation for embalming and burial. A punning allusion to the 'assay' or ceremony of disembowelling a deer after the hunt is noted by Humphreys.

109 in blood i.e. in the blood of the slain Hotspur. Humphreys points out that the Prince speaks truer than he knows, for a hunted deer, said to be 'in blood', is vigorously alive, like the shamming Falstaff.

109 SDS If Falstaff's resurrection follows a brief pause after the Prince's exit, it will surprise those in the audience who are ignorant of his trick and increase the anticipation of those who are not. If his 'death' is obviously faked through the whole se-

quence, Falstaff becomes a more theatrical clown, detached from the tragic implications of this sequence.

111 powder (1) embalm, (2) preserve (like venison). In both cases a process of steeping in brine was employed.

112 termagant savage or violent. The imaginary deity, Termagant or Mahound, represented in earlier miracle plays, became a by-word for bullying bluster. Compare Hamlet's criticism of the players for 'o'erdoing Termagant, it out-Herods Herod', *Ham.* 3.2.13–14. In Jean Bodel's widely known French version (thirteenth-century) of the *Ludus super Iconia Sancti Nicolai*, an actor concealed within 'Termagaunt' roars when this idol is beaten.

112 paid killed. Compare 5.3.45 and 5.4.42.

112 scot and lot in full, a commonplace (Dent S159). Falstaff puns on death as final payment, using a quibble on 'scot', meaning Douglas. Compare 1.3. 212–13.

116–17 The better . . . discretion Falstaff puts into memorable form the idea (compare Dent D354)

famous
line

better part of valour is discretion, in the which better part I have
saved my life. Zounds, I am afraid of this gunpowder Percy, though
he be dead. How if he should counterfeit too and rise? By my faith,
I am afraid he would prove the better counterfeit. Therefore I'll   120
make him sure, yea, and I'll swear I killed him. Why may not he rise
as well as I? Nothing confutes me but eyes, and nobody sees me.
Therefore, sirrah [*Stabbing him*], with a new wound in your thigh,
come you along with me.

depths
to heights

          He takes up Hotspur on his back

          Enter PRINCE [*and*] JOHN OF LANCASTER

PRINCE Come, brother John, full bravely hast thou fleshed   125
    Thy maiden sword.
LANCASTER   But soft, whom have we here?
    Did you not tell me this fat man was dead?
PRINCE I did, I saw him dead,
    Breathless and bleeding on the ground. Art thou alive?
    Or is it fantasy that plays upon our eyesight?   130
    I prithee speak, we will not trust our eyes
    Without our ears. Thou art not what thou seemest.
FALSTAFF No, that's certain, I am not a double-man. But if I be not
    Jack Falstaff, then am I a Jack. There is Percy!
          [*He lays the body on the ground*]

---

123 SD *Stabbing him*] Malone; *not in* QqF   124 with me] Qq; me F   124 SD.2 PRINCE *and* JOHN] Qq2–5, F; *Prince John*
Q1   125–6 Come . . . sword] Qq; *as prose* F   134 SD *He lays the body on the ground*] *This edn; He throws the body down* / *Var.*
1773, Capell subst.; not in QqF

illustrated by Cowl and Morgan from Vincentio
Saviolo, 'Of Honour', *Saviolo His Practice* (1595),
signature BB : 'The wisdom and discretion of a man,
is as great a vertue as his magnanimitie and
courage . . . without them a man is not to be accounted valiant, but rather furious.'
    117 **part** quality or role, as well as portion.
    122 **Nothing . . . eyes** 'Only an eye-witness
could prove me a liar' (Humphreys). The fact that
so many 'eyes' do observe Falstaff's actions always
shapes the playing of the scene.
    123 **thigh** The significance of the thigh has been
disputed. The armour would protect the front of
the leg, but probably not its rear. (Could this suggest that Hotspur was fleeing?) Fatal thigh wounds
were familiar to audiences in the 1590s: Philip
Sidney was known to have died of a thigh wound at
Zutphen in 1588; more mythically, Adonis dies of

such a wound inflicted by a boar in *Venus and Adonis*
(1593), 1052–3.
    125 **fleshed** initiated. The metaphor derives
from 'the practice of "entering" a young hound by
allowing it to taste the flesh of the animal it was
being trained to hunt' (Cowl and Morgan).
    133 **double-man** (1) apparition or wraith, (2)
two men (referring to his appearance with Hotspur
on his back).
    134 SD *He lays the body on the ground* Variants
of the stage direction, *He throws the body down*,
present vivid examples of an intrusive SD that has
strongly influenced readers and spectators for three
hundred years. It has, however, no early textual
authority other than 'There is Percy!' (134). A more
neutral verb in the SD permits readers and directors
to choose the degree of force in his gesture and the
tone in which he delivers the line.

If your father will do me any honour, so. If not, let him kill the next   135
Percy himself. I look to be either earl or duke, I can assure you.
PRINCE   Why, Percy I killed myself, and saw thee dead.
FALSTAFF   Didst thou? Lord, Lord, how this world is given to lying! I
grant you I was down, and out of breath, and so was he, but we rose
both at an instant, and fought a long hour by Shrewsbury clock. If   140
I may be believed, so. If not, let them that should reward valour
bear the sin upon their own heads. I'll take it upon my death, I gave
him this wound in the thigh. If the man were alive, and would deny
it, zounds, I would make him eat a piece of my sword.
LANCASTER   This is the strangest tale that ever I heard.   145
PRINCE   This is the strangest fellow, brother John.
    Come, bring your luggage nobly on your back.
    For my part, if a lie may do thee grace,   *generosity of spirit*
    I'll gild it with the happiest terms I have.
                A retreat is sounded
    The trumpet sounds retreat, the day is ours.   150
    Come, brother, let us to the highest of the field,
    To see what friends are living, who are dead.
                Exeunt [Prince of Wales and Lancaster]
FALSTAFF   I'll follow, as they say, for reward. He that rewards me, God   *cf*
    reward him! If I do grow great, I'll grow less, for I'll purge, and   *drunk as*
    leave sack, and live cleanly as a nobleman should do.   155   *a lord*
                Exit [bearing off the body]

148–9 For . . . have] *As* QQF; *an aside to Falstaff* / *Wilson, Humphreys*   150 ours] QQ2–5, F; *our* Q1   152 SD *Prince of Wales and Lancaster*] *Cam.; not in* QQF   155 nobleman] QQ4, 5, F; *noble man* QQ1–3   155 SD *bearing off the body*] *Capell; not in* QQF

140 at an instant simultaneously.

140 long hour . . . clock Mock precision, as if real warriors patiently timed their battles. But compare 1.3.99 (suggested by Brian Gibbons).

142–3 I . . . thigh Falstaff supports his lies with one true statement.

148–9 For my . . . I have Wilson and Humphreys regard this line as an aside to Falstaff. For examples of productions which treat the Prince's generosity as morally problematic, see Introduction, pp. 52, 56.

148 do thee grace help you to gain credit or favour. Evidently it does, because in *2H4* 1.2.148–9, the Lord Chief Justice tells Falstaff: 'Your day's service at Shrewsbury hath a little gilded over your night's exploit on Gadshill.'

149 happiest most favourable.

153 I'll follow . . . reward Wilson suggests that this expression links Falstaff to the hounds who are rewarded after the hunt with portions of the deer. Compare 108 above and n.

154 purge (1) become spiritually pure through expiating sins, (2) lose weight by taking purgative medicines.

[**5.5**]   *The trumpets sound. Enter the* KING, PRINCE OF WALES, LORD
JOHN OF LANCASTER, EARL OF WESTMORELAND, *with* WORCESTER
and VERNON *prisoners*

KING   Thus ever did rebellion find rebuke.
        Ill-spirited Worcester, did not we send grace,
        Pardon, and terms of love to all of you?
        And wouldst thou turn our offers contrary?
        Misuse the tenor of thy kinsman's trust?   5
        Three knights upon our party slain today,
        A noble earl, and many a creature else
        Had been alive this hour
        If like a Christian thou hadst truly borne
        Betwixt our armies true intelligence.   10
WORCESTER   What I have done my safety urged me to,
        And I embrace this fortune patiently,
        Since not to be avoided it falls on me.
KING   Bear Worcester to the death, and Vernon too.
        Other offenders we will pause upon.   15
                        [*Exeunt Worcester and Vernon guarded*]
        How goes the field?
PRINCE   The noble Scot, Lord Douglas, when he saw
        The fortune of the day quite turned from him,
        The noble Percy slain, and all his men
        Upon the foot of fear, fled with the rest,   20
        And falling from a hill he was so bruised
        That the pursuers took him. At my tent
        The Douglas is – and I beseech your grace
        I may dispose of him.
KING   With all my heart.
PRINCE   Then, brother John of Lancaster, to you   25

Handwritten margin notes:
judging as if a God
meant to go to Jerusalem to get forgiveness for death of Richard

talking about his treachery
rubbing hands – guilt

Act 5, Scene 5   5.5] Capell; *Scæna Quarta.* F; *not in* Qq   15 SD *Exeunt Worcester and Vernon guarded*] Theobald; *Exeunt
Worcester and Vernon* F; *not in* Qq   25–6 Then . . . belong] *As* Pope; Then . . . Lancaster, / To . . . belong QqF

Act 5, Scene 5

0 SD *trumpets sound* Although this is a triumphant royal entry, the trumpets may well be restrained in order to introduce the sober tone of the
opening lines.

  1 **rebuke** (1) disgrace, (2) reprimand.
  5 **tenor** habitual condition (*OED sb*¹ 3b).

5 **thy kinsman** i.e. Hotspur.
6–7 **Three . . . else** Shakespeare minimises the
casualties. Holinshed reports as slain on the King's
side 10 knights in addition to the Earl of Stafford,
and 1,600 soldiers; 4,000 were 'greevouslie
wounded' (III, 26).
20 **Upon . . . fear** In flight motivated by panic.

This honourable bounty shall belong.
Go to the Douglas and deliver him
Up to his pleasure, ransomless and free.
His valours shown upon our crests today
Have taught us how to cherish such high deeds,   30
Even in the bosom of our adversaries.
LANCASTER I thank your grace for this high courtesy,
Which I shall give away immediately.
KING Then this remains, that we divide our power.
You, son John, and my cousin Westmoreland,   35
Towards York shall bend you with your dearest speed
To meet Northumberland and the prelate Scroop,
Who, as we hear, are busily in arms.
Myself and you, son Harry, will towards Wales,
To fight with Glendower and the Earl of March.   40
Rebellion in this land shall lose his sway,
Meeting the check of such another day,
And since this business so fair is done,
Let us not leave till all our own be won.

Exeunt

32–3 I . . . immediately] Qq1–4; *not in* Q5, F   36 bend you] Qq4, 5, F; bend, you Qq1–3   41 lose] Q1 (loose)   41 sway] Q1; way F

---

26 honourable bounty the honour of bestowing the reward for honour (to Douglas).

27–8 Go . . . free The Prince's generosity contrasts with the King's severity in executing Vernon along with the more treacherous Worcester.

36 bend you direct your way.

36 dearest greatest.

40 To fight . . . March The play ends, as it be-

gins (1.1.38–40) with references to Mortimer and Glendower. In Holinshed, the King goes directly to York where he makes peace with Northumberland (III, 26).

43–4 And . . . be won The concluding lines may point towards a second play, however firm the closure provided by the victory at Shrewsbury.

TEXTUAL ANALYSIS

On 25 February 1598, *The First Part of King Henry the Fourth* (called simply *Henry IV*) was entered in the Stationers' Register to the bookseller, Andrew Wyse. The title page of the quarto printed later in the same year by Peter Short reads:

THE / HISTORY OF / HENRIE THE / FOVRTH; / With the battell at Shrewsburie, / *betweene the King and Lord* / Henry Percy, surnamed / Henrie Hotspur of / the North. / *With the humorous conceits of Sir* / John Falstalffe.

This first quarto, now generally known as Q1, and a fragment rediscovered in the nineteenth century, known as Q0, provide the only authoritative copy-texts for this play. Q1 appears to be an exceptionally faithful reprinting of Q0; both are widely acknowledged to be among the most carefully printed quartos of any play by Shakespeare. Their textual reliability is striking when compared with that of the six other good quartos of his plays which were first published in 1597–1600. For example, the earliest quarto of *King Richard the Second* (1597) omitted the deposition scene because of censorship; it was restored by the fourth quarto (1608) and much improved in the First Folio (F), printed in 1623, by collation with a manuscript presumably 'clean and superior to the quarto version' (Gurr, p. 176). Not only were there a great many press corrections to the only quarto of *The Second Part of King Henry the Fourth* (1600); the Folio also added 'eight longer passages, totalling over 160 lines', while omitting eight passages or twenty-three lines, most with 'marked sexual innuendoes' (Melchiori, pp. 190–1).

In contrast, subsequent quartos of *The First Part of King Henry the Fourth* (Q2, 1599; Q3, 1604; Q4, 1608; Q5, 1613; Q6, 1622) lack authority; they make minor revisions and add numerous errors. Each subsequent quarto is closely based upon the one preceding it. No recent editor takes seriously the claim of 'Newly corrected' on the title page of Q2. Q5 probably reflects some familiarity with actual performance in correcting the misattribution to Northumberland of Hotspur's lines at 1.3.199–206, and in clarifying Worcester's reply to Vernon at 5.2.3. Other improvements are negligible.

The Folio text (1623), probably based upon an edited copy of Q5, owes what limited authority it has to two factors: (1) a reflection of theatrical changes occurring subsequent to early performances, and (2) reliance on a copy-text characterised by spellings believed by some editors to be more typical of Shakespeare's usage than those in QQ01. F's act and scene divisions, which may well be evidence of Jacobean staging even if added by the F editors, have been generally adopted and are followed here, with the exception of the division proposed by Capell in 5.3 after line 100; F's 5.3 and 5.4 consequently become 5.3, 5.4, and 5.5. Selected examples of F's thorough but still incomplete excision of oaths and biblical passages, interesting primarily as evidence about responses to the 1606 law against profanity on stage, have been recorded in the

Collation at several points. F's other changes, including those which may depend on consultation of QqOI or which correct errors in Qq0–5, will be described in more detail below. None of these corrections, it should be stressed, adds or deletes passages longer than one line. They are accompanied by the perpetuation of old errors and the addition of many new ones, created by the processes of editing and printing the Folio text.

The printing of Q0 and Q1

Q0, an eight-page fragment found by J. O. Halliwell 'some years' before 1867 in the binding of William Thomas' *Rules of Latin Grammar* (1567) and now held in the Folger Shakespeare Library, provides the basic textual authority for 1.3.199 to 2.2.93. Charlton Hinman (1966) has shown that both Q0 and Q1 came from the printing-house of Peter Short. He observed that the same stock of types, including some distinctive ornaments, was employed for both quartos, and he surmised that Q1 'was printed directly from Q0' because the two texts share 'so many typographical and textual peculiarities' (p. viii), such as the omission of the speech heading 'Hotspur' at 1.3.199, leading to the misattribution already mentioned. That Q1 is an accurate reprint rather than the original text is indicated by its compression, which is relatively greater than that of Q0. Q1 ends with K4ᵛ, the final page of its tenth sheet, whereas Q0, according to Hinman, 'must have required at least one leaf of an eleventh sheet L'. Q1 makes only one clearly negligent error, omitting 'fat' from 'How the fat rogue roared' (2.2.93); it corrects 'whip' to 'whipt' (1.3.236) and replaces 'my owne' with 'mine owne' (2.2.29).[1]

The obvious care taken in printing Q0 and Q1, together with the unusually early publication relative to first performance, may have represented one means of assuring the Cobham family that the name of Oldcastle had been removed from Shakespeare's play. But such assurance seems to have been perfunctory. Although 'Falstaff' replaces 'Oldcastle' in dialogue and speech headings (Q of *The Second Part of King Henry the Fourth* preserves an 'Old.' speech heading at 1.2.96), Oldcastle lingers on in the Prince's address to 'my old lad of the castle' (1.2.34) and in Gadshill's cryptic reference to the safety of stealing in the good company of 'old Sir John' (2.1.55) and other 'burgomasters and great oneyres' (62): 'We steal as in a castle, cock-sure' (2.1.69–70). Other names which may well have given offence survive through QqF when Poins refers to 'Falstalffe Harvey, Rossill, and Gadshil' (1.2.130–1); Qq1–5 retain speech headings for 'Ross.' at 2.4.147, 149, and 153, corrected by F to 'Gad.'.

When Shakespeare completed the manuscript of a play, he turned it over, with or without revision, to his acting company. Authorial manuscripts, known as 'foul papers' (but not necessarily messy or 'foul') are believed to have furnished the basis for many quarto and for some Folio texts. Shakespeare or his company might also have arranged for a scribe to make a fair copy of his manuscript for the convenience of the 'book-keeper' or prompter.

That the manuscript of *The First Part of King Henry the Fourth* submitted for printing by Short was a scribal copy of Shakespeare's work rather than his own

[1] W. W. Greg in Hinman, Preface, p. vii.

corrected foul papers or revised transcription seems probable. Not only is it less likely that Shakespeare, as opposed to a scribe, could have overlooked and failed to replace 'Harvey', 'Rossill', and 'Ross.'. It is also doubtful that his company would have chosen to use the time of their major playwright on the large task posed by changing many names. (The *Textual Companion* editors judge that some 330 alterations would have been required.)

Controversy has arisen over two questions raised by the surmised existence of such a transcript: its proximity to the realities of staged performances, and its uncharacteristic orthography. The first of these matters requires a more careful consideration of how the manuscript might have functioned in the playhouse. The second has been linked with recent arguments for the validity of readings which are based on F. It will therefore be addressed as a key element in the current revaluation of F's authority.

The first quartos and stage practice

Surviving copies of playtexts which may have been used as prompt-books suggest that prompters were able to work directly from authorial handwriting; the actors would not always have needed stage directions which added to or clarified those provided by the playwright.[1] Individual actors' parts would have been copied out and distributed. In some cases, actors may have begun to study their parts and may have started rehearsals while the playwright continued to revise.[2] Approaching the copy-text for *The First Part of King Henry the Fourth* in the light of this complex theatrical process will help to explain its nature.

QQ01 exhibit features which are often found in quartos known to have been printed from foul papers, like *The Merchant of Venice* and *Much Ado About Nothing*. At the same time, they show signs of having been printed from a copy regularised by a scribal hand. Whatever the case may be, the quarto texts reflect a stage in the producing of *Part One* which is earlier than the revision of controversial names. The evidence that QQ01 originate from foul papers is not necessarily stronger than that for a fair, scribal copy, but it does highlight the question of the text's usefulness in the theatre. The two most conspicuous foul-paper characteristics have been thought to be (1) permissive or absent stage directions, and (2) indecisive treatment of minor characters. Recent editors seem to agree that had a play-book or prompter's copy served as the basis of the first quartos, these defects or oddities would not have been so apparent.[3] What this consensus may overlook is the possibility that some of the features deemed inadequate from an editorial viewpoint might not present great problems in the theatre itself.

QQ01's treatment of entrances and exits provides a number of examples which support this possibility. Act 3, Scene 3 omits four exits within fifteen lines, including a terminal exit for Falstaff, while 4.1 begins with no entrance formula whatsoever for

---

[1] See Scott McMillin, *The Elizabethan Theatre and 'The Book of Sir Thomas More'*, 1987, p. 49 and William B. Long, 'Stage directions: a misinterpreted factor in determining textual provenance', *TEXT* 2 (1985), 121–37.

[2] In *The Stability of Shakespeare's Text*, 1965, pp. 19–20, E. A. J. Honigmann mentions Sir Henry Herbert's criticism of actors for commencing work before their play-book had been officially licensed.

[3] See Hinman, p. ix, Humphreys, p. lxvi, and Bevington, p. 87.

Hotspur, Worcester, and Douglas. The omission of these exits, however, would be unlikely to confuse actors, while the omission of the entrance is, in theatrical terms, much more impracticable. This one is so plainly faulty that it is more likely to have been caused through a corruption of the manuscript by a scribe or compositor than by Shakespeare himself. Of the exits omitted in 3.3, two, those of Bardolph and Peto, are emphatically implied by the words of the Prince when he gives sharp orders, 'Bardoll. / Go beare this letter' and 'Go Peto, to horse, to horse.' For Bardolph or Peto to simply remain onstage might well cause raucous laughter and spoil the effect of the rousing couplet with which the Prince concludes his speech. This presumably signals his own exit, before Falstaff's final, antiphonal couplet, balancing the Prince's call to arms with a call for breakfast. Accustomed to a convention of separating scenes by general exits, an actor playing Falstaff would be unlikely to linger while Hotspur and the others come on.

QI repeatedly omits exits that clear the stage at the end of a scene, as do many other quarto and Folio texts. Skipping an exit direction which has been clearly referred to by speeches can seldom be judged a serious flaw in a script intended primarily for playhouse rehearsals. Shakespeare could have designed other scenes which obviously require exits but have left the timing indeterminate. For example, a contemporary editor must furnish exits for Bardolph and the Hostess in 2.4.399, where the action of the scene generates confusing bustle. Here we have evidence that Shakespeare, to quote Stanley Wells, was 'writing sketchily' as in 1.2 of *Much Ado About Nothing*.[1]

QqoI's omissions of entrances are potentially more disruptive for theatrical production. Characters left out of entrances preceding the first lines of scenes include Sir Walter Blunt (1.1), Bardolph (2.2), and Vernon (5.1). Douglas abruptly appears, without an entrance, eager to attack 'Another king', 5.4.24, after the Prince exits with his brother John and King Henry remains alone. In a more problematic example, the King's phrase, 'Here is . . . Sir Walter Blunt' (1.1.62–3) may be an implicit stage direction, indicating either that Blunt has been present from the beginning, or that he has entered belatedly (surprising the other lords, if not the King himself). Bevington and Oxford suggest that 'here' means 'here in the court' (and can therefore be no guide to action on the stage). Only a director can make a final decision about Blunt's stage presence. Bardolph, as the evidence of speech headings (see below) also suggests, provides fairly clear signs that Shakespeare was confused about a minor role, in ways which are similar to those found in foul papers. Shakespeare seems at first not to have distinguished him firmly from Gadshill or decided upon his function.[2] The cases of both Blunt and Bardolph, it might be noted, occur early, while Shakespeare could be trying out various possibilities. Those of Vernon and Douglas may be accounted for, in part, as theatrical casualties of the military crisis Shakespeare was orchestrating.

Three other features of QqoI suggest near-readiness for theatrical presentation: (1) lively, descriptive stage directions, (2) light punctuation, apt as a guide to pauses when speaking in the theatre, and (3) relatively accurate speech headings. Vivid directions are distributed throughout the text after the first Act: 'Enter a Carrier with a lanterne

[1] 'Editorial treatment of foul paper texts: *Much Ado About Nothing* as test case', *RES* 31 (1986), 13.
[2] See John Jowett, 'The thieves in *1 Henry IV*', *RES* 38 (1987), 325–33.

in his hand' (2.1), 'Here they rob them and bind them' (2.2), 'Enter Bardoll running' (2.4), 'He spieth Falstalffe on the ground', and 'He takes up Hotspur on his backe' (5.4). William Long regards such information as 'playwrights' advisory directions' which could be adapted or entirely ignored by experienced professional actors.[1]

Contemporary directors, notably Audrey Stanley, have argued that the punctuation of Q1 provides far more effective guidance to actors speaking verse than does either F or any modern text.[2] For example, Q1's comma in mid-phrase for 'what saies sir John Sacke, and Sugar Iacke?' (1.2.91–2) appears to suggest a balance of elements while leaving the syntactic distribution of meaning open to a range of voice inflections. This edition follows Q1 in deleting several commas from the King's speech at the beginning of 1.3, and in restoring a comma at the end of its penultimate line: 'And therefore lost that title of respect, / Which the proud soul ne'er pays but to the proud' (8–9). For silent reading, no pause after 'respect' is required. But to speak lines 8 and 9 on one breath might deprive the King's repetitive conclusion of its weighty and measured pace.

Speech headings in Qq01 are far more consistent, as well as more accurately adjusted to speeches and to speakers' names, than is common for plays derived from foul papers, particularly *The Second Part of King Henry the Fourth* (Humphreys, p. lxvii). But as Humphreys (p. lxviii) and Davison (p. 248) have argued, the exceptional necessity to revise names could have caused Shakespeare (or his representative) simply to make corrections on the foul papers themselves. Such confusion as exists pertains largely to Bardolph and Gadshill; the speech by the Prince at 2.4.146 is erroneously attributed in Qq01 to 'Gad', while 'Ross.' (the abbreviation for Bardolph's earlier name, Rossill), speaks lines at 2.4.147, 149, and 153 attributed by F to Gadshill. As in the case of Bardolph's missing entrances in 2.2 and 2.4, such errors are likely to have reflected Shakespeare's indecision as recorded in his manuscript. It is true that quartos set from foul papers generally reveal Shakespeare's propensity to tinker with the actual names of his minor figures (apparent in Hand D of *The Book of Sir Thomas More*, which is believed to be Shakespeare's writing). Their speech headings also tend to be more variable. Here the names themselves remain stable, while the slight changes in abbreviations and, occasionally, spellings of speech headings never interfere with a quick and reliable identification of a character.

Indeed, a cursory examination of the order of these headings shows that full or longer forms usually precede shorter abbreviations: Prince/Prin./Pr.; Falst./Fal.; Wor./Worst.; and Poines/Poynes/Poy./Po./Poin. Someone has taken the trouble to avoid confusing Pr. with Po. or Prin. with Poin., which in the italic face used for speech headings could easily mislead a reader, especially in 1.2 where both characters first appear. That this someone is more likely to have belonged to the theatre than to the print-shop is suggested by the fact that Po. does conserve space in some cases, as in the speeches beginning at 1.2.121 and 136, but that it also appears at 110, 142, and 154 where there was space to spare. And it was not used for 91 where it would have saved a line.

[1] Long, 126–7.
[2] Stanley supported her view in a lecture given at the Pacific Northwest Renaissance Conference, 1979.

The most conspicuous variant speech heading, 'Per.' for 'Hotsp.' and 'Hot.', could be assigned, with almost equal probability, to author or to compositor. This variant occurs ten consecutive times starting with his first speech in 4.1, before 'Hot.' reappears for the remainder of the scene. Because both forms of his name are used so frequently and regularly in *Part One* ('Percy' or 'Percys' forty-six times, 'Hotspur' ten times), the 'Per.' of Act 4 is unlikely to have expressed or caused confusion. Interestingly, neither 'Hotspur' nor 'Percy' occur in the dialogue of Act 4. Either Shakespeare or a scribe might simply have had the alternative form 'Per.' in his mind as he set down the speech headings.

One other feature of the play which may be mentioned in connection with the copy for Qq01 is the disappearance of Poins from the action after 2.4.419, and the sudden prominence of Peto as the Prince's attendant at the ends of 2.4 and 3.3. Fredson Bowers agrees with Dr Johnson's decision to replace Peto with Poins, on the theory that Shakespeare's original intentions can thereby be served. Bowers regards the 'substitution' of Peto for Poins in 2.4 as theatrically creaky, because, he reasons, the Sheriff would be more likely to recognise Peto than Poins (whom the Travellers of course never see).[1] He apparently forgets both the 'vizards' provided by Poins and the darkness before dawn at Gad's Hill, suggesting that Shakespeare's muddle with his thieves can become contagious for his bibliographers and editors.[2]

In summary, analysis of Qq01 suggests that their copy-text must have been more suitable for staging than many editors and scholars have judged. The manuscript submitted for printing omits a number of exits and entrances, but few of these omissions would have created confusion in the playhouse. In most cases, the manuscript seems to have been sensitive to stage requirements, clearly indicating exits through dialogue. An actor playing Falstaff does not need a stage direction after the Prince's 'Farewell, the latter spring! Farewell, All-hallown summer!' (1.2.128). Francis has to pop on and off because of his job. A degree of indecision about the coming and going of characters who serve as messengers, delegates, and followers might reflect the exigencies of a company sometimes reduced in size for summer touring, not merely the drafting phase of composition.

The facts that Shakespeare's company could easily add minor roles and that Shakespeare often handled such parts inconsistently are more problematic for editors than for actors.[3] More accurate and consistent speech headings such as we find in *Part One* have usually been considered characteristic of 'literary' fair copies rather than of playwrights' manuscripts. Surely, however, the preparation of parts clearly aligned with speech headings would have been more important for the players than for the printer, even if the Oldcastle controversy did provoke Shakespeare into more carefully identifying and renaming some roles in his play.

What, then, of the evidence that the copy for Qq01 could indeed have been a fair copy made by a scribe, rather than Shakespeare's corrected papers or a transcript

---

[1] 'Establishing Shakespeare's text: Poins and Peto in *1 Henry IV*', *SB* 34 (1981), 189–98.

[2] Compare the discussion of 'Russell/Peto', *Textual Companion*, p. 331.

[3] Arthur Colby Sprague repeats Cumberland Clark's view that Peto may have come into being because three men would not be quite enough for two to 'set upon' in 'Shakespeare's unnecessary characters', *S.Sur.* 20 (1967), 80.

incorporating his revisions and written in his own hand? To begin with, editors and textual scholars have noticed, following Alice Walker's *Textual Problems of the First Folio*, an occasional formality or stiffness in Qq01.[1] Where a more colloquial elision might well be expected, the text uses instead 'Before the game is afoote thou still letst slip' (1.3.272) or Falstaff's 'All is one for that' (2.4.130). Walker attributed such 'pedantry' to a compositor rather than a scribe. As Humphreys has shown, however, any argument from Qq01's treatment of elisions strongly confirms their authority as copy-texts. Where there are merely a handful of unelided and sometimes irregular forms, there are 'scores' of elided ones, correctly set, it would appear, by the compositors. Hereward Price has argued that Shakespeare exercised special care in eliding weak past verb forms for metrical purposes.[2] Humphreys applies Price's conclusions from *Titus Andronicus* to *The First Part of King Henry the Fourth*: 'of past forms in the verse portions (the only ones to which the test applies) Qq01 rightly elide 168 and rightly leave unelided 33; they wrongly elide 1 . . . and wrongly leave unelided 10'.[3]

Yet such accuracy need not exclude the hypothesis of a scribal transcript. Humphreys ruled it out because the text seemed to him better, in regard to punctuation and elision, than any transcript was likely to be, and because he considered that the revision of names would 'not appreciably mess up the MS or make it unusable' (p. lxviii). Recent bibliographical study of Qq01's orthography suggests that an exceedingly faithful scribal transcript has become a slightly stronger possibility than the alternatives. Particularly persuasive is the evidence amassed by the editors of the *Textual Companion*, which includes: Qq01's departure from Shakespeare's preference for 'between' in favour of 'betwixt'; its predominant use of 'prithee', when Shakespeare (before 1600) preferred 'pray thee'; its anomalously high incidence of 'ye' and 'y'; and its preference for 'yea', when Shakespeare's 'most authoritative texts' prefer 'I' ('ay').[4]

While no one would assert that editions should adjust Shakespeare's spelling in individual plays to match statistical norms for his entire career, the editors of the *Textual Companion* do argue that such norms, defined by computer study, may be employed as support for readings based upon the Folio text of *Part One* rather than on Qq01. By re-opening the question of the Folio's substantive authority, so emphatically denied by Hinman and earlier editors, they have reminded us that the Qq01 origins of the text cannot be the end of its story. The play, like Shakespeare's spelling, continued to evolve.

The Folio text

In her pioneering examination of the Folio text for *Part One*, Alice Walker classified the kinds of corrections and errors which could be attributed to its two compositors, A and B. Although the number of compositors responsible for what was thought to be

[1] Alice Walker, 1953, p. 111.
[2] 'The first quarto of *Titus Andronicus*', in *English Institute Essays 1947*, 1948, pp. 137–68.
[3] Humphreys, pp. lxviii–lxix.
[4] *Textual Companion*, pp. 329–30. See also MacD. P. Jackson, 'Two Shakespeare quartos: *Richard III* (1597) and *1 Henry IV* (1598)', *SB* 35 (1982), 173–91 and 'The manuscript copy for the quarto (1598) of Shakespeare's *1 Henry IV*', *N&Q* 33 (1986), 353–4.

A's stint has grown like Falstaff's men in buckram, Walker's findings remain a useful point of departure for considering the Folio text. She begins by listing twenty-six variants between F and its copy-text, Q5, which actually restore Q1 readings, later corrupted in Q2–5, such as 'fat' for 'faire' at 5.4.106. She also lists F's correction of cumulative Q1–5 errors.[1] F has long been credited with such minor improvements as replacing Q's 'present' (2.4.27) with 'president' (precedent) and 'Now' with 'Nor' (5.4.67). Although Walker's main contribution was to identify the extensive errors committed by Compositor B, she did show that F bore evidence of having checked earlier readings.

Yet in spite of having consulted its predecessors, the editors or copy-setters of F failed to supply many of the speech headings and stage directions missing in Qq01. Gadshill's 'Speak, sirs, how was it?' (2.4.146) has now been correctly attributed to the Prince, while Peto has been given a speech heading at 2.4.448. Falstaff is provided with an exit at 5.3.57 (although the scene remains undivided); so, too, are Worcester and Vernon at 5.5.15, while group exits have been added at the ends of 2.1 and 4.3. They have also been eliminated in several other places, repeating the omissions in Qq4–5. Douglas gets an entrance at 5.4.23, but the '*Etc.*' which probably included Bardolph at the beginning of 2.2 has been dropped. The exits of Bardolph and the Hostess in 2.4 are still unspecified, as are the entrances of Blunt in 1.1 and Vernon in 5.1. The inappropriate group '*Exeunt*' employed by Qq2–5 to conclude 3.3 has been kept, with the addition of a pointless '*omnes*'. The inference from F's treatment of speech headings and stage directions has generally been that the copy from which F was set contained some annotations based on familiarity with the theatre, but that a prompt-book cannot have been collated. Again, this consensus may reflect the doubtful assumption that the 'book' for a play would have given clear and consistent instructions to actors. Still, Bevington's observation about 'the First Folio editor's inability or unwillingness to provide any meaningful clarification of stage action' (p. 93) seems justified. The provision of an incorrect entrance for Poins at the beginning of 1.2 appears to be evidence of careless editing, although Qq4–5's mistaken treatment of Falstaff's welcoming 'Poins!' as a speech heading (1.2.86) probably added to the confusion. Another clearly erroneous entry is the inclusion of the offstage Westmoreland at the beginning of 5.1.

Although it would be pointless to cite the many misreadings introduced by F, it may be more fruitful to understand one of their causes. Paul Werstine has shown that Compositor B, thought by Walker to be the source of many substitutions, omissions, and interpolations in F, was relatively accurate in his work on other Folio texts, and that his mistakes on this text are partly caused by the way the copy he set had been previously cast off.[2] In casting off copy, a printer judges in advance the number of manuscript pages needed to fill a sheet or a group of sheets when they are printed. It seems that inadequate space in the overall sequence of plays was allotted for the printing of the last part of *King Richard the Second*, and the two parts of *King Henry the Fourth*, and that supplementary sheets had to be added, resulting in more space

[1] 'The Folio text of *1 Henry IV*, *SB* 6 (1954), 45–59.
[2] 'Compositor B of the Shakespeare First Folio', *AEB* 2 (1978), 241–63.

than the printers needed. The individual manuscript pages seem at this point to have been unevenly cast off, burdening the compositors with the task of adjusting copy to spaces which might be too great here, too small there. Some of the errors introduced under these circumstances were probably editorial. Werstine also points to one example which is of particular interest because it suggests that a proof-reading correction has been made which relies upon a corrected manuscript source. F's 'I, but tis like' seems to have been a late replacement for the Qq form 'Yea but tis like' (1.2.140), as is indicated by the abnormally large space which seems to have been left between the speech heading 'Prin.' and 'I'. Although we cannot exclude the correction of some other error as the cause of such a space, it does seem possible that one anomalous 'yea' typical of Qq01 copy has here been brought into line with F's preference for 'I'.

Whether such changes reflect in some degree the authority of Shakespeare or of his manuscripts as used in the theatre is the question that has been raised by the newest bibliography. F's revisions in 1.3, which Walker surmised to be signs of editorial intervention and, in fact, 'singularly pointless' (i.e. the replacement of Qq01's 'Either envie therefore' with F's 'Who either through envie' at 1.3.26) are believed by the Oxford editors to reflect 'deliberate authorial changes incorporated from the manuscript'.[1] Such judgements rely on the presence, within a few lines of the 'authorial changes', of undoubted restorations of Qq01, on the clustering of the changes in a scene where numerous elisions have been introduced, and on the editors' confidence in the statistical norms for Shakespearean spellings which diverge, as we have seen, from the usage of the first quartos.

Cruxes

In this edition, each word or passage considered to be a crux has been discussed in the Commentary when it appears. Of five cruxes that are particularly important, four – 'oneyres', 2.1.62, 'elf-skin', 2.4.203, 'scantle', 3.1.96, and 'estridges', 4.1.98 – are unlikely to have presented problems for audiences at early performances. In each case, the actor speaks an unusual word which is made roughly intelligible by its context. This edition has adopted the copy-text readings of these four words as both plausible and attractive.

One crux, however, at 2.4.410 presents a choice between familiar words and their senses: 'Thou art essentially made' (QqF1–2) and 'Thou art essentially mad' (F3). Not only would the words have been spelling variants in 1597; the actor playing Falstaff could also, through intonation and gesture, have delivered the phrase in very different ways. Indeed, the choice between conveying the sense of 'made' or of 'mad' might well have been the kind of decision which would vary from performance to performance. Not surprisingly, stage history seems to offer no clear examples of such choices in specific productions. Where original production is concerned, two points may be worth bearing in mind: (1) that we cannot be sure how actors would have pronounced

---

[1] *Textual Companion*, p. 333, note on 1.3.26; compare p. 333, note on 1.2.165.

the word, and (2) that Falstaff almost certainly means his phrase to be a compliment, whether he implies one or both senses of the word in question.

Lineation

The same pressure to save space that led the compositors of Qq01 to omit terminal exits and speech headings probably caused them at times to end one speech and begin another on one line. It has also been conjectured that Shakespeare's foul papers crowded speeches together. Junctures of two or three short lines (i.e. those having less than five metrical stresses) or of shorter with longer lines, all spoken by different characters, invite editorial decisions as to how such dialogue should be represented in contemporary editions: flush with speech headings near the left-hand margin, or distributed across the page on subsequent lines which have been visually linked to reflect the metre.[1] Given Shakespeare's growing tendency to use more short lines of verse, combined either with longer verse lines or with prose passages, and the fact that, as Wright shows, he 'modulates back and forth between the forms', it becomes evident that editors will often agree on the expressive variety created by his style, but disagree on how to represent it through lineation.[2]

Act 1, Scene 3 of *Part One* can illustrate the editorial options for representing short lines and suggest how such lines enrich dialogue.[3] If we consider only lines that begin and end speeches, Qq01 print twenty-nine lines as short. Of these, this edition prints twenty-six as shared between speakers (thirteen pairs), leaving only three as separate short lines which immediately follow the speech heading. Bevington uses ten pairs, leaving nine separate short lines, while Humphreys combines line 264 with 263 – thus including three speakers in a single line and leaving only two short lines separate. When an iambic line, however irregular, has apparently been divided between speakers, the separate components of the metrical unit have been spaced apart vertically but numbered as one line. For example, 210–11:

> HOTSPUR I cry you mercy.
> WORCESTER   Those same noble Scots
>   That are your prisoners –
> HOTSPUR   I'll keep them all!

Q1 prints Worcester's words, 'Those . . . prisoners –', as one long irregular line. F, apparently not pressed for space, splits Worcester's reference to the Scots where it is divided here, but like Q1, begins the speech immediately after the speech heading. F also gives Worcester (just before Hotspur's 'I cry you mercy') an extraneous short line, 'And list to me', which most editors reject. It thereby prints five short lines in a row.

Early in 1.3, Shakespeare uses a group of split lines in a way which quickly clarifies the troubled relationship between King Henry, Worcester, and Northumberland. At 14, the King cuts off Northumberland and seems to ignore his brief line, 'My

---

[1] G. Wright demonstrates that the use of short and of shared lines is an important part of Shakespeare's 'metrical repertoire' (p. 117).

[2] See G. Wright, p. 110.

[3] Other scenes of great interest in this respect include 3.1, 4.1, and 4.3.

lord –', in order to command the complaining Worcester, 'get thee gone . . .' The King then turns, seven lines later, to Northumberland with 'You were about to speak', a line which Northumberland completes: 'Yea, my good lord.' Northumberland's half lines dissociate him from his brother (whose haughty last line in 13 remains short even after Northumberland addresses the King with 'My lord – '). They also seem to frame the speech in which the King dismisses Worcester, pointing up the King's outburst and Northumberland's strategic obedience as he waits to say his piece in an attempt to justify his son.

Hotspur, interrupting again and again, is responsible for the largest number of short lines in this scene. Each of the eleven split lines from 128 until the end of Scene 3 includes a speech by Hotspur. These lines are often as unpredictable and energetic as Hotspur himself. Of particular interest are the linked speeches (210–11) which were cited above to illustrate typographical options. The use of split lines here suggests Hotspur's lack of control in the dialogue. Unable to keep the promise implied by 'I cry you mercy', he cries out in his next half line, 'I'll keep them all.' His interruptions here and at 216 seem to speed up the process by which Worcester becomes the wily historical expert, 'training' his nephew on. At 275, Worcester answers Hotspur's question, 'To join with Mortimer, ha?' and completes his line, 'And so they shall'. When Hotspur cuts off Worcester's, 'Hear you, cousin, a word', with the long and regular 'All studies here I solemnly defy', 225, he seems to ignore Worcester, as the King ignored Northumberland. But, unlike Hotspur, the King was keeping his channels of communication open. Northumberland and Worcester again complete Hotspur's short lines at 155, 185, and 214. By linking these exchanges, we have tried to make more evident the surprising interplay among the characters. Of course, no edition can hope to rival the theatre as a medium for expressing what Wright has called 'that condition of being bound together in a common action that the play as a whole affirms'.[1]

Hotspur's last words at 5.4.85, 'And food for – ', clearly break off without finishing his thought or his line. The Prince, who has refused to share glory with Hotspur, does however appear to share the thought with which he ends, 'For worms, brave Percy'. Yet he does not really split or divide a line with his rival after all. His own line continues, 'Fare thee well, great heart!', composing thereby a measured, independent pentameter which leaves Hotspur's 'for' hanging in the air – an extra beat which somehow assures us that the Prince cannot have fully mastered Hotspur's spirit.

Whether the stylistic contexts for short lines are verse, prose, or a mixture hovering between the two, such lines often signal swift and important shifts of emotion and purpose, as in 'I do, I will' (2.4.399). Although considerations of space may help us to understand why QqF printed part of the verse exchange between Hotspur and Lady Percy in 2.3 as prose, it is helpful to notice that their interview begins with a number of short lines. Early compositors could well have been responding to the near-indeterminacy and the lively imbalance of a style which fully exercises actors' voices and readers' ears.

[1] G. Wright, p. 139.

APPENDIX: SHAKESPEARE AND HOLINSHED

This edition treats as 'sources' for *1 Henry IV* those passages or details about characters or events which Shakespeare probably used. For Holinshed, however, there is special value in extending the possibilities of relationship between texts to include the methods and ambience of chronicle history. Often it will also prove illuminating to recognise what Shakespeare has left out of his play.

The Holinshed writers presented their readers with many opportunities to assess opinions which they recorded with little or no comment. This method served well the purposes of a playwright whose characters would not or could not obtain reliable information. A significant example of how Shakespeare adapted Holinshed's indecisiveness occurs in Act 1, Scene 3, where an argument over Mortimer provides one of the causes of eventual civil war. In the order of their occurrence, Holinshed's explanations for the defeat and defection of Mortimer are :

But coming to trie the matter by battell, whether by treason or otherwise, so it fortuned, that the English power was discomfited, the earle taken prisoner, and above a thousand of his people slaine in the place. (III, 20)

Edmund Mortimer earle of March, prisoner with Owen Glendouer, whether for irksomnesse of cruell captiuitie, or feare of death, or for what other cause, it is vncerteine, agreed to take part with Owen, against the king of England, and tooke to wife the daughter of the said Owen. (III, 21)

Thomas Persie earle of Worcester, whose studie was euer (as some write) to procure malice, and set things in a broile, came to the king vnto Windsore . . . and there required of him, that either by ransome or otherwise, he would cause to be deliuered out of prison Edmund Mortimer . . . their cousine germane, whome (as they reported) Owen Glendouer kept in filthie prison, shakled with irons, onelie for that he tooke his part, and was to him faithful and true. (III, 22)

Although Holinshed conveys the mystery of Mortimer's actions and attitudes, he leaves little doubt about the motives of English politicians. His King considers Mortimer's claim to the English crown before answering the Percys with the 'fraudulent excuse' that Mortimer deliberately gave in to Glendower. Whereupon Hotspur comments, 'Behold, the heire of the relme is robbed of his right, and yet the robber with his owne will not redeeme him' (III, 22). Shakespeare, however, turns the opportunistic rationalisations of the parties in Holinshed into a less premeditated, more volatile conflict by involving his characters personally in the Mortimer puzzle. The King's concern over Mortimer's lineage becomes an explanation offered by Hotspur only after the fact of the King's anger, which seems to be directed more at Hotspur than at Mortimer.

The King's surmise that Mortimer has indeed betrayed him emerges in connection with his statement, perhaps also news to the Percys, that 'as we hear', Mortimer has just married Glendower's daughter. Hotspur answers the King's surmise with a more generous one of his own, stressing the 'deadly wounds' Mortimer received during hand-to-hand combat with Glendower. In turn, Hotspur's justification of his brother-in-law enrages the King, who calls it a lie: 'I tell thee, he durst as well have met the devil alone / As Owen Glendower for an enemy' (1.3.114–15). Glendower's later statement (3.1.60) that he has fought off King Henry's attacks three times eventually makes possible a reassessment of how both the King and Hotspur behave: the King may have lost his temper in response to Hotspur's tactless vision of Mortimer as Glendower's military equal, provoking Hotspur into recollecting Mortimer's claim to the crown. In this instance, Holinshed's detached method of admitting uncertainty about Mortimer becomes a method of portraying characters who seem unable to tolerate uncertainty about one another.

As he condensed political events between 1400 and 1403, Shakespeare omitted materials which tended to simplify or sensationalise the rebellion. The Percys appear much more devious in Holinshed, where they are said to envy the King's 'wealth and felicitie' (III, 22). Worcester's 'studie was euer (as some write) to procure malice, and set things in a broile' (III, 22). Glendower, constantly 'robbing and spoiling within the English borders' (III, 20), is downright treacherous; his people contrive to hide a terrible device with 'three long prickes' of iron under the royal bed. Only by chance does Henry discover it before lying down. Holinshed comments at length upon the likely perturbation of a monarch who finds death in his 'secret chamber' and 'bed of downe': 'Oh what a suspected state therefore is that of a king holding his regiment with the hatred of his people, the hart grudgings of his courtiers, and the peremtorie practises of both togither?' (III, 18–19).

Holinshed's King has to reckon as well with sporadic danger from the French, who do cancel their plans to invade England when they learn of King Richard's death, but are later involved in attacks upon the Isle of Wight, Plymouth, and Cornwall. Twice in the period between 1400 and the battle of Shrewsbury, Richard himself is rumoured to be alive, by conspirators who 'wished the kings death' in 1402 (III, 19), and again by the Percys as they march towards Shrewsbury. This tale, says Holinshed, reflecting on the consequences of the usurpation and the ultimate rooting out of all the factions involved, 'bred variable motions in mens minds, causing them to wauer, so as they knew not to which part they should sticke' (III, 24).

Understandably, Shakespeare omitted details which might have detracted from the economy of his plot. Within the span of years his play dramatised, the English negotiated the return to England of Richard's Queen (who had been considered a desirable match for the Prince of Wales) and the King married the Duchess of Brittany. Holinshed also reports the visit of the Emperor of Constantinople who seeks help against the Turk, the business of successive parliaments, the burning of Lollards, the spectacular fiery comet of 1402, and the appearance of the Devil in an Essex church, dressed as a Grey Friar, which is linked to the conspiracy mentioned above. As the Devil behaves 'outrageouslie', the church roof blows off in a tempest (III, 20).

The England presented by Holinshed resembles Shakespeare's in being vulnerable to repeated invasions and disturbed by warring nobility. It differs because it seems to be in contact with a wider world, both political and spiritual. Because Shakespeare concentrates upon the King's responses to his limited options, Shakespeare's England may appear more parochial. Compared with Holinshed, Shakespeare seems to deprive the King of popular support; he emphasises Henry's disdain for 'vile participation' and omits all mention of how the people actively reinforced their King's authority by killing conspirators and beating away the French.

READING LIST

This list contains a selection from the books and articles referred to in the Introduction and Commentary, with some additions that may serve as guides to further study of the play.

Auden, W. H. *The Dyer's Hand and other Essays*, 1962
Bahktin, Mikhail. *Rabelais and His World*, trans. Helene Iswolsky, 1984
Barber, C. L. *Shakespeare's Festive Comedy*, 1959
Barber, C. L. and Richard P. Wheeler. *The Whole Journey: Shakespeare's Power of Development*, 1986
Barton, Anne. *Essays, Mainly Shakespearean*, 1994
Bate, Jonathan (ed.). *The Romantics on Shakespeare*, 1992
Bentley, Eric. *The Life of the Drama*, 1965
Booth, Stephen. 'The Shakespearean actor as kamikaze pilot', *SQ* 36 (1985), 553–70
Brennan, Anthony. *Shakespeare's Dramatic Structures*, 1986
Bristol, Michael D. *Carnival and Theatre: Plebeian Culture and the Structure of Authority in Renaissance England*, 1985
Brown, J. R. (ed.). *Shakespeare in Performance: An Introduction Through Six Major Plays*, 1976
Bullough, Geoffrey (ed.). *Narrative and Dramatic Sources of Shakespeare*, IV, 1962
Bulman, J. C. 'Shakespeare's Georgic histories', *S.Sur.* 38 (1985), 37–47
Bulman, J. C. and H. R. Coursen (eds.). *Shakespeare on Television*, 1988
Cox, John D. *Shakespeare and the Dramaturgy of Power*, 1989
Crowl, Samuel. 'The long goodbye: Welles and Falstaff', *SQ* 31 (1980), 369–80
David, Richard. *Shakespeare in the Theatre*, 1978
Empson, William. *Essays on Shakespeare*, 1986
Everett, Barbara. 'The fatness of Falstaff: Shakespeare and character', *PBA* 76 (1991), 109–28
Goldman, Michael. *Shakespeare and the Energies of Drama*, 1972
Greenblatt, Stephen. *Shakespearean Negotiations: The Circulation of Social Energy in Renaissance England*, 1988
Hapgood, Robert. *Shakespeare the Theatre-Poet*, 1988
Hodgdon, Barbara. *The End Crowns All: Closure and Contradiction in Shakespeare's History*, 1991
Holderness, Graham. *Shakespeare's History*, 1985
Hunter, G. K. *Dramatic Identities and Cultural Tradition*, 1978
'Truth and art in history plays', *S.Sur.* 42 (1990), 15–24
Ives, E. W. 'Shakespeare and history: divergencies and agreements', *S.Sur.* 38 (1985), 19–35

Johnson, Samuel. *Johnson on Shakespeare*, ed. Arthur Sherbo, 1968

Jones, Emrys. *Scenic Form in Shakespeare*, 1971
  The Origins of Shakespeare, 1977

Kahn, Coppelia. *Man's Estate: Masculine Identity in Shakespeare*, 1981

Kastan, David Scott. *Shakespeare and the Shapes of Time*, 1982

Laroque, François. *Shakespeare's Festive World: Elizabethan Seasonal Entertainment and the Professional Stage*, 1993

Lindenberger, Herbert. *Historical Drama: The Relation of Literature and Reality*, 1975

Mahood, M. M. *Bit Parts in Shakespeare's Plays*, 1992

McMillin, Scott. *Shakespeare in Performance: Henry IV, Part One*, 1991

Melchiori, Giorgio. 'The corridors of history: Shakespeare the remaker', *PBA* 72 (1986), 67–85

Montaigne, Michel de. *Complete Works*, trans. Donald M. Frame, 1958

Morgann, Maurice. *Shakespearean Criticism*, ed. Daniel A. Fineman, 1972

Muir, Kenneth. *The Sources of Shakespeare's Plays*, 1978

Ornstein, Robert. *A Kingdom for a Stage: The Achievement of Shakespeare's History Plays*, 1972

Patterson, Annabel. *Shakespeare and the Popular Voice*, 1989
  Reading Holinshed's Chronicles, 1994

Pechter, Edward. 'Falsifying men's hopes: the ending of *1 Henry IV*', *MLQ* 41 (1980), 211–30

Rabkin, Norman. *Shakespeare and the Common Understanding*, 1967

Rackin, Phyllis. *Stages of History: Shakespeare's English Chronicles*, 1990

Rossiter, A. P. *Angel with Horns: Fifteen Lectures on Shakespeare*, 1961

Saccio, Peter. *Shakespeare's English Kings*, 1978

Smidt, Kristian. *Unconformities in Shakespeare's History Plays*, 1982

Tillyard, E. M. W. *Shakespeare's History Plays*, 1944

Tomlinson, Michael. 'Shakespeare and the Chronicles reassessed', *Literature and History* 10 (1984), 46–88

Wilders, John. *The Lost Garden: A View of Shakespeare's English and Roman History Plays*, 1978

Wiles, David. *Shakespeare's Clown: Actor and Text in the Elizabethan Playhouse*, 1987

Wilson, John Dover. *The Fortunes of Falstaff*, 1943

Wright, George T. *Shakespeare's Metrical Art*, 1991